Weimar Germany

Weimar Germany

PROMISE AND TRAGEDY

Eric D. Weitz

PRINCETON UNIVERSITY PRESS • PRINCETON AND OXFORD

Published by Princeton University Press, 41 William Street,
Princeton, New Jersey 08540
In the United Kingdom: Princeton University Press, 3 Market Place,
Woodstock, Oxfordshire OX20 1SY

All efforts have been made to locate copyright holders of illustrations. If any have been missed, adjustments will be made in subsequent editions.

Endpapers photo: Potsdamer Platz from the Café Josty. SV-Bilderdienst / Scherl.

Library of Congress Cataloging-in-Publication Data

Weitz, Eric D.
Weimar Germany : promise and tragedy / Eric D. Weitz.
p. cm.
Includes bibliographical references and index.
ISBN-13: 978-0-691-01695-5 (hardcover : alk. paper)
ISBN-10: 0-691-01695-X (hardcover : alk. paper) 1. Germany—History—1918–1933. 2. Germany—Civilization—20th century. I. Title.
DD237.W47 2007
943.085—dc22 2007003791

British Library Cataloging-in-Publication Data is available

This book has been composed in Berkeley Typeface with Bauhaus display
Printed on acid-free paper. ∞
press.princeton.edu

Printed in Canada

10 9 8 7 6 5 4 3 2 1

To my father, **Charles Baer Weitz** (born 1919), and to the memory of my mother, **Shirley Wolkoff Weitz** (1925–2004), who first taught me the importance of learning

Contents

Illustrations

Color Plates (following p. 274)

Figures

Weimar Germany

INTRODUCTION

Weimar Germany still speaks to us. Paintings by George Grosz and Max Beckmann are much in demand and hang in museums and galleries from Sydney to Los Angeles to St. Petersburg. Bertolt Brecht and Kurt Weill's *The Threepenny Opera* is periodically revived in theaters around the world and in many different languages. Thomas Mann's great novel *The Magic Mountain*, first published in 1925, remains in print and, if not exactly a household item, is read and discussed in literature and philosophy classes at countless colleges and universities. Contemporary kitchen designs invoke the styles of the 1920s and the creative work of the Bauhaus. Postmodern architects may have abandoned the strict functionalism of Walter Gropius, but who can resist the beauty of Erich Mendelsohn's Columbus House or his Schocken department stores (only one of which is still standing), with their combination of clean lines and dynamic movement, or the whimsy of his Einstein Tower? Hannah Höch might not be as widely known as these others, but viewers who encounter her work today are drawn to her inventive combination of primitivist and modernist styles, her juxtaposition of African or Polynesian-style masks with the everyday objects of the 1920s. The deep philosophical speculations of Martin Heidegger and the layered essays of Siegfried Kracauer, both grappling with the meaning of advanced technology and mass society, still offer a wealth of insight into the modern condition. And what film buff has not seen *The Cabinet of Dr. Caligari*, *Metropolis*, or *Berlin: Symphony of the City*?

Weimar Germany speaks to us in other ways as well, perhaps most often as a warning sign. This was a society battered by economic crisis and unrelenting political conflict. World War I cast its long shadow over the entire history of the republic. However much present-day economists and historians have revised the notion that the Versailles

Peace Treaty placed excessive financial burdens on Germany, Germans of the time were convinced that they had been unjustly treated by the victors of World War I. Many were quick to blame the Allies and, following the stab-in-the-back legend, Jews and socialists at home for every subsequent disaster that ensued: civil unrest, hyperinflation, depression, bankruptcies, and any other kind of misery one can imagine. Weimar Germany conjures up fears of what can happen when there is simply no societal consensus on how to move forward and every minor difference becomes a cause of existential political battles, when assassinations and street fights run rampant and minorities become the easy scapegoats of antidemocratic forces. It is a warning sign because we all know how it ended: with the Nazi assumption of power on 30 January 1933.

Yet amid the conflicts and disasters, Weimar was also a moment of great political as well as cultural achievement. The destruction of the old imperial order in war and revolution unleashed the political and social imagination. For a time, Germans created a highly liberal political order with very substantial social welfare programs. The lives of so many ordinary people improved greatly: the working day was reduced to a more humane eight hours, at least in the first years of the republic, and unemployment insurance seemed to herald a new era that would protect workers from the vagaries of the business cycle. New public housing offered better-off workers and white-collar employees the chance to move out of old tenements into modern, clean apartments with indoor plumbing, gas stoves, and electricity. Women won the right to vote, and Germany had a lively free press. All sorts of plans were broached for creating the flourishing and harmonious society of the future, from nudism to communism. Sex therapists and popular activists asserted the right of everyone to a rich and fulfilling sexual life. Like the cinema, the spectacle-world of consumer goods conjured up the possibility of a different, more prosperous life, even if one had to return next morning at 7:00 AM to the workbench, office, or sales counter. Utopian beliefs emerged out of war and revolution. Surely the world could be completely transformed, whether—depending on the spokesperson—through modern architecture, photography, communal housing, or massed demonstrations in the streets: such confidence and conviction proved inspirational to so much artistic creation and philosophical rumination.

Germans were hardly alone in these endeavors. In the swirl and wake of World War I women won the right to vote in Britain; modern artists flocked to Paris; Dutch architects pioneered new building forms; and crowds and parties in Vienna, Budapest, and Petrograd overthrew antiquated imperial regimes and hoped for a bright political future. Germans watched and learned from these developments, for good and bad. But there was something particularly intense and concentrated about the German experience in these years. Unlike its neighbors to the west, Germany had lost the war. The economic, political, and psychological consequences were profound. Virtually every issue, every debate, was shadowed by the question of responsibility for the war and the cost of reparations. With no victory, there was no recompense for the sufferings men and women had endured for four years. There were no financial gains, no sense of the elation that comes from triumph after a struggle long endured. Unlike its Russian neighbor further to the east, Germany did not go through a total revolution that completely eliminated the power and prestige of the traditional elites. It steered a middle course with a revolution that most certainly democratized the country but left much of the old social order intact. The result was lack of consensus and constant debate. The most basic matters of how Germans would live together and with their neighbors were subject to unending strife.

The destructiveness of total war and the creativity of revolution—experiences that many Europeans shared, but that in Germany had a very particular coloration—propelled the work and thinking of Weimar's protagonists, whether they were visionary artists and architects, political reformers and revolutionaries on the left, or thoughtful, authoritarian-minded intellectuals on the conservative right. They were also animated by something deeper and of longer duration—the recognition that they were living amid the throes of modernity. Germany in the 1920s still had a very significant agrarian economy, many small shops and skilled handicraft workers, and elites of an older sort well ensconced in the officer corps of the army, the bureaucracies of the state, and the hierarchies of the Protestant and Catholic churches. But the old world, often idealized in retrospect, of aristocratic estates and peasant farming; of individual German states and a unified Germany dominated politically by princes, kings, and emperors; of rigid class distinctions—that world no longer existed unchallenged. The center of gravity had shifted to the city with its cacophony of sounds and images, to the factories and mines pounding out the products of an advanced industrial economy, and to the tensions and excitements of "mass society." This was a world in which most individuals worked for a wage or salary; people patronized the icons of a commercial economy and culture by reading newspapers, shopping in department stores, listening to prizefights on the radio, and going to the movies at least once a week; and politics included mass mobilizations to get out the vote, march on city hall or the nearby factory, and, sometimes, take up arms in revolution and rebellion.

All of Weimar's protagonists, whatever their political and cultural proclivities, grappled with this tension-bound world of modernity. There was no escape. Even when people tried to avoid it by living in isolation in the Black Forest or as semirecluses in apartments in Munich or villages in the Alps, or claimed to represent "traditional German values" in opposition to everything modernity signified, inevitably they used newspapers and the radio to convey their ideas and organized their followers in huge numbers to descend upon the voting booth or the marketplace. Others actively embraced modernity by advocating mass politics and industrial society or by developing new forms of expression—abstract art, dissonant music, architecture of clean lines and industrial materials—that they believed captured the tensions, conflicts, and excitements of the age. Weimar culture and Weimar politics spawned so much creativity precisely because its artists, writers, and political organizers sought to unravel the meaning of modernity and to push it in new directions, some emancipatory and joyous, others frightfully authoritarian, murderous, and racist.

Weimar Germany: Promise and Tragedy engages every major facet of Weimar life from 1918 to 1933—politics, economics, culture, and society, and the connections among them. I draw on an array of contemporary written, visual, and sonoral sources, as well as the very rich work in history and other scholarly disciplines.[1] Berlin as the cultural and political capital receives a good deal of attention, but I also address developments in rural society and in other towns and cities around the country. I strive to recapture the exciting, innovative elements of that conflicted, raucous, lively, and difficult period.

At the same time, I am very attentive to the severe constraints on Weimar society, whether imposed by the Allies, a sluggish international economy, the weight of Germany's own authoritarian traditions, or the emergence of a new, more dangerous, violence-prone radical Right. Ultimately, of course, I confront what went wrong, how it all ended so disastrously, and show that Weimar did not just collapse. It was pushed over the precipice by a combination of the established Right, hostile to the republic from its very founding, and the newer extreme Right. The established Right, composed of businessmen, nobles, government officials, and army officers, was powerful and well situated. Communists also sought to bury the republic, but it was the Right that always posed the gravest danger.

The twelve years of the Third Reich, however, should not color excessively the fourteen preceding years of the Weimar Republic. No historical event is predetermined, and most certainly not the Nazi victory. The conflicts and constraints of the Weimar period surely helped fuel the Nazi movement, but it is a travesty to see Weimar only as a prelude to the Third Reich. Weimar Germany was a rich, exciting moment, and many of the artistic works, philosophical considerations, and political imaginings created in its midst offered bright visions of a better world. Those visions continue to have meaning for us today.

Fig. 1.1 Wounded and dispirited German troops returning from Belgium at the end of World War I. In sharp contrast, the photos we have from August 1914 show German troops joyously departing for the front, showered with flowers and praise by waving crowds.

1

A Troubled Beginning

A defeated army on its return home is never a pretty sight. The bandaged wounds, the missing limbs, the hobbled walk on crutches seem even more ghastly shadowed by the sullen mood of the bedraggled soldiers (fig. 1.1). But on 10 December 1918, the chairman of the Council of People's Representatives, Friedrich Ebert, in office for just a month, sought to put a brave face on his greetings to the returning soldiers who had been defeated in battle.

> Comrades, welcome in the German Republic, welcome in the homeland, which has yearned for you. . . .
>
> Joyfully we welcome you back in the homeland. . . . No enemy has prevailed over you. Only when the opponent's superiority of men and matériel became ever more oppressive did we give up the struggle. . . . You have protected the homeland from the enemy's invasion. You have saved your women and children, your parents, from the murder and fire of war. You have saved Germany's fields and workshops from devastation and destruction. For that we at home thank you from the very depths of our being.[1]

Ebert, who had supported the war and had lost two sons to it, could not venture to critique the war as a tragic waste of human lives and material resources. He still sought meaning in the venture.

But he also sought to prepare the soldiers for the vast changes at home. The old rulers, who had weighed like a curse on Germany, have been shunted aside by the German people. We are now the masters of our own destiny, he claimed, and the future of German freedom rests on you, the returning soldiers. "Nobody has suffered more than you from the injustice of the old regime. We were thinking of you when we cleared out that doomed system. For you we fought for freedom, for you we've established the rights of labor." We cannot greet you with rich offerings and comforts. Our "unhappy country has become poor," and the victors burden us with harsh demands. "But out of the destruction we want to shape a new Germany."[2]

More than thirteen million men, 19.7 percent of Germany's 1914 population, served in the army during World War I. Nearly eight million of them were still in arms on 11 November 1918, when the armistice was signed.[3] They had gone to war, so they had been told, to defend the Fatherland against the barbaric Russians, who threatened to wreak chaos and destruction on German soil; against the Belgians and French, who had designs on German land and German women; against the British and Americans, who coveted German goods and feared German economic competition. Not all Germans had gone to war willingly; in the summer of 1914, stirring calls for peace and negotiations had also resounded in towns and cities. There were pacifists like the young architect Bruno Taut and radical socialists like Karl Liebknecht and Rosa Luxemburg, who opposed the conflict as the ultimate manifestation of capitalism's inhumanity. But those voices were ultimately drowned out by the headlong rush to war spearheaded by Kaiser Wilhelm II, his generals, and his civilian government. However much democracy had progressed in Germany in the decades before World War I, the army and the government still served at the behest of the kaiser, not of the Reichstag and certainly not of the electorate.

No soldier drafted into the German army in World War I began his march home on 11 November 1918 as the same man he had been in 1914 or 1916 or even in September and October 1918, when draftees were still being sent to the front. No returning soldier found his family and his village, town, or city in the same condition as he had left it. The sheer number of casualties had been too great. In Elkenroth, a tiny village of about 700 people in Rheinland-Pfalz, 91 men served in the army during the war, 21 percent of whom died and another 23 percent of whom came back wounded.[4] Every inhabitant of the village was directly affected by the loss of life or the physical and psychic damage of the war. All told, roughly 2 million German men were killed and 4.2 million wounded in World War I. Around

19 percent of the entire male population were direct casualties of the violence of the war.[5] Many of the survivors lived the rest of their lives with appalling physical and psychological wounds. Some were spirited away by their families or attempted of their own volition to endure life in bitter isolation from society. Yet the war-wounded, masks covering faces that had been blown away, dark glasses covering blinded eyes, wheelchairs replacing the gait of the walker, were everywhere visible on the streets of Germany's cities and towns in the postwar decade. Physicians had to deal also with a new "disease," shell shock, the autism and tremors that soldiers developed in reaction to ceaseless bombardments in damp and dirty trenches.

When the soldiers disembarked from the trains that eventually carried them home, they found that the women left behind had endured their own ordeal. Everywhere food rationing had been instituted by the spring of 1915, but food shortages nonetheless became the daily reality. In the winter of 1916–17, children five to seven years old in Essen were allotted only one-quarter liter of milk three times per week.[6] The city authorities noted that the bread was almost unpalatable because of all sorts of additives—bean flour and sometimes even sawdust—used to compensate for the shortages of wheat and rye.[7] The infamous "turnip winter" of 1916–17 was indeed reality for many Germans. Many years later, one man, a schoolboy during the war, remembered eating turnips for breakfast, unpacking the school lunch his mother had sent him to find turnips, and going home to a dinner of still more turnips.[8]

Women had also gone to work in the munitions factories. The extent of the transformation has often been exaggerated, since before 1914 large numbers of women already labored in Germany's industrial plants. But the demands of total war, of an economy and society that were completely mobilized to support Germany's army in the field, meant that many women moved into metalworking and munitions factories. Where once they had been few in number and hired only as helpers, now they became numerous and skilled machine operatives. At Krupp in Essen, Germany's major munitions factory, the company in August 1914 employed only 963 women out of a total workforce of 41,764. By mid-1917, the workforce had tripled in size, and one-quarter, 28,664 in total, were women.[9] Before the war most of the women had worked as cleaners and kitchen staff. By 1917, they were filling casings with gunpowder, polishing metal, and working the lathes and drill presses that kept production moving.

The work was hard, the conditions deplorable. Alfred Döblin, one of Weimar Germany's master novelists, in *A People Betrayed*, had one of his characters, Minna Imker, describe to her brother, newly returned from the front, the conditions she endured in a Berlin munitions plant. She worked long hours for minimal pay. Her hair had turned green from the gunpowder in the factory. But it was not only bosses and foremen and the extreme conditions of war that created such misery for her.

> We were doing piece work. The men were in charge of regulating the machines. Sometimes there would be six lathes to one man. In the meantime you just stand around and time passes and you know you'll get fired. He's happily working away at his girlfriend's lathe. The rest can wait. Ed, I've stood there sometimes so wild with anger. And when they're eating and drinking, what do they talk about if not the horses? Women. They passed the word to each other who was good in bed. They exploited our misery just like the owners. Or Wilhelm and his generals.[10]

Women also spent countless hours searching for food and fuel. Grandmothers and aunts took to the queues, waiting for meager rations of bread, while younger women worked their shifts in the factories. Hordes of women and youth spread out over railroad yards to pick up chunks of coal that had fallen from trains, or rummaged through fields like gleaners depicted in the Bible. As women engaged in more active protests, sometimes invading and looting stores or markets, the police reacted with a mix of exasperation, outrage, and empathy. The Berlin police reported as early as 1915 that "there are innumerable families who are going day after day without butter or other fats, and who are forced to eat their bread dry and to prepare their food without cooking fat. . . . Even good, faithful patriots have begun to turn into pessimists." The police admitted that they "hated [taking] drastic measures toward women." The "hours-long, often fruitless wait of housewives" made them easily susceptible to political agitation, in the view of the police.[11]

The burdens of industrial labor and food hunts were great, but far worse was the loss of loved ones, the husbands, brothers, and lovers who never returned from France, Belgium, or Russia. Those who did come home were often physically and psychically wounded. The pain of the loss would always remain, and was captured best, perhaps, by the artist and pacifist Käthe Kollwitz. She lost her only son in the first months of the war and spent years trying to exorcise her loss through her art. The sculpture *Mother and Son* (fig. 1.2), commonly known as *The Pietà* which she finally completed in 1937–38, is a searingly sad commentary on the waste of war. The artistic creation did little to assuage her own pain, which mirrored the ache felt by so many German mothers.[12]

Yet the experience of the war years, for all of the horrors at the front and difficulties at home, was also liberating for many women and men. The fury of war destroyed numerous social and artistic conventions. The Weimar era, with its heady enthusiasms, its artistic experimentation, its flaunting of sexuality and unconventional relations, its vibrant, kinetic energy, was a direct result of the vast disruptions of World War I, the distorted reverberations of its crashing destructiveness. An intense desire to grasp life in all its manifold dimensions, to experience love, sex, beauty, and power, fast cars and airborne flight, theater and dance crazes, arose out of the strong sense of the ephemeral character of life, of lives so quickly snuffed out or forever ruined by bullet wounds and gas attacks.

For many women, the factory and the city got them away from the strict gaze of parents, pastors or priests, and village gossips. As hard as the labor was, money in their own hands gave them a sense of emancipation that would carry over into the Weimar years. The forces of order—state officials, police, foremen and managers, even their own fathers, husbands, and brothers—watched all this with great trepidation. Together, they would try to ensure that the postwar factory would remain a man's world, but their success would be limited. Women would be removed from some sectors, like metalworking. But overall, the economy needed their labor—paid so much more cheaply than men's—and women needed jobs to support themselves and their families, so never was the entire female population consigned to the household.

The war also destroyed conventional notions of respectability and faith in authority. This was, after all, a war instigated by the elites of Germany and Europe. This was total war, the first of its kind, and the state assumed great responsibilities, managing everything in sight, including labor, raw materials, and the food supply. It also attempted

Fig. 1.2 Käthe Kollwitz, *Mother and Son* or *The Pietà*, 1937–38. The artist spent years trying to execute this sculpture and expunge her grief at the loss of her son in World War I. It now sits, controversially, in the Neue Wache in Berlin as the symbol of all German losses and victims in wartime. ullstein bild / The Granger Collection, New York.

to manage sexuality, threatening women who took lovers with the loss of their soldiers' wives' allowances. The state also promised great things, a prosperous, powerful Germany after the victory, a Germany that stood astride the continent. From that position of dominance, the benefits would flow to every member of the national community. But when, by the third year of war, the promises seemed increasingly hollow, many Germans began to attack the symbols and institutions that they had followed into war. Officials noted nervously the murmurings of discontent, the snide references to the once-sacred symbols of Germany, the imperial family and the officer corps, the disrespect shown to foremen and managers. The artist George Grosz captured these sentiments perfectly in many of his drawings and paintings, like *The Faith Healers* (fig. 1.3), which shows army officers and physicians declaring even a skeleton fit for military service. Grosz's distorted depictions of aristocratic army officers and self-impressed bureaucrats reflected the loathing that so many Germans felt for their elites. Never an easygoing character, Grosz had become utterly enraged at the uselessness of the war. For Grosz as for many Germans, the savagery of total war undermined deference toward authority, and obedience and respect would never be wholly restored in the fourteen years of the republic.

On 21 March 1918, the German army had launched its last great offensive on the western front. It threw everything possible into the battle: soldiers, reserves, munitions. The campaign lasted two weeks, and the army accomplished some advances but could never achieve a clear breakthrough of the Allied defenses. The malnourished German troops fell upon the provisions they found when they took the Allies' first lines, and all the threats of their officers could not get them to move on until they were satiated.[13] That was only one of the reasons that the German advance failed. Germany no longer had the human and material resources to do anything more than try to hold the existing positions. The military command ordered smaller offensives in the subsequent months, the last around Reims in July, and these were even less successful. In late July and August, the Allies regained the initiative and even sent German troops fleeing in panic with a tank attack near Cambrai on 8 August 1918.[14]

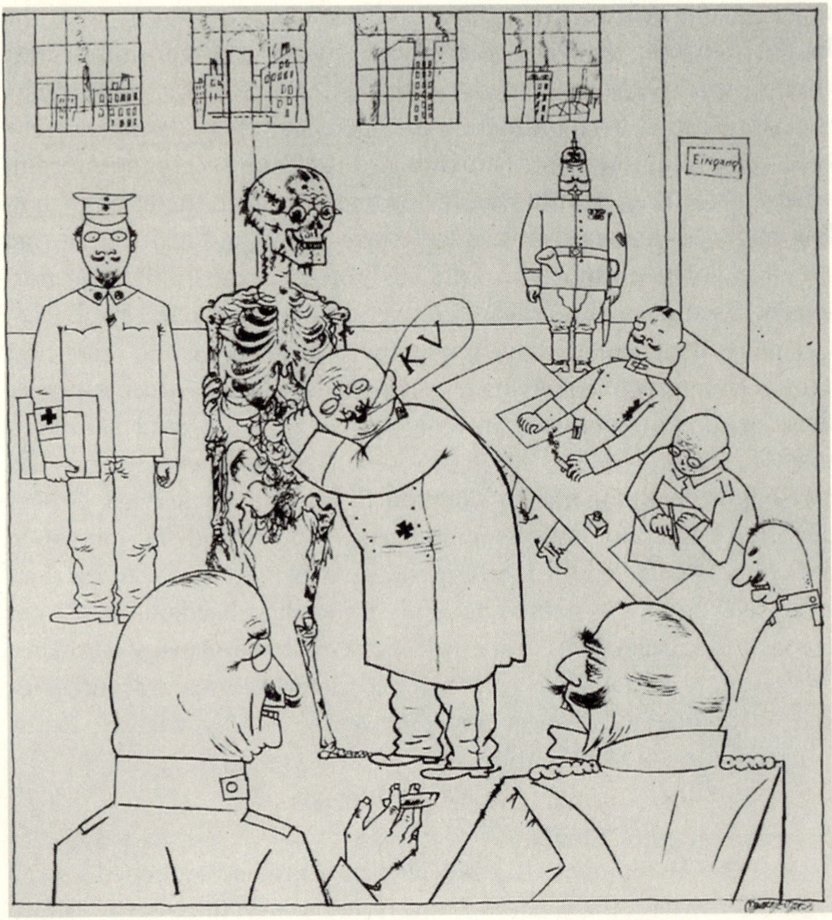

Fig 1.3 George Grosz, *The Faith-Healers*, or *Fit for Active Service*, 1916–17. The artist's cynical depiction of physicians' collaboration with the military. The doctor examining the skeleton declares it is "fit for service" while the officers complain that people are striking and inclined to revolution. Bildarchiv Preussischer Kulturbesitz / Art Resource, NY.

Still, it took weeks for the authorities to come to grips with the reality of Germany's desperate situation. At the very end of September, in a fit of panic—which they would later try to cover up—the two leaders of the Supreme Military Command, Field Marshal Paul von Hindenburg and General Erich Ludendorff, approached Kaiser Wilhelm II and told him that Germany had to request an armistice. Ludendorff had been aware for months of Germany's severe military and economic deficiencies, yet had hidden the truth from the kaiser and the civilian government. The German population, still promised great things, knew even less. But Ludendorff especially was already looking to the future, and wanted to foist the responsibility for the disaster onto a civilian government based on the parliamentary parties (and not just the kaiser's wishes), and thereby preserve the pristine stature of the officer corps and the German army. The kaiser, reportedly, was taken aback, but Hindenburg and Ludendorff insisted that he initiate contacts with the American government to bring the war to an end.

America had entered the war only in April 1917. In his famous "Fourteen Points" address to Congress on 8 January 1918 and in subsequent statements and speeches, President Woodrow Wilson had promised a just and lasting peace, one that ensured every nation the possibility of free development.

> There shall be no annexations, no contributions, no punitive damages. . . . National aspirations must be respected; peoples may now be dominated and governed only by their own consent. "Self-determination" is . . . an imperative principle of action, which statesmen will henceforth ignore at their peril.[15]

After Germany's blatant disregard of Belgian neutrality, and the ravages of French, Belgian, and Russian territory and populations, Ludendorff and Hindenburg knew that the only hope for a reasonable peace offer for Germany lay with the Americans. They understood that the Americans would need some sign of domestic reform before they would negotiate seriously with Germany. They also wanted to shift the blame for the impending defeat from the kaiser and army onto the parliament. In their hour of desperation, the two archauthoritarians, the generals who had spent two years directing a military dictatorship over Germany, initiated a process of democratization.

So on 3 October 1918 the kaiser called the liberal Prince Max von Baden to the chancellorship. He formed a new government from the majority parties in the Reichstag, which since 1917 had been seeking a negotiated peace. Two Social Democrats were among the members of the new government. For over two decades the Social Democrats had constituted Germany's largest party but had been barred from power by Germany's authoritarian elites. It was a profound sign of change that they were now admitted to the councils of state. The new government eased up on censorship and allowed some antiwar activists to leave the prisons to which they had been consigned. At the end of the month, the authorities initiated significant changes that made Germany into a constitutional monarchy with a government more fully answerable to the Reichstag than to the kaiser. They began a process of electoral reform designed to overthrow the highly inequitable suffrage law in Prussia, Germany's largest state. Prince Max's government also initiated contacts with the U.S. government, requesting an immediate end to hostilities on the basis of the Fourteen Points. Germany seemed on its way, finally, to achieving a liberal order that guaranteed political liberties and rights of participation, and, most pressingly, would bring the war to conclusion.

But it would not be so easy. After four years of killings, woundings, malnutrition, and overwork, popular anger ran red-hot. And the Americans were showing themselves to be not quite as magnanimous as they had promised. The exchange of notes between the German and American governments sent a deep chill through official German circles. The Americans seemed notably unimpressed by the domestic political changes to date. After all, the kaiser was still the effective and symbolic head of Germany, closely followed by his generals, and they suffered from the grand illusion that they could negotiate as equals with the Americans. They still refused to recognize that they came as the supplicants who had decisively lost the most destructive war in history. The Germans were shocked and angry to discover that the Americans were demanding rapid and immediate demobilization of the German army and its withdrawal from all occupied regions. On 5 and 6 November 1918, less than a week before the armistice, the army was still drafting new recruits.[16]

In these last days of October, when everyone knew that negotiations were under way between the United States and Germany, sailors in the port of Kiel were given orders to stoke the boilers and set out to sea. The German navy had fought a rather inglorious war. The British blockade across the North Sea had, for the most part, kept the navy confined to port. Its sole accomplishment had been to send out submarines that sank American-flag shipping and killed many of the passengers on board, thereby dragging the United States into the war. On board and in port the enlisted sailors suffered from wretched food. The officers, within hearing distance of the enlisted men, had quite satisfactory and well-prepared portions. The men, moreover, endured an extremely regimented disciplinary system. When the orders came to stoke the boilers, the men asked one another: Were the officers intent on engaging the British in one last desperate, and hopeless, battle? Were they going to scuttle the ships at sea, last-minute heroics according to someone's perverse notion of a fighting man's code of honor—better to die on board than to admit defeat? Indeed, the admirals were attempting one last great sea battle against the British to prove the mettle of the German navy and secure its future. Perhaps most important, they wanted to destroy the cease-fire negotiations that were under way with the United States and the accompanying domestic reforms. Better for the sailors to die at sea than accept a peace that, in the eyes of the fleet officers, was dishonorable.

But the sailors were having no part of it. On 29 October 1918 in the port city of Kiel they mutinied, and in so doing set off the revolution that would finally destroy imperial Germany. The revolt quickly spread from the sailors on board to the garrisons in town and then to workers all over the city. Seven demonstrators were killed in a clash with a military unit. A government delegation headed by the Social Democratic Party (SPD) leader Gustav Noske set off for Kiel in an effort to defuse the situation. The sailors at first demanded improvements in their own miserable conditions, but very quickly their efforts took on a more overtly political character as they began calling for an end to the war and the abdication of the kaiser. Within a few days, Kiel was in the hands of sailors, soldiers, and workers.

The sailors won some concessions. They also established the body that would be one of the key democratic institutions of the revolution: the council. These popular organizations had first been invented in the Russian revolutions of 1905 and 1917. The councils were a sign of desperate conditions and a search for new forms of political representation in the age of high industrialization and total war, when workers, soldiers, and sailors all across Europe became decisive political actors. The Russian model proved inspiring; amid World War I and its aftermath, councils emerged in many other European countries, including Italy, Hungary, and Austria. In Germany, there would be sailors councils, workers councils, workers and soldiers councils, even councils organized by artists and by agricultural workers. Their activities were often confused and chaotic, their politics inchoate. But they were, everywhere, a grassroots form of democracy that allowed a wider range of political participation, addressed a broader range of issues, than had ever before existed in Germany.

Typically, councils were elected at mass meetings of workers on strike, of soldiers defying orders, of artists planning the future of a gallery or a theater. The delegates would then go off to negotiate with the forces of order, be they bosses, foremen, city officials, theater managers, or army officers, and come back and report. They might be unceremoniously deposed by those who, hours or days before, had elected them. They might return to rousing cheers. Chaotic, loud, unruly, usually masculine, the mass meeting and the council served as very basic and important forms of democratic expression. Once institutionalized, the councils were usually content merely to supervise the work of regular civil servants or factory managers. But they also inspired great hopes and dread fears. To their mainly working-class supporters, the councils, especially in the most heated revolutionary moments, like the winter of 1918–19 or the spring of 1920, were the vehicles for bringing, at long last, democracy and socialism to Germany. To their opponents, including moderate Social Democrats, the councils were the very embodiment of "Bolshevik conditions," which, to them, meant political terror, insecurity, chaos, and economic disaster.

The revolution of 1918–19 spread from Kiel by railroad. Its movement can be tracked by railroad timetables as sailors set out from the port city to spread the word that they had had enough of war and had risen up against their officers. They went to Bremen, Hamburg, Bochum, Essen, Braunschweig, Berlin, farther south into Munich and Bavaria. The news of the mutiny found a warm reception as sailors called for an immediate end to the war, the removal of the kaiser and his generals, and a new, democratic government. Women and men laid down their tools, gathered in courtyards or in the main hall of the factory, and demanded the same. Calls went out for a general strike. Soldiers stationed at home began leaving their barracks. Even a few officers had come to recognize that the kaiser had to go. The chancellor, Prince Max, felt political control slipping through his fingers.

Events were moving too quickly. From the factories, mines, and barracks, striking workers and soldiers streamed into city centers. Everywhere they elected workers and soldiers councils. On 9 November 1918, with tens of thousands gathering in key public squares in

Berlin and many more still marching on the city, Prince Max, desperately hoping to maintain order in Germany, handed over the Reich chancellorship to Friedrich Ebert, the head of the SPD. It was a momentous event, yet Ebert and his comrades were unable to celebrate their triumph. The power for which they had so long campaigned came to them in an inglorious fashion—by the action of the last chancellor of the last imperial government at a desperate moment in Germany's history, when the burdens of war and the anxieties of defeat cast a dark pall over every thought and every action.

From the balcony of the Reichstag building, the SPD leader Philipp Scheidemann proclaimed a German republic. A couple of hundred meters away, from the balcony of the royal palace, the famed radical socialist and antiwar activist Karl Liebknecht proclaimed a socialist republic. Ebert was furious. He discounted Liebknecht, recently released from the kaiser's jails, as a wild radical who might just as well have languished longer in prison. But Scheidemann was his close colleague, and no recognized body, no government, not even a political party, had authorized the proclamation of a republic. There had not even been a discussion. Ebert longed above all for an orderly and just transition of power. He was even willing to countenance the continuation of the monarchy as an institution, if not the person of Kaiser Wilhelm II. But under the combined pressure of the Americans and the popular revolt, there was no saving the imperial family. So on 9 November, the kaiser abdicated, and no one ventured to install a successor. Wilhelm Groener, who followed Ludendorff as quartermaster general, told the kaiser, "The army will march home in calm and order under its leaders and commanding generals, but not by order of Your Majesty, because it no longer stands behind Your Majesty."[17]

Scheidemann, for the moment at least, was the cleverer politician. He had forced the situation, and on 11 November 1918 Ebert and his colleagues formed a new government with their more radical cousins, the Independent Social Democratic Party (USPD). They were reluctant powerholders, but they moved decisively to strengthen the democratic course. A spate of decrees established freedom of speech, freedom of religion, freedom of the press, equitable suffrage, including for women, and amnesty for political prisoners. It was a momentous transformation, spurred on by the mass movement in the streets and the workplace.

And the government moved quickly to bring the war to conclusion. Soldiers were still in the field in France, Belgium, Turkey, wherever Germany had gone to war. Negotiations with the United States had not been going well. Now at least Germany had a democratic government. The new government also placed its hopes in President Wilson. It accepted the ultimate American conditions for an end to the hostilities, which required the German army to evacuate the occupied regions within two weeks and hand over large quantities of heavy military equipment to Allied armies. The left bank of the Rhine, properly German territory, was to be occupied by Allied forces. The Brest-Litovsk Treaty, which Germany had foisted upon revolutionary Russia to grant Germany control over a huge swath of European Russia, was to be immediately revoked. The Americans made no promises about the character of a final peace settlement, refused even to prevail upon the British to lift the North Sea blockade. Although some officers (and even civilians) called for a French-style *levée en masse*, a mass mobilization of the population against the enemies, cooler heads prevailed. They would later deny it, but most of the leading officers saw no choice but to accept the Allied demands.

So on 11 November 1918, representatives of the new government traveled to Compiègne in France and signed the armistice that ended the hostilities (the formal peace treaty would come later). The officers stayed in their headquarters at Spa. The war that they had wanted, that they had prosecuted to such disastrous effect for four years, was brought to conclusion not by their signatures, but by that of Matthias Erzberger of the Catholic Center Party. Avoiding public responsibility for its own actions, the military would quickly claim that Germany was robbed of its victory by the traitors at home, the Social Democrats and Jews and even Catholics like Erzberger. The infamous stab-in-the-back legend, which would be used to stunning effect by Adolf Hitler, was launched even before the armistice had been signed.

By the end of January 1919, the German army, which at the time of the armistice stood at around eight million men, had been reduced to one million.[18] The demobilization was an amazing operation, and it was anything but well organized and disciplined.

Hundreds of thousands of men streamed back from France, from Russia, from Turkey. Many of them, consumed by the desire to get home, had simply started off on their own. Ominously, many soldiers did not give up their arms as they were required to do. German society was hungry, ragged, and dispirited. It was also, to a very significant extent, an armed society.

Not only soldiers were on the move. The great armaments factories also had to be demobilized. Germany had no need any longer of huge quantities of munitions and machine guns. By the tens of thousands workers were dismissed from their jobs, given a ticket and, if they were lucky, two weeks pay, and packed off on the next train to their home villages or towns. Millions of women, recruited into the factories during wartime, were now curtly told to make room for the men returning from the front. Krupp is again a good example. In an amazing logistical operation, the firm fired 52,000 workers and had them transported out of Essen by the end of November. Within ten weeks of the armistice, the total workforce was down to 38,000, about one-third its size at its maximum in 1917, and fewer than in 1914. Of the nearly 30,000 female workers in 1917, only about 500 remained.[19] Some of the women went willingly, of course, happy to leave behind the rigorous working conditions and crowded and unsanitary cities, and to return to their families in more bucolic settings. Others deeply resented the loss of their pay and the relative independence it had given them. Prussian officials later reported, in typical bureaucratic language, that

> [t]he removal of women [from the factories] was not accomplished without the overcoming of considerable difficulties. . . . [Women] proved themselves diligent and skillful, while the men were more choosy. They refused to accept heavy or dirty work or left it after a short time. Thus it required especially vigorous measures to remove women from the coking plants, where they were employed at jobs completely unsuitable for them.[20]

The authorities had problems with the owners as well, who often wanted to hold on to female workers because they were reliable and cheap. Not rarely, employers threatened to close the factories if they were forced to fire women.[21] But overall, the official policy of removing women from industry to make way for returning soldiers prevailed. Some women managed to remain in the paid industrial labor force, though not in the highly skilled positions they had occupied during the war years.[22]

As each trainload of returning soldiers pulled into a station, nervous city officials went out to greet them. The victory speeches rang hollow. More telling were the leaflets that advised the soldiers to keep moving until they reached home, that the towns and cities they passed through could offer them neither employment nor ration cards.[23] Officials feared unruly soldiers and sailors, many of them still carrying rifles over their shoulders.

What did returning soldiers do when they got home? The severely wounded Lieutenant Friedrich Becker, Döblin's major character in *A People Betrayed*, ambles aimlessly around Berlin, going from meeting to meeting, observing political rallies and demonstrations, listening to political speeches. He participates in little of it. His old colleague Krug pays him a visit and then goes to see the Gymnasium director. Replying to Krug's description of Becker, the director says, "The soldiers from the front all come back a bit peculiar. They have no use for those of us who belong to the pre-war days."[24] Recovering from his wounds, Becker goes back to his old Gymnasium. The director wants to hire him but cannot. Finances do not permit it, and, in any case, he eyes the war hero suspiciously, not sure whether his once-reliable teacher of classics, a cultivated man from a respectable family, loyal to the kaiser, can still be trusted. Finally, Becker just sits at home and suffers a severe mental breakdown. Erich Maria Remarque has Paul Bäumer, his main character in *All Quiet on the Western Front*, comment:

> Had we returned home in 1916, out of the suffering and the strength of our experience we might have unleashed a storm. Now if we go back we will be weary, broken, burnt out, rootless, and without hope. We will not be able to find our way any more.
>
> And men will not understand us—for the generation that grew up before us, though it has passed these years with us, already had a home and a calling; now it will return to its old occupations, and the war will be forgotten—and the generation that has grown up after us will be strange to us and push us

> aside. We will be superfluous even to ourselves . . . and in the end we shall fall into ruin.[25]

Many returning soldiers constituted Germany's lost generation. They never felt quite at home anywhere, were unable to seize the initiative and get their lives on course, and were plagued by the uncertainty of the future.

But for others, politics had become the stuff of life. Everywhere in the winter of 1918–19, soldiers encountered meetings, demonstrations, and strikes, and sometimes, unlike Lieutenant Becker, joined in. Germany was experiencing not only a sea of movement—demobilized soldiers, sailors, and workers traveling back and forth across the country—but also a tidal wave of protest. The orderly German, so frequently stereotyped and satirized, had become an unruly figure. Miners, hungry and overworked, went on strike demanding a seven-hour day, then a six-and-one-half-hour day. Factory workers gathered in yards and halls and demanded higher pay and recognition of their councils. Women harassed price-gouging merchants and demanded that city officials and army officers find them the bread that had been promised so many times. Actors, stagehands, and cleanup crews at theaters went on strike and also formed councils. Proclamations were written and read, printing plants seized and the printers ordered to set type for a revolutionary declaration. Through the winter, the demands became increasingly radical. Workers called for socialization of industry; soldiers demanded that their councils exercise the power of command in the military and that all insignia of rank be abolished. Others demanded the formation of a citizens' militia in place of the regular military. Even agricultural workers went on strike and organized councils. Sometimes, events turned violent—an officer unceremoniously thrown off a bridge, then shot while attempting to swim ashore; a hated foremen thrown into a wheelbarrow and dumped on a garbage pit or, even worse, down a mine shaft. Middle-class people formed their own paramilitary organizations, determined to protect property and livelihoods.

Artists and writers joined in enthusiastically. The elimination of censorship and the overall turmoil stimulated their outpourings. They founded collectives, organized councils, and issued manifestos proclaiming the overthrow of everything that was old and stultified.

They believed themselves the vanguard of revolution, those who could lead the masses.[26] Indeed they had an unprecedented liberty to express their wildest fantasies, from Bruno Taut's imaginings of new, extravagantly creative buildings atop the Alps to the expressionist theater of Franz Wedekind and Ernst Toller, which probed the deepest emotions and proclaimed a new emancipatory spirit.

All of these artistic trends had their beginnings before the war, but the revolution dramatically broadened the sense of new possibilities and the openness to new forms of culture. And they were tied in with young people: revolution and youth ran together. To some, the prospects were indeed horrifying. Young people engaged in all sorts of ill-disciplined and dissolute behavior and no longer respected their elders. The Munich literary scholar, Gymnasium teacher, and, until the revolution of 1918–19, state censor Josef Hofmiller reported the student councils' vote to the effect that students no longer had to greet the professors at the Gymnasium respectfully and submissively. The students demanded the right to read a variety of newspapers and to eat where they pleased, not just in the school cafeteria. Hofmiller was incensed more by their brash self-confidence than by their particular demands. He worried that they were living "above their intellectual level" and suffered from a kind of "brain flu" because of their enthrallment with contemporary fashion and mass culture—which included, the ultimate horror, reading authors like Dostoevsky![27]

The disdain for authority was also evident in the way revolutionary soldiers removed epaulettes and walked around with their shirts open at the collar, or raced through the city in open autos, blasting trumpets and horns. The *Münchener Neuesten Nachrichten* wrote about the "pandemic dance contagion," others about the continual "carnival atmosphere" that had gripped the city. The new eroticism that would draw the attention of so many writers in Weimar was already evident, even in Catholic Munich, during the revolution.[28] Not only youth and revolution, but sex and politics also seemed to run together.

The very act of revolution, of taking up arms, violating work discipline by holding a rally, striking, marching, talking, broke the limits of normal, everyday behavior. It gave ordinary people, if for only a brief moment, a sense of power, of participation in the shaping of their own world. The great poet Rainer Maria Rilke attended a mass meeting in the large hall of a hotel in Munich on 7 November 1918, two days before the proclamation of a republic in Berlin. He listened to the famous sociologist Max Weber, "one of the best brains and a good speaker," followed by the tense, excitable anarchist Erich Mühsam, then students and soldiers. The mix of participants was itself a sign of revolution. Rilke was taken with the event, with the crowd pressed close to one another so that the waiters could barely make their way; the air heavy with the redolence of beer and smoke and human bodies; the simple, open rhetoric of the common people. A young worker sprang up, addressing himself to Weber and other eminent individuals on the podium. He began his remarks with *Sie*, the formal "you" in German; then, stumbling to find the right form of address in a revolutionary moment, he switched to the informal *Ihr*. "Have you made the armistice offer?" he continued. "Then *we* must do it, not the gentlemen on high; let's take over a transmitter and we'll talk, the common people to the common people over there, and there will simply be peace. . . . Here, the gentlemen professors [addressing himself to Weber and others], they know French, they'll help us, so we say correctly what we think."[29]

That was the revolution: common workers finding their voice and a place to articulate their beliefs, searching for redress from the difficult situation—war, hunger, the harsh conditions of labor—in which they lived. Of course, not everyone was so taken with the movement as was Rilke, whose own enthusiasm would soon fade. The conservative writer Oswald Spengler also witnessed the revolutionary events of 7 November 1918 in Munich, if not in the same hotel hall as Rilke.

> I experienced the repugnant scenes of 7 November. . . . and am choking with disgust. And then the way that Kaiser Wilhelm was chased away, just like the way one throws out some lowlife [*Lumpenhund*] . . . after he had worked selflessly for thirty years and had sacrificed himself for the greatness of Germany. . . . Has the unruly lower class [*Pöbel*], which in other countries is vulgar beyond bounds, now reached us with its vulgarity? . . . I see that the German revolution has taken the typical course, slow destruction of the existing order, collapse, wild radicalism, chaos. We need some harsh punishments . . . until the time is right for that small group . . . to be called to leadership: Prussian

> nobles and Prussian officials, the thousands of our technicians, learned people, artisans, workers, all of them with Prussian instincts. . . . A lot of blood has to flow, the more the better.[30]

Liberals were also aghast at the chaos and disruption that the revolution spawned. Corresponding with her son Gerhard (who would later change his first name to the biblical Gershom and gain fame as a scholar of Jewish mysticism), Betty Scholem complained that the family's printing shop suffered strikes and demonstrations. She worried about the armed conflicts in the street and the absence of electricity.[31] But worse was yet to come. "We have an unbelievable week behind us, dismal to the highest degree. . . . [The Spartakus] reign of terror was fearful." A favorite public clock was shot up; bullets flew through the window of the local butcher shop. Ghostly groups of men hung about; the headquarters of the SPD newspaper, *Vorwärts*, was in a fearful state.[32] For Scholem, the revolution brought no promises of a glorious future.

Management would eventually reassert its power, the army preserve its officer corps—but the tastes derived from purposeful action on a scale beyond one's own four walls, those tastes lingered. And the reverberations sounded far beyond the soldiers and sailors and the working-class communities that were the centers of protest in 1918–19. The hyperactive vitality of Weimar culture, of its music, theater, film, photography, derived its intensity from the act of revolution, from the psychological sense of engagement, the heady enthusiasm, the notion that barriers had been broken and all things were possible. "With what hopes had we come back from the war!" wrote Arnold Zweig years later, remembering the revolution.[33] Like many others, he would soon be disappointed, but he threw himself into politics, then into his writing, like a demon. "I have big works, wild works, great, well-formed, monumental works in my head!" he wrote to his friend Helene Weyl in April 1919. "I want to write! Everything that I have done up until now is just a preamble."[34] And it was not to be "normal" writing. These are the times of galloping stallions and wide-open furrows, and talent is everywhere. War and revolution have drawn people out of the confining security of bourgeois life. "The times have once again placed adventure in the center of daily life, making possible once again the great novel and the great story."[35] As Zweig indicated, expressionism, cinema, literature, an explosive theatrical world—they all had their roots in the dual sensibility of the vast destructiveness of war and the powerful creativity of revolution. And they were sustained by the very fragility of Weimar's political order, which lent a continual sense of edgy nervousness to Weimar society that imbued the cultural realm.

Revolution was creative, but it was also chaotic. From the very moment he took office, the Social Democrat Friedrich Ebert worked feverishly to channel political energies down disciplined, regulated paths. More than anything else, Ebert feared that the Russian Revolution would be replicated in Germany. Ebert and his colleagues believed deeply in democracy and the replacement, eventually, of capitalism by a socialist organization of the economy. But what their Russian counterparts had accomplished, they also believed, was the creation of economic chaos and political terror, the very antitheses of democracy and a progressive social system. The massive project of restoring order and creating liberty in Germany required careful organization. Germans were hungry and cold; food and coal had to be procured, men put back to work, democratic institutions constructed. Germany would not, could not, tolerate "Bolshevik conditions," as he and his supporters repeated time and again.

Ebert believed that government had to be legitimated through democratic procedures, namely, the vote. German democracy had to be placed on a firm foundation, and only a new constitution could do that. Moreover, a free election and a new constitution would rein in his more radical coalition partner, the USPD, and would sap the councils of whatever legitimacy they might have acquired. To Ebert, the councils were not the embryonic form of a fully democratic society, one in which popular participation ran through all the institutions of society, including the workplace. He saw the councils, rather, as a dangerous radical experiment that smacked of Bolshevism. They had to be eliminated, but in the chaotic conditions of 1918–19, a direct assault threatened to backfire. With luck, elections and a constitutional convention would do the trick.

But the Social Democrats could not do it alone. They constituted Germany's largest party, but not a majority. They had to contend with five other major parties, plus workers and soldiers councils demanding some kind of participation in governance. Social Democrats had never before held national power. They had thousands of experienced party organizers, but not people skilled in running power and transportation networks, water and sewage systems. Ebert turned first to army officers, high-level bureaucrats, and capitalists, all those who, before November 1918, had by and large despised Social Democrats as traitors to the German nation. With each of these groups Ebert struck a deal. Army officers agreed to recognize the government and offered loyal troops for the suppression of the councils and the radical Left, and the socialist government agreed not to attack the integrity of the officer corps, nor to challenge its control over Germany's military. Capitalists agreed to recognize trade unions and grant the eight-hour day, and the government agreed to respect the rights of private capital and private property. The Social Democrats retained highly skilled civil servants, preserving their status and privileges, and they agreed to put their knowledge at the disposal of the government.

This was not Bolshevism, but a set of compromises aimed at steering Germany from the chaos of defeat and revolution toward democracy and economic revival. And they were fateful compromises. The forces of order were willing to work with Social Democrats in 1918–19 because they feared much worse, a Bolshevik tide that would engulf them. There was, to be sure, political activism and radicalism and chaos in Germany, but few prospects of a Bolshevik revolution. The old elites and the Social Democrats were, however, together in the grips of panic. They ran toward one another and embraced, but only temporarily. Once the sense of panic had passed, once officers, civilian officials, and capitalists felt the balance of power again shifting in their direction, they would look for other allies, which they found, ultimately, in the Nazi Party. The Social Democratic unwillingness, in the winter of 1918–19, to break the powers of their longtime adversaries would come back to haunt them from 1933 to 1945, the twelve long years of the Third Reich.

In mid-December 1918, the General Congress of the Workers and Soldiers Councils, with delegates elected from all over Germany, met in Berlin. It was the site of the great clash of ideas concerning the fate of the German revolution. The Social Democrat Max Cohen presented the government's side of things, to huge applause and loud catcalls all at the same time.[36] He spoke eloquently and movingly about the dire situation in which Germany found itself, but also of the promise of democracy and socialism. He quoted Marx and Heine. (Every German political speech had to quote one or another of the great nineteenth-century poets.) But, over and over, he called for order, production, discipline. Without those qualities—those traditional German qualities—there would only be more hunger, more chaos. Workers on strike were demanding more in wages than the total revenues of a firm, he claimed. It was ludicrous to imagine that the United States and Great Britain, the two most important powers with which Germany had to deal, would undergo revolution. There were real dangers that Germany would not survive as a country, that it would be dismembered by the vengeance of the Entente and by the separatist strivings of Germans themselves in places like the Rhineland. Socialism could take hold only when production was at a high level; otherwise the results would mirror conditions in Russia, where people were freezing and starving. "When production is halted, as it is with us, when neither raw materials nor factories are available: what is there actually to socialize? In these circumstances *immediate socialization is complete madness*. There is nothing whatsoever to socialize!"[37] Germany could progress only if all of its people moved together; the middle classes had to be brought along to socialism, and only a freely elected, national constitutional convention could manage that, not the workers and soldiers councils. And only with a legitimate government would the Allies negotiate.

Cohen's reasoned speech had the support of the majority of the delegates at the congress, but it also aroused ire and ridicule. Calm reasoning is not always in high demand during revolutionary moments. For some in the hall and beyond, the privations of war and the injustices of the old system demanded far more radical solutions. Not parliamentary elections that gave Germany's middle and upper classes representation, but a political system based on the councils was the way to go forward. Socialize now; rely on the revolutionary actions of workers in other countries and alliance with Bolshevik Russia. Seize the moment. As Cohen's antagonist at the congress, the

Independent Socialist Ernst Däumig, proclaimed: "Seventy years ago the poet of the revolution [Ferdinand Freiligrath] said *that the proletariat is called to destroy the old world and build the new one.* That task was not fulfilled in his day. But that is our task; that is the demand of this hour and this day."[38] This was the voice of revolutionary élan, of fire and brimstone and utter confidence in the ability of the working class to change the world from top to bottom. The rotten, decomposing state that Freiligrath had named and attacked in his day now had to be fully destroyed, and it would not be through the speeches of parliamentary delegates or the pencil pushing of trade union bureaucrats. Only the activism of the working class—which Däumig also labeled "*das Volk*," conveniently forgetting the two-thirds of the population that could not by any stretch of the imagination be classified as workers—would bring about the new day. That activism, according to Däumig, would find its political form in the workers and soldiers councils.

Despite the increasingly vibrant popular movement through November and December 1918, the Social Democrats triumphed at the congress and were able to contain the more radical potential of the councils. The delegates voted in favor of the quick convening of a constitutional convention via free and universal elections. The congress confirmed the government's powers. It also granted the Central Council oversight authority, though this soon became a dead letter. The mass movement was able to extract numerous concessions in the realm of wages and working conditions, and it certainly caused major disruptions, but it was too inchoate to become a true locus of power. That lay increasingly with the regular government headed by Ebert, the traditional bureaucracy, and the army.

From late December 1918 into the spring and summer of 1919, the military in particular regained the initiative. In numerous small-scale conflicts, some of them quite bloody, it suppressed the soldiers councils and also began to organize more cohesive and trustworthy units, some of them paramilitary formations that were given license to exercise extreme violence. Radical Berlin workers and the nascent Communist Party staged an armed revolt in January 1919, but this served only to marginalize the extreme Left and to enhance the Social Democratic government's reliance on the army and the right-wing paramilitary units that operated with the express approval of the government. The major Communist leaders, Karl Liebknecht and Rosa Luxemburg, were assassinated during the suppression of the revolt, the first in a series of terrorist acts carried out by the extreme Right that would continue to mar the public life of the republic. During a strike wave and workers' uprising two months later, the SPD defense minister, Gustav Noske, issued an order that "every person who is found fighting with arms in the hand against government troops is to be immediately shot."[39] It was a sad sign of the times, and of the government's terrible shortsightedness, that a socialist-led government authorized right-wing troops to shoot workers struggling for a more democratic and socialist Germany.

Amid this tense and unruly situation, Germans went to the polls. On 19 January 1919 they turned out in record numbers to elect a Constitutional Convention (which also assumed the interim role of the parliament). For the first time, women had full and equal suffrage. They were the great unknown in this election, and every party had its women's committee that sought to tailor the party's message toward women's interests. The largest portion of their vote went for the Catholic Center and the conservative parties, though they also contributed to a great victory for the Social Democrats. Yet Germany's political order remained deeply divided, and the SPD's support still fell short of a majority. The party constructed an alliance with the liberal German People's Party (DDP) and the Catholic Center Party, the three parties—known as the Weimar Coalition—most committed to turning Germany into a democratic order. When Chancellor Ebert gave the opening address to the Constitutional Convention on 6 February 1919, he faced constant interruptions and catcalls from the Right, though also rounds of applause from the Weimar Coalition delegates.[40] Ebert repeated his pleas for order, discipline, and hard work. He absolved the revolution and the government of responsibility for Germany's dire situation. Those were, instead, the results of a war, the mistaken policies of the old elites, and the vengeful attitudes of the Entente powers.

If one role of political leadership is to move along its constituency, then Ebert notably failed. He could never fully attack the old regime for the war, because the Social Democrats had supported it as well. Germany, in his rhetoric, appeared guiltless for the outbreak of the war. Instead of trying to shepherd the population to more reasonable expectations, he pandered to the Right and to its unbroken hostility to the Entente. Like his fellow citizens, Ebert was still full of illusions about what would be placed on the table at the peace talks. His rhetoric, certainly noted at the various embassies, was not likely to win any favors among the Allies.

> The war not only exhausted us. It also tremendously exhausted *our opponents*. And from this feeling of exhaustion comes their efforts to recover their losses from the German people and to bring the idea of exploitation into the work of peace. These revenge and rape plans require the strongest protest. (Bravo!) The German people cannot be made the wage slaves of other countries for twenty, forty, or sixty years. . . . The German people is resolved to hold responsible those who can be proven to have committed any intentional wrongs or violations. But one should not punish those who were themselves victims, victims of the war, victims of our previous lack of freedom.[41]

Ebert went on to complain that Alsace was being treated as French territory; Germans were being pushed out of lands they possessed; attempts were under way fully to control German finances and the German economy, leading to a "a general economic enslavement of the German people. . . . Now give us the Wilson Peace on which we have claim," he cried, but it would all be in vain.[42]

The delegates then went to work drafting a constitution—but in Weimar, not Berlin. The situation in the capital was still unsettled and dangerous, and the government thought that the "spirit of Weimar"—the symbol of classical, humanistic German culture—would help the republic win the acceptance of more conservative Germans and the Allies. Formally proclaimed on 11 August 1919, the Weimar Constitution protected basic liberties like freedom of speech and the press, declared the equality of women and men, and established free and equal voting rights for all German citizens from the age of twenty-one. The social reforms, some instituted by the first revolutionary government, others contained in the constitution, were no less significant: recognition of collective bargaining as legally binding, declaration of state responsibility for the unemployed and for the protection of mothers and children. The constitution also reestablished Germany as a federal system composed of eighteen states, though the central state had more power than was the case in the Kaiserreich and some small states were consolidated. The government, headed by the chancellor, was responsible to parliament, which was elected through a proportional voting system. A president was to be elected by popular vote every seven years, and he had the power to name the chancellor and the cabinet and, in extreme circumstances, to invoke emergency powers that would allow the chancellor to govern by decree.

The delegates produced a vital document that embodied the ideals held by liberals and democratic socialists since the mid-nineteenth century. The constitution drew the German political system more in line with liberal western and northern Europe than with the formerly imperial and soon-to-be dictatorial states of central and eastern Europe. There were flaws. The constitution had no stirring preamble that laid out a vision of a democratic Germany. The proportional voting system contributed mightily to the political fragmentation of Weimar. The electoral law that followed the constitutional mandate for a proportional voting system authorized representation in the Reichstag for every party that garnered sixty thousand votes. Deputies were far more dependent on their parties than on their constituencies. The powers granted to the president in emergency situations were too extensive. But the flaws in the constitution, so much debated as the republic entered its death throes in the 1930s and then after 1945, had less to do with the political system it established than with the fact that German society was so fragmented. A less divided society, and one with a more expansive commitment to democratic principles, could have made the constitution work.

While German streets were still engulfed by demonstrators and pickets, while paramilitaries operated at will, while German delegates drafted a constitution, the great powers convened in Paris to write the treaties that, they believed, would finally secure the peace for the future. Germans were not present at the initial meetings, and certainly not at the negotiations. This was a treaty that the victors had to negotiate among themselves: President Wilson of the United States, Prime Minister David Lloyd George of Great Britain, Prime Minister Georges Clemenceau of France, and Prime Minister Vittorio

Orlando of Italy. These were the Big Four, but the real power lay with the leaders of the United States, Britain, and France. Each was accompanied by an entourage of experts—officers, civilian officials, politicians, cartographers, demographers, agricultural specialists, and so on. Their task was daunting. The war had destroyed the old order. A century after the powers had convened in Vienna to reconstruct the European order shattered by the French Revolution and Napoleon, the victors of World War I had to create a new European order for the twentieth century. Boundaries had to be drawn, Bolshevism contained, new states established on the ruins of old empires. France and Belgium demanded recompense for the damages caused by the German army, and sought assurances that they would never again be threatened by their powerful neighbor to the east. In France and Britain popular sentiment demanded trials and even hangings of the kaiser and his generals. Representatives of colonies sought entrance to the proceedings to plead their case for independence. Would Wilson's rhetoric, a peace without annexations and indemnities, a world made safe for democracy, be fulfilled?

The victors summoned Germany's representatives to Versailles at the end of April 1919, and they would discover for themselves the fate of Wilson's promises. Their French hosts made a point of humiliating the 180-man German delegation by having their Berlin-to-Paris trains crawl slowly through the devastated French countryside. They were "brusquely loaded onto buses [in Paris] and sent under heavy escort to Versailles; their luggage had been unceremoniously dumped in the hotel courtyard and they were told rudely to carry it in themselves."[43] The head of the German delegation, the foreign minister Count Ulrich von Brockdorff-Rantzau, had been an advocate of a compromise peace and supported the new German government. But sporting a monocle and a haughty manner, he aroused the Allies' worst images of aristocratic, militaristic Germany. And like most Germans, he suffered from the delusion that Wilson, at least, recognized that a strong Germany would serve everyone's interests, and that America's views would prevail. A rather mild reprimand is what Brockdorff-Rantzau and the rest of the German delegation expected. In fact, the German delegation arrived in France with a small library of maps and detailed studies to serve as the basis, so they thought, for the negotiations.[44]

On 7 May 1919 the German delegation was summoned to a meeting at the Trianon Palace Hotel in Versailles. Clemenceau opened the meeting. "The hour has struck for the weighty settlement of our account. You asked for peace. We are disposed to grant it to you."[45] When it came time for Brockdorff-Rantzau to speak, he remained seated, a move that made the German minister a hero back home, but which the Allies viewed as a deliberate affront. His long, rambling speech only reiterated Germany's innocence and accused the Allies of adding to the number of German dead by deliberately postponing the peace treaty and maintaining the sea blockade. Brockdorff-Rantzau's speech was a disaster, one of the worst performances in the annals of diplomacy. Wilson, Clemenceau, and Lloyd George were all enraged. Wilson said, "This is the most inept speech I have ever heard. The Germans are really a stupid people. They always do the wrong thing."[46]

By evening, when they had had a chance to read the provisions laid before them, the German representatives reacted with stunned disbelief. The details were quickly published in the German press, and the sense of shock and outrage spread to the nation at large. The Germans were given two weeks to reply, and in that brief interval, only modestly extended, they managed to assemble detailed documentation and reasoned arguments protesting the harsh terms of the treaty. All for naught. Germany lost land in the west and the east, about one-seventh of its prewar territory, that virtually all Germans considered intrinsic to the nation. The losses included Alsace-Lorraine, the largest part of Posen and West Prussia, and the Memel region; the final fate of additional areas—notably Upper Silesia and the Saar, among others—was to be determined by popular referenda of the inhabitants. The treaty drastically limited the size of the military and required Germany to turn over to the Allies large quantities of existing matériel. It barred Germany from organizing an air force. Some diplomatic freedoms accorded most sovereign nations were denied to Germany, such as the ability to conclude certain agreements with Austria. Germany lost all its colonies and was denied admission to the League of Nations. Most glaring to Germans was article 231, by which Germany and its allies were compelled to assume sole responsibility for the war's outbreak. In the view of the Allies, the "war guilt clause," as it came to be known, established the legal basis for reparations claims. However, the amount of reparations was not established in the treaty, so Germany, in essence, had to sign a blank check.

The storm at home was violent. Even members of the governing coalition recklessly advocated refusal. The risk, though, was very great. It was all but certain that Allied armies would march in and occupy Germany should the government refuse to sign the treaty. Philipp Scheidemann, the first chancellor under the Constitutional Convention, took to the floor and, in words that could have come from the most conservative delegate in the chamber, cried out that all Germans, from whatever group (*Stamm*) or state (*Land*), stood together: "We are of one flesh and one blood, and whoever tries to separate us cuts with a murderous knife into the living body of the German people."[47] Scheidemann persisted in his overheated rhetoric: the treaty signified "pitiless dismemberment," "enslavement," "the creation of helots." "[This treaty] must not become the future book of law." "Sixty million [Germans] behind barbed wire and prison cages, sixty million at forced labor . . . [with] their own land made into a prison camp!" "The foot on the neck and the thumbs in the eye"—that was the meaning of the treaty. The stenographer recorded "stormy applause" and "active agreement."[48]

The speaker for the right-wing German National People's Party (DNVP), Arthur Graf von Posadowsky-Wehner, was even more scathing in his attack on the treaty. An old-line Prussian noble and bureaucrat, Posadowsky-Wehner labeled virtually every provision of the treaty "robbery." The loss of territory, the restrictions on the size of the military, the ban on union with Austria, the demand that the kaiser and his generals and officials be turned over to the Allies—everything was plain robbery, robbery of wealth, robbery of sovereignty. The seizure of Germany's overseas telegraph and telephone cables and radio transmitters grated especially hard on Posadowsky-Wehner and every other opponent of the treaty—it must have seemed like a particularly capricious and vengeful move, a rubbing of salt in the still-raw wounds. Posadowsky-Wehner claimed that a refusal to sign would lead to a "temporary evil," but Germany would retain its honor; and even if this meant the death of the German people, "after death, in our belief, comes resurrection." Acceptance would lead to the greatest misery for untold numbers of generations. The present generation must have "the ultimate courage

[*Todesmut*]" to bear the consequences for the sake of future generations. Posadowsky-Wehner was adept at marshaling history to his cause: Alsace was German to the core and had been stolen by the Bourbons; Upper Silesia had been separated from the Polish crown lands since 1253; the English swear by self-determination, but what about Ireland and India? And what can Belgium say to us after its shameful behavior in the Congo? And where are Wilson's promises? "This treaty is a Shylock treaty," he thundered to great applause, and Wilson was only the deceiver who covered his true intentions by posing as a friend to Germany.[49] The most the treaty supporters could muster in response was that Germany had no choice, and war, with all its dire consequences, would resume with an Allied invasion of the country should Germany refuse to sign.[50]

German efforts to have the conditions moderated, especially in relation to article 231, prompted the Allies to declare that Germany had "wanted and unleashed the war" and was responsible for the "raw and inhuman manner in which it was carried out."[51] The German fleet, interned at Scapa Flow in Britain, was scuttled by the crew, another grandstanding act that rendered the men heroes at home but only hardened Allied views of Germans as incorrigible militarists. The Allies gave Germany another ultimatum: it had five days to sign. With the threat of an invasion hanging over their heads, the government and the military command signaled their acquiescence, and the Constitutional Convention approved the treaty. But the entire government, including foreign minister Brockdorff-Rantzau, had resigned, and only with luck was Ebert, now the Reich president, able to form a new one. On 28 June 1919, exactly five years after the assassination of Archduke Franz Ferdinand, and in the Versailles Hall of Mirrors, where the German Empire had been proclaimed in 1871, two members of the SPD-led German government signed the peace treaty.[52]

By midsummer 1919, Germany had a democratically elected government, a new constitution, and a treaty that brought World War I to conclusion. Despite territorial losses, the country was intact, by no means a foregone conclusion in the fall and winter of 1918–19. One might have looked back over the preceding ten months with a sense of satisfaction and even some pride.

But everywhere the signs were worrisome. Only after the Versailles Treaty had been signed did the British lift the North Sea blockade, allowing more extensive imports required for production and basic domestic needs. Many cities still had food rationing in effect. The industrial economy was on the upswing, but not quickly enough, and inflation undermined the purchasing power of those who lived on fixed incomes. German soldiers were still stranded in far-off places like Anatolia and the Caucasus. Many regions of the country were governed under martial law. German paramilitaries had not only engaged in violent suppressions of strikes and demonstrations; they were also active in eastern Europe, fighting Communists and launching pogroms against Jews. The Right promoted a new style of politics that had emerged among the front generation—a style that glorified war and the trenches, that sought continually to re-create the sense of solidarity among men in battle, accompanied by a deep-seated, almost mythical fear and hatred of women. The Right was by no means the sole provenance of the culture of violence. Many of the supporters of the radical Left were also veterans of the war and had been moved by the heroic example of the Bolshevik Revolution. They, too, idealized male combat.

Moreover, Versailles left a host of problems that would cast a pall over the domestic and international politics of the 1920s and early 1930s. The reparations amount owed by Germany had not been specified. Numerous territorial decisions were contested. Despite the clauses for protection of minorities, almost everywhere in central and eastern Europe their status would become precarious over the course of the interwar years. And Germans never could accept the exclusive responsibility for the war assigned them by article 231. Throughout the fourteen years of the republic, Germans would fight and argue about every single issue. On only one item could all of them, Nazis to Communists, agree: Versailles was deeply unjust, a victors' peace that saddled Germany with enormous burdens to the benefit of foreign nations. The universal expression was the "dictate from Versailles." Many foreigners agreed. John Maynard Keynes, a member of the British delegation, quickly penned an eloquent essay against the treaty, which he denounced as a "Carthaginian peace." Keynes's book *The Economic Consequences of the Peace*, first published in 1919, would go through many printings and translations. It was, of course, welcomed in Germany.

Weimar would always be stalked by its opponents and would never be accorded full legitimacy by the population and institutions of German society. It would always be a site of the most intense contestation over every significant issue, every way of being in the world. Fear, loathing, and dissatisfaction found expression in the activities of right-wing military bands that engaged in assassinations and brutal repressions of strikes; in the endless discussions and plots of army officers for a military coup d'état; in the deliberations of business leaders who awaited the opportunity to roll back the power of workers on the shop floor and union leaders in negotiations. And they found expression in the constant needling, the unending damnations cast at the republic and its supporters—the "Jew-Republic," the republic of "traitors to the nation," of "stock-market hyenas," of monocled Prussian generals and frock-clothed priests. The Bolsheviks could kill their opponents and drive them into exile; German revolutionaries were more humane. The result was a contested legacy, a deeply divided civic and political culture. The success of the republic would hinge on its ability to manage Germany's precarious diplomatic situation and to oversee an economic revival. Achievements in both arenas were only intermittent. The environment in which the republic was founded, domestic and international, was hardly conducive to securing a democracy in the wake of a lost and disastrous war.

Still, as a result of the revolution, Germans lived from 1918 to 1933 in a political order more democratic than anything seen in Germany's past, certainly more liberal than what was wrought by the halting changes instituted by the last imperial government in the autumn of 1918. However troubled its beginning, however unsettled its life, the very fact that Germans had created a new political system, had forced the kaiser to abdicate, had won great social improvements—all that instilled Weimar with a vibrant, active spirit. The revolution and the founding of the republic unleashed one of the greatest periods of artistic and intellectual creativity in the twentieth century. "Moral renewal," "inner transformation," and "a new birth," the phrases that were voiced time and again among the revolution's partisans, found their way into the paintings, photographs, buildings, and philosophical ruminations that would define Weimar culture.[53]

2

Walking the City

Weimar was Berlin, Berlin Weimar. With more than four million residents, the capital was by far the largest city in Germany, the second largest in Europe, a megalopolis that charmed and frightened, attracted and repelled Germans and foreigners alike. In the 1920s it was one of Germany's and Europe's great cultural centers, the home of the Philharmonie, the State Opera, the Comic Opera, scores of theaters, and a cluster of great museums, all located in the center of the city. Berlin was a magnet for artists and poets, the young and ambitious. It had a glittering nightclub scene, including scores of homosexual bars, and a relentless fascination with the body and sex. Berlin was a great economic machine that churned out electrical goods, textiles, and confectionary products in huge quantities. It was the governmental center, and from the famed Wilhelmstraße, home of the Foreign Office, the Reich Chancellery, where the government sat, and the Reichstag, the parliament building, Germany's leaders and bureaucrats tried desperately to maintain order, promote prosperity, and revive the nation's international position. It was a city of leisure, with neighborhoods of elegant wealth and amusement parks, a zoo, and numerous lakes accessible by rail or streetcar to virtually all Berliners. Its infamous tenement blocks rivaled the slums of any great city for their darkness, congestion, and poverty. Tens of thousands of Russian émigrés, fleeing from communism, and Poles looking for work and business opportunities contributed to the city's international feel. Berlin's Jewish community was the largest in Germany, its main synagogue an elegant symbol of piety and prosperity. The Berlin Dom, the Protestant cathedral commissioned by

Kaiser Wilhelm II and completed in 1905, had a massive presence, its bombastic, late Renaissance style a testament to the pretensions and arrogance of the Hohenzollern rulers deposed in the revolution of 1918–19.

To walk the city is to experience voyeuristically all the varied, vibrant components of Weimar society, from the poor to the wealthy, the downtrodden to the powerful, architectural styles from neoclassical to modern, elegant shops and the everyday kitsch of working-class apartments with carved, cheap furniture and oilcloth table covers. To walk the city is to "feel" politics through the sight of street demonstrations, campaign posters, and party headquarters draped in banners. To walk the city is also to feel history—the various architectural forms, which in Berlin rarely predated the eighteenth century: the deliberate historicist style of nineteenth-century buildings; the museums that honored the past and sought to connect Germany to the wonders of ancient Greece; the monuments like the Brandenburg Gate and the Victory Column that glorified Prussian and German military victories.

To walk the city is, above all else, to sense modernity: the sight, smell, and taste of traffic congestion, industrial smog, polluted rivers and canals; the press of crowds jostling one another on the streets, train platforms, and subway cars; the relief of the cool breeze and clean water of the Wannsee, a weekend's escape by tram or railroad or auto with thousands of others; the glittering lights of movie theaters and restaurants, automobiles and traffic signals, illuminated advertisements, as night descends on the city; the seductive appeal of fashionable clothes elegantly displayed in shop windows. And after a long walk, one sits, the favored activity of city dwellers, perhaps Berliners especially. Wrapped up against the damp cold at the first, vague, elusive signs of spring, they linger over a beer or coffee and ponder and look—at the passersby, at the auto and streetcar traffic, at the stores across the way, at the gray sky.

We will start our walking tour at Potsdamer Platz.[1] Our guides will be two of Weimar Berlin's renowned *flaneurs* and *feuilletonistes*: Franz Hessel and Joseph Roth, complemented here and there by other great writers like Alfred Döblin, Thomas Mann, and Christopher Isherwood. We will try to make our way quickly, but like any Berliner, for that matter, any tourist, we might get diverted by the sites and attractions around us. It may take a while, but we will be richly rewarded. As Hessel described the joys of strolling around the city: "To walk slowly down lively streets is a great pleasure. The rush of others washes over you like a bath in the surf."[2] Once, as he was ambling through Berlin's elegant shopping district, he remarked:

> The Tauentzienstraße and the Kurfürstendamm have the elevated cultural mission of teaching the Berliner to stroll and gaze [*das Flanieren*]. . . . Strolling and gazing is like reading the street. Human faces, stalls, display windows, café patios, streetcars, autos, trees all become equally important letters that together make up the words, sentences, and pages of an ever-changing book. To stroll and gaze correctly, one should not have any particular plans. And because on the way from Wittenberg-platz to Halensee there are so many possibilities to eat or drink, to step into a theater or movie house or cabaret, one can risk promenading without any fixed goal in mind. Just follow the unplanned adventure that happens to capture the eye. Glass and artificial light help immensely; the latter especially as it competes with the last glimmers of daylight and dusk.[3]

Potsdamer Platz is the heart of Berlin, the most trafficked crossroads in Europe in the 1920s. Five major roads lead into it; each will take us to a very different part of the city. Twenty-five streetcars converge on Potsdamer Platz, along with untold numbers of automobiles, buses, taxis, horse-drawn carts, bicycles, and pushcarts—an average of 2,753 vehicles an hour according to an official count in 1928.[4] We start at the kiosk across from the tall traffic light. Five steel beams shoot out of a cement block and form a pentagon, connected high up by five rectangular steel panels, each holding a set of traffic lights facing the five streets that converge on Potsdamer Platz. On top is a slightly convex roof, a beacon at night as nearly one hundred individual lightbulbs shine upward. No ornamentation here: this is modern functionalist architecture in which the heaviness of the steel is balanced by the tower's light, open construction. The tower is a marker, visible a kilometer down each of the streets that lead into Potsdamer Platz. The clocks also serve as markers, the time regulators of modern society, reminding the passersby that it is the moment to return home, or make the opening curtain, or catch the train, or,

Fig. 2.1 Potsdamer Platz, the heart of Berlin, seen from the renowned Café Josty. The famed traffic light is in the middle, and all around is the hustle and bustle of modern urban life—cars, streetcars, trucks, and pushcarts, and everywhere people walking, talking, and watching. SV-Bilderdienst / Scherl.

just maybe, go off to work. Not everyone likes the traffic-light tower—one Berlin newspaper demanded its immediate destruction; another called it a "fool's play."[5] The city planners prevailed, however, and the tower, continuing its work, "watches over the play of the streets like a judge's seat at a tennis match"[6] (fig. 2.1).

Looking in one direction, we see the famed Café Josty; in another, the government district with its imposing buildings. Moving around the circle is fifty years' worth of transportation modes. A horse-drawn carriage carries kegs of beer. Automobiles are heading off to who knows where. A continual flow of streetcars stop to allow passengers to disembark; they are on their way to a café or theater, or just want to walk around the square to see what is happening. A few will while away some time before undertaking the short walk to the two major train stations, the Potsdamer right on the plaza, the Anhalter just a short walk away. Both connect Berliners to distant points east, west, and south, and also serve as mass transportation hubs. Each day tens of thousands of Berliners pour on and off the subways and commuter rails that run under Potsdamer Platz. Others climb the two or three steps up into the departing streetcar. A double-decker bus adds to the sense of a people in motion. A woman moves from café to café, selling flowers. Newspaper vendors are shouting the latest headlines, and, as the *Berliner Tageblatt* described the scene, they are the only ones who are standing still amid this bustle of movement. The array of offerings, representing all the political parties, left, right, center, and everything in between, has something for everyone. It is complicated, but why should life be simple? For every passerby who approaches with a few pennies, the vendors very nicely fold the newspapers, which offer "a little intellectual content to take away, a political opinion, a bit of information about the most recent events, a certain melancholy . . . of a summer evening . . . all the feelings and knowledge that the complete person needs for a weekday evening."[7]

At night the play of light is dazzling. The lights provide illumination, of course, but also stimulate desires, as the *Berliner Tageblatt* noted:

> What wonders of nature fill the plaza in the evenings? There is the evening red, for one. Also the evening green and an evening yellow. The glowing red can be explained scientifically by the fact that a large wine store has taken out a subscription with a firm that produces illuminated advertisements. The green and the yellow are similarly caused by a variety revue and a shoe factory. From the red light poets can already experience the fine qualities of the wine. The other colors also work powerfully on the imaginations of many people, so much so that what follows—the actual purchase of a pair of shoes or watching a show—feels like a mere shadow of the real experience.[8]

At night the lighted advertisements of the Kempinski Haus illuminate the square and, over time, accustom the passersby to the commercialization of daily life made possible by electricity. Soon they do not even notice the way their vision is both illuminated and assaulted by the self-advertisement of stores and cafés. As daylight comes, the ordered illumination of advertisements gives way to the utter chaos of painted and printed and unlit electric signs: on one building, the Pschorr-Haus, another sign, "Fight against cancer," directing pedestrians to a drug or health food store. It is election time; we see posters for the various parties, socialist, communist, liberal, Catholic, conservative, fascist, a panoply of images reflecting the diversity and chaos of Weimar politics. Around the corner there is an exhibit about the world war. In another direction, we see signs for offices to rent on the upper floors, and the ultimate, an advertisement for an advertisement, the solicitation to place a sign on a billboard.

Some observers loved the light in the elegant shopping district of Kurfürstendamm, not too far from Potsdamer Platz:

> The best thing . . . was the wonderful light which flickered over the boulevard. In the twenties there was much less bad and cheap lighting. There were candelabras on the Kurfürstendamm. The tree tops filtered the light and glimmering reflections of the advertisements gave the boulevard an intimate feel, which made every woman's face come alive. The streets did not thunder, they played music, a love song to the women of Berlin. In the twenties, Berlin was a gallant city.[9]

Even the buildings took on a different beauty with illuminated advertisements, which altered the passerby's sense of the structure's depth, height, and contour.[10] But all that, along with the many bars and cafés and new movie palaces, the sounds of jazz and the taste of ice-cream sodas, both imports from America, was rather too modern, too gaudy, for the older, wealthy generation. They still did their shopping on Leipzigerstraße off Potsdamer Platz.[11]

Some of those who arrive at the Anhalter Bahnhof and make their way in automobiles through Potsdamer Platz are ambassadors and ministers, generals and high-level officials. They could walk but are more likely to find a luxurious mode of transportation like a chauffeured car. Their destination is one of the more than twenty-five state buildings on Wilhelm- and Leipzigerstraße, both of which lead straight off Potsdamer Platz. Built over the course of the eighteenth and nineteenth centuries, and then rapidly in the fifteen years after unification in 1871, they house the Prussian and Reich state ministries, along with foreign embassies. Wilhelmstraße was home to the Foreign Office, the Finance Ministry, the British and French embassies, and many other major government buildings, all of them large,

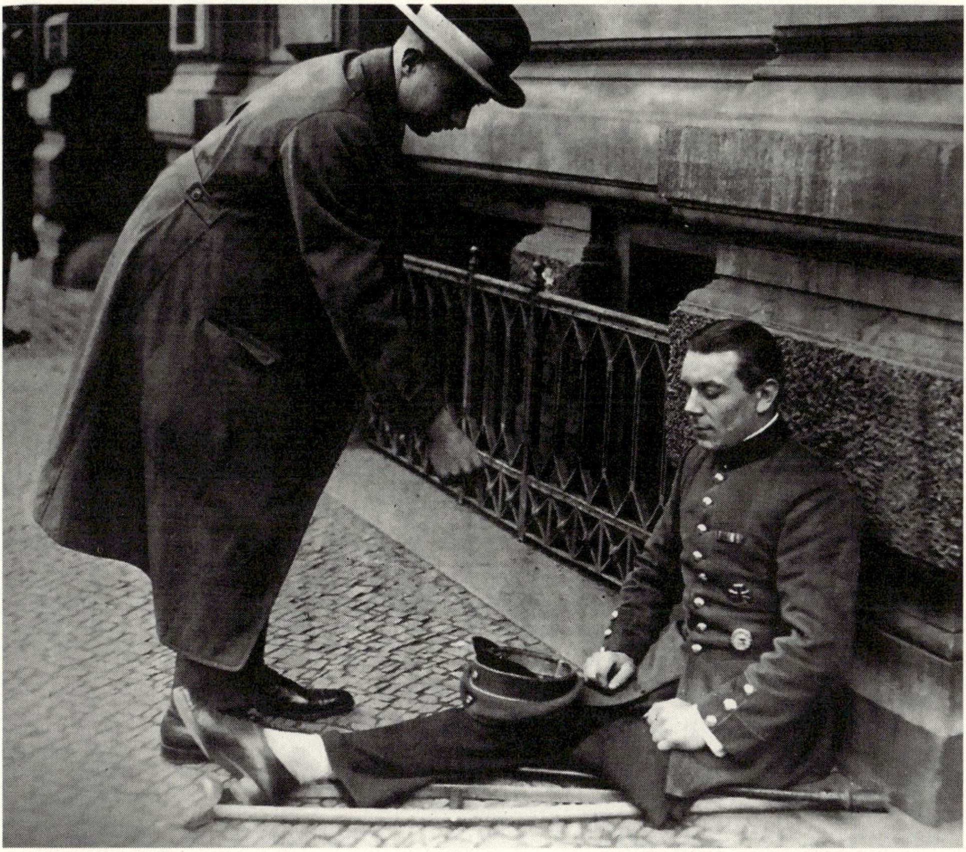

Fig. 2.2 The war-wounded were visible in every village, town, and city, here in Berlin.

imposing structures. The visitors, perhaps the individual state ministers of the interior, are on their way to a meeting with their Reich counterpart, or foreign diplomats to a reception at the Wilhelmstraße. But barely shielded from their vision, we see in the Anhalter Bahnhof, and everywhere else we walk, the war-wounded, the living testaments to the ravages of World War I—men without limbs, without part of their faces, without sight, sometimes begging, sometimes hobbling around, sometimes members of Berlin's legions of the homeless. Berlin alone had twenty establishments for the wounded. They, too, were a part of the street scene of Weimar Berlin (fig. 2.2).[12]

Railroad stations were the architectural glories of the nineteenth century, the monuments to the steel and iron and the fast pace of industrial society. The Anhalter, built between 1876 and 1880, was one of the most glorious in Europe. It loomed over the surrounding buildings, its heavy, powerful mass appropriate only for containing the strong steam engines of the railroads that carried Europe's leading diplomats and statesmen to Germany's capital. But the striking ornamentation of molded brick and terra-cotta, the pale-shaded sandstone used in part of the construction, and the semicircular arches that evoked Romanesque styles all lightened the weight of the structure. Inside—it is worth a detour from our street walk—the visitor finds not one, but four separate waiting rooms, divided by classes. To move from one to the other was well-nigh impossible: we have reached the first barrier on the walking tour. In addition, there were separate waiting and reception rooms for dignitaries, including the one that before the revolution was patronized by the Hohenzollerns.

From the Anhalter we might amble into any one of the dozens of beer halls and taverns in and around Potsdamer Platz. We decide on the Alt-Bayern. As the passerby quickly notices, this is definitely not Weimar modern architecture. Inside, there are many rooms and halls, most of monumental size. Ornamentation run riot defines the interior. Name an architectural style—Romanesque, Gothic, Renaissance, baroque—and you will find some imitation of it. Name a building material—plaster, wood, stucco, stained glass—and you will find it.[13] Nothing stops advocates of modernism faster in their tracks than the interior of the Alt-Bayern, though it probably does not stop them from ordering a beer there.

Still in need of entertainment, we stop at the Haus Vaterland—until World War I it was known as the Piccadilly, but the owners felt compelled to change its "unpatriotic" name.[14] The Vaterland offers patrons a virtual experience of Germany, Europe, and beyond. There is a Bavarian room, a Viennese room, a Rhineland terrace, an Italian room, and a French bistro, all with appropriate cuisine and decorations and waiters and waitresses decked out in "national" garb, gaudy red-and-white lamps for the Italian-inclined, lederhosen for the Bavarian aficionados, and so on. Those longing for a cruise down the Rhine listen to Rhenish choirs and watch artificial storms. Against a panorama of the Rhine from St. Goar to—where else?—the Lorelei on a sunny day, a variety of contraptions hourly let loose artificial thunder, lightning, and even rain. For those in search of something further afield, there is the Wild West Bar with its African American jazz band. Never mind the rather incongruous mix here—the patrons do not need to know that the great sounds of New Orleans, Kansas City, and Chicago were not quite situated in America's Wild West. Meanwhile, sixteen dancing girls wind their way through the various arenas of the Vaterland, changing costumes as appropriate. Four young men, garbed in the student outfits of the early nineteenth century, serenade the patrons with nationalist songs. Those with more refined tastes, or at least more money, head straight to the ballroom on the third floor. Along with dancing and cabaret revues, here the menu is more sophisticated and includes caviar, champagne, and pistachio ice cream. To aid patrons recovering from excessive alcohol consumption, the coffee bar offers supposedly genuine Turkish coffee. Perhaps no true Berliner would have been caught dead in the Haus Vaterland. Nonetheless, it does a lively business with the provincials who make their way to Berlin and want to experience the exotica of the city. But even for city dwellers, "for not much money you can get a breath of the wider world," as one Berlin newspaper put it.[15]

No doubt some of those who just enjoyed beer and a plate of pork hocks, feeling the residue of the fat swirling around their mouths, would like coffee and dessert. The Josty would be a good place to stop.[16] There are chairs and tables in front on the square, a garden in back, a glass-enclosed terrace, many rooms inside. Known for its pâtés as well as its confections, the Josty is crowded with the variety of bourgeois society—bankers and officials, intellectuals, society women and men, artists. All talking, looking, or, most often, doing both at the same time—the urban flaneur at repose. As the *Berliner Tageblatt* described it:

> What else does he need? A bit of refreshment for the body (in the form of a lemon ice), a little stimulation of the nerves (in the form of coffee), both are available here in the café's front garden. A little erotic can also be had.—Waiter, some erotic please, a half portion. At that the young lady seated at the next table crosses her legs together, and over there a young girl climbs the steep stairs into a bus.[17]

No nonsmoking sections here—cigar and cigarette smoke fill the air. But there are also the waiters, depicted by the writer Hans

Ostwald: “Suddenly a big, broad-shouldered gentleman comes over. His bony head with the gray-sprinkled beard and the red-speckled face, the large nose, the flickering eyes and the thick-lipped mouth—all that reminds one of a reactionary, agrarian representative in parliament, who makes huge profits from his industrial enterprises.”[18]

By evening it is time for more entertainment. The possibilities are limitless—plays from classical to modern, opera at one of the three major opera houses, classical music at the Philharmonie or any number of smaller venues. But less elevated entertainment is to be had as well, and here, too, the choice is staggering. We can find almost any kind of popular amusement somewhere between Potsdamer Platz and Kurfürstendamm. We can listen and watch sharp-tongued political cabaret written by famed satirists like Kurt Tucholsky, as well as many lesser lights. We can watch the “living theaters” of nude women, unless they happen to have been shut down by the police that evening for violating public standards of morality and decency. With Christopher Isherwood we might visit the Salomé, where in a gold- and red-painted interior, provincial Germans and foreign tourists come to eye the transvestites and lesbians. We can watch the Tiller Girls, whose dance line moves with military precision, at the more respectable Wintergarten theater. Or we can find a bit of almost everything, a mix of dance, music, and satire at the Schwarzer Kater on Friedrichstraße or the Linden Cabaret on Unter den Linden.

Perhaps we really want to hear some jazz, also easily available, but we will choose the real thing: an eight-piece band of African American musicians. They are playing the fast-paced syncopations of New Orleans jazz, interspersed with the windy, blues-jazz sound that evokes juke joints and smoke-filled bars up and down the Mississippi, a long way from the Kurfürstendamm and the Spree River. Why the Berliners' fascination with jazz? It is American and American means modern. The bending of trumpet notes, the interplay between trumpet and cornet, the strong rhythms provided by drum and piano echo the cityscape with its cacophony of autos, trucks, peddlers, and jackhammers. Jazz is the sound of the city elevated to art, and if Berlin does not have quite the same noises and rhythms as New Orleans, Kansas City, or Chicago, there is enough commonality that the musical form born in the very symbol of modernity, the United States, can be heard with such empathetic and knowing ears in Europe.

But jazz is not just American. It is African American, and that gives it an air of the exotic to Berliners. Except for the minuscule number of Germans who actually visited or settled in the country's overseas colonies before 1918, most Germans had encountered Africans only in the *Völkerschauen*, the traveling carnival exhibits that displayed darker-skinned people like animals in the zoo. The arrival on the World War I battlefields of African American and French colonial soldiers changed all that. Some African Americans, of course, lingered behind after the war or came back, musicians and artists especially, and they found Paris and even Berlin far more tolerant than the United States. But even for liberal and left-wing Berliners (along with many other Europeans), the fascination with African Americans went along with patronizing and racist attitudes. Jazz, in their understanding, was the immediate reflection of the "primitive" character of the "Negro," to use the polite language of the day. Jazz is loud and boisterous and childlike, closer to "nature," supposedly like the Negro himself. Unlike Europeans, "who can only dance with their minds," wrote one observer, responding to Josephine Baker's revue, "Negroes dance with the senses. . . . One can only envy them, for this is life, sun, primeval forests, the singing of birds and the roar of a leopard, earth. . . . [The Negroes] are a new, unspoiled race. They dance with their blood, with their life."[19] What better combination? Jazz was modern and "natural" at the same time; the rhythms of the city with the feel of the exotic, the expressionist and the primitivist bound up together.

Not far from Potsdamer Platz, in Berlin's less refined neighborhoods like Alexanderplatz or Hallesches Tor and many others, we can find more entertainment in untold numbers of bars and cabarets, many of them on the seedy side. Christopher Isherwood frequented them often. He was not yet a renowned author when he lived in Berlin in the late 1920s and early 1930s. His fellow lodger, Bobby, is a bartender at the Troika, which is far from the worst. It has a doorman and a cloakroom girl. But the place is nearly empty when Isherwood enters. A few young women lounge at the bar; employees yawn ostentatiously. The musicians talk among themselves. Suddenly a few tourists with money come in, anxious to experience Berlin's demimonde. The cigarette-boy and waiters descend upon the foreign guests. The three-piece band suddenly starts playing jazz. A few young men appear and begin dancing with the women from the bar. The "two flaccid gentlemen [the foreign guests] chatted to each other, probably about business, without a glance at the night-life they had called into being; while their women sat silent, looking neglected, puzzled, uncomfortable and very bored."[20] Everything is commerce and deception here, as it is with Isherwood's great character, Sally Bowles, a barely talented Englishwoman gone to the Continent to make a career for herself on stage and film. She also lives in an illusory world. She runs through scores of men, always looking for the one who can provide her with excitement and nice things. The men are all imposters—impoverished businessmen pretending to have money, supposed artists on the lam from the law in one country or another, aristocratic impersonators whose yachts and villas exist only in their imaginings, seedy doctors willing to perform abortions for a tidy fee. That, too, we see on our walking tour of Berlin.

Potsdamer Platz is not all for pleasure. By the 1920s, offices were plentiful, sandwiched in, between, and around hotels, beer halls, and cafés. In 1932 one of the fabled expressions of modernism, Erich Mendelsohn's Columbus House, opened right on the plaza. A nine-story marvel of concrete, steel, and glass, it stands out among the jumble of nineteenth-century structures. Its very name evokes America, the New World, everything modern. Far more massive than anything else on Potsdamer Platz, the building derives lightness from its smooth facade and extensive use of glass, both signatures of Mendelsohn's style, a huge contrast to the heavier, ornamented structures around it (fig. 2.3).

It is probably time to leave Potsdamer Platz. We will head out first on Leipzigerstraße, one of Berlin's most elegant streets.[21] Two small Greek temples, the work of the noted architect of the early nineteenth century Karl Friedrich Schinkel, mark the shift from Potsdamer to Leipziger Platz. The "temples" were originally the guard gates controlling entry into the city. They are small and elegant, with their carefully placed Doric columns evoking another world, far from the excess of the Haus Vaterland, the frenetic movement of traffic around Potsdamer Platz, or the modernism of Columbus House.

On Leipzigerstraße itself there are fine restaurants and cafés—none of the kitschy excess of the Haus Vaterland here. We pass by

Fig. 2.3 The bracing modernism of Erich Mendelsohn's Columbus House on Potsdamer Platz, built 1931–32. Note the contrast with the other buildings. SV-Bilderdienst / Scherl.

elegant shops, the grand Wertheim and Tietz department stores, impressive office buildings, powerful government seats—the Reich Post Ministry, the War Ministry, and the Prussian Herrenhaus, close to the Prussian Landtag. Some of the government structures, like the Herrenhaus, built between 1898 and 1903, were erected in an Italian Renaissance style—a construction, not just of stone and cement, but also, through the invocation of the past, of the power and legitimacy of the state. There are also a few private mansions, like that of the publishing magnate Rudolf Mosse, also built in Italian Renaissance style, complete with impressive collections of paintings and sculpture and a major library. Mosse even had himself and select guests painted in Renaissance garb, dining in an Italian villa. The painting, completed in 1899 and still hanging in the mansion in the Weimar period, reflected the self-confidence of the German-Jewish bourgeoisie and their identification with the icons of Western culture.[22]

The modern department stores like Wertheim and Tietz have little in the way of kitsch. That was a great relief to Franz Hessel. As he described them, most of their goods are sober: "proper is the adjective." The great stores have made a profession out of sales, and the young saleswomen have been well instructed how to handle the goods and the customers alike—so well that "we have no idea how skilled are the sales artists we encounter, how perfect the suggestions when the salesgirls of Wertheim and Tietz gently pull us into their magical realm." The modern stores are not chaotic bazaars but "clearly arranged, well organized theaters. They indulge their patrons with their high level of comfort. In bright courtyards and winter gardens we sit on granite benches, our packages in our laps. Art exhibits, which spill over into the refreshments area, break up the displays of toys and bathing outfits."[23]

The new generation, male and female, has learned that satisfaction and pleasure are to be found in refinement, not in huge quantities and colossal portions.

> The Berliner of yesterday, in his striving for pleasure, always runs the risk of excess, of quantity, of the colossal. His coffeehouses are restaurants of ostentatious refinement. Nowhere the cozy, unpretentious leather sofa, the quiet corner, so beloved by the Parisian and the Viennese. Instead of calling out "waiter," he always yells the stupidly titled "Herr Ober." Instead of a simple coffee, it's called double mocha. . . . Time and again new "Grand Cafés" with seats for a thousand patrons are opened. In the lobby there is a Hungarian band, on the second floor two dance orchestras perform. . . . Yes, one gets something for one's money.[24]

But that was yesterday. The new Berlin is more refined, more elegant, more Paris-like.

Almost everywhere at the meeting point of the Stadtmitte around Potsdamer Platz and Friedrichstraße and in the western parts of the city, one finds fashion—a famed fashion house where women sit at elegant tables while pretty mannequins languorously recline; expensive autos near the Tiergarten, "very well cared for, 'superior' quality, [are] rolled out of the stock of the automobile company in sparkling perfection down to the finest details." The chauffeurs wait for the "gracious ladies" (*gnädige Frauen*) to step out of the stores.[25] Fashion from Paris still rules, but Berlin's elegant women have come into their own.

> Along comes a new kind of women . . . the young avant-garde, the postwar Berlin woman. Around 1910 there must have been a few very good years. They produced women with slightly athletic shoulders. They move so nicely, almost weightless, in their clothes. Their lovely skin shimmers, illuminated only by a little makeup. Their smile is refreshing, with good-looking, healthy teeth. With self-assurance and in pairs, they cut through the afternoon crowds and congestion of the Tauentzienstraße and the Kurfürstendamm; they swim the crawl while others lag behind with the breast stroke. Sharply and clearly they steer toward the display windows. . . . These young women have begun to find a style that is far removed from the snobbism of a fine brand name or contentment with the same old thing. Is it really true what one hears ever more frequently: that the elegance of the Berlin woman ranks with the best Europeans?[26]

Of course, Hessel answered in the affirmative: Berlin was on its way to becoming "an elegant city."

Hessel was describing the "new woman" of the 1920s, an image of elegance and refinement, of activity and athleticism, and one that flowed from its bourgeois origins to working women, from the capital city to the provinces (fig. 2.4). After World War I, women were out in public in far greater numbers than previously. To be sure, working women, poor women, had always been out, fetching water from wells and pumps, provisions from the baker and the butcher, bringing their own household products to the market to sell. But bourgeois women of the nineteenth century had been more restricted. They might go on promenades, but almost always in the company of male relations. Evenings out were also escorted affairs, whether to the theater or to a relative's salon. Since the 1890s, even bourgeois women had begun to stake their claim on the streets. The department stores were the decisive innovation: they helped create the modern woman as spectator and consumer. Even the volume of wares on display necessitated what today's retailers would call

Fig. 2.4 A Berlin street scene 1926: the new woman out and about.

"traffic" through the store. In Germany, the Schockens, Wertheims, and other new entrepreneurs went to great lengths to make their palaces of consumption "safe" and "respectable" places for women. As Hessel noted, the "shopgirls" were carefully attired and trained in proper etiquette; the stores were well lit. At least in groups, or in the company of maids, bourgeois women breached the confines of the home to enter the spectacle-world of consumption. And when the department stores turned their wares outward to the street, when the new construction techniques of reinforced concrete and plate glass enabled them to develop broad window displays, as in Erich Mendelsohn's Schocken stores of the 1920s, they made the streets, not just the interior of the stores, "safe" for respectable women.

So walking the streets in and around Potsdamer Platz, we see women alone or in groups eyeing the dresses, linens, or shoes in individual shop or department store windows, enjoying an *Apfelkuchen* at Josty or drinking beer at the Vaterland. Later in the evening, we see the new female army of white-collar employees—shop clerks and secretaries, social workers and physicians—bustling down into the subway station to find their way home after work. A provincial visitor might still be shocked by these women, the flaneuses as well as the office workers, the short hair, the short dresses, the cigarette-smoking and gum-chewing visage, the air of recklessness and determination. The association of women and the streets no longer had to suggest the streetwalker of ill-repute. Here as with so much else, modernity meant diversity: the prostitute and the office worker, the female factory laborer and the physician. To the flaneur Franz Hessel,

> [t]he agile, erect city girls with their insatiable open mouths are indignant when my glance lingers on their sailing shoulders and soaring cheeks. Not that they have anything against being looked at. But this slow-motion examination by the harmless stroller unnerves them. They notice that with me, nothing is hidden behind my glance.[27]

Or so Hessel believed.

Oddly enough, it does not take us that long to walk through the government district, past the elegant streets and shops, then by the Berlin Dom, the Museum Island with its wonderful collection of ancient architecture and other worthy emblems of high culture, to reach the heavily Jewish Scheunenviertel. Jewish settlement here dated to the seventeenth century, when Friedrich Wilhelm, the Great Elector of Prussia, offered asylum to fifty Jewish families expelled from Habsburg Austria. Despite special taxes and restrictions on their activities, the Jewish community flourished. Beginning in the mid-nineteenth century, large numbers of East European Jews settled in the Scheunenviertel, crowding its tenements and streets. The dense press of people and the prevalence of Yiddish gives the Scheunenviertel a pronounced eastern European feel. Yet Scheunenviertel had its longer-settled German Jews as well. Reform and Orthodox Jews pass one another on the street; eastern European peddlers jostle with well-attired businessmen and shop owners. Then there are the petty thieves, prostitutes, gamblers, and pimps, who spill over into the Scheunenviertel from nearby Alexanderplatz, captured so well in Alfred Döblin's novel of the same name. The two districts together could easily be the setting for Bertolt Brecht and Kurt Weill's *The Threepenny Opera*, with its mix of beggars, prostitutes, ex-soldiers, police, and corrupt capitalists.

To Joseph Roth, the great journalist and novelist, it seemed strange that just a short walk from Alexanderplatz lay a neighborhood "whose grime and greasepaint don't so much conceal its Levantine-working-class nature as emphasize it." With no transition "you find yourself suddenly immersed in a strange and mournful ghetto world, where carts trundle past and an automobile is a rarity." Roth described a neighborhood bursting with activity, Polish children playing on the streets, adults rushing past to make business deals, men dressed so well that they would not look out of place on the elegant Kurfürstendamm, bumping against bearded, eastern European Jews wearing velvet hats. All sorts of business deals are transacted, maybe legal, maybe not, while off in the corner a pious Jew prays.[28] And mixed in with them are the refugees, the Jews from all over eastern Europe who are fleeing pogroms. Many want to move on, to America, Holland, or Palestine. Some came straight from Russian prisoner-of-war camps.

> In their eyes I saw millennial sorrow. There were women there too. They carried their children on their backs like bundles of dirty washing. Other children, who went scrabbling through a rickety world on crooked legs, gnawed on dry crusts. . . . A small minority [of the refugees] are young and healthy. . . . The boardinghouse smells of dirty laundry, sauerkraut, and masses of people. Bodies all huddled together lie on the floor like luggage on a railway platform. . . . The odd one among these people will have intelligence and initiative. He will go on to New York and make a million.[29]

Scheunenviertel has odd street names for a Jewish quarter. It was once home to the gallows of Prussian justice and the stables of the Prussian army. Along streets with names like Dragonerstraße and Grenadierstraße

> the men, with their ancient beards and sidelocks, walk slowly in groups; the black-haired butcher's daughters move along briskly, up and down their street speaking Yiddish. Hebrew inscriptions are written on stores and beer halls. These streets remain a world unto themselves and a kind of home for the eternal outsider. Until, that is, a new wave of people comes from

> the east and pushes out the old-timers, who, after not too long a time, are already so well adapted to Berlin that it is enticing for them to move to the western districts. There they strive to give up the very obvious signs of their particularities. That's a shame, because they look so much better as they roam around Scheunenviertel than later in their off-the-rack suits at the stock exchange.[30]

The center of Scheunenviertel is the New Synagogue on Oranienburger Straße, and had we bothered to take the commuter rail, the dome and spires of the synagogue would have been visible from kilometers away—a visual affront to Berlin's many anti-Semites (fig. 2.5). The Oranienburger Synagogue was completed in 1866 and could hold three thousand worshipers. It is the very symbol of the prosperity and confidence of the Jewish community in Berlin. At the same time, the Moorish style of the dome and two spires recalled Jewish roots in the Middle East and the golden age of Jewish life in Spain, while the spectacular organ symbolized reform Judaism's efforts to be modern by navigating two worlds, that of traditional Judaism and Christian German society. We walk past the Jewish boys' school, with its commemorative bust of Moses Mendelssohn, the famous Enlightenment philosopher and founder of the school, the more recent Jewish girls' school, the old Jewish cemetery, the Jewish hospital, and the Jewish old-age home. The Hochschule für die Wissenschaft des Judentums (the College for the Scientific Study of Judaism) is the intellectual center of reform Judaism, and many of the luminaries of German-Jewish culture, including Martin Buber, Gershom Scholem, and Rabbi Leo Baeck, received their training or at least attended lectures here. Like the synagogue, the Hochschule is a beacon for the Jewish community and a sign of its efflorescence in Germany in the late nineteenth and early twentieth centuries. Incidents of anti-Semitism were on the rise in the 1920s, and some Jews formed paramilitary defense organizations. Still, German Jews by and large enjoyed material prosperity and an expansive community life. Some of the intellectuals among them contributed to the revival of Jewish learning, others were in the forefront of the artistic and intellectual innovations of the Weimar period, and still others straddled and

Fig. 2.5 The New Synagogue on Oranienburger Straße, built 1859–66 in Moorish style, was the main place of worship for Berlin's Jews and a sparkling symbol of the community's prominence and self-confidence. The main chapel could seat 3,000 congregants. The building was largely destroyed by the Nazis on Reich Crystal Night in 1938, and then further damaged by Allied bombs. The facade, entrance way, and domes were rebuilt in the late 1980s and 1990s. Bildarchiv Preussischer Kulturbesitz / Art Resource, NY.

mediated both worlds, the specifically Jewish and the secular German and European.

When we have wandered enough through the elegant shopping district along Leipzigerstraße and the cramped and bustling Jewish quarter, have had sufficient beer and pork hocks, coffee and pastry, it is perhaps time to head home. A bank clerk among us walks back to the subway station at Friedrichstraße. With a couple of transfers and some luck, he arrives at his stop, Onkel Toms Hütte, in thirty minutes. Leaving the subway—here not really underground but below street level—he breathes in the fresh, cold, late autumn air, which snaps him to attention.

The area around the subway stop had been completely forested just a decade or so ago. The population growth pushed at the limits of available housing, and where there had been a forest and one pub, Onkel Toms Hütte (a play on the title of the famous American novel by Harriet Beecher Stowe), there now emerged one of the planned housing developments of the 1920s, an entire complex of buildings that was home, mostly, to the ever-growing white-collar stratum. Social reformers and government officials alike sought to create new, more hygienic, and rationalized apartments for the masses. The results were prodigious: 2.5 million new apartments were built in the Weimar era. In 1930, around 14 percent of the entire population lived in newly built apartments. The construction plans "recall the maps of [the army's] general staff," with sewage, power, water, transportation, schools all taken into account.[31] The architecture both reflects and molds the new-model family. The apartments are small but functional: two bedrooms, "rationalized" kitchen, living room, just the ideal for the modern family of two adults and two children.

As our clerk leaves the subway, he can stop—if it is not too late—in the stores beside the tracks: bakery, flower, food, shoe, also planned, so the residents coming home from the office can shop conveniently. Our clerk walks over the leaves that have fallen to the ground and takes in the smell of autumn, damp yet refreshing. He probably fails to notice the architecture of his own settlement, at least since the first days he moved in. But he knows it is modern, which suits his self-image, and he might even know the name of the

Fig. 2.6 Onkel Toms housing development, designed by Bruno Taut and built 1926–32. Note the smooth facade and recessed windows, signatures of the modernist style, and the slight curvature to the structure. Author's photograph.

architect, Bruno Taut. And he knows that his modern apartment is certainly more comfortable than the tenement from which he moved. The exterior of the three- to four-story building is flat, no ornamental protrusions, and it runs the length of a long city block. It has a sleek feel to it. If he bothered to stand at one end, he would notice the curve to the structure: it does not sit quite parallel to the straight street. As with Mendelsohn's Columbus House, the curvature gives the long building a dynamic quality, a sense of movement, accentuated by its recessed windows (fig. 2.6).

And, really, it is quite a pleasurable setting, a retreat from the noise and bustle of Potsdamer Platz, which is just what the architects and planners intended. Onkel Toms Siedlung is designed as a place of refuge where modern man can have a break from the nervousness of urban, industrial life. He is supposed to be able to find comfort and rest in a modern apartment guided by an efficient and loving wife. Indeed, the quiet is broken only by the noise of the subway or by children playing. A few meters from the apartment one can walk in the woods. Children's playgrounds have been built, and there is a central laundry facility and a kindergarten. Right nearby are churches, mostly Protestant, which many Germans, even Berliners, still attend on a regular basis. Modern amenities are important: each apartment has its own bathroom with hot and cold running water, central heating, and gas lines that fire the stove and oven—a huge improvement over the inner city districts where many residents still use common toilets in the hallway, pump water in the street, and haul coal or wood to light the oven. Sunlight streams into all the apartments, again quite a difference from the old *Mietskaserne*, the tenement barracks. In the daytime we see young mothers with their children in the park area, women stopping to talk as they go to the laundry room or to the market nearby. Onkel Toms Siedlung, like other new developments, is conducive to casual conversation; they establish a communications field among the residents, especially the women, while the men, after work, might be more prone to go to one or other of the nearby pubs: the community bans the sale of alcohol on the premises.[32] In the summer, Berlin's nearby lakes offer plentiful opportunities for swimming and boating. Onkel Toms Siedlung is indeed a refuge, one its residents desperately seek to protect. And our clerk might look at the long block of single-family attached houses that are also part of the development, not quite so modern in style, and imagine himself in this setting a few years hence.

Germany's modern architects were not content with designing just the exterior of developments like Onkel Toms Siedlung. They were interior designers as well, and they wanted the residents to live the functionalism that was on display. That meant a war against kitsch and clutter, against cheap oilcloth, frilly upholstery, and carved furniture. Our clerk and his wife did not rally totally to the architects' standards. They kept the decorations and furniture they had when they lived in a tenement. They choose to temper the modernism promoted by the architects and planners; in any case, they lack the money to outfit their new apartment with completely new furnishings.

In Onkel Toms Siedlung we are amid but not quite a part of the western districts, Grunewald, Dahlem, and Zehlendorf, Berlin's "better" neighborhoods. In the 1920s they are no longer "in"; they are just respectable, gleaning the respect that comes from wealth, status, and power.[33] Bankers, industrialists, high government officials, well-paid professionals and artists all live here. They were depicted by Thomas Mann as those for whom "the arrangement of life was so opulent, so manifold, so overdone, that there was virtually no room left for life itself."[34] After the opera, Sigmund, the main character in Mann's story "Wälsungenblut," has a caviar sandwich and a glass of red wine, elegantly laid out by the servants in the magisterial home that he and his twin sister occupy with their parents and an extensive staff of servants. Then he complains that "caviar and red wine are a barbaric combination."[35]

But there were other residents in the fashionable West End. Franz Hessel describes an evening he spent with an elderly woman, a member of the upper class. She is a secretary and archivist of the past, one who has held on to the artifacts of status of a bygone age. She shows him a large English doll clothed in fine muslin; the family book going back generations, with dedications and poems written in excellent penmanship; landscape paintings with hunters decked out in yellow jackets and riding boots. The bouquets of flowers in the pictures match the etchings on the porcelain plates and vases that bear the inscription "Royal Berlin." He is permitted to hold a bridal wreath from 1765, spun from green silk, also a tobacco box made out of agate. Family portraits grace the walls, "the heads of women with curled, lightly powdered hair and delicate, colorful shawls, men in wigs and dark blue tailcoats." She recalls four-poster beds "*à la duchesse* and *à tombeau*," nightcaps and night gloves, "wallpaper *en hautelisse* with figures copied from French designs." She brings out an unending array of possessions, daguerrotypes, carved and lacquered figurines, ink drawings. Suddenly Hessel notices "how tired I am from so much of Berlin." It is all rather too much—too much decoration, too much clutter, too much of the past, too many foreign influences. He leaves, hungry for the sights and sounds of the modern city.[36]

Berlin-West was open to new talent and new money, even if the individuals were subject to savage satire. The writer Carl Zuckmayer described the nouveau riche of the western districts as a successful confidence man who believed himself free of all ties to law and destiny. He is an independent "personage" who makes his way as he wishes. But all he really displays is the "impersonal, unprincipled, and conformist features" of this group. The older bourgeoisie, still tied to their traditional values and, perhaps, to the other parts of the country from which they hailed, were as distinct from the superficial, rootless nouveaux riches as a true painting from a smeary oil reproduction. In the "outmoded dignity of their clothing and bearing, there was something young, fresh, and lively about them."[37]

Franz Hessel, as much as he loved the modern city, also recoiled from the nouveaux riches. With fondness he remembered growing up in the "old West," and he recalled the texture of the homes: "So many memories are wound up in the sober, solid staircases with brown wooden banisters, the plain walls, and the figures etched in gray in the window glass, also by certain palace steps steeply rising to the main floor, smooth marble walls and pompous, colorful paintings on glass." It is easy to find the old world, even under layers of the modern:

> [B]ehind the cabinets that served as barricades was the glass sliding door, which once separated the salon and the Berlin room. We see on the sloped divan the shadows of the piano, which back then stood there with its velvet throw and the family photographs. Near the window, in a rather pitiful vase, we find something of the tropical world, a palm plant. From the step stool at the courtyard window of the Berlin room we look out onto the courtyard with the pale-colored grass shooting up between the stones. Only the old general's stable and coach house on the first floor have been pushed out by an auto repair shop.[38]

Even in odd places one could still find traces of elegance—a frieze of grapes, a sculpture of a female mask between two naked youths, a door frame made to mimic a temple gate. These were the last works of the great architect Schinkel's last students, part of the Prussian mimicry of Greek style, an effort to claim a line of succession from classical Athens to nineteenth-century Berlin.[39]

There was another kind of nostalgia, the setting less elegant than Hessel's West or the elderly aristocratic woman with whom he spent an evening, but no less poignant. Isherwood had a landlady who pined for the comforts she had once known. Long ago, before the war and the inflation, she had at least the means to employ a maid and spend summer holidays on the Baltic. Now, in the Berlin of the late 1920s and early 1930s, she is reduced to taking in lodgers of an ever lower sort.

> "You see, Herr Issyvoo [her mangling of his English name], in those days I could afford to be very particular about the sort of people who came to live here. . . . I only took them really well connected and well educated—proper gentlefolk (like yourself, Herr Issyvoo). I had a Freiherr once, and a Rittermeister and a Professor. They often gave me presents—a bottle of cognac or a box of chocolates or some flowers. And when one of them went away for his holidays he'd always send me a card—from London, it might be, or Paris, or Baden-Baden. Ever such pretty cards I used to get."[40]

Now she has as tenants a prostitute, a second-rate cabaret singer, a bartender in a run-down establishment, and an impoverished Englishman with literary ambitions. She lacks even her own room. Instead, she sleeps in the living room behind a screen on a small, broken-down couch, and does all the housework herself. All night long she is disturbed by tenants walking through the living room on their way to the bathroom in the hallway. Outside, at nighttime, prostitutes congregate, and everything appears worn and tired.

> From my window [Isherwood writes] the deep solemn massive street. Cellar-shops where the lamps burn all day, under the shadow of top-heavy balconied façades, dirty plaster frontages embossed with scrollwork and heraldic devices. The whole district is like this: street leading into street of houses like shabby monumental safes crammed with the tarnished valuables and second-hand furniture of a bankrupt middle class.[41]

There were many Berliners living, like Isherwood's Frau Schroeder, amid faded elegance and ever brighter memories of a bygone age.

The western districts were home to the well-off, but the development of mass transportation from the late nineteenth century on had opened their woods and lakes to all of Berlin's residents, and especially to the new middle class of the 1920s, who, at least in the latter part of the decade, have a Sunday and some spending money available to take in the pleasures of the sun and the water. Sunday, a day of rest, is to be spent with family or friends in the large stretches of forest and water, a respite from the noise and bustle of the city and its shops, offices, and factories.

On Saturday, we go early to the baker and butcher to buy some bread, cheese, and sausages to take with us, also some bottles of beer. We pack a rucksack and take the subway to the Krumme Lanke stop—the end of this particular line and one stop past Onkel Toms Hütte. Our goal is two small lakes, Krumme Lanke and Schlachtensee, and then the Wannsee, one of the glories of Berlin. It is a ten-minute walk from the subway stop to the woods. The streets are tree-lined, the gardens behind the high walls lush. Even fruit trees are to be found, along with the usual deep and colorful display of flowers that grace so many German homes. We see large brick houses of the nineteenth century, three stories high with impressive windows and balconies, all partly hidden behind brick walls and lush, verdant trees. But some of the wealthy residents of the western districts, perhaps patrons of the arts in their spare time, wanted a modern look. The great and near-great architects were kept busy in the 1920s, and we see some of the grand examples of the modernist style—straight, sleek lines without ornamentation and with large windows. To their detractors, the boxy style of modernist houses is hardly appropriate for the reputable life. For others, it is a break with the past and a badge of modernity. For Isherwood, the pretensions of the upper class were revealed in a riotous clash of styles. He gave English lessons in Grunewald, and he described the home of one of his clients:

> The hall of the Bernstein' house has metal-studded doors and a steamer clock fastened to the wall with bolt-heads. There are modernist lamps, designed to look like pressure-gauges, thermometers and switchboard dials. But the furniture doesn't match the house and its fittings. The place is like a power-station which the engineers have tried to make comfortable with chairs and tables from an old-fashioned, highly respectable boarding house. On the austere metal walls, hang highly

> varnished nineteenth-century landscapes in massive gold frames. Herr Bernstein probably ordered the villa from a popular avant-garde architect in a moment of recklessness, was horrified at the result and tried to cover it up as much as possible with the family belongings.[42]

But we do not get to see the interior of such houses. Instead, we hike in the woods for a while, then circle the Schlachtensee. The summer heat is not oppressive in this setting, and we know that the waters of the Wannsee will soon cool us off. From the path around the lake we see the villas of the very wealthy, who have a commanding view of the woods and water. We pass all sorts of people walking, sitting on the benches—lovers nestling into one another; children running up and down, attempting to skim rocks in the lake; older couples sitting quietly and watching, taking it all in—every other person with a dog large or small, often let loose to run around. And everyone studies everyone else, furtive and not-so-furtive glances with which they attempt to decipher the lives behind the gait and the visage of the passersby. Some people have rented boats and are rowing across the lake; a few people are actually fishing from the banks. We decide it is time for a snack and take out a *Käsebrötchen*, the crusty roll that is a Berliner staple, smeared with butter, layered with cheese and cucumbers. Or a *Schinkenbrötchen*, graced with a thin slice of smoked ham, or perhaps with one of those indefinable salami-type meats, the cheaper concoctions that Berliners consume by the thousands of pounds. A slice of *Apfelkuchen* finishes off the snack—no Berliner would call this a meal.

We circle the Schlachtensee, but to get to Wannsee we have to leave nature—pruned and cared for as it may be—and walk some way along the street and past people's homes. But soon the large lake opens out before us. The lake area is packed with people—many picnicking or lying in the sun, children playing, everyone swimming—as are so many of the beaches around the lakes in the western districts (fig. 2.7). Class differences, so finely articulated among Berliners in work, dress, and speech, are not so clearly noticeable, at least not from a distance. We sit down against one of the canopy seats, stretch out for some of the season's last rays of sunlight, sleep a little. Then it is off to the boat rental; we take a rowboat, which is not very expensive, and make our way in between and around the

Fig. 2.7 A weekend at the lake in Berlin West, looking out at the Wannsee. People swim, sail, and sunbathe, a respite from the hectic pace of urban life. Bildarchiv Preussischer Kulturbesitz / Art Resource, NY.

sailboats. There must be hundreds of boats out on the lake, and it is refreshing to be away from the bustle of the city center. The winds are westerly , which is good—the clean air of the North Sea and the Brandenburg countryside sweeps over us before it has a chance to mingle with the factory, coal dust, and automobile pollution of the city. Out in the middle of the lake we can stow the oars and just drift, eat or drink a little more, relax. We could go further out, where the Wannsee connects to the Havel, and make a grand tour around the river and the many small lakes that connect to the Wannsee. But it is Sunday and we are content not to row too strenuously, so we drift.

Before we know it, it is early evening. The sun sets late, so there are still hours of daylight. We make our way to shore, then to a beer garden. Sausages, rolls, beer are the fine accompaniment to the waning hours at the lake. Then it is off to the subway. Monday is a workday. We head back to the city and think drearily about a Monday at the drill press, on the sales floor, or at the desk, and dream about the next weekend.

Berlin is also a working city. For some of those, perhaps just a few, who had ventured out to Wannsee on Sunday, the return meant going back to the heart of the city, to Wedding, one of the centers of proletarian Berlin. Factory workers from the nearby electrical and machine-building plants live here, along with day laborers, teamsters, seamstresses, washerwomen—the whole array of working-class Berlin, along with the netherworld of thieves, gang leaders, and prostitutes. Though predominantly poor and working-class, Wedding, like most Berlin districts, had something of a mix of residents. Even before World War I it was known as "Red Wedding" because of the strong Social Democratic presence in the neighborhood. During the Weimar era Communists dominated the area. By the time of the Depression, Nazis and Communists battled for control of pubs, courtyards, and streetcorners. Everywhere in Wedding we see the signs of politics. Hammer-and-sickle emblems and swastikas are pasted on kiosks. Electoral posters depict Adolf Hitler or Communists marching over the ruins of Germany's upper classes. Storm troopers and Red Front Fighters eye one another warily. Communists march singing Hans Eisler's 1929 composition "Red Wedding," which summons the working class to the battle against capitalism.

> Red Wedding greets you, comrades.
> Keep your fists ready!

Hold tight the red ranks,
For the day is not far off!
We struggle as socialists
Finally in one, united front!
Working brothers, Communists,
Red Front! Red Front! . . .

Left, left, left, left!
The struggle continues
Left, left, left, left!
A scoundrel, whoever capitulates!
We spread the truth from house to house
And chase the lies out the chimney,
As Karl Marx and Lenin taught.
And even if the enemy kills the best of us,
Wedding will come back, Berlin will remain red,
So that Germany belongs to the Germans.[43]

But Wedding was not so uniformly politicized as Communists would have liked. Poverty crushes the spirit as often as it arouses people to organize and fight. In Wedding we walk past the infamous *Mietskaserne*, the large, six-story housing blocks that were built beginning in the 1880s to house Berlin's fast-growing working class. The apartment blocks are built around a seemingly endless maze of internal courtyards. We walk past the men leaning against the wall of the first courtyard, the children playing a game, and enter the first level. We walk up a couple of flights of stairs, noticing the toilet in the hallway. Fortunately, there is at least running water in the apartments, but we have to make way for the coal man coming down the stairs. On his back he carries racks of coal that the residents use for cooking and, in winter, for heating. Berlin's winter blue haze is not the result of factory pollution alone, but also of the burning of coal in thousands of homes and apartments. We enter a two-room flat. The family is fortunate because they are on the outer ring of the block, and they get sunlight through the windows. The kitchen is open into the sitting room, which also doubles as the bedroom for the children (we count four), while a curtain shields from view a bedroom used by the parents. The woman of the house tries to maintain some order and cleanliness, but with wood floors, a coal-burning stove, and open shelves for the dishes, along with the endless routine of cooking and caring for four children and a husband, it is a nearly impossible task. On the table is an oilcloth and a cheap glass vase with some flowers. An oil painting of a hunting scene hangs on the wall, but no picture of the former kaiser or of Bismarck—this is a communist household, and we see copies of *Rote Fahne*, the communist newspaper, lying around. Two upholstered chairs, covered with a cloth, are the prized possessions of the family. The man of the house takes us over to visit a friend of his, who lives in one of the inner rings. Again two rooms, but the stifling heat seems even worse, and no furniture beyond the bare wood chairs and table grace the dwelling. No sunlight ever penetrates this apartment, and it is no wonder that the men every night go down to the local pub, where there is some relief from the summer's heat or the winter's cold. The women meet with their wash basins by the water pumps, around the peddlers who come through the district, and at the market.

Isherwood captured life in Hallesches Tor, another working-class quarter much like Wedding and only a reasonable walk from Potsdamer Platz. He enters Wassertorstraße, a "deep shabby cobbled street, littered with sprawling children in tears," then finds his way up the five flights of stairs to the Nowaks' apartment, where "a stifling smell of potatoes fried in cheap margarine filled the flat."[44] The living room has two beds in it, as well as a table and chairs; all the family's activities are conducted here, especially since there is no separation from the kitchen. Things are crowded in everywhere. The roof leaks; the courtyard, dark and humid and full of trash, offers little relief. Frau Nowak tries desperately to keep the cramped apartment tidy, while two of her children, a male teenager and a twelve-year-old girl, run wild, yell at each other, or sit around doing nothing while she slaves over the stove, fetches wood, and mops the floor. Two working adults, her husband and their oldest son, do not earn enough to provide the family with better living arrangements. Frau Nowak is ailing with the scourge of the working class—some kind of lung disease that makes her breathing difficult and gives her terrible coughing fits.

Poor himself, Isherwood moves in as a boarder, adding to the chaos. To reach the bed in the living room that he is given, he has to climb over all sorts of pieces of furniture. The first dinner consists of lung hash, piles of potatoes, and fake coffee. To get to the bathroom at night, he has to make his way around all the furniture in the living room and through the kitchen, and then tries to skirt the beds of all the family members. He hears everything in the inner life of the tenement world—the streetcar driver leaving early for work, the baby crying, a door or window closing. Politics is as coherent as the living arrangements: Frau Nowak is a monarchist, the older son a Nazi, the terrible teenager a Communist of sorts. Outside on the streets the swastika competes with the hammer and sickle.

Days and weeks go by, indistinguishable one from the other.

> Our leaky stuffy little attic smelt of cooking and bad drains. When the living-room stove was alight, we could hardly breathe. When it wasn't we froze. The weather had turned very cold. Frau Nowak tramped the streets, when she wasn't at work, from the clinic to the board of health offices and back again: for hours she waited on benches in draughty corridors or puzzled over complicated application-forms.[45]

Wedding and Hallesches Tor are populated mostly by a less skilled, poorly paid, and sometimes itinerant working class. To their west and north lay Siemensstadt, founded just before World War I and home of the giant Siemens works, Berlin and Germany's great electrotechnical company. Its many factories in Berlin alone churned out electrical products large and small, lightbulbs and appliances for the home and giant generators for power plants. In 1925 it had more than sixty-six thousand employees in its Berlin plants, more than half of the firm's entire labor force.[46] As one of the high-tech firms of its day, Siemens relied greatly on the knowledge and abilities of its engineers, technicians, and most skilled workers. By the mid-1920s, it was a leading proponent of rationalization, the application of scientific methods to the production process, which also entailed ever closer supervision of the workers on the shop floor and ever more finely grained pay schedules based on individual workers' productivity.

Siemens was also a pioneer of paternalism. From its early days in the nineteenth century it provided health benefits and pensions to its workers. The firm recognized that if it wanted loyal and productive workers, it had to meet their needs; it also had to shape their mentalities, and not only for the eight, nine, or twelve hours that they labored inside the factory gates. It also had to shape their family lives, helping them with food, providing them with entertainment through company-run sports leagues and recreation facilities, and, for a very small group of the privileged few, offering them low-cost housing designed for the modern, nuclear family. The "intimate connection of work and home," said Fritz Richter, the Siemens executive responsible for its housing construction policies, is ultimately "justified . . . by production considerations."[47]

So as we make our way into Siemensstadt, we notice, amid the many factory buildings, warehouses, and offices, the well-designed, clean-looking apartments and homes that the company has just finished building. Most of the buildings rise to three stories, but there are also single-family houses. Garden plots are available for all the residents, enabling them to supplement the wages expended in the market with homegrown vegetables and fruits. We see soccer fields and playgrounds. As we enter one of the apartments, we notice that they bear a modern stamp, like those in Onkel Toms Siedlung. They are small but functional, with two bedrooms—ideal for husband, wife, and two children, but no more—and a kitchen divided off from the living area. Light streams in, a huge advance over the tenement blocks in Wedding. All of the apartments have their own bathrooms and central heating, a far cry from Christopher Isherwood's experience with Frau Nowak. Most of the units even have balconies, and more electrical outlets than anyone had ever seen—this was Siemens, after all. The design also encourages the functional division of family life: rest, recuperation, and work, yet another aspect of modernity. Only a tiny portion of the firm's employees can partake of these advantages—in 1932, only some 1,790, 5 percent of the entire Siemensstadt workforce. But these were, to the firm at least, the critical element, the highly skilled workers, technicians, and office managers who kept the factories running.[48]

For Weimar modernists, there was beauty to be found inside these factories. Hessel left the streets of Berlin and entered the AEG turbine factory, the main competitor to Siemens. Designed by the architect Peter Behrens and completed in 1910, it was one of the early modernist buildings in Berlin. Hessel described the factory as a "temple of the machine . . . [a] church of precision." He goes up to the gallery and, looking down, feels he has the same sight line as if he were standing at the top of a cathedral. He is overwhelmed by the sight of "lengths of steel and casings, gear cylinders and pulleys waiting to be worked on, pumps and generators that are half completed, pieces that have been cut and drilled and made ready for construction, machines large and small that are being checked on the workbench, parts of turbo generators spinning in the vessel of the centrifuge made out of concrete."[49] He watches as steel pieces are hammered, drilled, lathed into shape, for what exact purpose he has no idea. The entire hall is "a chain of labor"; the pieces move unceasingly from one workbench to another, one floor to another. Then they are measured, inspected, and packed. Everything possible is done by machine, humans spared any unnecessary exertion. Workers have become just the starters and tenders of machines. For Hessel, the factory is a symphony, or perhaps a collage, various parts strewn about, all making up a greater whole. But this symphony, this collage, is constantly in movement, a perpetual motion machine that requires little human intervention. Everything is orderly and rationalized, even the drinks during the coffee break.[50] Whether the AEG workers share Hessel's enthrallment is, of course, another matter.

For many Germans, our walking tour would not have been a pleasant experience. Accustomed to the slower pace of smaller cities, the quiet of the village, the darkness of the countryside at night, they experienced Berlin as artificial, parasitical. With so many people out day and night, who actually worked? Why were the natural rhythms of sunrise and sunset challenged by the glow of streetlights? And what could be more terrible than the display of bodies, lightly garbed, provocatively moving?

Ludwig Finckh, a conservative Swabian author, loudly proclaimed, "*Berlin is not Germany*." The capital was inhabited by "visionaries, dreamers, and adventurers . . . [who] live in a delusion." They call for the brotherhood of all peoples while Germany's adversaries laugh away. The Social Democrats "teach respect for every opinion," and are thereby at best indecisive, at worst traitorous, while the military renounces the reason for its own existence by failing to use force. Finckh even called for a new German capital, one that would evoke "the spirit of Germany" against the "spirit of Berlin."[51] Similarly, the conservative journalist Wilhelm Stapel complained about the "cesspool of the Republic, the spoiler of all noble and healthy life." Even worse was the desire of small-town residents to replicate it, to make "every little rathole in all of Germany . . . a microcosm of Berlin." Stapel did not refrain from voicing the deepest fear of conservatives—deracination: "All too many Slavs and all too many altogether uninhibited East European Jews have been mixed into the population of Berlin. It is an embarrassing mixture; it determines through sheer quantity the character of this city."[52] The enemy has taken over:

> the lip; the saucy airs, more precisely, self-aggrandizement; the insolent self-righteousness and the endless cackle of irony; the snobbish imitation; the shrill prattle; and the extravagances of the freshly civilized immigrants, the balkanized Parisianisms. . . .
>
> It is today a decisive question for German culture whether the countryside will choose to tolerate the presumptions and impudence of Berlin intellectuality. . . .
>
> The spirit of the German people rises against the spirit of Berlin. The demand of the day can be summarized like this: the rebellion of the countryside against Berlin.[53]

Joseph Goebbels in 1928 took over the leadership of the Nazi Party in Berlin. He fumed at the lit-up city; the confusion between night and day signified its degeneration. The noise of the city, the lights, prostitutes, the confusion of gender roles caused by homosexual men and modern, nonmaternal women, the babble of languages—all were markers of an immoral and degraded world where people pursue bodily pleasures. Sex and drugs define their lives. Degenerate Berlin feeds off working Berlin, exploits the solid citizenry who toil away, only to see the fruits of their labor dissipated by the flaneur, the sophisticate, the Jew, parading around the city, whiling the time away in cafés, looking and feeling but doing nothing productive. Ominously,

> the other Berlin is lurking, ready to pounce. A few thousand are working days and nights on end so that sometime the day will arrive. And this day will demolish the abodes of corruption . . . [I]t will transform them and give them over to a risen people.
>
> The day of judgment! It will be the day of freedom![54]

The fear and resentment that gripped a villager from Upper Franconia or the Harz Mountains, a town dweller from Baden, upon his arrival in Berlin, was mirrored by the contempt of the Berliner for the "provincials," a rather typical attitude of the sophisticated urban dweller toward those moved to discomfort by the sights and sounds of the city. The writer Erich Kästner expressed well the city dweller's snide contempt. The visitors stand unsettled in Potsdamer Platz, finding Berlin too loud, too direct, too wild:

> Out of fear they're bent-kneed
> And do everything wrong.
> They smile painfully. And they wait, dumb,
> And stand around Potsdamer Platz
> Until they are run over.[55]

The famed satirist Kurt Tucholsky depicted Germany outside Berlin as a place ruled by "provincial philistines" and other assorted reactionaries, a world of "surreptitious Catholicism" and superstition, of dim-witted peasants and aristocrats and craven officials. The solution? The light of Berlin had to illuminate the darkness of the provinces.[56]

So what was Berlin modern? The writer Matheo Quinz depicted the famed Romanische Café in 1926.[57] Wealthy producers sit at their tables while struggling actors and artists look for loans. Communists debate in their "Talmudic" fashion; right-wing journalists gather at their own table nearby. Artists have a penchant for drawing cartoons of one another—easier, no doubt, than the hard work of producing great art. Conversations can be overheard in which Picasso, chocolate, and fascism all run fast one into the other. Doctors and psychiatrists gather. Do they talk over cases, or observe their patients in different surroundings? In the early morning hours, the other Berlin takes over—the gamblers coming out of their haunts, the lovers emerging from the hourly-rate hotel rooms. Also fast-paced Berlin, tinged with an edge of sadness and exhaustion.

The Romanische was the common meeting ground for all the elements of Berlin's intellectual life, yet each moved to its own wing, its own table within the café, the perfect symbol of Weimar politics and society—lively, democratic, engaged, and divided and divisive, unable to speak beyond its own circle. Everyone looks, but no one talks over the divide.

Foreign observers were also attracted to the rapid pace and cultural vibrancy of Berlin, and fell in love with it. The British diplomat and author Harold Nicolson, pondering what gave Berlin "its charm," described a city so restless that at night even the animals in the zoo pace around, while trains dash along the tracks and traffic lights pulse. "For in the night air, which makes even the spires of the Gedächtniskirche flicker with excitement, there is a throbbing sense of expectancy. Everybody knows that every night Berlin wakes to a new adventure." While Parisians and Londoners are soundly asleep in their beds, Berliners are looking for the next excitement.[58]

Berlin modern was all this and more. It was the sights, sounds, and smells of the city, the fast-paced, hyperactive, glittering metropolis of Potsdamer Platz and the overcrowded, dark, eternally damp neighborhoods of Scheunenviertel or Wedding. It was the sparkling brilliance of the Romanische Café, where artists and intellectuals and their managers and dealers gathered, and the rationalized, clockwork pace of the Siemens or AEG factory. It was active and engaged women moving about the streets, proudly asserting their place in public, and political brawls between Communists and Nazis. It was the elegance of the Tietz department store and the peddlers hawking their wares in Wedding, the woods and lakes open to all and the new apartment complexes, each unit carefully designed for a nuclear family, hopefully one that abhorred kitsch and clutter. It was the look of Columbus House and the experience of the cinema and weekend escapes to Wannsee, and the sight of eastern European Jews in Scheunenviertel, well-heeled businessmen and professionals in Grunewald, émigré Russian aristocrats keeping up the pretense of wealth and power, and women's bodies on display in revues and cabarets.

Berlin modern was a kaleidoscope of diversity and excitement. Other cities in the 1920s—New York, London—had the bustle and energy of Berlin. Some, like Paris, had all that and were also far more beautiful and charming. But there was something particularly intense about Weimar Berlin. It was the capital city of a country defeated in war and the center of ongoing, high-stakes political conflict. It was also a new city, one that had been, until the last quarter of the nineteenth century, a sleepy, swampy royal residency and seat of the Prussian government. After German unification in 1871 it grew rapidly in every possible way. Its factories boomed and population soared; it became the capital not only of the state of Prussia, but also, for better and worse, of a major European power. In the 1920s Berlin finally came into its own as a great cultural center as well, one that easily rivaled Paris, London, and New York. Somehow, the city drew on all these diverse, even contradictory sources. Hope and despair born in war and revolution, unceasing political strife, fast-paced growth in the age of high industrialization combined with the still-visible presence of old wealth and old power, the crush of people and buildings in a major urban setting coupled with bucolic havens around its many lakes and woods—all that gave Berlin the particular energy and creativity in the 1920s that every observer, foreign and domestic, noted.

Weimar was Berlin, Berlin Weimar. The capital city was the symbol and pacesetter. For the rest of Germany it was too far in front. It was a magnet that attracted ambitious and talented people from all over the country and beyond, but it also inspired dread and loathing. Yet it mirrored Weimar Germany in one, absolutely essential fashion: no single group, no individual, could claim Berlin as its own. No one dominated Berlin, and no consensus reigned. That, too, was Berlin modern.

3

Political Worlds

In 1925 the great Weimar journalist, essayist, and novelist Joseph Roth wrote a feuilleton, "The Kaiser's Birthday." Roth celebrated one of the great achievements of the era—the kaiser had been deposed.

> If the republic had only given us the possibility of forgetting the kaiser's birthday, it would already have accomplished a great deal.
>
> "Nothing has changed." "Everything has remained the same." But one thing has changed: The Old One [the kaiser] is no longer around.
>
> And this one thing provides the comforting certainty that History is right. This one thing: the possibility of looking up to the throne and finding it empty, of knowing that no majesty can interrupt the direct link between God and me.

Roth knew, of course, that the German population was so deeply divided politically, and many yearned for the return of the Hohenzollerns. Still, it was wonderful that they had to send their birthday greetings to Holland, Kaiser Wilhelm's place of exile, not to Berlin. The kaiser's birthday was the single true republican holiday, according to Roth, precisely because one realizes that there is no longer a kaiser. Moreover, his departure made people understand how fragile are the trappings of power despite the appearance of solidity.

> This generation has seen how regal purple deteriorates into a plain overcoat worn on a journey. . . . We have seen with our

> own eyes how what we took for marble was just plaster. We have experienced the great marvel of demystification. . . . Never again will a kaiser come, as he was. . . . The chain is broken, the atmosphere cleared, the stage props destroyed.
>
> That is the achievement—for the time being—of 1918.[1]

The kaiser was gone. And as a result, a broad realm of possibilities opened up before Germans, who took to the streets and the polling places in a flurry of activism. Weimar politics were loud, contested, unruly—and strikingly democratic. Almost any political party could muster enough votes to find representation in the Reichstag. Weimar's deepest enemies, let alone its supporters, published their newspapers and gathered their followers in demonstrations. Women won the right to vote and joined political organizations unhindered by legal restrictions. Parties and movements of all stripes used the new media and new art forms of the 1920s—radio, photomontage, microphones, and, finally, film—to carry their messages to the most isolated villages and furthest corners of the country. Politics became "mass" in an unprecedented fashion. Probably no other country in the 1920s—certainly not the United States, with its stark repression of the Left, vicious antiunion policies, and legally enshrined racism—had so wide a range of free speech, such a vital public sphere, as Germany.

And yet: periodic states of emergency led the state to close down the publishing houses of the Communist Party, and even Adolf Hitler was banned from public speaking in virtually all German states from 1924 to 1927. White terrors—the extreme violence exercised by the right wing—resulted in the summary execution and internment of thousands of radical workers, especially in the early years of the republic. Political assassinations conducted by shadowy yet well-connected right-wing groups were commonplace between 1919 and 1923. The courts were notorious bastions of conservatism that barely prosecuted acts of terror committed by the Right, while they assiduously pursued the Left. As in any market-driven economy, those with wealth had far greater access to the government than did the middle class and the poor. The wealthy were able to limit sharply the scope of Weimar's social welfare programs while they whined unendingly and bitterly about a system that, so they claimed, encouraged the unproductive and the indigent rather than those who were hardworking. On the extreme right, a brand of politics emerged that idealized violence and racial anti-Semitism, and even the Left, influenced by the Bolshevik Revolution, adopted a militaristic style.

Huge obstacles continually challenged the great democratic promise of Weimar. Ultimately, they proved far greater than the republic's potential. World War I left an enormous burden that no European country in the 1920s could easily resolve. But defeat in the war coupled with the roughly two million deaths and 4.2 million wounded made the economic, social, and psychological problems much more acute in Germany. The loss and debility of so many men in their prime working age placed a drag on the economy, disrupted family patterns, and weighed upon the support and counseling services provided by the state and private charities. The Versailles Peace Treaty incessantly kindled the anger and resentment of virtually all Germans, and it was the republic that was saddled with the blame for its harsh provisions. Versailles also placed a drag on the international politics of the 1920s, since the great powers were continually preoccupied with its unresolved issues, notably, reparations. Meanwhile, the political leadership of the republic was notably old and stuck in a political mind-set that proved unable to deal with the new problems presented by the post–World War I era. The economy, though retooled for peacetime faster than anyone could have imagined, proved highly unstable, with a few intermittent years of expansion interspersed with severe crises. The collapse of international commodity prices, mediocre rates of productivity, and high levels of unemployment even in good years placed severe constraints on every government and made miserable the real-life circumstances of millions of Germans.

Throughout it all, Germany remained deeply divided politically. No individual party or movement, no single set of ideas or commonly held beliefs, prevailed in Germany in the years after World War I. No one, no thing, exercised hegemony. No party until the Nazis in the end phase of the republic proved able to attract support beyond a limited base. Instead, high-stakes contention ruled Weimar politics, and even minor issues were elevated into existential questions. And the "democratic deficit"—the reluctance to embrace democracy, even more, the downright hostility to it on the part of so many Germans, perhaps even a majority, endangered the republic from its very founding.

Weimar's political history divides easily into three broad phases, two periods of crisis sandwiching a brief five years of relative stability. In each phase, a particular political configuration dominated and offered its own version of order and progress. In 1918–23, it was the Left and center; 1924–29, largely the center Right; 1930–33, the authoritarian Right. The first two, at least, demonstrated Weimar's promise; the last, Weimar's pathologies. Each phase ended amid a combined, catastrophic economic and political crisis. Each political configuration, in the end, failed; each fell victim to the concerted attacks of its opponents and its own ineptitude. In the end, Weimar's deep-seated problems proved far greater than the ability of its political leaders to forge consensus and establish hegemony.

The first phase, 1918 through 1923, indelibly marked the character of the republic. The constitution established a highly democratic political system, including free and equal suffrage, proportional voting, and basic political liberties. The constitution also called for social rights, and the programs instituted by the Social Democratic Party (SPD) during the revolution, and then maintained and expanded afterward, gave teeth to the rhetoric. Alongside the pillars of the German social welfare system that Chancellor Otto von Bismarck had instituted in the 1880s—health insurance, pensions, and workers' accident insurance—the SPD governments established the eight-hour day and trade union recognition. All over the country, municipalities that came under Social Democratic control or influence founded health clinics and expanded educational and job-training opportunities. The SPD's partners in these ventures were most often the German Democratic Party (DDP) and the Catholic Center Party. Together, these three, known as the Weimar Coalition, provided the strongest base of support for the republic in its fourteen-year existence. Alongside its national role, the Weimar Coalition dominated many individual state and municipal governments for virtually the entire history of the republic, including those of important states like Prussia. It influenced virtually all the governments of the first phase, even when the Social Democrats chose to avoid the responsibilities of high office.

The republic was the creation of the mass movement of 1918–19 and the Weimar Coalition parties. It was their child. The SPD was the largest of the three coalition members. More so than any other German party, it had an unquestioned commitment to democracy, though it was more than willing to use force against the radical Left. It was oriented toward workers in "heavy metal," the coal and steel industries of the classic industrial age. But its class-oriented viewpoint, its rhetorical idealization of the proletariat, profoundly limited its appeal. The SPD could never command a national majority with Marxist-laden terms like "the fighting community for democracy and socialism," "class struggle," "the transformation of the entire capitalist economy into socialism, an economy driven by the goal of providing for the well-being of all," and the "international union of the proletariat."[2] Its imagery of powerful workers triumphing over the detritus of class society, including priests, officers, businessmen, and Communists, resonated with those who were already receptive to the social democratic message (fig. 3.1).[3] It is doubtful that it convinced anyone else. At the same time, the SPD's abandonment of socialism to some distant future alienated the substantial, though circumscribed, group of radical workers and intellectuals. The party's advocacy of women's emancipation also limited its appeal—class was always more important than gender, and even the flaming banner of youth could never be lofted by women alone: men had to be present as well, indeed, in the lead. The party's symbolism was awash in red—banners, sashes, flames—and accorded with long-standing imagery in which socialism stood for illumination of mind, spirit, and life itself (see plate 1). However, for many Germans, red simply linked Social Democrats with Communists, enabling them to lump the two Marxist parties into one convenient box despite the sharp differences between them.

The DDP was the progressive liberal party and drew to its side many middle-class professionals, including the small but mostly well-situated Jewish population. It advocated the *juste milieu*, that is, balance in politics and society. It decried extremes of all kinds and firmly advocated discussion and negotiation, at home on the basis of the constitution, abroad by Germany's inclusion in the council of nations (fig. 3.2). The DDP opposed both monopolies and socialization, supported individual initiative as well as social welfare measures to correct gross inequalities and injustices. It affirmed "the law" as a "part of

Fig. 3.1 "Vote for List 1—Social Democracy" The powerful male worker carries the banner of socialism and triumphs over all its corrupt and nefarious antagonists—officers, priests, communists, and tightfisted capitalists. Hessisches Landesmuseum Darmstadt.

Fig. 3.2 "For Everyone: Honorable Labor in City and Countryside. Against Dictatorship from Left and from Right. The German Democratic Party." The DDP positions itself as the party that pursues a reasonable middle course based on law and justice. Hessisches Landesmuseum Darmstadt.

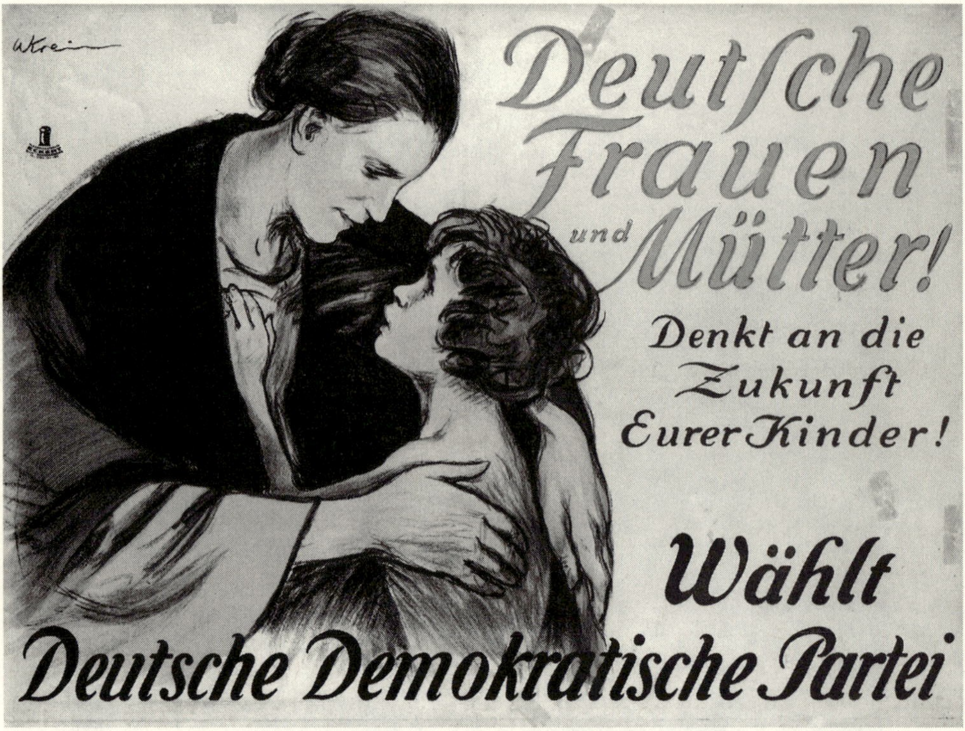

Fig. 3.3 "German Women and Mothers! Think of the Future of Your Children! Elect the German Democratic Party." Every political party sought to appeal to women, and all of them used maternal imagery, as does here the liberal German Democratic Party. Hessisches Landesmuseum Darmstadt.

the national culture" and called for a national militia to replace the old authoritarian army.[4] Like all German parties, it called for close ties with and protection of Germans outside the territory of the state, but at least demanded the same protections for minorities (mainly Jews and Poles) in Germany, a provision the conservative parties would never even contemplate. The DDP, again like all the other parties, faced a new political reality with female suffrage. Many women professionals found a political home in the DDP, and many of the leading female parliamentarians of the republic were DDP members. Its self-presentation as the protector of women had, unfortunately, little popular resonance (fig. 3.3). Indeed, popular resonance of any kind the DDP had only in the election to the Constitutional Assembly. After that, it suffered a slow continual decline to virtual irrelevance, the epitome of what contemporaries and one present-day historian have called the "dying middle" of Weimar politics.[5]

The SPD and DDP were limited by class, the Center by religion. Catholicism saturated the party. Priests and bishops played leading roles in its internal affairs; Catholic teaching shaped the program. But the Center also provided a fruitful avenue of activism for lay Catholics, including women and youth. Despite its very prominent role in the republic—four chancellors and many other leading officials came from the Center Party—Catholics retained in the 1920s their sense of grievance in a Protestant-dominated country. Many Germans viewed Germany, for good or bad, as a Protestant creation in which Catholics had to struggle to make their voices heard. Catholic memories of the Kulturkampf, Bismarck's attack on Catholic influence in politics and society, were long. Schools and education were at the core of Catholic concerns in Weimar. The Center vigorously monitored and jealously guarded the church's right to provide religious instruction in the public schools. "Religion and Fatherland must be at the center of education and instruction," proclaimed the Center.[6] Like the other parties, it worried about the moral degeneration of youth and called on the state to protect it from *Schmutz und Schund* (filth and trash). It claimed to be above class and to represent all *Berufsstände* (professional estates). Industrial workers, artisans, salesmen, landowners—all were united by religion and nation and all were welcome in the Center (fig. 3.4). But the image of unity under the church belied the deep internal divisions in the Center Party between a liberal-social reform wing and a conservative-authoritarian one. The liberals predominated in the first two phases of the republic, the conservatives in the last.

The Weimar Coalition parties were the mainstay of the republic. But their vision, collectively and individually, hardly went uncontested. The coalition's commitment to parliamentary democracy, social welfare, and state involvement in the economy—with socialism (on the part of the SPD) consigned to some distant future—found powerful antagonists on the right and the left. In the eyes of these groups, the very character of Weimar state and society had not been settled by the constitution. In the eyes of virtually everyone, including the Weimar Coalition parties, the very territorial boundaries of Germany had not been definitively resolved by the Versailles Treaty. The most basic issues about how Germans would live together and with their European neighbors were on the table and

Fig. 3.4 "Through Sacrifice and Labor to Freedom! Elect the Center Party." Every party tried to rally support through imagery of the strong, upright German farmer or worker. Here the Catholic Center party joins together honest labor and Christianity by depicting a peasant behind a plow with the Cologne cathedral in the background. Hessisches Landesmuseum Darmstadt.

vigorously contested through every political phase of the republic's history.

On the left, Communists and assorted other radicals demanded a political and social system dominated by labor—or by the parties that claimed to represent the historic mission of the working class. "Proletarians!" "Working Men and Women," "Workers" began virtually every leaflet, every appeal of the KPD. Powerful men, working at a lathe or a drill press, dominated the imagery of the party. In the early years, the workers and soldiers councils stood at the heart of its vision. The councils would supplant parliament, and democracy would run through all the realms of society, including the workplace. With the elimination of the profit motive, wealth would be shared and all members of society would prosper. Women would become free and equal, first through their entrance into the paid labor force. "Socialization of industry and agriculture" served as the sum total of the Communists' economic program. Over the course of the Weimar period, the loyalty that the party always displayed toward the Soviet Union turned increasingly into sheer mimicry and dependence. For Communists the enemies were omnipresent. They were bosses, bureaucrats, and priests, but also fellow workers who aligned themselves with the SPD or Center. Communist language was harsh and exclusionary; it spoke to the experiences of some workers, but never a majority.[7]

Three times in the first phase of the republic Communists were involved in armed uprisings against the state—January 1919, March 1921, and October 1923. Each was a bigger fiasco than its predecessor. In between, Communists actively fomented labor unrest and sought to turn every vague manifestation of protest into a general strike against the republic. All these efforts failed. The only successful general strike in German history—against the right-wing Kapp Putsch in March 1920—was called by the trade unions, not the Communist Party.

But the revolts and strikes demonstrated a number of key points. They showed that seething discontent reigned among a segment of the working class that joined communist revolts and strikes. Many workers found inspiration in the KPD's vision of a prosperous, egalitarian, and peaceful future. The party offered them a place to broaden their horizons and develop their talents and abilities. In contrast, none of the lofty promises and hopes of the republic's founders penetrated very far among workers who had endured the privations of World War I and a difficult postwar economy. Despite rapid retooling and economic expansion, work could still be hard to find and inflation undermined whatever money workers accumulated. For those with jobs, the internal workplace regime in factories and mines seemed as harsh as ever, with bosses and foremen lording it over workers, despite the eight-hour day and trade union recognition. Presumably, if the republic were able to promote economic progress and provide avenues of political participation, at least some of these workers could be won to its side. But not the Communist Party and not communist workers. From its founding, the KPD was committed to continual confrontation with the republic. On the left, then, the Weimar Coalition would always face a sharp antagonist with some significant popular support, but never one that could command a majority even of workers. "The flame of revolution" was not an idea that most Germans found inspiring; instead, it conjured up fears of chaos, instability, and Russians (fig. 3.5).

But it was the Right, not the Left, that posed the real threat to the Weimar Coalition and to the very existence of the republic. Numbers alone were a factor—probably more Germans stood on the right than the left. Even more important, the Right was powerful, well connected, and lodged in the major institutions of state and society—business, the civil service, the army, the universities, and the churches. It had its street-corner agitators and barroom brawlers, but also its bankers, businessmen, colonels, professors, and clerics. The Right was, to be sure, highly heterogeneous and divided. It would not cohere into a single force until the very end of the republic, when it coalesced—actively and passively—behind Hitler and the Nazis.

The major parties of the Right were the German National People's Party (DNVP) and the German People's Party (DVP). The latter cooperated intermittently with the Weimar Coalition parties. But it never gave full-fledged, unconditional support to the republic or even to the idea of democracy. It always hedged its commitments based on whether its concerns were adequately reflected in governmental policies. That meant, primarily, a probusiness policy that signified limited taxation, the affirmation of private property rights, the revision of Versailles, and, especially, the rollback of the gains won by workers in the revolution. Rhetorically the DVP claimed to support cooperation of workers and employees with entrepreneurs to ensure the well-being of the workforce. But management had to retain the business and technical control of the enterprise. The DVP viewed an independent middle class as decisive for the stability of the nation and the growth of the economy. It wanted "a political and economic reconciliation of nations, but believes this is impossible so long as our enemies trample on the honor of the German people, prevent the unity of Germans, and support the victors' peace that was imposed upon us." The DVP wanted a reassertion of "the spiritual and moral values" that defined the "national particularities" of Germans. As the party stated in its "Basic Principles" of 1919, the DVP "struggles against every destructive effort that seeks to replace the devotion to the national-state and the German people with cosmopolitanism. It opposes every effort to repress our German sentiments for some kind of worldly convictions that are foreign to our very being. The moral

Fig. 3.5 "The Flame of Revolution May Not Be Extinguished! Therefore Elect Communists List 4." A powerful male figure serves as the symbol of Communism, while masses of male workers form behind him. Hessisches Landesmuseum Darmstadt.

and economic reconstruction of our people can succeed only if we return to those old, basic principles of loyalty, honor, impartiality, and incorruptibility in public service, trade, and commerce. The German People's Party struggles against every other way of thinking."[8] Without being openly anti-Semitic, the DVP nonetheless articulated the anti-Semitism that was widespread in Germany. Everyone understood "cosmpolitanism" as a code word for Jews. The "flooding of Germany with people of foreign origin" had also to be struggled against, according to the DVP, and that, too, was code language for Jews.[9]

The grand fulminations against the republic came from the DNVP, powerfully rooted in the old Prussian landowning nobility, certain business segments, army officers, some high-level state officials, and assorted others who despised democracy. At one time, before the war, they had been monarchists. But most of the DNVP crowd had abandoned monarchism—despite rhetorical affirmations of loyalty to the Hohenzollerns—during World War I, when the ineptitude of Kaiser Wilhelm II became clear even to them. They spent the first, second, and third phases of the republic searching for some kind of authoritarian alternative, usually of a military kind. Whatever their claim to support "tradition"—Protestantism, the close ties among family members through the generations—the DNVP had actually embarked on a radical right-wing campaign (fig. 3.6). Many of its members supported the attempted right-wing putsch in March 1920 led by Wolfgang Kapp and an assortment of present and former army officers. Others took a hands-off attitude, waiting to see whether the putsch would succeed. In any case, like the putschists, the DNVP demanded a powerful Germany with expanded borders, a clearly designated hierarchical society in which the wellborn prevailed, and social welfare for the elite, not workers and the poor, in the form of protective tariffs, government-supported industrial cartels, and agricultural subsidies. "The liberation of the German people from foreign coercion" and "[to build] a new, strengthened Reich on free soil, to unite with the Reich the German territories that were ripped away" were among the provocative, vengeful ideas it loudly proclaimed in its 1920 statement of principles. Its positions were openly nationalist and aggressive, and it demanded that only those with a "a reliable German way of thinking" be allowed to work in the foreign service.

Fig. 3.6 "We Hold Firmly to the Word of God! Elect the German National [People's Party]." The conservative nationalist DNVP's appeal to women: Christian unity across the generations. Hessisches Landesmuseum Darmstadt.

Military service was a desideratum for all men; Germans had to be reminded how great a debt of gratitude they owed the army and its leaders for propagating correct values and securing Germany's rise to a great power.[10]

For the DNVP, Germany's sorry state was a result of its betrayal at home since 1914 by Jews and socialists, and even by Africans in the service of foreign powers. "Germans! Protect the Borders of Your Fatherland against the Russian Bolsheviks!" or "Bolshevism Brings War, Unemployment, and Hunger Misery" were typical slogans, complete with monstrous images of bloodthirsty hounds, apes (often with caricatured African features), or Asians setting Germany aflame, or of the spirit of death representing communism and threatening to descend on Germany. The supposed enslavement of the German people through the Versailles Peace Treaty, the Dawes Plan, the Locarno

Fig. 3.7 "Locarno? Elect the German National [People's Party]!" The DNVP bitterly and brutally attacked Streseman's policy of fulfillment by raising racial fears of French colonial troops towering over Germany and creating a swath of destruction. Hessisches Landesmuseum Darmstadt.

treaties (to be discussed below), the Young Plan, and virtually every other international agreement provided the Right with unending political fodder and melodramatic posters with biblical allusions to enslavement (fig. 3.7). Jews represented a "corrosive, un-German spirit." Since the revolution, there existed an "ever more fateful, increasing dominance of Jews in government and in the public sphere." It had to be challenged and vanquished. Only a "deepening of Christian consciousness" could bring the moral rebirth of the German people. The DNVP struggled against "trash and filth . . . against the spirit of decadence." Private property rights and private initiative were at the core of any productive economy. "We reject Marxist class-struggle thinking as the destroyer of culture. Our goal is not class struggle, but peaceful labor grounded in a notion of responsibility."[11]

In the first phase of Weimar, the DNVP simply hammered away at the republic. In the Reichstag and the state parliaments, in its newspapers, in every conceivable public venue, it attacked Weimar and its supporters with the most virulent rhetoric. This was a radicalism of the powerful and well-situated—and they trafficked with those still further to the right. All over Germany, and especially in Bavaria, extreme right-wing groups emerged almost in pace with the revolution and the founding of the republic. The extreme Right was a highly diverse concatenation. It included the Freikorps, paramilitary bands formed in the winter of 1918–19 by officers with good connections to the upper ranks of the officer corps. They were, at first, accepted and even welcomed by the Social Democratic government, which desperately needed a security force. But it was a foolhardy, tragic decision, because the Freikorps could never be won over to the side of democracy. The Freikorps repressed strikes and fought against Communists up and down eastern Europe. They also exercised summary justice against radical workers—they lined up striking workers and left paramilitaries against a wall and shot them—and pogroms against Jews. The literate and literary among them infused their leaflets, stories, and novels with hatred of Jews and women and admiration of the rifle and the machine gun.[12] Their vision stood completely opposed to democracy; it was, instead, a fascist ethos that they espoused and practiced.

Tens of thousands of ex-soldiers found their way into the Freikorps in the early years of the republic, and from there they moved on to the netherworld of extreme right-wing groupings and parties of the first phase of the republic that included but went far beyond the Nazi Party (formally, the National Socialist German Workers Party, or NSDAP). Their members were ideologues and agitators. They were, in the early 1920s, not quite respectable, too wild and unpredictable for the nobles and businessmen of the DNVP or for the right-wing clerics, officers, and state officials who dominated Bavaria. But many of them found a few wealthy individuals to provide funds for their activities and army officers to spirit weapons to them. Not respectable, perhaps, but also not beyond the pale. The more upper-class and well-situated Right and the less respectable radical Right shared a common belief system and a common language marked by nationalism, anti-Semitism, and hatred of the republic.

A profusion of simpleminded yet effective slogans captured the essence of right-wing politics and linked the established and the extreme Right. The first was, of course, the *Dolchstosslegende*, the stab-in-the-back legend, which the army's supreme command had already begun to propagate in the weeks before the armistice. Germany had never been defeated on the battlefield, but had been betrayed at home by Jews and socialists. The enemy was clear. Many of the right-wing groups spoke about some form of socialism, about "working people" (*Werktätige*, rather than *Arbeiter*, as the latter was more associated with the Left) and "socialization through the national people's community."[13] They talked about overturning the "dictate of Versailles," about a "German rebirth," and the "reconstruction of a strong German armed force." And they talked about breaking "the Jewish domination of the state, economic, and cultural realms."[14] As yet another right-wing group, the Deutschvölkische Schutz- und Trutzbund, stated: "The Bund strives for the moral rebirth of the German people through the awakening and promotion of its healthy character. It sees in the oppressive and corrosive influence of Judaism the main reason for the collapse. Removing this influence is the precondition to the reconstruction of state and economy and the rescue of German culture."[15] As with the DNVP, all sorts of other anti-Semitic slogans were the common stuff of the extreme Right: "Jewish Bolshevism," the "Jewish world conspiracy," the "Jewish republic," the "Jewish corruption of the German people."[16]

All of this indicates that Adolf Hitler invented nothing in terms of right-wing ideology. His great innovations lay in the organizational and rhetorical realms. It also indicates that anti-Bolshevism was as significant as anti-Semitism, and the merger of the two was one of the Right's great innovations. Conservative intellectuals like Oswald Spengler wrote about "Prussian socialism," Ernst Jünger of "front socialism." Hitler trumped them all by adopting the slogan "national socialism." These were all efforts to harness the collectivist strains of socialism to the cause of the nation and race, and to decouple socialism from egalitarianism and internationalism. This was a socialism tied to the Darwinian struggle for survival, now couched in national and racial rather than species terms. "The entire nation is a class," as Oswald Spengler put it.[17] This nationalist rhetoric was often tied to a notion of Germany as a "young" nation, like Italy and, sometimes, Russia.

More than anything else, the string of political assassinations that so marred the early years of the republic demonstrates the common ground shared by the established Right and the radical Right. In the first six months of 1919, right-wing assassins killed Rosa Luxemburg, Karl Liebknecht, Leo Jogiches, Kurt Eisner, and Hugo Haase, all esteemed leaders of the socialist and communist movements, Eisner even the minister president of Bavaria. Luxemburg and Liebknecht were murdered in particularly brutal fashion by a Freikorp unit, the others by individual assassins. But none of the murderers ever served more than a token sentence, protected as they were by conservative judges and officers and other well-connected members of the establishment.

Then the terror spread to representatives of the Weimar Coalition parties. Matthias Erzberger, the leader of the Center Party, advocated during World War I a negotiated settlement to the war. He signed the armistice, an act for which the Right never forgave him, and was a strong supporter of the republic. The reform program he engineered modernized the financing of the central government and placed it on solid footing. He was gunned down in August 1921. His death caused profound grief and demonstrations of sympathy, but also pronounced glee on the right. The *Kreuzzeitung*, a DNVP organ, proclaimed that "nothing is cheaper than to condemn the assassins," while the *Oletzkoer Zeitung*, a local organ also connected to the DNVP, wrote:

> Erzberger . . . has suffered the fate which the vast majority of patriotic Germans have long desired for him. Erzberger, the man who is alone responsible for the humiliating armistice; Erzberger, the man who is responsible for the acceptance of the Versailles "Treaty of Shame"; Erzberger, the man whose spirit unhappily still prevails in many of our government offices and laws, has at last secured the punishment suitable for a traitor. . . . [T]he majority of the German people breathe a sigh of relief at this moment. A man like Erzberger, who carried the primary responsibility for the misfortunes of our Fatherland, was a standing menace to Germany so long as he was alive. . . . We must learn to hate our enemies abroad, but we must also punish the domestic enemies of Germany with our hatred and our contempt. Compromise is impossible. Only extremism can make Germany again what it was before the war.[18]

These were the words of "respectable" elements of German society. The unbridled hatred and the call to violence were fearsome signs, even if thousands of others, workers especially, poured into the streets to protest the assassination.

Ten months later, on 22 June 1922, other assassins killed Walter Rathenau, the foreign minister of the republic, a renowned businessman and writer and scion of a prominent Jewish family. Like Erzberger, Rathenau was hated because of his commitment to the republic, and because he was smart, cultured, and Jewish. The respectable Right, with its emotional, overwrought rhetoric, charged him with betraying Germany. Rathenau, they claimed, was in the pay of the Entente; indeed, he was not truly German, even if he represented Germany abroad. The assassination caused another outpouring of grief and countless demonstrations all over Germany in which millions affirmed their support for the republic. There were also gut-wrenching assessments of the poison that had entered into German public life. At a stormy Reichstag session following the murder, Chancellor Joseph Wirth gave one of the most forceful and moving political speeches of the Weimar era. He knew that the assassins had not acted alone, knew that they operated in an environment that had made such terror acts *salonfähig*, that is, acceptable in polite society. Wirth vociferously attacked the men on the right, quoting from articles published by individuals sitting in the chamber before him. He asked why they had not condemned outright the assassination and charged them with creating a "murderous atmosphere" in the country. "We are experiencing in Germany a political brutalization." Wirth pleaded for democracy, for patience in working to ameliorate the strictures of Versailles, for a more reasoned atmosphere in Germany, for an end finally to the "atmosphere of murder, of rancor, of poison." And he concluded: "There stands the enemy (to the right), who drips his poison in the wounds of the people—There stands the enemy—and about that there is no doubt: the enemy stands on the right!"[19]

Wirth was correct—the enemy did stand on the right. In a flurry of grief and determination, the Reichstag passed a law establishing commissars in each of the states with responsibility for maintaining public order. But the impact was slight, and while the commissars monitored the Right, they were far more concerned with the Left.

The conservatism of the judiciary and bureaucracy hollowed out the law. The assassins, like those who killed Erzberger, were spirited out of the country to safety, protected by their connections to the established Right.

The Weimar Coalition had already suffered its first defeat in spring 1920. In the wake of the Kapp Putsch, the coalition's suppression of strikes, workers' militias, and political demands for an all-workers' government cost it support on the left. Many people who had voted for the SPD or DDP in 1919 because they feared far worse from the left retreated to their more normal political stance in the center and on the right. Unable to command a majority, though still the largest political party in Germany, the Social Democrats withdrew from the government. For the next few years the SPD and DVP were in and out of the governments; only the DDP and Center formed a constant presence. The succession of diplomatic conferences designed to deal with the reparations problem added to the political difficulties faced by every German government, since none of the negotiations succeeded. Indeed, when the businessman Hugo Stinnes spoke at the Spa conference in 1920—the first postwar conference at which Germany was invited to participate—his opening words were "I rise in order to be able to look the hostile delegates straight in the eyes." He called the Allies "our insane conquerors."[20] The Allies were appalled; the Right at home cheered the provocative and irresponsible words.

From Spa onward there extends a long litany of failed international meetings designed to resolve the lingering postwar issues. At London in 1921 the Allies delivered to Germany a substantial reparations bill that only further undermined the republic and gave the Right more ammunition. But far worse lay ahead.

An inflation had begun in 1914 because the government financed the huge expense of war largely via loans, expecting that conquered territories and vanquished foes would provide the resources to pay off the debt. Instead, Germany lost the war. By 1919 the value of the mark had fallen by one-third.[21] Yet in the initial postwar period, the inflation had beneficial effects. The depreciated currency made German goods attractive on the international market and enabled businesses to meet worker demands for higher wages. But then inflation kicked into hyperinflation (discussed in more detail in the next chapter), the likes of which have rarely been seen in the annals of national economies. Only part of the blame can be laid at the Allies' door. They were convinced that Germany was dodging its reparations obligations by delaying shipments of gold, timber, and coal; overvaluing the assets it did transmit; and, not least, deliberately manipulating its currency to pay in devalued cash. Not all of this was true. Nonetheless, in January 1923, France and Belgium moved troops into Germany and seized key assets. They occupied the Ruhr, Germany's industrial engine, a concentrated one-hundred-mile stretch of coal mines and steel mills and other manufacturing enterprises. The government declared a policy of passive resistance: whenever French or Belgian troops moved into a factory or an office, the workers and employees were to lay down their tools or pencils and go home. By June, the economy in the Ruhr had come to a virtual standstill. Germans fumed at the French, the Belgians, and their own government. Meanwhile, the government printed money to support passive resistance, which sent an already incredible hyperinflation into the stratosphere. By the end of November 1923, a single U.S. dollar bought 4.2 trillion marks, a barely comprehensible exchange rate.

It was a wild, dispiriting year. Communists attempted a revolution; the Nazis attempted a march on Berlin to seize power. Both were fiascoes. Large segments of the population saw their life circumstances deteriorate drastically. In the now-legendary stories that have come down to us, Germans carried suitcases and pushed wheelbarrows full of money—to buy a loaf of bread or a pair of shoes. They swarmed over the countryside and railroad yards like biblical gleaners or latter-day thieves, gathering potatoes that had been left behind in the field or coal that had fallen off train cars, or they dismantled fences and took the wood for heating. Prices changed two and three times a day. The police sometimes just threw up their hands, overwhelmed by the unending popular actions that they had to face and, at times, sympathetic to the plight of their fellow citizens. On occasion crowds plundered stores and markets and paid what they thought were appropriate prices: they paid 2 marks for a loaf of bread instead of 5 or 6, 15 to 20 for shoes instead of the 200 to 300 that was posted, 1 mark per pound for fruits and vegetables instead of 4 to 5.[22] Neither businesses nor individuals could plan because inflation on this scale destroys the possibility of any rational economic calculation. Just five years after the end of the war, Germans were again plunged into misery. Many took out their resentments on an assortment of enemies that were believed to have profited handsomely from the disastrous situation—bosses, neighbors who seemed better off, Jews, foreigners, the French, the "cursed republic," Bolsheviks.

Finally recognizing the disaster at hand, the government abandoned passive resistance in September, paving the way for serious discussions with the Allies. A series of complicated, multilevel negotiations ensued, involving not just the elected representatives of Germany, but spokesmen from heavy industry as well. Extraordinarily, the republic permitted private individuals and business interests to negotiate for the country. With gusto, the Right seized on the opportunity presented by a republic terribly weakened by foreign occupation and hyperinflation. In November, the government—now again including Social Democrats—introduced a new currency, the Rentenmark, a bold and devastating move. In one fell swoop, the government established financial stability, yet again to the grave disadvantage of large segments of the population, who found their currency holdings essentially expropriated. Over the course of the following year, the French and Belgians agreed to withdraw from the Ruhr in return for a promised schedule of reparations payments that Germany committed itself to meet. Business, with the support of the government, rolled back many of the social gains of the revolution. Government employees were laid off in substantial numbers, an unprecedented development. By February 1924, factory workers were back on twelve-hour shifts, miners on eight and one-half hours. A miners' strike in late spring 1924 constituted a last-ditch effort to hold on to the workday achievements of the revolution, but the miners went down to bitter defeat.

In 1924, then, the entire political constellation shifted to the right, opening the second phase in Weimar's political history. The visions of the various political groups remained, for the most part, constant. The Weimar Coalition parties still advocated democracy and social welfare, but they were increasingly weakened by their loss of voters to the Right, in the case of the DDP and the Center, and to the Left in the case of the SPD. The Center had the most stable electorate, but its internal divisions became ever more pronounced, and conservatives were moving to the forefront of the party. The DNVP also became more divisive internally, with one wing willing to make compromises with the system in order to influence governmental policies. But in 1928 the right wing gained the upper hand, exemplified by the selection of businessman Alfred Hugenberg as party leader. Under his direction, the DNVP kept up its drumbeat of hostility and vitriolic rhetoric and moved closer to the Nazis.

Weimar's politics became ever more fragmented. In 1928, six major and eight minor parties won representation in the Reichstag; an astonishing forty-one parties had contested the election. Germany had the distinction of having the first mass-based communist party outside of the Soviet Union. On the right the soaring rhetorical attacks on the republic continued, and both prominent and insignificant figures discussed incessantly how to forge an authoritarian alternative.

But a certain calm reigned as well. There were no putsch attempts, no armed rebellions. Strikes were fewer, the working class and the trade unions exhausted by the more open battles with employers and the state that had been waged in the first phase of the republic. And high unemployment made workers wary of strikes, because there was always someone down the road ready to take the job. Aside from the DNVP, the radical Right, including the Nazis, had become marginal, almost irrelevant specks on the political spectrum. The 1928 Reichstag election brought a shift back toward the center and left, and the SPD returned to the government and even assumed the chancellorship. The Dawes Plan, named for the American banker Charles G. Dawes, revised Germany's reparations bill and schedule of payments, easing somewhat the crisis over the country's postwar obligations. The Reichstag accepted the plan on 24 August 1924. As a result, American capital flowed into Germany and fueled an economic expansion that gave many Germans, at long last, hope for the future.

The conservative DVP and the Catholic Center set the tone of the governments in the middle phase of the republic. The major figure was Gustav Stresemann of the DVP, who sat in every government of this period in the key position of foreign minister. Stresemann was one of the few individuals in the bourgeois parties who had risen from middling origins to a leadership position. He was as committed as anyone to overturning the hated Versailles system. Yet he believed the goal could be reached by a policy of "fulfillment," through Germany's meeting its treaty commitments and, at the same time, negotiating their revision. He believed the Allies could be won over to recognize the injustice of Versailles. Stresemann injected a note of reason and compromise into the always heated, highly ideological atmosphere of Weimar politics. But Stresemann remained a German nationalist, a conventional figure who strove unstintingly not for an international order of cooperation and compromise, but for a revival of Germany's great-power status.[23] Like his colleagues in the DVP, Stresemann was realistic enough to tolerate the republic. But all of them lacked an emotional and intellectual investment in democracy; it was always, in their minds, something imposed upon Germany by Social Democrats and foreign powers.

Party strife and cooperation, however, did not constitute the full range of Weimar politics. In Weimar Germany, hope and progress, as well as despair and defeat, always went hand in hand with raw, deep-seated conflicts over the very nature of culture, society, and politics, and these were fought out not just in elections and in the Reich and state (*Land*) parliaments. Politics in Weimar also meant popular mobilizations like rallies and mass demonstrations in the streets and petition drives and letter-writing campaigns. Through these measures, all sorts of associations, from socialist youth groups to middle-class teachers' organizations, exercised sharp pressure on the formal institutions of governance. This was democracy in action, even when the specific goals of various pressure groups were profoundly antidemocratic. At the same time, the old elites continued to exercise influence through their prominent role in major institutions like the army, the churches, and the state bureaucracy. Weimar politics were intensely modern, as the high level of popular mobilization signifies; at the same time, there existed profound residues of traditional power. There was no easy and clear Left-Right distinction in this regard: the extreme and even, at times, the established Right adopted all the forms and techniques of modern mobilizations and propagated the modern ideology of race, while liberals advocated a more traditional politics that supported elections and the rule of law, but also promoted the deference of the lower classes to those higher on the social and educational scale.

A range of issues and events that unfolded in the second phase of the republic—new laws that permitted the censorship of "filth and trash" and that established comprehensive unemployment insurance; international negotiations that brought Germany, finally, a modicum of recognition and relief; veterans' demonstrations and communist marches; army scandals and achievements—all became flash points of conflict over the most basic political values and beliefs, over what precisely should be the character of Germany in the twentieth century. These issues and events also demonstrate the highly public nature of politics in Weimar Germany, the intertwining of movements, interest groups, and institutions in political decision making, in short, the uneasy mix of modernity and tradition that contributed to Weimar's particular intensity.

On 3 December 1926, the Reichstag passed one of the most controversial measures of the republic, the Law to Protect Youth from Trashy and Filthy Writings. The campaign for such a law had emerged well before 1914 and attracted a diverse array of supporters. Teachers, clerics, social workers, and all sorts of other conservatively minded people fumed about penny novels and other forms of cheap literature. The writings were, sometimes, pornographic, but more often were simply heart-thumping, horseback-mounting, detective-revolver-packing romance and adventure stories. Their wide availability and great popularity were signal features of modern, urban life. Enterprising publishers and authors spotted a lucrative market; high-volume printing presses, accustomed to churning out hundreds of thousands of copies of newspapers every day, could easily be adapted to pour out mass-market, cheaply made books or brochures. From pulpits and classrooms around Germany pastors, priests, and teachers spoke out against the dangers of *Schund und Schmutz* (trash and filth) and their portrayal of the excitement of the bright lights of the city, alcohol, bodies rubbing close to one another, sex. The writings appealed, so the critics said, to the most base human instincts and destroyed respect for authority. They were directly responsible for the frightening rise in criminal behavior, promiscuity, and sexually transmitted diseases. The works had no aesthetic value, the law's advocates claimed, and were often the product of foreign, notably Jewish, authors. Reading them undermined young people's ability to appreciate the great works of German literature and the deeper truths they revealed. One Protestant minister defined *Schund und Schmutz* as rooted in "Jewish Manchesterism," blending anti-Semitism, anti-free-market capitalism, and anti-British sentiments into one phrase.[24] Those explicitly on the right, like DNVP backers, blamed the republic for the very existence of trash and filth, just as they blamed it for Versailles and every other ill affecting German society. Hermann Popert, a Hamburg juvenile court judge and one of the most prominent campaigners, railed against the "overstimulation of the imagination" produced by filth and trash.[25] This was poison. Young people had to be protected from such things, and the state had to be the guardian enforcer.

Some of Germany's leading intellectuals spoke out against the law as a blatant act of censorship that violated the constitution. As Thomas Mann wrote: "Every literate and knowledgeable person recognizes that the need to protect our youth from filth and trash . . . is nothing more than a pretext. The law's drafters want to use the law's penetrating power against freedom, against intellect itself."[26] But intellectuals never mounted the successful public campaign that the law's supporters mustered. The proponents were lodged in powerful institutions and successful pressure groups—the Protestant and Catholic churches, the teachers' association, the librarians' association, middle-class women's groups, and many others. For all their claims to be representing "traditional values," they spearheaded a modern political mobilization. They campaigned on the local level, organizing exhibits, demonstrations, and rallies, which gelled into a national movement. They had direct social and personal links to the major centrist and conservative parties. Weimar was a democracy, and the formal political institutions were porous—they could be influenced from the outside, in this case, by conservative pressure groups.

It took three readings and a fractured majority before the government could muster the requisite votes in the Reichstag. But the bill did pass. As a result, a governmental board was established by the minister of the interior in cooperation with the state governments. The board had the power to ban a work from being displayed or sold to anyone under eighteen, though it turned over enforcement to local officials. The effects of the law, however, were minimal. By spring 1932, 143 items had been placed on the list, hardly a dent in the flood of cheap literature on the market.[27] Nonetheless, the establishment of a formal censorship board demonstrated the Right's ability to wage a mass campaign that led to triumph in the legislative arena—a rather ominous sign for the republic.

A comprehensive unemployment insurance program was somewhat less controversial. Ultimately, on 16 July 1927, the Reichstag passed it by a wide majority (356 to 47, with 16 abstentions). The law superseded a maze of local and regional measures, and turned unemployment insurance into a right of workers, rather than a benefit that they could gain only by proving need. The law provided for benefits for 26 weeks, with the possibility of extension to 39 weeks, at the rate of 35 to 75 percent of the basic wage one had received. The benefit was financed by a tax divided between employers and wage earners. On the same day, the Reichstag, also by a large majority, extended a law that protected women's jobs six weeks prior to childbirth to six weeks after as well (though without pay). The six-week postpartum period could be extended with a doctor's certification that the mother's health would be adversely affected if she returned to work.[28]

Both provisions lay within the scope of social welfare programs initiated by Bismarck in the 1880s. More immediately, the unemployment insurance law represented a revival of the corporatist coalition of 1918–19: trade unions, employers, and the state all proved willing to support social welfare in conjunction with high productivity. Employers had given up their opposition to the program and, at least at this point, were not willing to challenge directly the Weimar system. At the same time, the unemployment insurance law provided the government with the popular support it needed and balanced its generally probusiness policies.

All the parties, even the unions, feared any provisions that might undermine the incentive to work. As a result, the unemployed could claim support only for a limited period of time and at rates well below their earned wages. Like similar programs that would emerge in other developed countries, especially after World War II, the German unemployment insurance law segmented the population. The law benefited those workers employed in industrial enterprises. Excluded from support were workers in agriculture, still a very substantial segment of the labor force, those who labored in small shops, and the long-term poor. Nonetheless, the unemployment insurance law was a milestone of social welfare that ameliorated some of the instabilities and inequities of the capitalist labor market. It protected workers from bouts of unemployment. And its easy passage provided one more hopeful sign of the era of relative stability. In 1927, no one envisioned the catastrophic levels of unemployment that would hit Germany just three years later. For that crisis, the 1927 law would prove totally inadequate, and it would then become the touchstone of conflict, the first step in the demise of the republic.

Stresemann was a forceful and effective advocate of fulfillment, and he found a willing partner in the French foreign minister, Aristide Briand. The Locarno treaties, signed on 1 December 1925, marked their first great success. Germany, France, and Belgium renounced the use of force to alter the boundaries between them. Germany thereby recognized its western borders, including the loss of Alsace-Lorraine; France effectively renounced any annexationist strivings in the Rhineland. France also promised to evacuate its troops from the Cologne region. Germany still did not recognize its eastern borders, but it at least promised that it would not alter the German-Polish boundary by force. Germany was also promised admission to the League of Nations, a promise that was fulfilled on 10 September 1926 and included a permanent seat on the organization's governing council.

A number of other international agreements continued "the spirit of Locarno" through the second phase of the republic. The Geneva Convention banning the use of poison gas was signed on 17 June 1925 and ratified by the Reichstag on 5 April 1929. In the Kellogg-Briand Pact, named for the U.S. secretary of state and the French foreign minister and signed on 27 August 1928, fifteen countries renounced the use of war to resolve conflicts and achieve political goals. Germany joined the initial group, which would later grow to sixty-three signatories. And the reparations crisis eased somewhat. On 7 June 1929, the various powers, including the United States, concluded the so-called Young Plan (named after the American banker and chief negotiator Owen D. Young), which set Germany's final reparations payments at 137.3 billion goldmarks, payable over fifty-nine years. The last payment would have been due in 1987. At the same time, the Allied powers and the United States gave up the lingering controls they had exercised over the German economy through the Dawes Plan, though areas of the Rhineland remained under occupation.[29]

So toward the end of the second phase of the republic, Germans could look at the international situation with some optimism. Germany had been incorporated into the League of Nations and had won some relief from its reparations obligations. A large dose of distrust still colored Allied attitudes toward Germany, but the country was no longer a pariah.

None of this, however, sufficed for the powerful right wing in Germany. Like Erzberger and Rathenau before him, Stresemann was hounded by the Right as a traitor to the nation. But in 1925 in the Swiss town of Locarno, crowds had cheered the successful, initial signing of the treaties. Erich Eyck, leading DDP political figure and later historian, reported on the scene at the final meeting after Briand and Stresemann had both given moving speeches.

> Outside, from all the churches of Locarno and even from the little chapel of the Madonna del Sasso, bells were ringing a welcome to the new era of peace that was about to spread across Europe. In the square in front of the town hall the citizens of Locarno were gathered in applauding, jubilant approval. Paul Schmidt [the Foreign Office interpreter for the German delegation] recalls: "As we descended the few steps of the little stairway with Stresemann and Luther, the crowd exploded in another roar of acclaim. Then suddenly everyone was still. All the men in the crowd removed their hats and formed a silent, immobile double row through which we, deeply moved, proceeded to our carriage."[30]

For their achievements, both Stresemann and Briand were awarded the Nobel Peace Prize. In his speech before the League of Nations in Geneva (10 September 1926) and then at the Nobel Prize ceremony in Stockholm (10 December 1926), Stresemann eloquently advocated an international order of law, justice, and peace, though he also, always, proclaimed the sovereignty of the nation and its particular culture.[31] At Geneva, Stresemann was followed by Briand, who spoke in similar fashion and asserted that bloody conflicts, especially those between France and Germany, had been put to rest.

It is easy, decades later, to react cynically to the scenes at Locarno, Geneva, and Stockholm, or to shake one's head in amazement at the naïveté of the diplomats and the crowds that applauded them. Did they not have any prescience of the disasters that lay ahead? Yet in 1925 and 1926, just a few brief years after the armistice, only two and three years after the chaotic and crisis-filled year of hyperinflation in Germany, the "spirit of Locarno" at least gave people hope that human and material devastation on the scale of World War I would not be repeated.

However, the reactions in Germany were by no means uniform. There were, to be sure, supportive comments in the liberal and socialist press. But when the German delegation arrived from Locarno at Berlin's Anhalter Bahnhof, they found no cheering crowds, only a few ministers and hordes of police. After all, Stresemann's predecessor, Walter Rathenau, had been assassinated just three years earlier. The police were there to protect the republic's representatives from the republic's population. Stresemann was vilified just as Rathenau had been before him, only spared, because he was not Jewish, the anti-Semitic vitriol. Far from taking pride in Stresemann's receipt of the Nobel Peace Prize, the Right viewed it as the ultimate proof that he was hostage to the interests of foreign powers.

At the end of the second phase of Weimar's history, it should have been clear to all involved that the Right could never be brought along to accept the republic. Only the total and complete defeat of the Right could ensure the republic's health and well-being. That might have been possible in 1918–19, but not in 1925 or 1929. And much worse was yet to come.

The spectacle of Germans marching in disciplined military formation, waving flags and banners, and, sometimes, battling it out with counterdemonstrators and the police, suffused Weimar society. Franz Hessel, our guide on our walking tour of Berlin, also depicted a communist demonstration he encountered:

> Red Whitsun. They have come from all over Germany. Textile proletarians from the Erzgebirge. Miners from the mines in Hamm and the armaments city Essen, which has become a Red Front fortress, also red marines from the northern coast. But also other, distant parts of Europe and the wider world send

> their representatives—the Protective Guard of the Swiss workers and the Czech Labor Defense march with their flags and posters. Reverentially they greet the Soviet standard. In long columns they marched in from the outskirts of the city, at the head a curious collection of musical instruments. Trumpets with many gaping mouths, jazz tubas, Negro drums. These fighters are wearing uniforms just like those whom they want to overthrow. The gray shirts and the brown jackets are belted in warlike fashion. And as once the eyes scanned over the stripes of noncommissioned officers, now they gaze over the sea of red armbands worn by the men on the wings, firmly leading the columns of marchers. Even the children are wearing uniforms.[32]

Walking along with them, Hessel noted how the iron of the railroad overpasses echoed the cries of "Red Front!" and "Be prepared!" From the balconies of bourgeois apartments, men and women watched sullenly as the Communists marched by. But from the side streets with the shabbier apartments, red flags hung from the windows.

As Hessel noted, everyone was a part of the event, those who marched and those who watched with scowls on their faces. The Communists made their presence felt, and that, after all, is the point of a demonstration. But was Hessel right to draw a connection between parading Prussian troops and columns of uniformed workers marching on the city? The historical lineage perhaps traces more to the Bolshevik Revolution than to the Prussian cavalry. German Communists, like all those around the world, absorbed the mythology of the storming of the Winter Palace in Petrograd in October 1917, that is, the understanding of revolution as a military act. The march toward the communist utopia depended, in this view, on the complete and violent triumph over multitudinous enemies of the working class—bosses, capitalists, clerics, and the state (fig. 3.8). This fascination with things military penetrated deeply into the communist movement and beyond. Even Social Democrats and liberals organized paramilitary formations, and Jews self-defense groups, and all of them—especially the Communists—gave a combative tenor to public life in Weimar Germany.

But it was the Right that had a special affinity for the military style. There were, by some counts, more than two hundred paramilitary groups in Germany in the 1920s and hundreds more right-wing

Fig. 3.8 "Everywhere in City and Countryside: Red Unity for Antifascist Action!" The Left marches: Communists also conveyed a militaristic spirit with images of strong men parading in unison, ready to fight Nazis and policemen.

associations and circles.[33] They organized millions of Germans into a new form of politics that was modern and combative. In 1922, the Deutschvölkschen Schutz- und Trutzbund alone counted close to

Fig. 3.9 The Right marches: The veterans' organization parades in 1930 in Koblenz on its self-proclaimed holiday, the "Reich Front Soldiers Day of the Stahlhelm." Weimar was engulfed by demonstrations honoring the military. Bildarchiv Preussischer Kulturbesitz / Art Resource, NY.

two hundred thousand members.[34] Some of them playacted, to be sure. They donned uniforms and marched around as if they were tough, proud military heroes. But others were positively dangerous, well-armed and prone to engage in barroom brawls, streetfights, and armed combat. They recruited many World War I veterans, who were then joined, in the late 1920s, by younger men who regretted that they had missed the action on the battlefields of 1914–18. They read with delight Ernst Jünger's loving depictions of battles, sniper hunts, and the technology of warfare in such works as *Storm of Steel*, *Copse 125*, and many, many others. They marched in events like "German Day," established in 1921, which brought together scores of right-wing paramilitary organizations, each marching under its own flag and all joined together. The Stahlhelm, the veterans' organization, was the largest, but by no means the most dangerous. The paramilitaries carried truncheons, metal splinters, and revolvers, sometimes clandestinely, sometimes not. They wore jackboots and military jackets with insignia of rank (fig. 3.9). Their disciplined formations often degenerated into brawls, especially when bystanders jeered at them. Ultimately, the Nazis would absorb all of these groups, giving them a much firmer ideological direction. But the style and the meaning of militarism had already been developed all over the right-wing spectrum in the 1920s.

The militaristic tones of Weimar society were not the result of the paramilitary formations alone. The German army had a storied past and remained an honored institution despite its defeat in World War I. In the Prussian tradition going back to the seventeenth century, the army was admired, fawned over, and well supported. Some Germans no doubt mistook the tone of the famous remark of the eighteenth-century French philosophe Mirabeau—"Prussia is an army with a state, rather than a state with an army"—seeing it as a compliment and missing his irony. Any visitor walking around any German town immediately encountered one monument after another to the Prusso-German military. In Berlin, one of the major thoroughfares ran from the Brandenburg Gate to the Victory Column, linking the eighteenth and nineteenth centuries to the present via the army.

The Versailles Treaty had placed sharp limits on the German military. Germany could have a Reichswehr (the new name for its army) of only one hundred thousand men and no air force whatsoever. The treaty also severely limited the size and heft of the navy. Thousands of officers and enlisted men had to be fired, to the great chagrin of the military command. The army chiefs spent a good deal of time surreptitiously circumventing the Versailles strictures, generally with the connivance of the Reichswehr ministry, led for a good part of the 1920s by Otto Geßler, a member of the DDP. The army secretly recruited men above and beyond the one hundred thousand limit into the so-called Black Reichswehr, and received additional, also secret, budget appropriations. A series of agreements with the Soviet Union provided for the construction of German arms factories on Soviet soil and granted the Reichswehr training facilities in the Soviet Union.

All sorts of ties—personal, professional, political, class—bound the regular army to the wide array of right-wing paramilitary formations that so marred the political landscape of Weimar Germany. Many of the paramilitaries were commanded and staffed by officers who had been cashiered in 1919 and 1920 because of the Versailles Treaty.

Regular officers visited and sometimes trained the paramilitaries; arms flowed to them from army and police stocks. Only the total chaos of 1923 and pressure from the Allies led the Reichswehr minister to force the army to withdraw its active support of illegal recruits and paramilitaries, though these activities never entirely ceased.

The key figure for about half of the Weimar period was the chief of the army command, Hans von Seeckt. He was a typical Reichswehr officer who had grown up under and served the old regime (fig. 3.10). According to the historian and onetime DDP political figure Erich Eyck, Seeckt was "a strong personality of outstanding military capabilities and he dedicated his tireless and intelligent labors to creating and equipping the new army."[35] But he was never a democrat, never a committed supporter of the republic, and only reluctantly did he accept the new order. His only virtue politically was that he was too realistic and hardheaded to believe in the many plots, ventures, and dreams of the radical Right. But his ideas were not so far removed from theirs. His ambition was to restore the might of the army and, with it, Germany's great-power status. When asked his position during the Kapp Putsch, Seeckt famously replied, "Reichswehr does not fire on Reichswehr," words he repeated during the Hitler Putsch in 1923.[36] The republic, however, needed more from its army than a stance of neutrality during right-wing putsch attempts. Seeckt's major concern was always to protect the integrity of the Reichswehr, not that of the republic.

Seeckt's downfall came in 1926, in yet another Weimar minicrisis that was so revealing of the fault lines in the society and polity. In June 1926 the former crown prince asked Seeckt to allow his son, Prince William, the opportunity to take part in military exercises. The revolutionary government had exiled the entire imperial family to Holland, but within a few years only the former kaiser was permanently barred from stepping on German soil. A request of this order was quite outrageous. What thriving democratic system would allow the heir of a deposed monarchical and imperial family the right to participate in the maneuvers of a republican army? The point is, of course, that the army was far from being republican, and its officers from the top down, Seeckt included, barely tolerated the republic. Instead, they viewed themselves as the true bearers of the German spirit and the German state, and were only biding their time until something different, whatever that might exactly be, replaced the republic.

Fig. 3.10 Generals Hans von Seeckt (right) and Werner von Blomberg, the very epitome of the Prusso-German officer corps, in uniform with jackboots and medals. Seeckt sports a monocle, a much satirized accessory of the nobility. Small wonder that contemporaries wondered about the army's commitment to the republic.

Seeckt approved the request. The news generated a public outcry that ultimately let to his dismissal. Nor was this the end of army scandals in 1926. At the end of the year, the British press exposed the ties between the Reichswehr and the Soviet Union. The first scandal revealed how fragile was the republic if it could not count on its own army to steer clear of the Hohenzollern family; the second demonstrated how thoroughly the army was still able to shape the budget and foreign policy of Germany, even under a republic.

Seeckt was not the only military figure with a powerful public presence. The president of the republic since 1925 was Field Marshal Paul von Hindenburg. Often depicted as an ineffectual, bumbling figure who exercised merely symbolic functions, Hindenburg in fact played an active role in the politics of the republic. His election to the presidency generated deep misgivings abroad and at home. The reaction of the foreign press was universally negative: Hindenburg was, indeed, the very embodiment of Prussian militarism. On 7 April 1926, he celebrated his sixtieth (!) year of service in the Prusso-German army (fig. 3.11). Hindenburg had fought in the Austro-Prussian War of 1866 and the Franco-Prussian War of 1870–71. In World War I, along with Erich Ludendorff, he commanded the army that drove back the Russians in East Prussia. The two of them then exercised virtual dictatorial powers as the Third Supreme High Command from August 1916 until Germany's defeat in the war. Theodor Wolff, the editor in chief of the liberal *Berliner Tageblatt*, wrote about Hindenburg's election: "The republicans have lost a battle. . . . We are ashamed of the many millions who are revealed to the world to be so politically immature. The . . . election was a test of intelligence before the world gallery. Before sympathetic, horrified friends and scornful enemies roughly half of the German people have failed the test."[37] Others were more sanguine, especially after Hindenburg had declared himself ready to abide by the constitution. Stresemann's impression was that Hindenburg was more rooted in the time of Wilhelm I than in that of Wilhelm II, meaning that he would abide by the precepts of a constitutional presidency and would not be very prone to reckless actions. Presciently, he wrote that "the main thing is [to ensure] that uncontrollable people do not gain influence upon him."[38]

But there was little to be happy about if one were a convinced democrat. At the celebration of Hindenburg's years of service, Reichswehr Minister Geßler emphasized the continuities between the

Fig. 3.11 Field Marshal and President Paul von Hindenburg, also in uniform, complete with jackboots, medals, and sword. Not the ideal president for a republic. Bildarchiv Preussischer Kulturbesitz / Art Resource, NY.

kaiser's army and the Reichswehr.[39] It might have been a mollifying speech to the military, but it was yet another sign of how beholden the republic was to the antidemocratic forces on the right.

Among Hindenburg's other contributions to the republic was a decision that German diplomatic and consular representations abroad as well as German-flag ships should carry both the black-red-gold flag of the republic and the imperial black-white-red flag (with a black-red-gold insignia in the inner upper corner). Hindenburg also exercised pressure on the building of cabinets, making clear in 1927 to Chancellor Marx, for example, that he was opposed to the participation of Social Democrats in the government and favored those who were on the side of "the interests of the Fatherland." The result was the entrance of the DNVP into the government. And he ostentatiously appeared at the dedication ceremony for the Tannenberg Monument in Hohenstein (East Prussia), the site of the successful German counterattack against the Russians in late August 1914. The monument was, in fact, a large fortress. At the dedication ceremony on 18 September 1927, Ludendorff was also in the lead, followed by some seventy thousand people, including large columns of various right-wing paramilitary organizations, like the Stahlhelm, the Jungdeutsche Ordnen, and Nazi groups. In his speech, Hindenburg denied the charge that Germany had anything to do with the outbreak of World War I. "We, the German people, all its classes, reject with one voice the charge that Germany is guilty of this greatest of all wars! . . . With pure hearts we came to the defense of the Fatherland. With clean hands the German army took up the sword."[40] The speech, along with the militaristic character of the ceremony, caused great consternation at home and abroad, but domestically it clearly had strong support as well. At the same time, Hindenburg refused to observe any celebration of the German revolution that had blazed the path to the republic.[41] Indeed, Hindenburg played a major role in stoking revanchist sentiments in Germany. In his 1929 New Year's message, he wrote, much as he did every year:

> The entire German people greets today the beginning of the new year with deep bitterness, because a great part of our land is denied the freedom on which we have just claim—just in God's eyes and in man's eyes. We have long hoped for its attainment.

> And we still want to hope, despite harsh disappointment, that in the new year the German people will be given back its full right of self-determination.[42]

At least Hindenburg was able to say that Germany "sincerely welcomes" the Kellogg-Briand Pact. But as for real support for Stresemann's policy of fulfillment—not a word from the president, a fitting response from a man who was also an honorary member of the right-wing veterans' group, the Stahlhelm.

The German military, with its conservative, authoritarian traditions, infused Weimar politics and society. The army chief of command and the second (and last) president of the republic exercised major influence on governmental policies. Their reserved—at best—attitude toward the republic was common knowledge. The symbols of the military were everywhere, in festivals, monuments, and parades. Precious few officers were convinced supporters of the constitution. This was a republic without a republican army, a situation tolerable—though barely—during the more stable, second phase of the republic's history from 1924 to 1929. But the army was ready to pounce as soon as the conditions changed and it was again possible to imagine an authoritarian alternative to democracy.

The interim period of Weimar politics at least brought some stability and economic progress. By 1928, Germany's factories and mines were producing at high levels. New department stores were opening up in major cities, a sign of the revival of commerce and consumption. Many individuals had seen a turn for the better in their personal circumstances, although structural unemployment remained high and many middle-class families had still not been able to recapture their standing of 1914. But it was possible to look forward with cautious optimism. The national election of 1928 resulted in a turn back toward the center. The SPD returned to the government at the head of a large coalition that excluded only the DNVP, which, under Hugenberg, was taking a decisive lurch to the extreme right.

And then came the world economic crisis. It began, of course, with the stock market crash in the United States in October 1929, which turned first into a banking and then a production crisis. It spread quickly to Germany because so much of the economic upturn of the preceding years had been fueled by American capital. When American banks called in their loans, German banks quickly fell into a liquidity crisis, which then sent the entire economy into a tailspin. Probably no country was as deeply affected by the crisis as was Germany. In mid-1932, the depths of the Depression, fully one-third of the labor force was unemployed.

Revolution, Versailles, putsch attempts, hyperinflation—now this. How could the republic ever hope to win the loyalty of the German population? Quickly, the economic crisis became a legitimacy crisis of the political system as well.

In the coalition government, each of the parties rapidly reverted to form and sought to protect its own constituency. The funding of the unemployment insurance system—one of the great achievements of the republic's second phase—became the focal point of conflict. The system had been financed by tax contributions from employers and workers. It was designed to tide workers over episodic bouts of unemployment. Absolutely no one had envisioned unemployment on the scale of the Great Depression, and the unemployment insurance fund quickly went bankrupt. Social Democrats demanded an increase in business taxes and continued support for workers, who, after all, had lost their livelihoods through no fault of their own. The majority parties in the government demanded a retrenchment of government spending as the quickest means of reviving the economy. They wanted unemployment and other benefits curtailed and more stringent criteria applied to the applicants. The parties failed to reach agreement, and the government fell. The president, Paul von Hindenburg, appointed a conservative member of the Center Party, Heinrich Brüning, as chancellor. Divided on every key financial and political issue, the Reichstag fractured into an unworkable institution. President Hindenburg invoked article 48 of the Weimar Constitution, which allowed the chancellor to govern by decree.

For the next three years, until the Nazi seizure of power, Germany was governed by a presidential dictatorship. There were still elections—many of them, in fact—still constitutional protections of basic liberties, and Germans took to the streets and the press in large numbers to express their views. This was a strange sort of dictatorship, one based upon the inability of a democracy to function rather than on an outright overthrow of power and abolition of a constitution. But as the presidential dictatorship developed, it became less a series of stopgap measures and more an elaborated effort to overthrow the republic from within and cast off the limitations of Versailles so Germany could regain its great-power status. Brüning's vision was of an authoritarian system, perhaps a clerico-military dictatorship, that would carry out an antilabor, antidemocratic, and somewhat anti-Semitic policy.[43] This was still the Weimar Republic, but, at least politically, it was Weimar hollowed out, a system that deprived the republic of all meaning connected to the word, a governmental system that had jettisoned the progressive vision (however varied) of the republic's founders. Had the presidential system survived, it no doubt would have led to the suppression of trade unions and the Communist Party, the suspension of elections, and the most severe limitations on the freedom of the press and of speech.

In 1932, the nadir of the Depression, Germany experienced two Reichstag elections, two presidential elections (counting the runoff), and three chancellors, as well as numerous state and local elections. Every election revealed the extreme fragmentation of the society. No party could muster a majority. Brüning and his successors in 1932, Franz von Papen and Kurt von Schleicher, governed with the tolerance, but not the support, of the Reichstag. The first fatal step had come in 1930, when Brüning called elections in a fairyland belief that he, a sitting chancellor in the midst of a depression, would win widespread popular support. It was a political blunder of the first order, which led to the surge of the Nazi Party. That party won 17 percent of the vote and 107 seats in the Reichstag. A political system that was already fragmented and indecisive became completely paralyzed. The Reichstag was unable to decide on any major issue, and Hindenburg kept invoking article 48. Brüning, then, had a free hand to follow the deflationary path that he believed would lead Germany out of the Depression. He sharply curtailed government spending by significantly reducing social welfare benefits and firing and cutting the salaries of civil service workers. Such policies only increased the disaffection of large segments of the population and did nothing to revive the economy. If anything, they worsened the economic situation.

Economic depression and political fragmentation and paralysis largely destroyed whatever faith Germans still had in the Weimar system. Even the Weimar Coalition parties had a hard time exuding confidence and rallying their supporters. The situation was perfect for the republic's opponents, the Nazis now in the lead. They had ample ammunition to attack the republic—what was left of it—and to claim the mantle of the nation, as we shall see in more detail in chapter 9.

The kaiser was gone, Joseph Roth wrote. His contemporary, the famed satirist Kurt Tucholsky, wrote about a lion being gone, having escaped from the zoo. Tucholsky described the government's reaction:

> In the army ministry a subcommission of the investigative committee met to check over its own indispensable character, when the horrifying report came. The breakfast—sorry, the meeting—was immediately broken off. Two general staff officers worked hip-hop with their assistants on a new battle plan for fighting the lions and demanded immediately:
>
> 2 army corps,
> 1 press office,
> 24 staff officer positions outside of the regular budgetary appropriation,
> 1 canon,
> 1 battleship

The parties also reacted:

> The German People's Party was, as always, at its post. In a half hour loud blue posters were pasted on all kiosks and trees:
>
> FELLOW CITIZENS!
> THE LION IS LOOSE!
> WHO IS GUILTY?
> THE JEWS!
> ELECT THE GERMAN PEOPLE'S PARTY![44]

Roth portrayed the great achievement of Weimar. Tucholsky, with his inimitable style, captured the underside, the powerful, if bumbling, role of the bureaucracy and the army, the pervasiveness of militarism, and the quick resort to anti-Semitism.

Weimar politics was all that and more. No single description can ever capture its diversity or its conflict-ridden character. It was startlingly democratic, yet infused with profound authoritarian elements. Most important, Germany was a liberal democracy. Whatever its flaws, the constitution established the rule of law, equality under the law, political liberties, and procedures for democratic voting. Politically Weimar was fragmented and chaotic, capable of producing peaceful, egalitarian, and humanitarian visions of the future alongside dreams of violent revenge against Jews, foreigners, and supposed domestic degenerates.

Weimar politics had profound links to the past. Virtually all the major parties were continuations of the dominant parties of imperial Germany. The army and bureaucracy, populated at the upper levels by the wellborn and the well-connected, were barely refashioned under the republic and continued to command power and loyalties. Yet there was also a freshness to Weimar politics, for good and bad. New parties and movements emerged on the right and the left, and the style of confrontational mass politics that they promoted influenced every other political group. All of them had to contest elections in a raucous public sphere and learn how to use the new media to their advantage. The Right had come to understand that politics could no longer consist solely of deals made among men of the "better classes" in their clubs, boardrooms, and offices. In the age of mass politics and total war, a nationalist politics had to find a popular base. It had to win the support of millions of people who would march behind elite men: followers who would vote, march, and rally; would read, write, and propagandize their views. The Right followed the pioneering insight of the Left: there was power to be found in mass mobilization.

The new parties on the extremes, the Communists and Nazis, did it better than anyone else because they were less hobbled by tradition. They added paramilitary organizations and street battles to the repertoire of political contention, lending a sharp edge to Weimar politics that enhanced its "mass" character. In cities and towns, Germans were literally assaulted with slogans and starkly drawn poster images and with marching men. Crowds of both genders lined the streets to gaze; flying teams of agitprop players performed skits on streetcorners and then rapidly moved on, before the police or rival groups appeared. Processions moved this way and that, and sometimes culminated in the seizure of the city hall, a company's headquarters, or the marketplace. This was a politics of display and spectacle, suitable for an era of mass media and a society and polity deeply divided. It was also a politics, Right and Left, defined by militancy, by hostility to the existing social order of inherited privilege and of the status that came with education and property. Neither Communists nor those on the extreme Right displayed any deference to established authority and its status symbols. They broke the boundaries of politics as they had existed before 1918. Ultimately, of course, the NSDAP would be the beneficiary of these trends. But its success would also result from the widespread support it received, passive and active, from the established Right.

At the same time, in the wake of World War I, many Germans had developed a deep revulsion against violence. They helped make Erich Maria Remarque's *All Quiet on the Western Front* an immediate best seller. They signed antiwar petitions and supported the KPD's campaign against the increase in military budgets. They joined pacifist organizations and admired antiwar artists like Käthe Kollwitz, whose searing woodcuts, drawings, and sculptures depicted the immense sorrow of war, or John Heartfield's powerfully political photomontages, which called on Germans to fight militarism. But many Germans, right, left, and center, were attracted by the spellbinding image of powerful men ready for combat. It was not a sensibility conducive to democracy.

Women's suffrage, women's activism, and the reforming impulse of the Weimar Coalition also added a new dimension to politics. Each of the parties now had to contend with female as well as male voters, the greater public presence of women, and women in their own ranks. Social Democrats were especially worried about what they saw as the religious and conservative inclinations of women. Indeed, there was some rightward tug as a result of female suffrage, but not—as many contemporaries claimed—to the far right. Women also won seats in the Reichstag, though their numbers declined over the course of the era. But in municipalities women won representation and found avenues for their talents and abilities in the expanding social welfare realm of the republic. Women worked as welfare inspectors, child and family counselors, and health officers. In the

Reichstag and the various Landtage they served especially on committees dealing with health and education. They had a profound impact in these areas, and also in the newly professionalized field of social work. But the major ministries and offices—economics, defense, interior—remained closed to them. Weimar as a welfare state was, in part, a woman's state, in terms of personnel as well as policy. And when the attack came upon Weimar, it was very much an attack on women, or at least on women in the public sphere, including the world of politics.

Weimar politics was not all innovation. There were also deeply etched lines of continuity with the German past, and one of them was no doubt the powerful role of the bureaucracy and the military within the state. Weimar was a democracy, and unlike those in imperial Germany, the ministers were responsible to the Reichstag. But civil servants and army officers had technical expertise. At the upper levels they were granted lifelong tenure and could be removed only in a declared fiscal crisis or national emergency. They exercised a decisively conservative, antirepublican influence on Weimar politics, most evident in the army's equivocal attitude toward putsch attempts and the judiciary's solicitous treatment of right-wing terrorists. Yet the judiciary permitted all sorts of frivolous and inflammatory lawsuits against the republic's leading figures, like Matthias Erzberger and Friedrich Ebert. It was a low, mean business, and it wore down the republic's defenders. Perhaps it is no surprise that so many Weimar politicians died young, cut down by either stress-related illnesses or assassinations. Ebert, Stresemann, and Rathenau were in their early fifties, Erzberger in his forties. The socialist and communist leaders assassinated in 1919—Luxemburg, Liebknecht, Eisner, Haase—were all in their late forties or early fifties.

The legacy of World War I was perhaps the republic's greatest obstacle. It hobbled developments at every turn and gave the enemies of democracy endless rounds of ammunition. The revolution had failed to break the powers of the antidemocratic forces in German society, lodged as they were in the powerful institutions of the army, bureaucracy, universities, and business. The republic required a long breathing space to make convinced democrats out of so many Germans. It needed an expansive economy and diplomatic successes. But none of the cards would play out well for Weimar democracy.

4

A Turbulent Economy and an Anxious Society

"Die Wirtschaft ist das Schicksal" (the economy is destiny) wrote the industrialist, visionary, and foreign minister Walter Rathenau.[1] He was, to a very significant extent, correct. In the best of circumstances, the creation of a developed democracy in Germany would have been a very difficult enterprise, one always hounded by powerful antidemocratic forces all across the social and political spectrum. But the best of circumstances never existed for the Weimar Republic. It was founded in the shadow of World War I and amid the crossfires of revolution and civil war. If it were ever to win the loyalty of the majority of the German population, the republic would require a stable and expansive economy. This it was not to have. The years of economic growth were fleeting, and their achievements were built atop severe structural weaknesses; the years of crisis were many and mind-boggling in their effects. Germans of the Weimar period experienced a "world turned upside down," and not just once, but thrice—postwar readjustment, hyperinflation, and depression.[2] Small wonder that by the end, a majority could not be mustered for the republic.

Germans suffered economically, and they fought vociferously over economic matters large and small. Taxation, reparations, trade union representation, technological innovations, the very notion of private property rights—all these matters were deeply contested. And not just as mere policy disputes, whether the tax rate should be a bit higher or a bit lower, whether one, two, or five union representatives should be able to sit on a company board. Virtually every economic issue went to the heart of how Germans should live together and with other countries in the post–World War I era; every policy dispute had the potential to become an existential crisis of "the system," as Weimar was pejoratively labeled by the Right. There occurred, to be sure, some moments of consensus, particularly among those involved in the productive sector: business, unions, and the state. In the early years of the republic, they came together in support of inflation until it ran completely out of control. In the middle phase, they all supported rationalization. But the numbers of Germans adversely affected by inflation and rationalization, let alone depression, were legion, and their grievances found a ready voice on the right and the left. Politics and economics ran tightly together: Weimar's economic problems were enormous and unprecedented, the solutions sharply contested.

Through all the highly charged disputes and amid the turbulence of economic booms and crashes, Germans lived in an era marked by "relative economic stagnation" and "accelerating modernization."[3] The two designators seem to stand in direct contradiction to one another, yet by their coexistence they reveal, once again, just how conflicted and complex were the Weimar years.

Compared to the periods before 1914 and after 1945, Weimar's real growth rates were meager and the macroeconomic effect of technological innovations limited. No leading-sector innovations with a broadly stimulating impact on the economy emerged in the 1920s. There was nothing comparable to the impact of textiles production in the early phase of industrialization, or innovations in the steel industry in the 1880s or in the chemical industry from the 1890s to 1914—or, for that matter, of computers in the 1980s and 1990s. In addition, the poor performance markers resulted from Germany's retreat (in step with other developed economies) from the globalizing trends of the nineteenth century. World War I put a sharp brake on the movement of goods and capital across borders. The war's huge costs and legacy of indebtedness left only the United States in the advantageous position of a credit holder. The postwar disputes concerning the entwined problems of inter-Allied debt and Germany's reparations obligations further disrupted the flow of capital, and eased only between 1924 and 1929. Then the world economic crisis destroyed capital, and what was available again largely retreated into national markets. Germany always had to import significant amounts of food and raw materials. It required foreign currency and foreign capital to pay for its imports and to finance economic development, and needed export markets for its own products. While many Germans gleefully advocated the retreat toward a more closed national economy, such a position could not, in the long run, serve Germany's interests.

At the same time that Germany's economy, in relative terms, stagnated, it also became more modern. The proportion of the population engaged in industrial labor continued to grow and reached one statistical high point in the mid-1920s. Young women fled the farms for the greater independence of the cities and factory labor. Every observer commented on the exponential growth of the "new middle class," the legions of white-collar employees who staffed the offices of government and business; the display floors of department stores; and the laboratories of hospitals, factories, and research institutes. The baby boomers of the age cohort born around 1900 were everywhere, pressing on the very limited, sometimes nonexistent, jobs in industry and government. Engineers and business owners wrote rhapsodically about rationalization, streamlined production techniques that would increase output with less labor. And the era of mass consumption arrived. Beautifully designed department stores artfully displayed an array of goods, and advertisers lured Germans with a dreamworld of fashionable prosperity.

Weimar's economy was, then, a bundle of conflicts and contradictions. And like its politics, its economic history divides easily, though roughly, into three phases. The first phase, 1918–23, was the era of inflation; 1924–29, of rationalization; 1929–33, of depression.

The inflation had begun previously, during the war, as the government borrowed to finance its hugely increased expenditures. Germans bought bonds on the promise of steady returns on their investment and on the presumption, of course, of military victory. Any temporary difficulties, they were led to believe, would be followed by an era of unprecedented prosperity as German economic and political might spread across the continent. That was not to be. Instead, at war's end, Germans had a depreciated currency, factories almost completely dependent on military contracts, and severe shortages of both the basic necessities of life and the raw materials needed for production. Millions of returning soldiers had somehow to be reintegrated into civilian life. The British maintained their naval blockade until the summer of 1919, worsening the already dire situation in Germany.

To almost everyone's surprise, the immediate postwar readjustment and recovery proceeded smoothly. Amid the chaos of revolution, the army rapidly demobilized and German industry quickly switched over to peacetime production. Inflation bore much of the credit. Rising prices for goods stimulated investment and the expansion of manufacturing. German products were relatively inexpensive abroad, resulting in an export boom. Business and the government were able to meet incessant demands for wage increases with depreciated currency. A short-term shift to tighter monetary policies, from spring 1920 to spring 1921, interrupted the upward swing of the economy—and served as a warning signal to business, unions, and the state, all of which resumed their proinflation policies.

But in tandem with inflation loomed the reparations issue, threatening this surprisingly positive picture. In fact, reparations and inflation became entwined in a complicated and, ultimately, utterly disastrous fashion.[4]

As the economic historian Theo Balderston explains it, reparations can be understood as a "tax collected from German citizens by the German government acting as the Allies' fiscal agent." However, this tax lacked the "moral legitimation" that normally accompanies tax collection.[5] Both the German government and the German citizenry felt Allied claims were completely unjust. When the Allies finally delivered the bill on 5 May 1921 in the so-called London Ultimatum, even moderate Germans were shocked. The Allies set Germany's reparations commitment at 132 billion goldmarks, 50 billion to be serviced immediately in the form of bonds that Germany would pay off at the rate of 2 billion goldmarks per year plus the value of 26 percent of German exports.[6] Yet another political crisis ensued in Germany. The government, faced with a virtually universal opposition to higher taxes, was effectively bankrupted and had to look to the capital markets for the necessary funds. There it found no takers. In essence, the German government faced a strike by both taxpayers (relayed in the refusal of the Reichstag to vote for tax increases) and wealthholders (relayed in the government's miserable credit rating and the absence of purchasers of government bonds).[7]

The London Ultimatum resulted in long, wearying negotiations, numerous conferences, notes back and forth, promulgations, declarations of disaster soon to be at hand. The Germans claimed an incapacity to pay; the Allies demanded that Germany meet its obligations. A stream of high-ranking German visitors descended on London. (Paris, everyone knew, was a lost cause in terms of exercising German influence, and the Americans had withdrawn behind their two oceans.) The Germans managed only to sow confusion. Some supported the policy of fulfillment—meeting Allied obligations while working diplomatically to revise the reparations bill downward. Others argued that Germany simply had no capacity to pay, and tried to convince the Allies of this reality. Still other Germans were just recalcitrant and demanded sheer refusal—no negotiations, no payments, nothing. Like the extreme nationalists at the end of World War I, they were prepared to let the worst happen. Let everything—economy, society, the republic—crash to smithereens rather than deal with the reality that Germany had started the war, had lost the war, and now had to pay for the war.

While Germany pleaded poverty and an inability to meet its reparations obligations, many foreign observers noted what inflation had wrought—a manufacturing revival, restaurants and nightclubs filled with patrons, and a lively export trade. Only if they peered more closely did they see extensive pockets of unemployment and soup kitchens as well. But then inflation crept into the danger zone, where the beneficial effects were undermined by wild speculation, deteriorating living standards, and the inability to plan in any kind of rational manner. For Germany in the early 1920s, such developments inevitably complicated the already difficult matter of reparations and the country's foreign relations.

In the summer and fall of 1921, rising prices set off another round of demands for wage increases. Germans had learned the efficacy of mass protests during the revolution. All across the economic spectrum, from coal miners to civil servants, workers and employees demonstrated and went out on strike. By and large, they succeeded. They won significant wage increases, which government and business could meet by paying in depreciated currency, and business, at least, by raising prices. A galloping wage-price spiral emerged, a kind of contagion in which entire industries as well as individual businessmen abandoned any restraint. The government, unable for political reasons to raise taxes or to counter wage demands, printed currency and used other methods to increase the money supply. At home and abroad, confidence in the German economy deteriorated, stimulating speculation rather than more reasoned economic calculations. Everyone, it seemed, who had some currency holdings began speculating—would the mark go up or down against the pound sterling, the franc, and the dollar? All of this only further weakened the mark and intensified inflation.[8]

Then, in the summer of 1922, galloping inflation kicked into hyperinflation, accompanied by a business slowdown, declining exports, and rapidly escalating unemployment—the worst of all possible worlds. Businesses faced a liquidity crisis, and everyone faced a shortage of paper currency. The Reichsbank was convinced that it had to ensure the availability of credit for business and paper currency for daily transactions. Only these measures, it believed, would keep the economy humming and maintain social peace. So by various instruments it continually increased the money supply, which of course only provided more fuel for inflation. All the economic indicators pointed to disaster. By the end of the year, the value of exports—the key to the successful recovery in 1920 and 1921—had declined substantially. In October 1922, one dollar bought 3,180 marks. In November 1922, the index of living costs, pegged to 100 in 1913, stood at 15,040.[9] In December, the Prussian statistical office concluded that unskilled chemical workers were earning only 69.4 percent of the minimum existence requirement for a married couple with one child; for skilled workers, it was 76.1 percent, and printers, a traditionally well paid occupation, earned only 58.2 percent of the required minimum.[10]

The Allies watched all this with grave concern. They claimed that Germany was deliberately manipulating its finances in order to dodge its reparations and war bond obligations, or to pay them off in devalued currency. But the situation was so risky—and, in any case, the reparations burden was denominated in goldmarks—that the Allied view hardly suffices as an explanation. Rather, hyperinflation resulted from a combination of factors: the wage-price spiral, in which no party saw any need to exercise restraint; speculation fever; and the drastic deterioration in confidence in the German currency and the German government, exacerbated by Allied pressure.[11]

But the French and Belgians were not bothered by these complexities. They wanted to be paid. Convinced that Germany was deliberately undermining the reparations process by manipulating its currency and refusing to turn over material goods and other assets, they moved in troops on 11 January 1923 and occupied the Ruhr, Germany's major industrial region. The government proclaimed a policy of passive resistance. Whenever Allied troops moved into a factory or mine, everyone was to stop work. If they moved into a governmental office, civil servants were to pack up and go home. By the summer of 1923, production had essentially ground to a halt in the Ruhr. Since so much of the rest of the economy was dependent on the Ruhr, the effects of the regional collapse spread through the entire national economy. With business activity so limited, tax revenues declined dramatically. To support the policy of passive resistance, the government provided unemployment benefits to workers and giant welfare payments to companies. The government made available to businesses in the Ruhr a huge range of credit instruments, while various ministries and agencies paid out wages for unproductive work, unemployment benefits, and welfare support. By the end of June, the government had guaranteed 2.5 *trillion* paper marks' worth of credits to business, and had provided another 5.2 *trillion* marks in the form of subventions to the railroad and postal service and social supports.[12] The government had neither the gold reserves, the moral legitimacy, nor the real economic production required to meet its obligations. But it had printing presses, and these it used with abandon.

The result was a wild escalation of prices, the likes of which have been matched in only a handful of instances around the globe. The Reichsbank issued paper currency in ever larger denominations, finally a 100-trillion-mark note on 2 November 1923. Toward the end of the month, the mark had reached the unbelievable exchange rate $1 = 4.2 *trillion* marks.[13] Germany's sacred hard currency had become worthless. The "inflationary consensus," the agreement among business, labor, and the state on the beneficial effects of inflation, shattered as hyperinflation destroyed any kind of economic or even personal predictability.

The situation had reached a crisis point in the summer of 1923. The living circumstances of large segments of the population had become, once again, just five years after the end of the war, desperate. In market squares, women plundered stalls and stores. The unemployed occupied municipal offices. Crowds fought with the police. Swarms of urban dwellers descended on the countryside, stealing potatoes, chickens, and whatever else they could find. Tavern owners and farmers who protested found themselves unceremoniously roughed up, sometimes stripped of their clothing. Wildcat strikes ran through all sorts of industries. By the fall, workers were being paid every two or three days, and sometimes twice a day. Firms used multipliers to calculate wages—one day, the set wage times 27 billion; a few days later, the set wage times 67 billion.[14] Merchants did the same, or switched to a foreign-currency calculation or simply bartered. People bought up goods as quickly as they could, since the money became even more worthless within hours. Pianos, bicycles, sewing machines, motorcycles, stocks of shoes: better to have real goods than cash savings.[15] The nervous tension that ensued could not be quantified, but it was very real: the long hours on line for food, wages, or unemployment relief; the frantic running from one office to the next; the ceaseless mental calculations about what bills to pay or what items to buy with billions of worthless currency in one's hand; the recognition that the bonds one had bought in 1914, 1915, and 1916 to help the war effort had lost all value; the mental and sometimes physical search for the enemies who supposedly had caused it all and had profited at the expense of good Germans (fig. 4.1).

For the poor and the unskilled, living on relatively fixed welfare payments and wages, the situation was utterly catastrophic, and the more children to feed, the more difficult the situation. Homeowners who rented out rooms and apartments, along with pensioners, found their incomes evaporated by the scale of the inflation. Those with savings accounts—a financial cushion generally not found below the thin stratum of the most highly skilled, well-paid workers—watched the value of their hard-earned savings rendered worthless. Health conditions plummeted. Infant mortality rates increased, the average life span declined, and communicable diseases like tuberculosis

Fig. 4.1 The great inflation 1923: satchels and baskets loaded with nearly worthless money.

spread more rapidly. As one observer wrote, "From everywhere in the Reich, the doctors report that the children are anemic, listless, weak and subject to illness."[16]

The overall effect was not only a general and mostly disastrous decline in living standards, but also a severe disruption of the boundaries between social groups, much to the chagrin of the middle class in particular. To find a skilled worker, perhaps, or a speculator living better than oneself, to discover one's liquid assets reduced to nothing, to be repaid in worthless currency for loans granted to friends, relatives, or business associates, to be placed in the demeaning position of waiting on line for hours on end to purchase a loaf of bread—all that was very difficult to accept and became seared into the memory of these people, shaping their behavior for decades to come. For anyone who had possessed even a modicum of status—the civil service employee, the teacher, the old middle class of shopkeepers and the new one of the technically trained—the damage to their standing was as wounding as the real material want that they suffered. As the newspaper of one of the white-collar unions put it: "The great mass of white-collar employees will have to admit—with shame—that their income does not even begin to approach that of a twenty-one-year-old woodworker."[17] By one calculation, upper-level civil servants had an income in 1922 on average only 1.35 percent higher than unskilled workers—a sad situation indeed for a group that considered itself the bearer of German culture.[18]

The middle class, to so many Germans the stable core of society, seemed to be disappearing before their very eyes. Middle-class households sold off their porcelain, silver, upholstered antique chairs, and anything else of value. One British observer noted:

> It has certainly been a shock to me to see how the middle class lives, what terrible poverty there is to be found behind closed doors. In well-furnished houses there are chairs devoid of leather which has been used for shoes, curtains without linings, which have been turned into garments for the children, and a woman student lucky enough to possess a nightdress or two has cut them up to wear as chemises, using the odd bits from the sleeves and hem to make pocket handkerchiefs. This sort of thing is not the exception but the rule. I know many families where before the war two servants were kept, now they do their own housework; and instead of dinner in the evening they have plain brown bread and weak tea without milk or sugar, and only one meat meal a week.[19]

Many spoke about a social "leveling," a "proletarianization" of the middle classes, and a general "immiseration."[20] Gustav Stresemann, reflecting a few years later on the impact of the inflation, remarked that "the intellectual and commercial middle class, which was traditionally the pillar of loyalty to the state," had become proletarianized and completely uprooted.[21] From their secure and reasonably prosperous position before the war, academics found themselves impoverished, their high status masking a downward slide in their economic fortunes. Many had to sell their libraries, often to foreigners, and professors and students alike took manual jobs on the side in order to maintain their families.[22] Germans and foreigners worried about the consequences for German culture, still held in such high regard around the world. How could students learn, professors research and publish in such circumstances?

But some people did quite well in the inflation. Mortgage holders and other borrowers could pay off their debts in devalued currency. Thomas Mann found himself among the victims: having loaned a substantial amount of money to a friend to enable him to buy a country house, he was chagrined when the friend paid off the debt in essentially worthless currency.[23] Holders of foreign currencies also prospered. Businesses or individuals with American dollars or British pounds went on buying sprees throughout Germany, gobbling up factories and mines and luxury consumer goods for a song. Physicians and psychiatrists in Berlin were thankful to have British and American patients who paid for consultations in their national currencies. A postal inspector who stole $1,717, 1,102 Swiss francs, and 114 French francs was able to buy two houses, install a girlfriend in an apartment (complete with the requisite piano), and donate money to his church. A Munich artist was able to get his hands on one dollar and with that could buy some items for the house, pay his dental bills, and stock up on food.[24] Farmers who exported sometimes did quite well, and even those tied to local markets could at least ensure that they and their families had enough to eat and products that they could barter. Two pounds sterling bought an entire winter's supply of potatoes for a village.[25] Foreigners crossed over into Germany from the border regions and wiped out markets with their purchases, since German goods were so inexpensive for them. Dutch farmers bought entire herds of cattle and drove them over the border back home.[26]

Social resentments, never far below the surface in Weimar, became acute. Industrialists blamed workers for high wages, laziness, and burdensome social costs. Workers charged businessmen with benefiting from speculation. City dwellers attacked country people, who supposedly gorged themselves on sausages while those in the city starved. Everybody, it seems, blamed civil servants. "The foreigner," some kind of Slav or especially a Jew, who lived as a speculator, profiting off German misery, was an ever-present image.[27] Such suspicious characters were to be found among the newly monied, often depicted as stereotypically Jewish, or as a monocled nouveau riche, cigarette dangling, driving a late-model automobile, accompanied by a short-haired, short-skirted new woman. They aped a cultivated lifestyle but were constitutionally incapable of true cultivation. They spoke too loud and, for the most part, dressed sloppily; even if they dressed well, something was always off-key, as were their efforts to play music, which usually descended into stylized African or African American rhythms. The country had not only suffered a lost war and an unjust peace; now it was also prey to all sorts of devious foreigners and social-climbing locals. The historian Hermann Oncken worried that the nouveaux riches could "color the lifestyle of the entire nation, especially since so few of the traditional social counterweights have remained."[28] Even Thomas Mann worried about this "new type." When he purchased a couple of art objects as a hedge against inflation, he described the art dealer: "The man, blond-Jewish and elegant, mid-thirties, with monocle and fat, white, manicured hands, dressed in quilted robe and polished slippers, was perfect as an example of the international, cultured, capitalist profiteering class."[29] In Germany in 1923, there was precious little empathy for others.

Everyone, it seems, tried to dodge the law; the better-off just did it in a more genteel fashion. While small-scale retailers might try to doctor their books or stash money in a milk can, big business speculated in the international markets and hid assets abroad or in ghost subsidiaries. For individuals and businesses, it also became impossible to establish the most rudimentary life plan. Some level of predictability, that necessary precondition to any kind of future planning, had been completely destroyed by hyperinflation. In 1922 and 1923, the situation had reached the point where "it is considered a crime to maintain credit balances at the banks and making debts is viewed as the height of business wisdom," as an internal Reichsbank memo put it.[30] The industrialist Hans von Raumer summed up the grim situation: "We in business can no longer live from the depreciation of the currency. That has exhausted itself. At the beginning we lived from the outside world falling for our mark. . . . Then we lived from the capital of our pensioners. That has also been used up. Then we lived from the reserves of our enterprises. You only have to look at the liquidity of the plants to realize that this is also gone."[31] The entire Ruhr struggle was turning into a disaster for both businessmen and workers.

By the summer of 1923, confidence had collapsed not only in the mark. The government had lost all credibility as well, domestically and internationally, and rightly so. Hamburg businessman Wilhelm

Cuno served as chancellor and, in the period from November 1922 to August 1923, presided over a government of the center Right; Rudolf von Havenstein was the president of the Reichsbank. The crisis situation required far more competent leadership than either of these two individuals was capable of providing. It was a sorry comment on the Weimar system in general that, at a moment of grave national crisis, it generated leadership of such poor quality.

In mid-August 1923, the Social Democrats withdrew their support of the government and Cuno resigned. The president, Social Democrat Friedrich Ebert, appointed as chancellor Gustav Stresemann, head of the German People's Party, and he formed a coalition government that again included the SPD. On 26 September 1923, the Stresemann government unconditionally ended passive resistance. The way was now open to negotiation with the Allies, since the occupation was becoming increasingly expensive and pointless for the French and Belgians, who also had to contend with the opposition of the British and Americans. At the same time, Germany had finally to come to grips with the inflation. And it also had to contend with an array of very serious political threats: a communist revolution, a Nazi-led revolution, separatist strivings in the Rhineland, and—perhaps most dangerous of all—a military dictatorship or some other kind of authoritarian solution promoted by some business leaders, aristocrats, and conservative intellectuals. Strikes, mass demonstrations, mob actions, sometimes directed at Jews—the sense of disorder was palpable. From every side, the republic was under assault.

The government wanted emergency powers to deal with the multiple crises, which required the Reichstag to pass an enabling act. Stresemann's government, including the SPD and the conservative, business-oriented DVP, was inherently unstable. The SPD delegates in the Reichstag refused to support an enabling act that permitted the suspension of the eight-hour day. The government fell, but Stresemann managed again to put together another coalition. On 13 October 1923, the Reichstag passed an initial enabling act—minus the revocation of the eight-hour day and other social provisions—that granted the government emergency powers; subsequently, the law would be renewed and expanded. This was not the first time in the short life of the republic that government-by-decree had come to pass, but this episode was the most extensive and far-ranging to date.

Given the crisis situation, it was probably necessary, but it was a dangerous precedent and a sad sign of the state of the republic.

Through the winter of 1923–24 and on into the spring, the governments essentially ruled by emergency decrees. First under Stresemann, they governed with the explicit participation of the SPD. Then at the end of November 1923, a more conservative shift ensued. The Center Party leader Wilhelm Marx took over as chancellor, and the SPD moved to a position of tacit parliamentary support for the government. The SPD did not want to take direct responsibility for the social provisions that were sure to come and were certain to outrage the party's working-class base. Together, the Stresemann and Marx governments successfully placed the country on even keel, but at enormous costs. The republic would never fully recover from the combined damage of hyperinflation and stabilization.

Emergency measures enabled the governments to beat back the attempted revolutions by the Communists in October and by the Nazis in November. The first moves toward political stability had been taken. Most significantly, on 15 November 1923 the government established a new currency, the Rentenmark, backed by the country's industrial and agrarian assets and issued by a new (ultimately temporary) bank, the Rentenbank. The bold move had an almost immediate impact. It halted the inflation and thereby placed the country on a stable financial footing. The government demonstrated new resolve by ruthlessly pursuing any violations of currency regulations. Then it slashed the size of the public payroll by nearly one-quarter. Temporary employees and married women were the first to go; higher-level employees with tenure (*Beamte*) were relatively protected. By the end of 1923, those civil servants still employed were earning in real terms about 40 to 75 percent of what they had earned in 1913, and weeks went by when they were not paid at all.[32] Then came major reductions in the social welfare system. The government cut all sorts of subsidies and payments to the poor, the unemployed, and the underemployed.

On two major fronts, the government virtually yielded its role to the representatives of major industrial and financial interests. By allowing certain laws from the revolutionary period to lapse, it threw the issue of the workday to the private sector. Employers were on the offensive; workers were battered and worn down by the economic crisis. The mine owners had taken the lead in September 1923, and every major industry quickly followed. By spring 1924, the prewar work shift, twelve hours in the factories, eight and one-half in the mines, had been reestablished. Employers also won greater freedom to fire workers at will and to ignore labor representation within the workplace. The crisis of hyperinflation enabled business to destroy—not totally, but to a significant degree—the social measures it had only reluctantly conceded in 1918–19.

In the critical realm of foreign policy, the government, challenged on so many fronts, also essentially gave major industrial and financial interests a free hand.[33] In the fall of 1923, coal and steel industrialists had begun negotiating with the French, a rather unseemly private assumption of the diplomatic tasks generally left to the state. As a result of these talks, German firms agreed to send goods from the Ruhr to the French and Belgians as partial payment on Germany's reparations obligations. In this way, production could resume in the Ruhr, an outcome the industrialists desperately desired. Moreover, the German government, in a huge concession to business interests, promised to recompense industry its portion of the reparations bill. At the end of the year, discussions began again in official diplomatic circles and this time included the Americans (though through "private" individuals, as opposed to government officials, in order to placate an isolationist Congress). On a British initiative, an experts' panel, headed by the American banker Charles G. Dawes, convened to assess Germany's ability to pay.

The Allies and Germany accepted the Dawes Plan at the London Conference in July–August 1924. The plan then passed in the Reichstag, albeit narrowly. While not reducing the overall reparations figure of 132 billion goldmarks, the Dawes Plan delineated a more reasonable schedule of payments. It also provided for an Allied Agent-General, seated in Berlin, to supervise the payments, the German budget, and the Reichsbank, though with less aggressive intervention than previously. In conjunction with the plan, France and Belgium agreed to withdraw their troops from the Ruhr over the course of the next year.

For Germany, the Dawes Plan and the concomitant withdrawal of French troops constituted the final pieces of the stabilization program. Yet the reparations issue was still far from resolution. Another round of negotiations in 1929 led to the last formal agreement, the

Young Plan (again named for a U.S. banker who led the negotiations), which lowered the overall burden and set up a schedule of payments that would be fulfilled, finally, in 1987.[34] The link between reparations and inter-Allied war debt was clearly in evidence here, because French debts to the United States were scheduled to be paid off one year later, in 1988. Through the Young Plan, the Allies also gave up their supervision over German finances. Germany was out of receivership. But hard on the heels of the Young Plan came the Depression. U.S. president Herbert Hoover initiated a one-year moratorium on reparations and war debts, and in June 1932 at Lausanne the European Allies agreed to let their claims on Germany lapse and then essentially defaulted on their own war debts to the United States.

An inglorious end to a miserable chapter of international finance and diplomacy. By best estimates today, reparations, had they been fully paid, would have amounted to 10 to 12 percent of Germany's national income each year.[35] Although that was surely a substantial percentage, it was manageable in strict accounting terms. But it was not manageable politically. As Gerald Feldman notes, "the paradox of reparations was that they imposed demeaning obligations on the German state while undermining the legitimacy and stability required by the state to fulfill them."[36]

Reparations was an issue handed on a silver platter to all the forces opposed to Weimar democracy. Powerful voices raged against every reparations plan, from the London Ultimatum to the Dawes Plan and the Young Plan. "The dictate of Versailles" and the "slave-labor" results of reparations, which supposedly impoverished hardy and sober Germans, made great political propaganda. Such propaganda rendered the creation of a democratic majority, difficult in any case in Germany, almost impossible. It sapped the political will and determination of even reasonable politicians, who were ground down by popular outrage and political grandstanding against reparations. Leading and powerful individuals, like the industrialist Hugo Stinnes and the Reichstag delegate Karl Helfferich, kept up a steady drumbeat of assaults on the Weimar governments, Helfferich in particular attacking every hint of a settlement as a sellout of German assets, German interests, and the German people themselves. (This is the same Helfferich who so viciously slandered Matthias Erzberger, contributing to a climate of hatred that resulted, finally, in Erzberger's assassination.)

Stinnes played his own game, traveling to Britain and France as a private individual and engaging in talks, all the while bad-mouthing Weimar political leaders and their supposedly irresponsible policies.[37] Helfferich labeled the Dawes Plan a "Second Versailles," and the rabidly conservative and ragingly irresponsible Stinnes told a collaborator that "only a war can bring us out of our situation." He was confident that Germany would triumph over France and would regain all its lost territories and more, even though "our beautiful Ruhr district will be completely destroyed in the process."[38]

The Right could never be won to the side of the republic. More tragically, Weimar would never fully regain the trust of the middle class that had lost so much in the inflation. As a result of court decisions, the government was forced to agree to revaluation measures, which, theoretically, would benefit holders of mortgages and other debts. But the ultimate decisions on the rate of revaluation helped only slightly, and never altered the basic fact that middle-class assets had been destroyed and, in desperation, consumed in the inflation. And the republic lost a great deal of working-class support. Inflation was bad enough. Then came the decline in wages, long stretches of unemployment, and the loss of the eight-hour day, a terrible blow substantively and symbolically. Workers' wages would rise and hours of work sink over the next few years, but the republic could never fully restore its credibility among workers. As for the agricultural sector, farmers benefited initially from the inflation—they could pay off their mortgages with depreciated currency, could extract favorable terms of trade from desperately hungry city dwellers, and had good export markets. But inflation did nothing to ameliorate the long-term structural problems of German agriculture. The Great Depression came earliest to the agrarian sector, and farmers, too, blamed their woes on "the system."[39]

The Weimar Republic lost the middle class in the inflation and the working class in the stabilization, and it never had very much at all of the agrarian sector—something of an exaggerated characterization, but broadly accurate nonetheless.

Still, the stabilization program carried out in 1923–24 had its successes. It secured the territorial integrity of Germany and put an end to revolutionary attempts on the extreme right and left. It gave Germany a sound currency, first with the Rentenmark and then, in the fall of 1924, with the Reichsmark, which was placed on the gold standard. All of this created the conditions for an economic revival, financed by the influx of American capital. German companies, along with municipalities and state governments, were eager customers for relatively inexpensive American loans. Business invested in plants and equipment; municipalities built housing stock and opened clinics. The gross national product increased from 71,145,000 Reichsmarks in 1925 to 88,486,000 in 1928.[40] In 1927 total industrial production finally reached the 1913 level and surpassed it in the following two years.[41] In 1927 and 1928, the Reich government arbitrated many wage disputes and began again to force down the length of the workday and increase the hourly wage. For many industrial workers the workday again approached the hallowed eight hours.

These were the storied "golden years" of the Weimar Republic, evident in statistics but also in lifestyles. Germans went on a consumption binge, and they did it with modern flair. Even workers were looking for display and style, and more and more people were prepared to buy on credit. Rigid class lines dissolved around consumption, as a department store manager revealed to a Reichstag investigative committee. He noted that even middle-class people were buying on credit, whereas before the war only the poorest had gone into debt for consumer purchases. "The better-off workers feel themselves today to be more or less lower middle class, and they have taken on the requirements of the earlier lower-middle-class person without having the latter's firm foundation of assets. . . . In general, the sense of thrift has relaxed. People . . . want to enjoy something from life, and they spend their money today on clothes and externals of every kind."[42] Others reported that even poor people bought butter instead of margarine, and everyone looked for good-quality meat.[43] Shopkeepers, legislators, government inspectors, social workers—they all had the explanation: war and inflation. People had suffered enough deprivation; as the department store manager said, they wanted to enjoy themselves. In war and inflation they had learned that assets and goods, even life itself, were ephemeral. What had value one moment could, in a flash, depreciate to nothing. All that was solid melted into the air—not, as Marx said, under capitalism in general, but under the crisis conditions of total war and hyperinflation.

Better to enjoy life now than live for the future. It was an attitude both well suited for and cultivated by the advertising industry, which blossomed in this era of mass consumption. Advertisers merged the appeal of sex with the clean lines of modernist design. The advertisement for Kaloderma soup used a vaguely Asian, Madame Butterfly–type female figure and a heavy but modern typeface. Montblanc pens were promoted with a mix of montage and a play on politics: "After the revolution, Montblanc remains the king of fountain pens." Vogue used a prototypical elegant and attractive new woman and a modern typeface to promote its perfume (see plate 2).

The line between advertising and art was quite indistinct. Many artists worked for advertising firms, and intellectual journals like *Die Neue Linie* adopted covers that could just as easily have been product endorsements.[44] The architects of the new department stores, like Erich Mendelsohn, devoted great energies to interior design to ensure that the goods were displayed attractively and seductively. Outside, new construction techniques of steel, reinforced concrete, and plate glass allowed for ever larger display windows. Window dressing became a recognized profession, complete with formal apprenticeships, exams, and licenses. All over Berlin and even in provincial towns one could see on the streets the display of wealth and the penchant for modern design and consumption.

Even bourgeois, middle-of-the-road publications like *Die Gartenlaube: Illustriertes Familienblatt* conveyed an image of modern consumption. The magazine dated back to the 1850s and was directed at middle-class women (or those aspiring to join their numbers). It presented a mix of popular genres, including a few pages of current news with a large dose of photojournalism. It published serialized novels and short stories, all with a dash of suspense but with positive endings—certainly no *Schund und Schmutz* in its pages! *Die Gartenlaube* carried, inevitably, columns on health and beauty and cooking, and displayed on its covers drawings and photographs of children and families in bucolic settings, such as picnics overlooking—what else?—the Rhine. Royalty entranced the magazine's editors, but so did modern sports competitions and travel to exotic places to the east.

Die Gartenlaube sought to be modern, but always with a sense of bourgeois decorum and propriety, in both its articles and its advertising pages. A Persil soap advertisement trumpeted:

> Healthy women—a healthy people!
>
> Can it promote good health when our women stand at the washtub in a contorted position and, in antiquated fashion, rub and mistreat their laundry? It is so unreasonable, so silly. In this age of modern health education, Persil offers the possibility of making the wash snow-white and sparkling!
>
> Women, wash with Persil![45]

And how much more modern this would be when the washing was done by machine rather than by hand! Older women could learn modern methods from the younger ones:

> You young women have it good!
>
> How the wash tormented us when there was no Persil! Even today not all of the old ones among us have adapted. And it is so convincing when one really tries it without prejudice:
>
> *With Persil the wash is half the work it was before and comes out as beautiful as it can be!*[46]

Summing it all up, another advertisement ran: "Persil is the deliverance from toil, bother, and aggravation. Persil is the laundry method for the modern woman."[47]

As these examples indicate, advertisers targeted women especially. They both drew upon and created the image and reality of woman as consumer. They deployed the allure of elegance, style, and sex to sell anything and to suggest the possibilities of a consumer's paradise, a utopia of plenty in which possession of objects would serve as the path to self-fulfillment. Advertisers did not think much of women's intellectual faculties, as one contributor wrote in the advertising trade journal:

> Women tend to think in strongly personal terms. Nevertheless they are easy to influence. Their first questions will always be: is there a use or advantage in it for me? They relate everything directly to their appearance, their happiness, their sympathies. General facts, logical reasons, abstract considerations,

> and technical details do not say much to them. Statistics and politics leave them cold in the moment of a purchase. They demand instead that their immediate desires be understood. . . .
>
> Women love a simple and personal language, however modern they might be in their professions and progressive in their opinions. With things that touch them personally, they are first of all women.[48]

Hence the need for advertisers to stop thinking in masculine terms, to refrain from sarcasm and humor—neither of which were natural to or cultivated by women.

Modern consumption was one sign of the golden years of the Weimar Republic; "rationalization" was the other. The term meant, most basically, the application of scientific methods to production in order to expand output, with less labor. Technological and managerial improvements were all the rage. Businesses combined, mechanized many processes, and shed workers. More than seven hundred institutes—state, private, and mixed—were involved in researching and planning rationalization.[49] For all the talk, few pathbreaking innovations were implemented in the 1920s. Mechanizing the filling of cement bags was a major improvement, especially for those who labored in dusty, lung-destroying cement plants, but it was hardly the profound and pathbreaking innovation that could fuel a sustained economic expansion.

America was the very model of rationalization.[50] In the 1920s, hundreds of businessmen, engineers, and trade unionists traveled to the United States. They barely noticed its natural beauty, rarely ventured to New England, the West coast, or the South. They docked in New York and headed straight to the industrial Midwest to get a look at America's production facilities. They wanted to see up close the world's most advanced industrial economy. They investigated and wrote about its innovative technology and its revolutionary organization of production, notably the assembly line. The pace and efficiency dazzled even the most sober and jaundiced German businessman.

Nothing drew them like the iconic Henry Ford and the Ford factories, Highland Park and River Rouge, in Detroit. In Germany, Ford's autobiography was reprinted countless times, reviewed everywhere. He was the epitome of America—the self-made man, the brilliant engineer who created an economic powerhouse. In comparison, Germany seemed static and hidebound. Where would one find a German farmboy who had created his own company and risen to the top echelon of business executives? Nowhere. Germany's class system would never allow such a thing.

Engineers like Franz Westermann gushed about the "powerful experience" of his visit to Ford, "that gigantic production facility created in a short time by human hands which not only impresses the eyes by its size and the manner of its technical construction but whose living spirit is palpably present . . . so it simply draws people into its orbit."[51] Westermann extolled the "work rhythm that sweeps everything along with it, just as a band carries along the legs of the marching troops and even the spectators," while others described the production process as a "symphony" or a "spiritual bond." Each worker knew his part, and they all fit together in some magnificent whole.[52]

Westermann was responding to the assembly line, Ford's great innovation. Some critics recognized the monotony involved, but others claimed that the assembly line was less grueling than other forms of manufacturing labor and therefore beneficial to workers. In any case, monotony seemed a beneficial trade-off for the glories of high wages and mass consumption, which enabled American workers to buy durable goods of which no German worker could dream. That, too, was part of the American innovation, because low-cost production on the assembly line also meant relatively inexpensive products that could be sold on the seemingly limitless American domestic market. German visitors—businessmen, engineers, and worker representatives alike—marveled over the American workers who could buy a house and even trade up from a Model-T to a fancier Nash automobile.[53]

For some visitors, it was precisely the attention to service in the vast domestic market that they found so impressive. For Felix Deutsch, the chairman of the electrotechnical giant AEG, this was America's great achievement: the customer was king. Responding to an inquiry from the *Vossische Zeitung*, he wrote that what comes across in America in every conversation, every set of business guidelines, and every prospectus is the significance of good service, an orientation toward the wishes of the customer and his psyche.

> The commitment to service in America has become a kind of business religion. It's not just talk, but also reality. The care with which one is served in every single business in America is extraordinary, and continues even after the shop assistant has for hours shown you all sorts of things and you finally leave the store without buying anything. Also fantastic is the willingness to exchange or take back goods that have already been sold but have been found unsuitable.[54]

As Deutsch well knew, none of this would ever happen in Germany, just as a farmboy would never rise to the top of the entrepreneurial class.

Few German visitors peered more deeply into the substantial wealth disparities within American society and, especially, the racial divide. Businessmen in particular were hardly troubled by Ford's vicious antiunion policies, racism, and anti-Semitism. What they saw in the 1920s was the "American system" that would reach such heights in the 1950s and 1960s—high-tech, low-cost production; mass marketing; and high wages.

It was a formula that dazzled, that needed to be watched carefully. But could it be successfully imitated at home? Few thought so. Germany, many businessmen and engineers claimed, lacked the huge domestic market that America possessed and could not afford American wages. Moreover, Germans engaged in "quality work" (*Qualitätsarbeit*), they asserted, which relied on highly skilled craftsmen and precision labor. Instead of adopting the assembly line, German businessmen, engineers, psychologists, and sociologists focused on time-motion studies and psychological techniques designed to enhance the productivity of labor. These new efforts to "engineer" the modern worker involved modern psychology and changes in the technology and organization of production that vastly diminished the autonomy of skilled workers on the shop floor. Workers were to be tested, observed, trained, and managed—incessantly. As a result, managers assumed more power and the pace of work intensified.

The rewards—as with Henry Ford's high-wage–high-consumption model—were supposed to come in the form of economic prosperity for all, and it was on that basis, and because of their commitment to technology, that Social Democrats supported rationalization. But the social benefits were never to emerge, at least not at the level at which they would have a highly beneficial impact on the broad mass of workers. Certainly, major companies deployed an array of welfare programs designed to bind workers to the firm. But major benefits like company housing were generally limited to an elite stratum of the workforce. For the rest, it was sports teams, parks and playgrounds, churches, cultural events, newspapers, and recreational associations, all sponsored by the company and dedicated to creating a loyal workforce. The companies directed many of their efforts at women—not female workers, but the wives of male workers. The presumption was that as the caretakers of the "orderly family," widely understood as the bedrock of society, women would benefit from advice on how to conduct household labor more productively, which would also signify efficient use of the wages brought home by the male worker. A cozy, comfortable, and rationalized household would give the men the rest and recuperation they needed to perform well day in and day out, by the drill press, the mine seam, or the blast furnace.

Rationalization, far from bringing prosperity to workers, only made their lives more difficult. While wages did rise between 1924 and 1929, so did unemployment, and employed workers found the intensified pace of work nerve-rattling and destructive of their health. Any worker who objected was quickly told that there were thousands of others outside, ready to take his place. At one brass foundry, the size of the workforce at the end of the decade was 60 percent of the 1923 level, while output had risen 50 to 60 percent. The Ruhr mining workforce declined by 33 percent from 1922 to 1928 while production rose significantly.[55] By one measure, productivity per working hour between 1926 and 1930 rose 25 percent in metals processing, 18 percent in mining, 15 percent in basic steel, and 13 percent in chemicals.[56] How was this possible? In the mines, longwall mining—gang labor on one seam over a relatively long stretch—enabled managers to supervise workers more consistently and permitted the more extensive use of new, power-driven machinery. Both developments—tighter control over the labor process and increased mechanization—led to an expansion of output with fewer workers. Piecework, far more than the assembly line, expanded throughout industry and was perhaps the most essential means of raising productivity. It also meant the enhanced exploitation of labor. Piecework rates were always set just low enough that workers were compelled to labor ever more rapidly and efficiently in order to receive even a halfway reasonable wage. The health costs could be high—a faster pace of work and longer hours resulted in more industrial accidents, sometimes of the most serious nature, causing amputations, damaged lungs, and scalding burns. Industrial labor remained long, hard, and dirty, and now became more intense and dangerous.

Female workers faced even more daunting circumstances. In 1928, the textile workers' union staged an essay contest and asked its women members to report on their lives. The submissions came primarily from women who were, in some way, active in the labor movement and were not, therefore, typical of the vast majority of women workers. Nonetheless, the compilation of their writings, *Mein Arbeitstag, mein Wochenende* (My Working Day, My Weekend), gives an unparalleled insight into working women's lives in the Weimar era.[57]

Women depicted a life of monotonous routine governed by the alarm clock, the factory whistle, the clang of the machinery in the textile factories, and endless household labor. They described a nation populated by the sleep-deprived: never enough rest, always awaking groggy, usually at 5:30 AM or even earlier, and not getting to bed until 11:00 PM or even later. Before they took their places at the loud, fast-moving looms or spinners, they had already made beds, swept and dusted, prepared meals, washed dishes, wakened children and gotten them ready for school. Some ran home at lunchtime to put the hot midday meal on the table for children, parents, and brothers, and then ran back to the factory in time again for the afternoon blast of the factory whistle. If a woman's fellow worker took a brief break to wolf down a buttered roll or run to the bathroom, she ran her neighbor's machines as well as her own. Some were on their feet all day; others had to bend awkwardly to tend the machines. They reported working conditions and physical ailments little different from those described in the early stages of the factory system in nineteenth-century Britain. "You leave the factory feeling worked to death and completely exhausted," wrote one.[58] In the evening, supper had to be prepared, dishes washed, laundry folded, children attended to. Wages, certainly women's wages, were too low to support a family, and piecework pay only added to the frenetic pace of life and labor.

Everyone contributed to the household, and if fathers or husbands had become disabled or were laid off, the situation became dire indeed. Saturday was a half-day's labor in the factory, and household work consumed even a good part of Sunday. Laundry day—sometimes as infrequent as every fourth or even sixth week—fully destroyed the weekend. Men, whether brothers, fathers, or husbands, expected to be served their meals and have their clothes laundered; it was the rare woman who reported that her father cooked or her husband helped with the household tasks. Living conditions were often cramped:

> We are a family of six, a nine-year-old boy and three grown daughters nineteen, twenty-five, and twenty-eight years old. The entire family life plays out in two rooms. . . . Even at night there's no peace; the one is always disturbing the other. *The beds—and we only have four—are right next to one another. When one or the other wants to get in bed, he has to climb over the others who are sleeping.* If someone is sick, the situation is even worse.[59]

Mothers worried about the hours their children were left alone, and longed to be able to take walks with them rather than run off to the factory. In the evening they desired only calm and rest, but these were not to be had:

> With taking care of the fire, preparing dinner, checking homework while cleaning and cooking the vegetables for the next day, airing out the bedding and then making the beds, many days washing the floors down, washing the dishes—by then it is certainly 8:00. *Now comes the wonderful moment that I have been waiting for the entire day, the one enjoyable hour when I can eat my dinner and read the newspaper.* I look at the clock—9:00. I'm tired, my baby is sleeping, and I would also love to go to bed, but not yet. I'm still not finished with my work. I have to get out the sewing machine. . . . Since I sew most of our own clothes,

> I can't leave everything to Saturday afternoon or Sunday. My factory job provides us with only a pitiful existence, despite the fact that we're paid by piecework.[60]

If they worked the late shift, they came home to husbands and children already asleep, and the household work still before them into the early morning hours. Even small children knew the rhythm of the work week and looked forward to the Sundays that their mothers and fathers were at home with them.[61] But exhaustion was their constant companion: "*I say it all the time: the loveliest thing the worker has* (and not everyone has it) *is a bed. At least when sleeping he is freed of worries.*"[62]

The surge of layoffs, even in the so-called golden years of the republic, meant that young people had an extremely difficult, and sometimes impossible, time finding a footing in the labor market. At the same time, older workers could not always keep up with the new, intensified pace of labor. Just prior to the onset of the Depression, management at the Leuna chemical works established criteria for layoffs that targeted the "over-age and less productive" in order to hold on to "young, more vigorous people."[63] A Krupp official later bemoaned the fact that the firm had had to lay off older and loyal skilled workers, but there were no alternatives, since with the "intensified demands of the new methods of work, they burdened the firm all too much with their deficient productivity."[64] The Communist Party was not far off the mark when it described German rationalization as "*American factory and exploitation methods, American profits, but no American wages, only German hunger wages.*"[65]

Germany's highly modern economy ran not just on the labor of production workers. It also needed trained technical staff in offices and laboratories. White-collar workers had been "discovered" shortly before World War I. Emil Lederer before 1914, Hans Speier, Theodor Geiger, Siegfried Kracauer in the 1920s—acute observers all—published pioneering studies.[66] There was much to go on: between 1885 and 1925, the number of white-collar workers had increased fivefold, while that of manual workers had not even doubled.

Strikingly, in 1930, only one-fifth of salaried employees had fathers who pursued a similar occupation.[67] In other words, white-collar labor was one of the few realms of significant social mobility in Germany.

They were different from the older middle class of shopkeepers and highly skilled artisans, who still constituted a very significant segment of the population. According to the 1925 census, there were roughly 11 million independent proprietors and "supportive family members" among the 35.8 million Germans who earned a livelihood. But of those 11 million, 7 million were in the agrarian sector. That left roughly 4 million independent proprietors in manufacturing, commerce, and the professions.[68] Many of these were shopkeepers and artisans who, by definition, owned their own stores and workshops. They were the very embodiment of the hallowed qualities of "independence" and the supposed mainstays of German society, as Stresemann and virtually every other observer to the right of the Social Democrats claimed. But their real-life circumstances were often miserable, and not only because of the inflation. Their numbers were substantial; economically they had long been under pressure from industrial producers and large-scale commercial retailers. By the 1920s, few artisanal shoemakers or hat manufacturers could compete with the factories that daily churned out thousands of such products; not many clothing shops could compete with the prices and offerings of the Schocken and Wertheim department stores. Politically, many members of this old middle class would move more and more to the right in the Weimar years, and they would ultimately find their way to the Nazis, who cultivated them assiduously.

The new middle class attracted the most commentary in the 1920s and early 1930s—precisely because it was new. And its numbers, roughly 5.3 million in the 1925 census, surpassed the roughly 4 million members of the old middle class and the independent professions.[69] Like the vast majority of production workers, they were dependent employees who labored for a wage—even when it was called a salary as a sign of their status above manual workers. Siegfried Kracauer described in his book *The Salaried Masses* their rigidly ordered work regime.[70] In every one of its aspects the modern office workplace was like the military, disciplined and hierarchical.

Owners and managers prized subordination above all else. Before hiring, they subjected potential employees to batteries of aptitude tests. For sales positions, young women had to demonstrate a friendly demeanor; for office positions in banks and large firms, they had to display polite servitude and demonstrate efficiency at the typewriter and telephone. If their typing speed was not up to the standard, the firm gave them lessons accompanied by martial music, as Kracauer, partly bemused, partly horrified, reported.

Like the rationalized factory, the modern office was large and anonymous, the work automated and specialized. Workers were so numerous that few managers could know their underlings' names, much less any personal details of their lives. The employees were like line infantry, an anonymous and servile mass, like the proverbial German figure, his head bowed in subordination and obedience to his superiors while he tramples on those beneath him. The work had become automated. Typewriters, calculating machines, mechanical letter openers and sealers, addressing machines, card punchers hummed along, and messages shot through pneumatic tubes from one end of the office to the other. In accounting departments young women sat for hours typing out punchcards that were fed into tabulating machines, the forerunners of the modern computer.[71] A typist would not become an accounts specialist, nor a salesperson an office employee. As office work became automated, women increasingly staffed the positions—and office work suffered a decline in status at the same time. Female white-collar workers were paid, on average, around two-thirds of men's salaries.[72]

The modern office was extremely hierarchical. Firms claimed that they offered possibilities for advancement, but these were usually few and far between. At the very top sat an impenetrable elite, linked by family, education, status, and class. While they lingered in their positions until comfortable old age, many employees found themselves unemployed at forty, victims, like their blue-collar colleagues, of their inability to keep up with the faster pace of work.

At the same time, companies sought to win the loyalty of white-collar employees through all sorts of social welfare programs and morale-building events. Kracauer commented on a race through the streets of Berlin, with each of the teams representing one of the major German companies—cheap advertisement, and also a way to bind employees to the company. He also noted the depiction of a firm outing at its rowing club, quoting from the company newsletter:

> [It was like] a family party . . . in the setting of the rowing club . . . all a colourful medley, many leading gentlemen from our establishment with their ladies . . . and, as a special honour for us, the chairman of the board of directors, Privy Counsellor X, who nodded affably to the dancing couples and appeared to feel entirely at his ease. No reserve, no separation, a purely human get-together for the pride and pleasure of the coming generation. "Refined informality" was the watchword of the evening.[73]

Kracauer could not resist a sardonic gloss: "Hard to decide which is more pitiable: the confusion of joviality with a purely human get-together, or the over-zealous triumph at the fall of barriers. Probably not everyone had the good fortune to feel at ease in such circumstances."[74]

Still, the divide between salaried employees and industrial workers was just as great. All middle-class parents were bound and determined that their sons and daughters should marry up, not down. The workplace of the new middle class also tried to project a certain demeanor of bourgeois comportment. One department store publicity brochure noted that many of its employees lived in cramped and dark apartments and socialized with those who were ill-educated.

> In the store, however, the employees for the most part spend their time in cheerful rooms flooded with light. Contact with refined and well-educated customers is a constant source of fresh stimuli. The often quite awkward and self-conscious girl trainees more quickly accustom themselves to good behavior and manners, they take care about their speech and also their appearance. The varied nature of their work broadens the sphere of their knowledge and improves their education. This facilitates their ascent to higher social strata.[75]

Kracauer noted that the "distinct mania in bourgeois German society to raise oneself from the crowd by means of some rank, be it only an imaginary one, hampers solidarity among salaried employees themselves. . . . A chasm of impressive depth yawns likewise between, for example, technical and commercial employees in industry."[76] Commercial employees treated technical employees in the same firm with disdain, while the technical employees thought they were the only ones who were truly productive. Civil servants, in turn, looked down upon employees in private industry. Many white-collar employees were union members, yet that fact did not automatically translate into solidarity with manual workers; nor would the devastating impact of the Depression weaken their fierce attachment to the markers of status, however minor their effects on real living conditions.

The proportion of the working population engaged in agriculture had been on a steady decline for decades. But the 1925 census counted 30.5 percent of the working population involved in the agrarian and forestry sector, still a very significant segment.[77] The agrarian situation varied so greatly across the country that it is hard to make generalizations. No area represented only one kind of land tenure and social system, though there were prevailing trends. In East Prussia large estates worked either by tenant or sharecropping systems or by agricultural laborers still predominated, though there were many small peasant holdings as well. Saxony had a mix of estate and peasant holdings. The south and southwest had primarily peasant holdings, and the same was true of the north and northwest where dairy farming predominated. All of the farmers hated the system of market and price controls imposed during the war, which continued in uneven form for some years afterward. Most of them dodged, bent, and undermined the system by black market transactions and felt no compunction.[78] All the farmers benefited from the fact that they controlled basic products for which there was great demand. The distortions of the market as a result of controls and inflation gave the agricultural sector relative power, and enraged city dwellers especially, as well as a huge range of officials who were trying to steer the economy toward recovery. At all the crisis moments—1918–19, 1920–21, 1923—rumors ran rife that farmers were hoarding huge stocks of grain, meat, and dairy products. And sometimes they were, betting on higher prices or more lucrative goods for which they could barter. Then the collapse of world commodity prices sent agriculture reeling into depression as early as the mid-1920s. The "golden years" certainly did not apply to Weimar's agrarian sector. And farmers were quick to blame socialists and Jews for all of their woes.

Indebtedness was the scourge of agriculture. Farmers climbed out of debt during the inflation and managed almost immediately to sink back in. Always eager to buy more land, they invested too heavily when the terms of trade were in their favor, and suffered when prices collapsed and they could no longer carry their mortgages. Moreover, they bemoaned the shortage of labor that they endured, especially the paucity of girls and young women willing to put up with the strain of agricultural labor. On the farms girls and women endured sixteen- to seventeen-hour working days, dirty conditions, and heavy lifting, all under the ever-watchful eye of the owner of the farm and his wife. The revolutionary government in 1918 had abolished the highly repressive labor codes (*Gesindeordnungen*) that gave agricultural employers nearly feudal powers over their farmhands, male and female. But in reality conditions had improved little and, in some ways, had gotten even worse. Intensive farming, in a sense the rural variant of rationalization, was all the rage, the solution, as touted by state officials and farm organizations, to the crisis of agriculture. Government officials, physicians, and social workers developed courses and brochures that showed women how to swing a hoe or churn butter in an upright position. The notion was that such techniques would not only ease the strain on women's backs and thereby make their labor power more efficient; other expected outcomes were that agriculture would become more productive, women more fecund, and Germany more lavishly supplied with its own foodstuffs.[79]

All to no avail. The cry for intensive farming and rationalized labor came at precisely the moment when a labor shortage appeared in the countryside. To the utter dismay of farmers and officials, thousands upon thousands of young women fled the rural areas for factories and the city. The work may have been no easier, but at least they did not suffer under the constant gaze of their employers. They felt freer, while farmers and officials foisted upon them the blame for the crisis of agriculture. While young women enjoyed the dissolute life of the city, they claimed, the very basis of the nation's vitality—a healthy agriculture and a thriving family farm—were being undermined. But the argument carried little weight with young women. In places like Saxony, where the agricultural and industrial areas were close to one another, the new city women, sometimes just weeks removed from the countryside, looked down their noses at their compatriots who were still cleaning out livestock stalls and shoveling muck.[80]

All the positive economic signs of the Weimar Republic's middle period—high-level production, rising consumer demand, technological innovations—came to a screeching halt over the winter of 1929–30. The U.S. stock market crash in October 1929 set off a banking crisis that quickly spread to Germany as U.S. banks called in their short-term loans. The financial crisis rapidly turned into a production crisis that spiraled downward as firms laid off workers, government revenues declined, and demand collapsed. By the beginning of 1932, six million Germans were officially unemployed, about one-third of the labor force. But the statisticians probably failed to count another two million "unofficially" unemployed: all told, roughly an almost unbelievable 40 percent of the workforce. German unemployment rates were higher than even those in the United States. In specific industries the picture was still worse: 41.9 percent unemployment in iron and steel, 48.9 percent in machine building, and 63.5 percent in shipbuilding. From a GNP high of 88,486,000 RM in 1928, the figure plummeted to 55,544,000 RM in 1932.[81]

Eleven years after the end of the war, just six years after the inflation and stabilization, Germans experienced yet another crisis, unforgiving in its effects (fig. 4.2). Once again, an economic disaster quickly became a multifaceted political conflict as well, an existential crisis of the Weimar system. Just under the veneer of every policy debate lurked the fundamental questions: Was the liberal republic even capable of resolving the country's immense economic problems? Or was it, perhaps, part of the cause? For the Right especially, unrelenting in its hostility to Weimar, the Great Depression (or, as Germans tend to call it, the World Economic Crisis) provided a golden opportunity. Now it could again contemplate seriously the overthrow of the republic.

The initial point of contention, as discussed in chapter 3, was the imminent bankruptcy of the unemployment insurance fund. Unable

Fig. 4.2 A Depression soup kitchen. The two men on the right are trying to maintain appearances as well-dressed, respectable individuals, though the clothes look tattered. Probably they were among the legions of white-collar employees also thrown out of work.

to reach an agreement on whether to cut benefits or raise taxes to maintain it, the SPD-led government fell. In spring 1930, President Hindenburg named as chancellor Heinrich Brüning of the Center Party. He faced the looming bankruptcy of the entire government. Tax revenues were dropping precipitously, and the state's creditworthiness was so limited that it could not raise money in the capital markets, either nationally or internationally. The Reichsbank, though recently freed from Allied supervision, still pursued a restrictive monetary policy (and indeed was mandated by law to do so), so it could not, as in 1922 and 1923, simply print money to finance the government's obligations. Moreover, Brüning followed the conventional economic wisdom of the day. The way out of a crisis was to adopt deflationary policies. The state had to slash public expenditures of all sorts, business had to cut labor costs, and prices had to fall. Once things had bottomed out in this fashion, business would again have incentives to invest, and the economy, now on a sounder basis, would revive. Although all sorts of proposals were raised, especially in the popular media, for work-creation programs and what would later be dubbed Keynesian pump-priming policies, none could pass through Brüning's opposition or the like-minded conservatism of most of the German elite.[82] Even Social Democrats accepted the necessity of deflationary policies and argued only about how the burdens were to be distributed. Virtually everyone had the experience of 1923 in mind: the dangers of inflation, in their view, far outweighed the deflationary policies pursued by the Reich. Like Herbert Hoover in the United States, Brüning would pay a political price for his narrow-minded policies, but the political outcome in Germany would be far more drastic and frightening.

From spring 1930 to spring 1932, when he was deposed by the president, Brüning essentially ruled by decree under article 48 of the Weimar Constitution. This was the outcome of a completely paralyzed political system in which no effective majority, either electorally or legislatively, could be formed for any set of policies to deal with the Depression. The Social Democrats, holding on to the shreds left of their republic, tolerated the government. But Brüning was temperamentally well suited to governance-by-decree, which he viewed as a stepping-stone to a more fundamental, authoritarian reshaping of the republic. He was also temperamentally well suited to follow a set of deflationary policies that spared business and exacted an ever-increasing toll on the population at large. To be sure, wages had gone up in the last part of the "golden years," and firms also paid out substantial sums in legally mandated social welfare benefits, such as apprenticeship training and taxes that funded unemployment, health, and accident insurance. These were the result of Germany's long-standing social welfare policies, which were significantly expanded under the republic (and were not fully rolled back even in 1923–24). State expenditures on social welfare were also quite substantial, much higher than in the pre-1914 period and even higher than in comparable developed countries. In 1913, social welfare accounted for 19.3 percent of all public expenditures in Germany; in 1929–30, that figure had reached 40.3 percent.[83] These were the kinds of social benefits that would become typical all over western Europe after 1945, but they were much more difficult to carry in an era marked by relative economic stagnation and intermittent economic crises. But they were not the cause of the Depression, which was to be found, ultimately, in the collapse of demand that followed the financial crisis initiated by the U.S. stock market crash.[84]

So ruling by decree, Brüning raised taxes, cut social welfare benefits, slashed the number of government employees and cut the salaries of those who remained, and forced localities to balance their budgets. His immediate successor in 1932, Franz von Papen, did much the same, only in more sinister fashion (as we shall see in chapter 9). The last chancellor of the republic, Kurt von Schleicher, lasted in office only a month, not long enough to test a new set of policies. All in all, the government's very restrictive fiscal policies only worsened the impact of the combined banking and manufacturing crisis. For so many Germans, the Depression meant yet another social catastrophe with very immediate consequences, the third such catastrophe in fewer than twenty years. Their living conditions plummeted, yet again; their ability to plan for the future was shattered, yet again; their hopes destroyed, yet again. Unemployment insurance provided some support for close to a year; then it was welfare. As the German saying went, "Too much to die and too little to live."

In 1932, three young sociologists, Marie Jahoda, Paul Lazarsfeld, and Hans Zeisel, who would soon have to flee Nazi Germany and would go on to very distinguished careers in Great Britain and the United States, observed life in Marienthal, an industrial suburb of Vienna shattered by unemployment. It was Austria, not Germany, but their observations and insights concerning the social and psychological effects of unemployment have resonance far beyond the specific community they investigated. Matters would have been no different in any industrial town or village in Germany.[85]

The three sociologists depicted a community consumed by the struggle to find sufficient food and clothing. Schoolchildren had lunches packed only on the day when welfare payments were disbursed; otherwise they went hungry. Some families held themselves together with dignity in the most trying of circumstances, while others disintegrated. Men drank more heavily; women suffered under the increasing burdens of providing for a family with fewer and fewer resources. Some men simply absconded, or went off in search of work. People tried their hands at breeding rabbits, which became a veritable craze, or were thrown back on growing their own vegetables on meager plots. Cats and dogs disappeared, slain and cooked by the malnourished.[86]

The social and psychological effects were just as devastating. People were worn down by poverty and hopelessness. The three sociologists aptly titled one of their chapters "A Weary Community." The residents of Marienthal had become bored and listless. Without jobs to structure men's lives, their days became an empty void—one minute, one hour, blending into the next without demarcation. Over time, their walking pace slowed down; their posture became more stooped. The surroundings had deteriorated as well, the factory now a shambles, the once well-tended park overgrown with weeds. Although there was a public library and people had time on their hands, fewer patronized it: even reading seemed pointless. Once-vibrant cultural organizations lacked for members and involvement. Men stayed in bed for hours on end, or hung around in stairwells and courtyards. "Nothing is urgent anymore; they have forgotten how to hurry."[87]

For the women, though, the day still had demarcations: they still had to cook and clean and tend to the children. Their labor had become more intensive and oppressive, because they now had to scrounge for food and fuel, keep tattered clothes together by mending, and take in wash to earn at least a little for the household. Although factory work had been difficult, somehow they had managed to complete their household labor as well. Many women still longed to return to the mill. "If I could get back to the factory it would be the happiest day of my life. It's not only for the money; stuck here alone between one's own four walls, one isn't really alive. . . . Since the factory closed down, life is much harder. You have to rack your brains to think what to cook. The money doesn't go far enough. You are shut up inside all day long and never go out anywhere."[88]

The situation was no better for members of the middle class who suffered unemployment. The sense of despair ran very deep. The Federation of White-Collar Employee Unions sent around a questionnaire on unemployment, and, as Kracauer reported in his study, got back these sorts of responses:

> Thirty-nine, married, three children. . . . Three years earned nothing. Future? Work, madhouse, or turn on the gas.

> Before the war, several businesses of my own, which I had to give up as a result of the war and my call-up. When I came home my wife died. All my savings were stolen away by the great national fraud (inflation). Now I am fifty-one years old, so everywhere I hear: "We don't take on people of that age." The final step for me is suicide. The German state is our murderer.

> I am spiritually broken and sometimes entertain thoughts of suicide. Moreover, I have lost confidence in all men. Thirty-eight years old, divorced, four children.[89]

Unemployed white-collar workers sometimes tried to open a shop or make a go of it as sales agents living off commissions. They all led miserable existences, like one who went

> begging from door to door [and] whose rank and standard of living fell even below that of the proletariat [even though he] was an independent, but his independence consisted in the necessity of bearing his misery alone, without the social protection enjoyed by wage earners.[90]

That was the reality of life at the end of the republic, a consequence of a global phenomenon—the world economic crisis—and the policies pursued at the national level by the right-wing German governments that ruled from 1930 through 1932.

At the end of World War I, Germans, like other Europeans, longed for a return to normalcy. For many, that meant the prewar world of stable—or at least only moderately increasing—prices, a world where bondholders knew the real rate of return they would receive on their investments, landlords could calculate effectively their mortgage payments and the rents they would receive, those with savings accounts could rest assured that they were protected should a family emergency arise, and wage earners knew whether or not their pay was sufficient to put food on the table and roofs over their heads. Instead of prewar stability, they got postwar turbulence. It had its moments of glory, to be sure, when Germans indulged their desires through consumption in magnificent shops and department stores. As in any market-driven economy, some people proved quite adept at taking advantage of fast-moving speculative opportunities. There was money to be made, even during the inflation and the Depression.

But the overall impact was one of disruption and immiseration. Germans had never seen anything like the hyperinflation of 1922–23 or the Great Depression of 1930–33, and it was much worse than what many of their European neighbors experienced. No other country carried the combined political and economic burden of reparations that Germany did. Few other societies were so highly industrialized as Germany's. When the Depression hit, many Italian and even French industrial workers could go home to their villages. German workers, by and large, were too many generations removed from their villages to be able to find refuge in the countryside. Village life in the 1930s was hardly paradise, but the plight of poverty in an urban, developed setting has its particular material and psychological costs. Coming right after the war, the economic crises made Germans jittery and desirous of nothing so much as security. Inflation and depression, different economic phenomena, both make daily life incalculable and the future unpredictable. They throw everything off keel. The aversion to the republic, the ready attraction to promises of German grandeur and prosperity, the search for the demons that had caused the situation—all that had its powerful grounding in the disruptive experience first of hyperinflation, then of depression.

Could it have been different? Certainly, the blockages were substantial. World War I left an immensely burdensome legacy. The costs of the war carried over, and Germany's bill was not only its own but the Allies' as well, in the form of reparations. The Allied governments defended their own national interests and took sustenance from the vengeful mood of their constituents at home, but that did not make for smart and productive politics. Allied policies only weakened the democratically elected German governments, making any kind of progress so much more difficult. The long-term economic trends—the relative stagnation in between the high growth rates prior to 1914 and after 1945—did not provide an auspicious setting for macroeconomic policies. And at key moments, Weimar lacked imaginative and creative economic leadership. The governments and the Reichsbank pursued policies that facilitated both hyperinflation and depression.

But the trends of the Weimar years were also the result of policy choices that gave major industrial and financial interests preponderant influence over the economy. In the revolutionary moment of 1918–19, more forceful and imaginative policies on the part of the SPD could have reined in big business, which, after all, was not just antisocialist, but largely antidemocratic as well. Instead, the SPD banked everything on a quick revival of production, which necessarily meant caving in to business interests. Business, unions, and the state all supported the inflation until it went sour in hyperinflation; in the crisis situation that ensued, business was able to reassert its powers and roll back many of the social achievements of the revolution. And in the Depression, a right-authoritarian government pursued the deflationary strategies that business also supported. Of course, not all businesses prospered. They, too, had to live with unpredictability, and many made poor calculations. Whatever the concessions to their interests, not even in the best years were they enamored with Weimar.

Many Germans blamed the crises they endured on the republic, on socialists, on Jews, but the real problem was much closer at hand. It was the German Right, in which heavy industry and major financial interests exercised preponderant influence, and which promoted policies of inflation, stabilization, and deflation that worsened the real-life circumstances of so many Germans.

5

Building a New Germany

"If you don't long for the impossible, how can you achieve the possible?" wrote the artist Hermann Finsterlin in 1920.[1] He was a member of a group of architects and artists brought together by Bruno Taut, who expressed their visionary hopes in a series of letters to one another, the "Crystal Chain," as they called it. Writing amid the enthusiasm of revolution, they imagined a world in which art reigned supreme. Humanity's great aesthetic achievements would no longer be mere ornaments tacked onto the everyday world, fleeting glimpses of beauty amid the drone of daily life. Art would penetrate the very pores of individual and collective existence. Art would mold society, reshape humanity. Art and life would be one.

Many of the Crystal Chain artists and architects were exponents of expressionism, that sprawling, loose-knit style that probed the psychological depths of individuals and societies, often exposing harrowing experiences of violence and disorientation. Bold strokes of color and figures set awry from their surroundings characterized many expressionist paintings (see plate 3). But expressionism also had a utopian tenor, a bold imagining of a harmonious and beautiful future, which the Crystal Chain letter writers articulated. The expressionist sensibility ran from the depths of despair to the heights of joy, and evoked the trauma of World War I and the initial, glorious hopes of the revolution. Both histories and both sensibilities—war and revolution, despair and hope—fired the creative imaginings of painters, writers, and architects. They made art, like politics, a "serious thing" in Weimar Germany. Politics was not just about whether a sales tax should be 6 or 7 percent, and art was not about decoration and prettifying this or that corner or canvas. Weimar art was about the totality of being and was infused with powerful, utopian visions of transforming society—and humanity—once and for all.

By 1924, a new, more sober-toned artistic style—"New Objectivity"—had emerged, which challenged and tempered the expressionist advocacy of the extremes. New Objectivity, with its modulated tones and clean lines, seemed more suitable to the middle phase of the republic, the era of relative political stability and strong economic development. But expressionism never quite died off, and in many instances and among many working artists, no sharp break divided the two styles and the two periods. Especially in architecture, some of the most fully realized creations of the Weimar period, like those of Bruno Taut and Erich Mendelsohn, were the results of holding together in dynamic tension the utopianism of expressionism with the restraint of New Objectivity. Both architects challenged conservatives, whose unease with modernity and paucity of ideas resulted in buildings that endlessly evoked the past, and functionalists like Walter Gropius, whose adherence to strict rules and formal design principles resulted too often in a sterile architecture that seemed to forget human beings. All three of them, Taut, Mendelsohn, and Gropius, prolific writers as well as builders, believed fervently that the structures they designed—notably, Taut's apartment blocks, Mendelsohn's Einstein Tower and department stores, and Gropius's Bauhaus building—heralded a new, modern era, a world that would be creative, joyous, and dynamic, in harmony with both nature and frenetic urban industrial life. Their buildings evinced the very best of the Weimar spirit.

Taut had had a difficult career marked by many professional disappointments. He was a well-trained architect and had entered numerous competitions, but in the years before World War I he received very few commissions. His one great success was a highly innovative glass house exhibited at the Cologne Werkbund exhibit in 1914. He lived modestly and sometimes in dire straits, primarily in Berlin and Stuttgart. Taut's intellectual orientation no doubt created problems with potential clients who were more staid, more conservative in their politics and their aesthetics. Taut, in contrast, was a great and eclectic searcher: he sought deep meanings in Christian-tinged spirituality, in

Japanese culture, in socialism. He put all these tendencies together in somewhat inchoate fashion, but a thread ran through it all: his belief in the possibility of creating a more humane society, and the leading role that a new architecture would play in that creation.

A deeply committed pacifist, Taut had managed to avoid army service during World War I, though at the personal moral cost of working in war-related production. As with so many artists, the revolution offered opportunities that had been closed off to him in Wilhelmine society. He was already a prolific writer, and with the revolution he threw himself into a bustle of activities. In the winter of 1918–19, Taut seemed to be present in virtually every artistic pronouncement and organization, however ephemeral. He cofounded the Works Council for Art, drafted countless manifestos, initiated discussion circles, and published his writings and drawings that had languished for years.

Taut's beliefs are vividly expressed in *Alpine Architecture*, published in 1920, though he had been working on the project since 1917.[2] It is a wild, fantastic collection of drawings and paintings based on his imaginings of building all around the Swiss Alps, even setting some structures atop the largest mountains. Taut had never even seen the Swiss Alps; he based his work on tour guides and artists' renderings of the mountains. The images convey a strong mystical and religious tone. Many of the drawings and paintings concern the Christian themes of pilgrimage, ascension, and redemption; in line and color, they are also quite sensual, and are sometimes run through with sexual symbolism. Seen in its totality, *Alpine Architecture* is a cri de coeur against the brutality of World War I and a search for spiritual integrity through beauty—of landscape, of design, of sexuality. Taut wants to place humankind in an environment that marries the dramatic, natural landscape of the Swiss Alps and the human-made technology of construction. It is an organic vision of peace, in sharp contrast to the utter destruction of landscapes and lives by the mechanized warfare of World War I (fig. 5.1).

Many of the same themes also emerge in the Crystal Chain letters, a running correspondence among thirteen architects and artists, some of whom would go on to prominent careers, that Taut initiated in 1919. The group was a kind of secretive brotherhood that fancied itself the pioneer of a new age. The members adopted meaningful pseudonyms—Taut's was "Glass," reflecting his lifelong fascination

Fig. 5.1 Bruno Taut, *Crystal Mountain*, 1919, from his *Alpine Architecture*. Taut fantasized about building glass and crystal structures in the Alps, creating a utopia that combined natural and man-made beauty. Stiftung Archiv der Akademie der Künste, Berlin. © Erbgemeinschaft Bruno Taut.

with its many-sided beauties—and shared their musings only with one another. They were given to flowery manifestos and provocative nonsense, to fanciful architectural drawings and paeans to spiritual renewal. Like Taut's *Alpine Architecture*, the Crystal Chain reflected the despair of the war, and the confidence that the old society had been destroyed and a new one was waiting to be born. It required only the determined imagination and commitment of great artists. They called themselves knights, gods, and creators—women need not apply—and at the same time planned socialist collectives and new cities of artists and craftsmen. In the dire political and economic situation of 1919 and 1920, all they could do was dream since virtually no buildings were being constructed. Taut turned the desperate situation into a virtue. As he wrote in the very first letter, a call to arms to his fellow architects:

> Let us consciously be "imaginary architects"! We believe that only a total revolution can guide us in our task. Our fellow citizens, even our colleagues quite rightly suspect in us the forces of revolution. Break up and undermine all former principles! Dung! And we are the bud in fresh humus.[3]

The new architecture would be a collective accomplishment, not the work of any single man. In Taut's third letter, he quotes the revolutionary leader Karl Liebknecht:

> Storm, my companion,
> you call me!
> Still I can do nothing,
> still I am in chains!
> Yes, I am also the storm,
> part of you;
> and the day will come again
> when I shall break the chains.
> I shall rage anew,
> rage through the worlds,
> storm around the earth.
> Storm through the lands,
> storm mankind,
> his brain and heart,
> storm-wind, I am like you.[4]

Through Liebknecht, Taut gave vivid expression to the revolutionary hopes and sensibilities of the era. One of the other prolific correspondents in the group was Wenzel Hablik, a successful textiles and interior designer. He shared Taut's utopian fantasies.

> Your ideas should be as irresponsibly free as a bird. . . . Let us create a fresh atmosphere, a pure aura of spirit, wit, and joy. Many an idea comes to life through another spirit and matures into fact. . . .
>
> Come and join the struggle against all things negative and corrupting.
>
> Join the struggle, preach, rejoice, blow the trumpet! Speak out in a hundred persuasive tongues. Sacred duties await you—speak out.
>
> We should be teaching people how to be happy—man and woman, girl and child. Speak out! Speak out! Delight in existence—in the universe—in being and in perishing. We should be expunging the thought of war from the hearts of all mankind!
>
> Where are you, prophets?—the heralds of the new life, telling of the new suns—moons—and stars!
>
> The millions await you![5]

Naive sentiments? To be sure. But such great longing, the powerful belief in the possibilities of the future, inspired the work of so many creative artists, including those among the Crystal Chain participants who doggedly pursued their paintings, sculptures, designs, and poetry despite minimal success, and those who would go on to highly successful careers. Even Hans Scharoun, after 1945 West Berlin's powerful building commissioner and codesigner of the new Philharmonie, the home of the Berlin Symphony Orchestra, could, in 1919 and 1920, lapse into rhapsodies about

> let[ing] the fantasy that springs from asceticism shine forth. Not seeking but storming, not wanting one path to the goal but a universal goal. Infinity is not outside us, is not a star that we can force down to earth, but twinkles delicately in every stirring of the artist's fantasy. In creating we are gods, in understanding sheep.[6]

Storms, illumination, trumpet sounds—these were the images the artists summoned to evoke the promising future. Taut put it most succinctly: "Long live Utopia!"[7]

Hablik, Scharoun, Taut, and the others in the Crystal Chain expressed the grand ideas and the brimming self-confidence, and also the shadows of despair, that define revolutions. Taut believed in "socialism in an unpolitical sense . . . [meaning a society] free from every form of domination and [characterized by] the simple, unpretentious relationships of people to one another. . . . Socialism, fraternity, develop through the devotion to an idea, through idealism."[8] In 1919 and 1920, he was given to sketching out idyllic communities of small producers in which money would not be needed, idle chatter would disappear, and everyone would live in harmony. The nineteenth-century anarchists Pierre-Joseph Proudhon and Peter Kropotkin (whom he quotes) would have felt at home in Taut's village.[9]

But Taut learned to control his most fervent longings in order to realize some of the most important public housing developments of the Weimar era. As an architect balances elements in the design of a great building, Taut managed to combine visionary beliefs with practical concerns in the service of social reform. In 1921, he was named building commissioner (*Stadtbaurat*) in Magdeburg, a medium-sized, heavy-industrial town with an SPD-led city council. That post was (and is) a powerful position in Germany, because the commissioner has to approve all building plans. An energetic official could initiate all sorts of projects; it is no accident that the great buildings and the great housing developments in Weimar arose in cities with energetic, reform-minded commissioners who had the political support of Social Democratic–led local governments.

Taut had a rocky tenure in Magdeburg. Despite the SPD-led city council, he faced huge obstacles from more conservative city officials and the building industry. In fact, nothing got built in Magdeburg, but the political trials served as good experience when he received a call to Berlin to serve as consulting architect to a newly founded, mixed-financed cooperative company established with a mission to build low- and medium-income housing. Taut took up his new post in 1924 and would remain there for six years. He worked closely with Martin Wagner, another pioneering architect who had been appointed Berlin's building commissioner. It was an auspicious time: the hyperinflation was over, and the economy boomed with the help of American capital. German municipalities and state governments borrowed on the American markets. Germany's long-standing, catastrophic housing crisis cried out for redress, and inspired reformers now had the political backing and the financial means to undertake major projects.

And build they did. In Stuttgart, Frankfurt am Main, Hamburg, Berlin, and many other cities, housing developments large and small were constructed. Usually cooperative building societies took the initiative. Typically these were limited-profit companies with a high degree of public involvement, generally from the municipalities. Their financing came from a variety of sources, including tax revenues, municipal governments, trade unions, foundations, and churches. They could not alleviate the housing crisis in total, but in certain areas they had a profound impact. "*Licht*, *Luft*, *Sonne*"—light, air, sun—were the bywords, and they signified everything that the large, dark, and dank *Mietskaserne*—the rental barracks that we visited in chapter 2—did not have. Now many Germans for the first time had indoor plumbing, electricity and gas, and clean apartments open to the sun and greenery. Members of the new middle class—the army of white-collar workers in government and business—and a few well-paid skilled workers poured into the new apartment blocks, usually designed in modernist fashion with clean lines, flat roofs, and recessed windows. Modernism was not always to the liking of the residents, who sometimes pined for the more typical two- or three-story German house with sloped roof, balcony, and window boxes full of flowers (at least in the summer). But the new apartments were a great advance over the old *Mietskaserne*.

The statistics themselves tell one part of the story. As noted in chapter 2, overall 2.5 million new dwellings, housing about 9 million people, were built in the Weimar era. In 1930, around 14 percent of the entire German population lived in newly built apartments. Frankfurt am Main, the city with the most extensive construction program and, in Ernst May, another visionary building commissioner, added 15,000 new dwellings between 1924 and 1933. Between 1924 and 1929, Berlin alone built 135,000 units.[10] The construction plans were like a *Gesamtkunstwerk* (a total artwork)—the architects provided for adequate infrastructure and playgrounds, gardens, and schools for leisure, rest, and self-development. The architects devoted great attention to interior design, which was intended to make family life far more "modern" and "rational" than it had been in the past. The apartments were geared toward the small, nuclear family with two children (as we saw in the course of our walk around Berlin), most definitely not toward a multigenerational extended kin group or even a two-generational household with a slew of children. The two-bedroom unit was standard, and the kitchen was closed off from the rest of the apartment, a result of the architects' and planners' conviction that modernity meant a complete, even spatial, division of work and rest. The door dividing the kitchen from the more open combined living and dining room was de rigueur.[11]

Taut's achievements in Berlin were a part of this story. At least in this period, he proved himself an adept, politically savvy, and economically efficient architect. He kept his more utopian longings in check; instead, he designed housing that provided many people with the first reasonably sized, sun-drenched apartments in their lives, also equipped with many modern conveniences that lessened some of the most trying elements of women's household labor. And he did it all in the most cost-saving manner possible.

Two of Taut's greatest developments were—and are, since they are still standing and in very good condition—the Onkel Toms Siedlung in Zehlendorf in Berlin's southwest (which we visited in chapter 2) and Britz, with "Hufeisen" (Horseshoe) the core element, in the southeastern part of the city. On both of these projects, Taut collaborated with other architects, and they generally divided the work into sections, each designing a particular part of the settlement. The Onkel Toms Siedlung—named after a local tavern and subway stop, themselves named in playful allusion to the famous American novel by Harriet Beecher Stowe—was built in stages between 1926 and 1932. The buildings are typically three and four stories high with recessed windows (see chapter 2, fig. 2.6).[12] They run a long way down the block, providing a strong horizontal line, accentuated by the recessed windows. When they curve along the street, as many of them do, they project a dynamic sense of movement. Single-family homes were also built on the site, also in modernist style. True to his fondness for nature, Taut ensured that the pine trees native to the area remained, which gave the residents quick and easy access to wooded areas. All of the buildings backed onto green stretches, and the entire area is virtually adjacent to Berlin's lovely Grunewald and the lakes Krumme Lanke and Schlachtensee. Playgrounds and a school were also incorporated into the development.

Taut's fascination with color, so vivid in *Alpine Architecture*, was evident in the multihued exterior stuccos, from brown-red to gray-green, that he had splashed onto the buildings. A variety of color schemes accented the window and door frames: green exteriors had yellow, red, and white accents; red exteriors had white, yellow, and red. Taut rejected the white dogmatically promoted by pure functionalists, and the gray of so many nineteenth-century buildings. In Germany's dreary climate and smokestack-heavy economy, wrote Taut, white quickly turned "a dirt-ingrained, dead gray. Or alternatively—and this is even worse—a white house after a certain time looks as if it is wearing a dirty white shirt. . . . [T]he same pure white that in Mediterranean countries produces such perfect harmony . . . in our latitudes fails completely."[13] Color provides "a certain warmth and depth," especially on dull-gray days (of which there are, of course, many in Germany). Used properly, color also deepens perspective, creating the illusion of expanse. Color "can make the wall of a house appear to recede . . . to come forward to meet the observer; it can calm or relax the eye or, contrarily, it can disconcert or dazzle the eye."[14] It can make buildings appear in harmony with their natural surroundings, or it can set off the buildings in opposition to nature. The overall effect of a carefully designed color scheme imparts a "feeling of stability . . . [of] decisiveness followed by unconditional avoidance of all sentimental combinations and mixtures."[15] And he worked out the details: deep, rich colors to enhance the sense of space between buildings, balconies painted white to reflect more brightly into the living room, darker colors where buildings faced west and received the warmer afternoon sun.

Taut showed here his deep sensitivity to the real living circumstances of people, even though he shared the modernists' arrogance: they were going to design the way people *should* live, whether they liked it or not. Meanwhile, strict functionalists considered his innovations with color merely decorative and therefore a swipe against the modernist ethos.[16]

The principles Taut realized at Onkel Toms are evident also in Berlin-Britz, which was built between 1925 and 1927, almost contemporaneous with the Zehlendorf settlement. Taut was the lead architect on Onkel Toms; Britz was a collaboration between Taut and Wagner. Britz was the name of a noble family who owned the land, still agricultural until the city purchased it in 1925. So the site could be completely planned; the Berlin city council and the local Neukölln authorities took charge and turned the project over to Taut and Wagner. Along a green thoroughfare (Fritz-Reuter-Allee), they designed four-story, block-length apartment buildings, a kind of living wall that defined the area. Behind them and separated by gardens, they built two-story row houses. Taut designed the buildings west of the green thoroughfare in modernist style with flat lines, recessed windows, and repeating patterns. His structures have no ornamentation, no historical references. East of the thoroughfare, a different architect and construction company built more traditional-looking apartments and houses, with sloped roofs and outcroppings. As at Onkel Toms, Taut and Wagner broke up the monotony of modernism through the use of various exterior colors and some variety in the architectural forms. Some blocks, for example, had curved exteriors for the staircases on either side of the apartments (fig. 5.2).

Both sides, the modernist and the traditionalist, made some compromises at Britz that, finally, complemented each other well. The more traditionalist buildings had recessed windows, not the bay windows typical of the older structures in Berlin's bourgeois districts, and some of Taut's blocks had partly sloped, tiled roofs and attic rooms. Some of the construction elements were prefabricated in an innovative effort to hold down costs, and for the first time a construction firm used heavy machinery on a housing site. Taut drew on the ideas of the garden city movement, developed especially in Britain with echoes in Germany before the war, but now joined them to a large-scale urban development. All told, Britz had 1,027 residences, of which 472 were single-family homes. The main area, the Hufeisen, was shaped in a horseshoe (as signified by its German name), which provided sunlight for all the residents and was also supposed to demonstrate social equality and the residents' sense of community.[17]

Fig. 5.2 Bruno Taut and Martin Wagner, Berlin-Britz housing development, built 1925–27. A fine example of the drive to build housing that offered residents "light, air, and sun." Berlin-Britz is also modernism with a difference: note the rounded corners and stairwells, anathema to strict functionalists who prized straight lines and ninety-degree angles. Author's photograph.

A large structure, it nonetheless gained a free, airy feel from its open architecture and large green areas in front and back (fig. 5.3).

As in many of his other designs, Taut incorporated the existing natural areas into the construction. Green areas abound in Britz, and the gardens are, relatively speaking, large—easily the size of *Schrebergärten*, the highly prized garden plots on the edge of German cities; these also serve to interpose significant space between the blocks of buildings. To emerge from the subway at Blaschkoallee after the traffic, bustle, and noise of Kurfürstendamm or Alexanderplatz or Friedrichstraße—Berlin's central commercial and shopping zones—is to find oneself suddenly in a quiet, peaceful neighborhood, an area unlike so many parts of the city. Especially on a summer day, one can breathe in the smell of flowers, grass, and trees. It has an utterly calming effect, as it must have had on its residents in the 1920s and early 1930s, even if not all the vegetation was yet so fully grown. Later on, families could walk their children to school, to play areas, to the local clinic, all the social institutions that reform-minded planners like Taut and Wagner had envisioned.

At both Onkel Toms and Britz, Taut and Wagner devoted as much attention to the household interior as to the exterior design. The new apartment was to be the site of the "rationalized" household: the language and program of Weimar economics had made their way into the family and the home. Explicitly referring to time-motion studies that sought to enhance labor productivity, Taut happily called this new development "the application of the Taylor System to the home."

Fig. 5.3 Bruno Taut and Martin Wagner, Hufeisen (Horseshoe), part of Berlin-Britz, built 1925–27. Taut believed that the interior sightlines into other apartments would inspire a sense of community among the residents. Today's residents and observers might think first about the loss of privacy. ullstein bild / The Granger Collection, New York.

Newly designed apartments with their streamlined architecture, he claimed, would allow "the woman . . . a way to improve her performance." She would organize her daily household labor according to plan, with, of course, "sufficient time for going on walks and sleeping." Order would always prevail, so the parlor, where unexpected guests had to be kept while the mess was hurriedly picked up, could be eliminated. Each room would have its specific function, and would serve that function alone.[18]

The architects targeted the kitchen for the major overhaul, as was most famously expressed in the "Frankfurt kitchen" designed by Margarete Schütte-Lihotzky. But the same principles were at work in Taut's and many other new housing developments. To minimize bending and stretching, the architects designed countertops at the appropriate height; they replaced open dish racks with cupboards, minimizing dust collection. Metal and brick replaced wood, which was both hard to clean and subject to rotting. Racks eliminated the need for drying the dishes; preset flour dispensers obviated measuring. Perhaps most important, the kitchen was to be closed off from the rest of the apartment or house, eliminating the congestion and dirt of the open room that had served both functions. And a separate bathroom for every family, small as it had to be, became de rigueur. In addition, all sorts of useless ornaments, the knickknacks so beloved by the lower middle class and working class, were to be eliminated. Even a floor lamp, with its large and ornate lampshade, had to be expunged because it collected dust and, well, just looked so awful, as did the oil paintings of German landscape scenes or of the kaiser. Taut and other modern architects also hated the carved, ornamented Victorian-style furniture that was so prevalent in Germany. Spare, sleek, efficient—Taut's apartments embodied the modern ideal.[19]

And modern also meant a clearer division of labor between men and women. Taut and other progressives advocated the formal equality of women, but when it came to the home and the family, that was still women's sphere. The small, efficient, and closed-off kitchen was her space, from which she would emerge into the dining area, voilà!, wholesome dinner in hand. Taut did make some moves toward egalitarianism by suggesting that men and children make the beds and clean a bit. Apparently, they needed help to figure out these tasks: he recommended that cumbersome featherbeds be replaced by simpler blankets or duvets.

Still, Taut's architecture always had a humane element at its core. Despite the large size of the developments at Onkel Toms and Britz, they retain a human scale, unlike so much modern architecture with its coolly rational and scientific form. The horseshoe design ensured that all the residences received sunlight. By exposing the exterior of virtually every apartment to the line of sight of everyone else, Taut emphasized social equality and hoped to create a communal sense among the residents. Later generations might think first and foremost that the building all too easily enables the surveillance of people in their apartments and limits their privacy. But Taut saw only the progressive, socially egalitarian character of the design, which would help create the more compassionate men and women of the future society. At Onkel Toms, Taut designed the doors and windows not only according to the formal aesthetics of modernism, but also with human action in an urban environment uppermost in mind. The doors offer ease of entrance and egress; the windows enable the residents to peer out, elbows on the ledge, at the activities on the street below. Taut created "a kind of alliance between man and architecture," in the words of one critic.[20] And he always thought of architecture as a collective enterprise.

In this sense, Taut's more wildly utopian writings and drawings between 1917 and 1921 and his designs and buildings between 1924 and 1930 are intimately linked. He did not have two distinctive phases that can easily be parsed into expressionism and New Objectivity. Both his early and his later work are marked by an intimate interrelationship of environment, building, and life; by a similarity in design forms, such as the horseshoe, a symbol of openness, that appears in both his drawings in *Alpine Architecture* and the Britz development; and a rejection of universal rules and pure logic and rationality as a basis of design. Taut was always more of a humanist than his modernist contemporaries Walter Gropius, Ludwig Mies van der Rohe, and Le Corbusier, whose dogmatic adherence to strict design principles sometimes resulted in sterile, anonymous buildings.

On 9 November 1918, the day when masses of workers, returning soldiers, and onlookers gathered in huge demonstrations all across Berlin, the day when Philipp Scheidemann proclaimed a German republic and Karl Liebknecht a socialist republic, Erich Mendelsohn founded his architectural office. Mendelsohn, too, had just returned from the front, and he was hardly oblivious to the events going on around him. But even the chaos and upheaval of revolution could not impinge on his enormous self-confidence or inhibit him from launching his career. It was a step he had daydreamed about all the while he languished in the trenches on both the eastern and western fronts, and he wasted no time upon his return.

Mendelsohn, like so many other figures of Weimar culture, understood the distinctiveness of his times, its dilemmas as well as its possibilities, the trauma of war and the hope of revolution. "Revolution is not only in politics," he told a small group of well-placed listeners, gathered in the salon of Molly Philippson, in the winter of 1918–19. It has an entire complex of conditions; it is dramatic, chaotic, and forceful, moving and exciting, and also wonderfully embracing.[21] In the complex character of revolution, Mendelsohn lectured, we find a drive toward human fulfillment that cannot be met or limited by claims to power and daily concerns, and reaches far beyond the territorial borders of a state. Mendelsohn advocated a kind of creative internationalism, a play of fantasy and aesthetics that might be based in national conditions but, in its working out, dissolves borders and brings people together. It was no surprise, he continued, that an era of general want and misery—the war and its aftermath—had fostered the creation of a new consciousness. Its spiritual triumph would also be a triumph of form, of a new architecture.[22]

Mendelsohn was no socialist and, indeed, always cultivated very close relations with businessmen. After all, he needed commissions. By the late 1920s, he had become perhaps the most successful architect in Germany, a man who presided over a firm with forty employees and was designing some of the most distinctive commercial and private architecture in the world.[23] Yet his rhetoric in 1919 and his involvement in revolutionary artists' organizations like the November Group and the Works Council for Art were not mere flirtations. He always spoke in terms of revolution, of new beginnings, of great possibilities, in Germany and beyond. A new art, a modern art, was needed that reflected the spirit of the age and did not merely seek to replicate nature or reproduce the styles of the past. The new art had to be a total art.

And that, of course, is where Mendelsohn the architect comes into the picture. The modern architect will give shape to this new spirit in the fixed form of new buildings. He has to be a "whole person," possessed of practical as well as theoretical knowledge, of the humanities as well as the sciences, a veritable Renaissance man.[24] The fantasy of his creative genius will render the materials of the modern age—steel, plate glass, and reinforced concrete—into beautiful and distinctive structures that, at one and the same time, stimulate and soothe the senses. The new buildings will arouse the aesthetic sensibilities and ease the tensions of frenetic urban life for all those who live, work, or shop in the structures, or simply pass by and observe them. The buildings themselves will inhabit and challenge the cityscape of ornamented, traditional buildings; if built in rural or wooded areas, they will blend into and depart from nature. The great architect, in all his designs, will be able to balance these complex tensions. His work will be, in a word, "organic," that term beloved by so many Weimar figures, whatever their aesthetic or political inclinations.

Great modern architecture will create a sense of dynamic tension, of movement and calming stasis. Mendelsohn often used the metaphors of music and "force-field" (*Kräftespiel*) to illustrate his ideas.[25] The "organic cohesion" for which the architect strives can take a "harmonic direction or a contrapuntal direction," which can be realized horizontally or vertically.[26] It is especially in counterpoint, where several different melodies are pieced together to create a unified composition, that Mendelsohn identified the essence of architecture.[27] But his love for the organic beauty of a Bach fugue or a Gothic cathedral did not prevent him from seeing the same possibilities in the "hard clang" of a machine's movements, the "metallic sheen" of its material, and the "precision of its rotations."[28]

Certainly, Mendelsohn was a firm defender of the modern. To businessmen, fellow architects, and an educated public he trumpeted the excitement of the present, with its new construction techniques and materials, mass consumption, automobiles, and advertising. "It is unthinkable," he wrote in 1923, "that we can turn back time. . . . Unthinkable that we leave unused the greatly broadened possibilities of technology. That we see the machine as the enemy of humanity, instead of as our powerful tool that we need to master. . . . That we found our personal lives on some original and ancient fatherland [*Urväterland*], instead of trusting the house key to modern times. For this *modern* time is our *own* time."[29]

But modern times also create a distinct nervousness and unease among men. Only through his "will to reality," through his domination of the natural elements, can man become master of his modern unease.[30] Like so many other brilliant Weimar figures, Mendelsohn sought to resolve the tensions of modern life by grasping, not rejecting, modernity. Like Taut and Gropius, he claimed that architecture was the most unified of all the arts, hence the medium best suited to stimulate as well as to calm, to establish the balance. And the structural form it has to take is very clear: "The man of our time, with the nervous excitement of his fast pace of life, can find his equilibrium only in the calming effect of the horizontal dimension." The dynamic sense of movement must also create a sense of harmony to calm the nervousness of the modern age.[31] A great building has to project a balance of emotional effects. It is precisely through his advocacy of balance and harmony that Mendelsohn tempered his expressionist, perhaps even Nietzschean, excesses, found in his use of terms like "vitality," "emotion," "feeling for life," "mastery over nature," and in his utter conviction concerning his own genius.

His great structures—the Einstein Tower, the Schocken department store in Chemnitz, the Universum movie palace in Berlin, and the Columbus House on Potsdamer Platz in Berlin—brilliantly realize his theories. They create a sense of dynamic movement that also has a calming effect. Mendelsohn's Einstein Tower, his very first building, remains one of the best expressions of his ideas (see plate 4). Built in Potsdam in a scientific park that housed a number of research institutes, the Einstein Tower contained a telescope and laboratory (and is still today a working observatory and laboratory). It was intended to test Einstein's theories through research on the light spectrum of the sun. Built in circular and spiral fashion out of a variety of materials, the Einstein Tower arises seamlessly out of its low-slung base. The horizontal base situates the building in the surrounding field; the vertical tower mimics the upward thrust of the trees that envelop the site. Its recessed windows ensure that no outcroppings disrupt the symmetry of the structure. Mendelsohn spent almost as much effort on the interior of the building, one of his signature approaches. He designed the working rooms without ornamentation and with a great deal of natural lighting. Darker-toned furniture played off the light-colored walls and richly stained wood doors and railings.

The Einstein Tower has a remarkable, unmistakably distinctive appearance yet somehow creates a sense of harmony with its surroundings. The building is fully integrated into its setting, the wooded park and other nearby research institutes, and thrusts upward to the heavens.[32] Upon seeing the structure for the first time, Einstein himself said one word: "Organic!"[33] And so it is, as overused is the term. As Mendelsohn glossed Einstein's expression, "organic" signified that "one cannot take any part away from it, neither from its mass, nor from its motion, nor even from its logical development, without destroying the whole." Organic means that "exterior forms express their interior structure . . . [and] use, structure and architectural expression coalesce to an organic whole, where scientific facts and creative vision combine to an unbreakable pattern."[34]

This one building conveyed (and still conveys) harmony both with nature and with the built environment, and the quest for spiritual and scientific truth. It is also remarkably playful, in stark contrast to the strict functionalism of Bauhaus, which took itself so very seriously. However, playfulness is probably not what Mendelsohn had in mind: he also took himself so very seriously and always claimed to have been influenced in his art by Einstein's theory of relativity. The design of the building was not meant simply to be beautiful and organic, but to be an expression in concrete of relativity theory. Mendelsohn was influenced by his friendship with the physicist Erwin Finlay Freundlich, who was Einstein's assistant and whose book *Die Grundlagen der Einsteinschen Gravitationstheorie* (The Fundamentals of Einstein's Gravitational Theory) served as a kind of primer to relativity theory. Mendelsohn was especially interested in the premise that energy carries mass and the two exist together, and that every kind of material contains latent energy. "Dynamic tension" and "function and dynamics," the terms Mendelsohn used so often to describe his own architecture, derived directly from his reading of Freundlich and conversations with him and with Einstein, who would later be a frequent guest of the Mendelsohns.[35]

The Einstein Tower did not succeed as an expression of relativity theory. And certainly not every contemporary was overwhelmed by the building, or by Mendelsohn's self-confidence in his own genius. Predictably, Potsdam officials had initially rejected the design as unsuitable to the site and were only reluctantly dragged along into acceptance. Reactions were decidedly mixed, and the cutting observations of the art critic Paul Westheim were shared by many who saw in the structure only the self-aggrandizing expression of a dilettante. The Einstein Tower, Westheim wrote, is

> not thought through according to the objective standards of the engineer, but flirts embarrassingly with elements of engineering. Despite modernist touches, it has a monumentality that suits the style of the memorial to the war of liberation [*Völkerschlachtdenkmal*] and of the Bismarck on the Rhine monument. This tower in Potsdam is a gigantic poster. It is an advertisement less for the observatory than for the originality of the builder. It is a Mendelsohn Tower. . . . If he had more of an architect's skills, his building style would have more structural consistency, yet at the same time it would have fewer distracting flourishes, through which he directs attention to himself. He has the grandiose self-consciousness that unites genius and dilettantism. He is unskilled, which prevents him from being a master builder in the true sense, but it enables him to manage the material in the kind of naive fashion from which the skilled tradesman, thinking about the practical and purposive design, would inevitably shy away.[36]

The Einstein Tower also did not succeed as construction. Within five years it had to undergo significant repairs, and many more followed, not always with the best results. (A full-scale, complex, and highly scientific renovation in the late 1990s finally restored the building to its original glory.) Mendelsohn's fascination with concrete and reinforced concrete ran ahead of the technical capacities of the materials. In fact, the building ended up as a mix of materials, including brick, cement, and reinforced concrete, and they did not always adhere well to one another, a principal reason for the building's structural problems.[37] The stucco exterior created the appearance of a building made totally out of concrete, but that was, in fact, a modernist deception.

Nonetheless, the Einstein Tower is a brilliant building. Even the inconsistent use of concrete hides the load-bearing features of the construction, giving the structure a smooth, dynamic character, and also permitted the rounded features of the building and the sense of an upward-escalating spiral. The sharp angles and ninety-degree corners of the vast majority of other buildings were metaphorically consigned to history by Mendelsohn. The Einstein Tower is like an elegant sculpture rendered in great mass. Its deceptive lightness and proportionality constitute a vivid expression of the questing spirit and sparkling creativity of Weimar culture.

These qualities are also evident in the department stores Mendelsohn built in the 1920s and early 1930s, especially for the Schocken brothers in Nuremberg, Stuttgart, and Chemnitz, as well as his Columbus House on Potsdamer Platz in Berlin. In these works, Mendelsohn tamed the expressionism so vividly conveyed in the cement and stucco of the Einstein Tower, yet his basic design principles remained constant.

It was a perfect partnership with Salman Schocken, who wanted not a luxury store but a temple of mass consumption. The store in Chemnitz, designed and built from 1928 to 1930, is the best of the three and Mendelsohn's most fully realized building. It is a massive structure, nine stories tall and seventy meters long, yet light and dynamic. Built on a large plot in the city center, it was marked off from all the surrounding structures by its bracing modernism (fig. 5.4). Mendelsohn achieved its light, dynamic effect through the use of the modernists' favored materials, reinforced concrete and glass. The five rows of repeating, equally sized windows lighten the feel of the building and also permit streams of daylight to bathe the goods on sale inside. On the two ends, the main staircases, the twenty-five narrower windows that Mendelsohn designed contribute a sense of greater height and vertical dynamism. The top four stories are recessed in a steplike fashion, also lightening the feel of the building. But the most profound effect is the curvature, which, in combination with the repeating glass, lightens the massive structure and endows it with dynamic movement. The cantilevered construction meant that no load-bearing vertical columns or steel I-beams interrupted the continuous flow of the facade (figs. 5.5 and 5.6). Mendelsohn's design contrasted enormously with the heavy stone constructions of earlier department stores. With the Chemnitz store he achieved the

Fig. 5.4 Erich Mendelsohn, Schocken department store, Chemnitz, built 1929–30, aerial view. Like his Columbus House (fig. 2.3), the building is an almost shocking assertion of modernism amid the traditional structures all around it. Schloßberg Museum Chemnitz.

"dynamic tension" he so often wrote about, the apparent contradiction that the static mass of a building, firmly tethered to the earth by steel and concrete, can nonetheless be dynamic. It is as if the very condition of modernity, the tension between stasis and movement, tradition and progress, had been rendered in this one building.[38]

And it was a department store, a temple of consumption. As mentioned, the bands of windows provided streams of natural light to heighten the allure of the displayed goods. The color of the products played off well against the light shades of the walls. Carefully designed electric lighting also brightened the merchandise and the entire experience of shopping. The elevators and escalators looked stylish and elegant. From the outside, the constant lighting gave a modernist glow to the buildings and also provided a place for advertisements; internally it bathed the goods in an enticing shimmer. The ability to use ever larger display windows also opened the building to the street, with passersby able to look in, not only to the display, but past it to the arrangements of goods in the store's interior.[39] All design elements, interior and exterior, were not mere ornamentation. They had functional purpose—to enable people to move easily through the store, from one display of goods to another, from one section to another, and thereby to enhance sales, "to move the merchandise," as American retailers would say.

For Mendelsohn, as for Taut, there was no strict line of division between his earlier, expressionist phase and his later work. The Chemnitz store is certainly more restrained than the Einstein Tower. But many of the design principles that Mendelsohn championed are evidenced in both—the curvature of the structures, the absence of

Fig. 5.5 Erich Mendelsohn, Schocken department store, Chemnitz, built 1929–30, full view. The use of steel I-beams and reinforced concrete enabled Mendelsohn to hide the load bearing features of the structure and open the outer wall to repeating sheets of glass. As a result, an aura of lightness belies the building's mass. The curvature gives it a dynamic sense of movement. Staatliche Museen zu Berlin, Kunstbibliothek.

Fig. 5.6 Erich Mendelsohn, Schocken department store, Chemnitz, built 1929–30, night view. The extensive use of glass allowed natural light to bathe the goods on display inside. At night, the effect was reversed. Artificial light beamed outward from the store, giving the building a compact glow. Staatliche Museen zu Berlin, Kunstbibliothek.

ornamentation, the smooth exteriors, and the attentiveness to lighting. Mendelsohn transformed the playfulness of the Einstein Tower into the pleasure of shopping in Chemnitz. But both buildings were designed to elicit joy as well as wonder, and to evoke the cry of "Organic!" that Einstein had (perhaps) voiced at the sight of his tower.

Both Mendelsohn and Taut departed from strict functionalism with its hard lines and absence of color. Mendelsohn had an affinity for curves; Taut happily used color and, along with Wagner, introduced some quirky elements into his designs, such as the towerlike stairwells in some of the Britz buildings, to disrupt the monotony of totally clean and straight lines. Both Taut and Mendelsohn were also keenly aware of the larger environments in which they situated their structures, unlike so many modernists who just plopped down their aesthetically refined buildings with no attention whatsoever to the surroundings. Their buildings might just as well have landed from Mars, or so thought many critics. Not that Taut and Mendelsohn believed that their buildings should be subsumed by the environment. Both built highly distinctive, even dramatic structures that were impossible to ignore. But Taut was always attentive to the wooded areas and green spaces in which his housing developments were built. They provided a serene respite from urban life and broke up the monotony of repetitive rectangular structures. Mendelsohn always sought to make his buildings relate to the sidewalks and the streets of city life. They were built with the cityscape in mind, the movement of pedestrians and vehicles at the site of the building, which he often curved so as to calm the "nervousness" of the modern city and also to enhance the flow of movement around the building. As he wrote about one of his early triumphs, the expansion and renovation of the Mosse publishing house in Berlin, the building "is not a disinterested spectator of the rushing cars and of the advancing and receding flow of traffic; rather, it has become an absorbing, cooperating element of the motion. . . . The balance of its forces soothes the frenetic pace [*Nervosität*] of the street and of the passersby. . . . By dividing and guiding the traffic, the building, despite all tendencies of its own towards movement, becomes an immobile pillar amidst the turbulence of the streets."[40] In Chemnitz, the street in front of the Schocken department store was widened and curved to reflect the curvature of the structure, bringing building and cityscape into a unified whole.

Mendelsohn's resistance to strict functionalism explains his deep admiration for Frank Lloyd Wright. The two met in 1924 during Mendelsohn's first visit to the United States. They developed an immediate bond—both great architects, both egomaniacs, each unquestionably convinced of his own genius, both certain that they were forging not only a new aesthetics but a new way of being in the modern world, attuned to its characteristics yet also attentive to history. For both, great architecture would be aware of tradition yet expressive of the times. It would be intellectual and intuitive, creative yet responsive to its environment, whether a natural landscape or the cityscape; it would work with the available materials yet not be limited by them.[41] Each of them forged a highly distinctive style—Wright's Prairie School style, Mendelsohn's "architectural dynamics" (as he termed it)—that, indeed, blended these diverse elements and came to be expressed in some of the most distinctive buildings of the twentieth century.

In many of his writings and speeches Mendelsohn developed an articulate critique of strict functionalism. His unnamed target was Walter Gropius, the famed founder of the Bauhaus school and another legendary twentieth-century architect. Right after World War I, Gropius, too, was imbued with utopian hopes. He collaborated with Taut on a number of manifestos and projects during the revolution of 1918–19. Like so many others, Gropius believed that the utter disaster of World War I marked an irreparable break with the past. Artists and society were at sea, searching for a new way forward. As he wrote in 1919: "Today's artist lives in an era of dissolution, without guidance. He stands alone. The old forms are in ruins, the benumbed world is shaken up, the old human spirit is invalidated and in flux toward a new form. We float in space and cannot yet perceive the new order."[42] At this moment especially, to indulge in historicist architecture would be a foolish exercise in nostalgia for a world that could never be re-created. Better to grasp reality, deepen the breach with the past and create something new, something that would reflect and mold the modern condition. A highly effective exponent of the new architecture, Gropius, too, was convinced that modernist aesthetics would transform man and society, ushering in a new age of harmony and creativity.

The famous Bauhaus school that Gropius founded in 1919 with the support of the SPD government of Saxe-Weimar would be the main vehicle for his ideas. The school, in Gropius's design, would break down one barrier after another: between the different fields of art, arts and crafts, teachers and students, machine and man, and art and society. As he wrote later, education at the school should develop "the individual's natural capacities to grasp life as a whole, a single cosmic entity."[43] The curriculum entailed instruction in artisanal crafts as well as the more traditionally defined arts like sculpture and painting. Students applied themselves to metalworking, typography, photography, and carpentry as well as design, drafting, weaving, and pottery. The instructors, some of whom were already or soon would be among the foremost artists and architects of the twentieth century, included Wassily Kandinsky, Paul Klee, László Moholy-Nagy, and Mies van der Rohe, among others. They were given the title of master, rather than professor, to invoke the artisanal world of apprentices, journeymen, and master craftsmen, and to try to create a more informal social attitude than that which prevailed in the universities and art academies of Germany. Creativity at the school would be encouraged by "friendly relations between masters and students outside of work; therefore plays, lectures, poetry, music, fancy-dress parties. Establishment of a cheerful ceremonial at these gatherings."[44] Compared to the extreme hierarchy and gaping social distance between professors and students at German universities, that kind of exchange alone was revolutionary—even if one is left bemused by the idea that students and instructors had to be ordered to have fun.

Like Mendelsohn and Taut, Gropius believed that architecture, because of its distinctive characteristics, had a unique role to play in the forging of a new art and a new society. The fruit of architectural creativity—the building—was not consigned to the mausoleum museum, as a painting or sculpture would be, but was visible to all in daily life. It required the services of artists in varied media, and also skilled craft labor, for its construction. Architecture was therefore the truly "organic" art form, into which all the others would be subsumed. Architecture would synthesize and surmount the existing division between artistry and artisanal labor. The workshop would be the site of this union, where "the mere drawing and painting world of the pattern designer and the applied artist [would] become a world that builds again." Gropius called on architects, sculptors, and painters to "return to the crafts! For art is not a 'profession.' There is no essential difference between the artist and the craftsman. . . . Together let us desire, conceive, and create the new structure of the future, which will embrace architecture and sculpture and painting in one unity and which will one day rise toward heaven from the hands of a million workers like the crystal symbol of a new faith."[45] Even Taut could not have said it more fancifully.

But this was not mere whim on Gropius's part, the flush of revolutionary enthusiasm in 1919. As with Taut and Mendelsohn, his views and designs became somewhat moderated, and more successful, in the latter half of the 1920s, but his oeuvre cannot be divided into two distinct phases, an expressionist or utopian beginning abandoned for New Objectivity. His own development was, shall we say, "organic," his best buildings dependent on the imagination and fantasies inspired by the revolution and the opportunities offered by the republic. He always condemned the "dead architecture" that was prevalent before the war, which was focused only on reproducing the past and pretty ornamentation.

> This kind of architecture we disown. We want to create a clear, organic architecture, whose inner logic will be radiant and naked, unencumbered by lying facades and trickeries; we want an architecture adapted to our world of machines, radios and fast motor cars, an architecture whose function is clearly recognizable in the relation of its forms.[46]

This was the modernist program that Gropius advocated tirelessly and effectively. The beauty of a building should derive from its function; indeed, beauty and function should form a unified whole. Instead of an exterior covered with a riot of disruptive ornaments, the new architecture would have clean lines and smooth surfaces that reflected the function of a building, whether it be a residence, office, or factory. Beauty should also derive from the very nature of the materiáls used in construction. There should be no historical references in a building, no imitation of past styles, whether of classical Athens, Renaissance Rome, or baroque Vienna. A building's only reference would be to itself, its function and the modern times of which it was a part.

As Gropius wrote and lectured in various venues, during and after

Weimar, new industrial materials—steel, reinforced concrete, and plate glass—technically opened up new possibilities. Architects could design much lighter structures. The load-bearing capacity of the building is moved from the exterior walls to the steel skeleton; the external face of the building is reduced to a screen to protect the inhabitants from noise, rain, and cold. Windows are no longer holes that have to be cut out of massive stone walls, but a continuous sheen of glass separated only by the thin steel frames. "[The] sparkling insubstantiality [of glass], and the way it seems to float between wall and wall imponderably as in the air, adds a note of gaiety" to modern buildings.[47]

> The New Architecture throws open its walls like curtains to admit a plenitude of fresh air, daylight and sunshine. Instead of anchoring buildings ponderously into the ground with massive foundations, it poises them lightly, yet firmly, upon the face of the earth; and bodies itself forth, not in stylistic imitation or ornamental frippery, but in those simple and sharply modeled designs in which every part merges naturally into the comprehensive volume of the whole. Thus its aesthetic meets our material and psychological requirements alike.[48]

Similarly, flat roofs hide some of the ugly features of a building, like gutters; are useful as play areas; and are more efficient because they reduce maintenance-heavy surface areas.

In the realization of this new architecture, "organic" was the critical term for Gropius, as it was for Taut and Mendelsohn and so many others. It meant the complete unity of all things in a state of balance, and harmony between a building's form and its function.[49] Properly ordered and integrated with one another, form and function, not decoration, create beauty. Properly designed, the building would express the beauty inherent in the very materials used in construction. The work would be the creation not of an isolated genius, but of a collective that joined together artists and craftsmen. The result would be eminently modern, a building that was "precise, practical, free of superfluous ornament, effective only through the cubic composition of the masses."[50] A modern building, he wrote later, "should derive its architectural significance solely from the vigor and consequence of its own organic proportions. It must be true to itself."[51] And because architecture is the major expression of the spiritual qualities of an era, an organic architecture would both reflect and create the inner cohesion of the epoch.[52]

Gropius firmly advocated machines and mass production. This was modern reality, and students of the arts had to be trained to work with that world; they must not flee into a nostalgia for the past of the supposed individual artistic genius, working away in isolation on his canvas or sculpture. The modern artist had to design lamps, chairs, hinges, everything for mass production. Buildings had to make use of prefabricated materials and standardized plans and modules. Gropius envisioned the factory system moved to the building site, a viewpoint he shared with Taut and others.[53]

Gropius's Bauhaus building, so often remarked upon, was—and is, since it is still standing and in good condition—a fine expression of his design principles and one of the greatest creations of the Weimar era (fig. 5.7). The building is composed of functionally related elements, three cubes linked together by enclosed bridges. Each cube serves distinct functions: workshops and auditorium; classrooms, offices, and library; and studios, dining room, and dormitory. True to modernist principles, the load-bearing structures are hidden, so the exterior becomes a playfield of airy lightness. The horizontal plane of glass interrupted only by light steel is striking. As a result, the workshops and studios were flooded with natural light; when lighted in the evening, the building gave off a compact glow. The Russian writer Ilya Ehrenburg captured the remarkable thought processes and design elements in the building: "When I finally saw the Bauhaus which seems to be cast of one piece like a persistent thought, and its glass walls which form a transparent angle, united with the air and yet separated from it by a distinct will—I stopped instinctively . . . [in] admiration. . . . [It is] a triumph of clarity."[54] The linkage of the cubes is clearly evident, a stirring emblem of Gropius's belief in that hallowed word "organic": all parts are intimately related and no individual element can stand on its own. In addition, Gropius designed houses for the staff and director that are related in style to the main building. In Dessau, Gropius realized his total vision.

But Mendelsohn must have thought that Gropius had gone rather overboard, even if this one building was successful. All his talk of collective work, standardization, and mass production seemed to promote those very aspects of modernity that Mendelsohn feared most, namely, the creation of a society marked by monotony and dominated

Fig. 5.7 Walter Gropius, Bauhaus Building, Dessau, built 1925–26. The most famous building of the Weimar era, the Bauhaus was (and is) a triumphal statement of the modernist aesthetic. Its beauty derived from the materials used in the construction and the building's function. Like Mendelsohn's Schocken store, the repeating bands of glass lighten the structure and provide a wonderful light source for the studios. The building is still in use as a design school and, after a number of renovations, in good condition. Author's photograph.

by the stultified masses. Both were modernists, but Gropius's encompassing vision challenged Mendelsohn's Nietzschean belief in individual creative genius. Moreover, functionalism, according to Mendelsohn, constituted only the preconditions of architecture, the technical requirements with which one begins. But this foundation alone "despite great measurements and clear relation to the technical means does not create great architecture."[55] Great architecture unites function and dynamics. "But only out of this interrelationship between function and dynamic, between reality and unreality, consciousness and unconsciousness, between reason and feeling, calculation and thought, between limits and infinity can emerge the active, living desire for creation, the architect's infatuation with space."[56] "Architectural dynamics," as he later put it, expresses "the tension innate to elastic building materials, of movement and counter movement within the immovable stability of the building itself."[57] An architecture that expressed these tensions, according to Mendelsohn, was a great architecture suitable for the modern condition.

Many others went even further than Mendelsohn in his criticism—and, indeed, included him among those whom they castigated for creating a sterile, materialist, mechanistic architecture that tore men and women from their rootedness in tradition. For many critics the "spiritual revolution" that Taut, Mendelsohn, Gropius, and many other modernists promoted through their writings and their designs was nothing but the factory brought to living quarters, the triumph of "mechanistic" civilization over the true spirituality represented by specifically German culture and history. The modernists, in this view, degraded man to a mere material being; modern architects had not transformed the degradation of the age but had succumbed to it, indeed, fostered it. For the critics, beauty and history were inseparable; a beautiful building had to evoke timeless values and historical rootedness. The modernists had performed radical surgery, shorn modern buildings of every association with a deeper, spiritually endowed past. The modernists were not artists; they were merely engineers.

Many critics, for example, found the efficient, airy, predesigned houses of Taut, Gropius, and Le Corbusier sterile and cold, the banning of knickknacks and older furniture a sign of a failed sensibility, one that gave no credence to history and tradition. One critic claimed that only a rootless intellectual, a nomad, could feel at home in Le Corbusier's concrete and glass structure, part of the famed Weissenhof Siedlung in Stuttgart. It seemed disconnected from everything around it, as if it had only "condescended to land for a moment on earth." It was not everyone's desire, he opined, to fold away the bed during the day and live without a bedroom in which to make love, rest, dream, conceive, give birth, and die. Dramatic, yes; livable, no.[58] Another critic claimed that Weissenhof had been "designed and executed in complete ignorance of all the things a family needs to make a dwelling a home." The interiors of the houses crafted by Mies van der Rohe lacked appropriate landings and railings, and this omission, along with immense, drafty windows, made the homes downright dangerous to children. Facing south, they allowed in too much sunlight, sure to spoil food in the kitchen, while stoves were positioned right in the way of traffic, and no place was provided for weather-drenched clothes.[59] Artistic, yes; sterile, also yes. And Taut's design for the Onkel Toms Siedlung set off the "Zehlendorf roof war," as the newspapers dubbed it, with conservative critics charging that the flat roof was distinctly un-German.

The Bauhaus itself had been subject to withering critique from its very founding, and Gropius was ultimately forced to move the school from Weimar to Dessau.[60] Even worse, the attack on the modernists became entwined with ever-growing race thinking. In 1926, Emil Högg, a professor of architecture at Dresden, attacked the new buildings as representing a "nomadic architecture" that would lead to "uprootedness, spiritual impoverishment and proletarianization."[61] The total break with the past that the modernists promoted was nothing less than "bolshevist" architecture. In contrast, Högg lauded the architects who based their work on traditional buildings even as they developed new designs. This was a truly German "folk architecture." The words Högg applied to modern architecture—nomadic, uprooted, bolshevist—were the very terms that the Right used in relation to Jews and the republic in general. The conservative architect Paul Schultze-Naumburg, one of the modernists' main adversaries, was even more blatant. Modern architecture, he wrote, was a direct reflection of the Jewish blood that had despoiled German racial stock. The modernists were not "real" men; they were "the uncreative men, formless and colorless, the half and quarter men, unbeautiful men who desire no beauty, who set their stamp upon our time."[62] What they build represents a "soulless, godless, mechanical world." The truly German house, he claimed, "gives one the feeling that it grows out of the soil . . . like a tree that sinks its roots deep in the interior of the soil and forms a union with it. It is this that gives us our understanding of home [*Heimat*], of a bond with blood and earth."[63] For those like Högg and Schulze-Naumburg, the modernist project was a nightmare of dehistoricization and spiritual impoverishment. Only the purification of the race could lead to a true revival of art and architecture.[64]

Taut, Mendelsohn, and Gropius went about their work with the greatest of expectations. A new, innovative architecture, rooted in the conditions of modernity, they believed, would surmount the fragmentation of contemporary life. Modern architecture would heal the rift between technology and beauty, man and nature, the individual and society. It would evoke life rather than the mass death and destruction of total war, and would fulfill the revolution's promise—as they understood it—of renewal and rebirth. Organic, crystalline, spiritual—these are the terms that coursed through the writings of Taut, Mendelsohn, and Gropius.

And they were hardly alone. They were members of an extraordinary generation of European architects, all of whom were born in the 1880s. In addition to Taut, Mendelsohn, and Gropius, the list includes Le Corbusier, Ernst May, Mies van der Rohe, Martin Wagner, Hendricus Theodorus Wijdeveld, and many others. All of them were strongly influenced by the great political and cultural debates and movements in the years before World War I. In architecture, that included the first stirrings of modernism and extensive discussions about housing reform, in Germany and in many other European countries. As a student in Munich, Mendelsohn moved in the circles of the Blue Rider group with Franz Marc, Wassily Kandinsky, and others. Taut was among the avant-garde artists who frequented Der Sturm (The Storm) gallery, which promoted expressionist and abstract art. Taut especially was influenced by anarchist and socialist writers, and both Taut and Mendelsohn read Leo Tolstoy very seriously, not only for his great literary talents but also for the spiritual and nonviolent beliefs that marked the great novelist's later years. Gropius worked in the office of Peter Behrens, Germany's first great modern architect. And all three were influenced by Dutch and Belgian architects, notably Henry van de Velde, who before World War I were starting to forge a modernist architecture with reformist social impulses. The cultural world of the generation of the 1880s was European, not just German, and even American if one includes Frank Lloyd Wright (born in 1867, a bit older than the others), who strongly influenced Mendelsohn and Gropius. This was also the generation that very directly experienced World War I, that sensed the shattering of the world by the massive loss of life and material destruction of the war. They knew that the pre-1914 world was gone forever. The German and European revolutions of 1917–21 gave them new possibilities, and they believed that now, finally, they could help create a more peaceful and harmonious world through the design of homes, factories, research institutes, and stores—all in modernist fashion.

Taut and Mendelsohn resisted the absolute functionalism of Gropius, Le Corbusier, and other great architects of the twentieth century. They worked with the same materials and designed the same clean buildings, but they moderated the hard lines of functionalism and, sometimes, added playful elements to their structures. Not everything they built was wonderful. Some of Mendelsohn's buildings of the 1920s are fairly mundane examples of commercial architecture. But his best work vibrantly expressed the possibilities of the age, whether oriented toward science (the Einstein Tower) or business and consumption (the Schocken department store), with poetic grace and verve. Some of Gropius's designs prefigure the worst of post–World War II architecture, as does Taut's Carl Legien housing development, built in 1929–30 in the Prenzlauerberg neighborhood of Berlin. The Legien buildings resemble an earlier, smaller version of the anonymous, sterile, large-scale public housing developments built after World War II all over the Western world and beyond. But Gropius's Bauhaus school remains the signature work of Weimar modernism, and Taut's best work, at Onkel Toms and Britz, joined together social reform and an aesthetic sensitivity to create a model of engaged architecture. And even the Carl Legien apartments were well designed to receive plenty of sunlight.[65] Many Germans who moved into the new housing developments recalled, years later, a great improvement in their living conditions. They have fond, even warm, memories of the apartments and the communities—even if, to the chagrin of the architects, they kept their oil paintings and ornamented furniture, even if the residents endured flat roofs and strict regulations that, for example, banned cats, allowed wash to be hung out only on particular days, and banished bars to the surrounding neighborhood.[66]

In the early 1930s, Erich Mendelsohn began collaborating with his fellow architect Hendricus Theodorus Wijdeveld, from Holland, and the French painter Amédée Ozenfant to found a new arts and crafts school, the European Mediterranean Academy. It drew other prominent participants from a variety of European countries, including the composer Paul Hindemith. The academy would be an advanced arts school that would teach architecture, painting, sculpture, ceramics, textile design, typography, theater, music and dance, and photography and film.[67] The subject matter that would be taught would be similar to that of the Bauhaus, but Mendelsohn and his collaborators were not so rigorously antihistoricist as Gropius and other Bauhaus artists. They deliberately chose a Mediterranean location for their school so they could draw from the historical heritage of the ancient world. Mendelsohn and many of his collaborators were modernists with a difference; they forged their own special blends of expressionism and functionalism. But they founded the European Mediterranean Academy at a highly inauspicious moment. It was 1933, just about the low point of the world economic crisis and the year the Nazis came to power. The academy never came to be.

Just a few years earlier, in 1930, the Mendelsohns had moved into a house in Berlin that he had designed. It was (and is—it still exists and is privately owned) an elegant, modern building situated near the Havel in one of Berlin's western districts. Its rectangular structure ran horizontal to the ground and let in streams of light. The interior was decorated with furniture specially designed by Mendelsohn. A terrace offered a lovely view of the Havel and, in the summer, was the setting for many concerts, including performances by the architect's wife, Luise Mendelsohn, an accomplished cellist. The house became a meeting place for many of the great intellectual figures of Weimar Germany, as well as visiting intellectuals. Einstein was a regular guest, and the early proponents of a European union, like Richard Coudenhove-Kalergi, also visited. On 31 March 1933, two months after Hitler's assumption of power, the Mendelsohns each packed a suitcase and left the house, and began an exile and a peripatetic existence that took them to Holland, Britain, Palestine, and, finally, the United States.[68] They never returned to their home.

Bruno Taut was abroad when the Nazis took power on 30 January 1933. He soon returned to Germany to find the situation drastically altered. He was thrown out of the Prussian Academy of Arts, along with Erich Mendelsohn and other exponents of modernism. From reliable sources he heard reports that he was a wanted man, and on 10 March 1933 he fled Germany, first to Switzerland, then to Japan, where architectural colleagues offered him the opportunity to lecture and write, and finally to Turkey, where Martin Wagner had also fled. Taut had never been of the hardiest constitution and often lived on scant means. In exile his health deteriorated seriously, and he died in Istanbul in 1938.

Walter Gropius had left the Bauhaus for private practice in 1928. But he was shaken when the Nazis closed the school in April 1933, just three months after they had taken power. In the Nazi view, the Bauhaus epitomized modern, "degenerate" art. Gropius tried to keep his practice going in Germany, but in 1934, he, too, went into exile. In Britain he had a difficult time finding commissions; in 1937 he left for America, where well-placed allies helped him get reestablished. A major Bauhaus exhibit at the Museum of Modern Art in 1938, heralded by lavish praise from MoMA's fabled director Alfred H. Barr, Jr., contributed greatly to America's enduring fascination with the Bauhaus and its founder.

But in exile, none of the three was able to equal the best of his work of the Weimar years. None of Mendelsohn's later buildings, whether in Palestine or the United States, has quite the verve and excitement of the Einstein Tower or the Schocken department store. In Japan and Turkey, Taut was unable to build at all. Gropius had a very eminent career as a high-flying international architect and chairman of the Architecture Department at Harvard. But none of his later structures had quite the restrained elegance of the Bauhaus building in Dessau, and some were total disasters. The ugly apartment blocks he designed between 1964 and 1968 in the Britz-Buckow-Rudow district of West Berlin are typical examples of drab and sterile post–World War II housing. Even worse is the Pan American building (now Metropolitan Life) in New York City, which he designed with Pietro Belluschi. Opened in 1963, the skyscraper rises like a huge, ugly abscess that covers up the beautiful Beaux-Arts Grand Central Terminal and destroys the elegant sight lines of Park Avenue.

Torn by Nazi repression from their grounding in the turbulent excitement and hopeful optimism of Weimar Germany, Taut, Mendelsohn, and Gropius could never quite find their bearings again, never produced buildings that matched their greatest creations of the 1920s and early 1930s. Nor would modern architecture, later on, be so fully devoted to the public realm as it was in Weimar Germany.

The great buildings of Weimar were not corporate office towers, the self-displays of business wealth and power; they were housing developments, department stores, and educational and research institutions. Sun-drenched apartments, enticing places to shop, and stimulating spaces to learn—that, too, was the promise of Weimar.

6

Sound and Image

Weimar was a cacophony of sounds, a dazzle of images. A couple visiting Berlin from the provinces, emerging from the Anhalter Bahnhof and walking the short stretch to Potsdamer Platz, would feel assaulted by the noise of the traffic and the riot of posters displaying cigarettes, political slogans, cabaret performances, and candidates for the next presidential election. At night, they would be awed by the electrification that lit up the city. Berlin before the war had not been so hectic, so noisy, and so brightly illuminated.

But there were other sounds and images that, by the end of the 1920s, offered new, exciting, and sometimes troubling experiences to both our provincial visitors and urban Berlin sophisticates. In small towns and in the city, Germans attended the cinema regularly and watched melodramas, comedies, travel adventures, and newsreels in grand, newly built movie palaces. They listened to the radio, which caught on like wildfire after its introduction in 1921. Radio brought music, plays, sermons, and news reports into bars and dance halls, and into the privacy of people's homes. Just like Berliners, our visitors from the provinces read the very popular illustrated magazines, splashed throughout with photographs from around the world. They might have visited a gallery that ennobled photography as art, or purchased one of the new, more compact and inexpensive cameras and joined the local photography club. And in both Berlin and the provinces, they listened to records on the plug-in phonograph, which during the 1920s replaced the hand-cranked gramophone. In their homes and even on the beach they listened to American jazz, Italian operas, and German symphonies (in short excerpts, given the limits of the 78 rpm record).

All of these media technologies had been developed before 1914. Photography stretched back to the 1830s and had begun to move into the amateur realm at the end of the nineteenth century. Cinema had emerged in the 1890s, the gramophone a bit earlier, and both had become increasingly popular down to World War I. The army used primitive radios during the war. Lithography, linotype, and other printing advances had allowed for the development of illustrated weeklies in the decades before 1914 as well.

But Weimar was most definitely the boom period for all of these new forms of communication and expression, which proliferated rapidly and proved immensely popular. Major technological improvements enhanced the quality of reproductions and transmissions, whether over the airwaves, on a very large screen, or on pages printed by newly developed, rapid-fire printing presses.[1] As consumer costs came down, many Germans were able to purchase radio sets, phonographs, and cameras. These new technologies appeared in a society that was already "mass," a society in which the majority now lived in urban areas, most people acquired their daily needs through paid labor and purchases in the marketplace, and at least minimal public education was virtually universal. The combination of technological advancements and mass society diffused the new sounds and images into the very pores of German life in the 1920s and early 1930s. They exposed Germans to worlds beyond their own borders—to photo images of strikes in Shanghai; the sounds, broadcast with only a few minutes' delay, of a heavyweight boxing match in New York or a concert in Paris; or the sight, produced in Hollywood, of Charlie Chaplin facing the elements and his brutal adversary in frigid Alaska.

The widespread diffusion of new sounds and images also raised profound and troubling questions. Were films and photographs art, or just crass commercial items? Who should determine what Germans heard over the airwaves or purchased at their newsstands? Did hearing classical music on a flat disc spinning around on an electrical device degrade the experience of listening? The churches, the state-run schools, the art academies, the censorship office—all the official and semiofficial institutions that, before 1918, controlled the words and images that Germans encountered in the public sphere—suddenly found their authority undermined, first by the revolution and the creation of the republic, then by the flourishing of the new mass media. Photography and film, recordings and radio became yet another battlefield of conflict over the scope and meaning of modernity. All the while, Germans flocked to the cinema, turned on their receivers, bought magazines, and danced to the strains of recorded jazz, and some of Weimar's greatest cultural figures created entirely new genres of visual and sonoral artistry.

For decades cameras were big, boxy items whose cost and complications put them well beyond the reach of the average person. The large cameras of the past had to be laboriously transported and set up. The subjects had to remain still for minutes on end as the chemically treated plate became exposed to light. Virtually the only shots possible were set pieces: the married couple with the wife sitting, the man standing very erect behind her, the no less carefully arranged image of an entire family, situated in the garden with the house in the background, a symbol of bourgeois prosperity and propriety. Occasionally, a photographer like August Sander might lie in wait with his tripod and box and suddenly capture three young, unsuspecting farm men in their dapper best, on their way to a dance (fig. 6.1). Sander's photo communicated the unexpected, the spontaneous moment when the subjects' eyes met the camera lens. But an image of this type was a rarity, even for so accomplished a photographer as Sander.[2]

All that had begun to change in the 1880s and 1890s, when George Eastman's company in the United States, ultimately named Eastman Kodak, started to develop roll film for cameras to replace the bulky plates used to capture a single image. Eastman Kodak, as well as many of its competitors in the United States and in Europe, also started to produce smaller cameras specifically designed for the new kind of film. As with computers at the end of the twentieth century, high-end items for professionals remained very expensive, but in the 1890s, smaller, more compact cameras became affordable at least for the middle classes. As yet there existed no uniform design or film size. But just before the war, the motion picture industry adopted 35 mm film as its standard. An enterprising New York businessman recognized that leftover lengths of movie film could be

Fig. 6.1 August Sander, "Young Farmers on the Way to a Dance," Westerwald, 1914. One of Sander's most famous photographs in his effort to capture the full range of German life. © 2006 Die Photographische Sammlung / SK Stiftung Kultur—August Sander Archiv, Cologne / ARS, NY.

purchased for one-third the normal price. Manufacturers all over Europe and the United States, including Eastman Kodak, followed his lead and adopted 35 mm film as the standard for most cameras.

But the truly great technical innovation came in 1925 with the introduction of the Leica by the German firm Leitz, based in Wetzlar. The camera had been under development since 1911, and the final version was a marvel that merged compact size, easy-to-use 35 mm roll film, and outstanding optics. The Leica was so small that it could be hidden away under a man's jacket or vest, and could be whipped out in an instant to capture the action at hand. Photojournalism and the Leica developed together, though it took a few years for the camera really to catch on. Then it spawned countless imitations from manufacturers all around the world.[3] The Leica itself was (and is) quite expensive; the imitations sometimes were not, and they, too, contributed to the spread of photography as an amateur hobby.

Photography is, of course, a reproducible medium.[4] A painting or sculpture is executed once. A photographic negative can be printed many times, and a skilled photographer can alter the tones and effect of the image in the printing process. Nothing disseminated photography so much as the illustrated magazines of the 1920s. The first and most successful was the Ullstein house's *Berliner Illustrirte Zeitung* (*BIZ*), which had been founded before World War I. The *Münchener Illustrierte Presse* followed in 1923, and the *Kölnische Illustrierte Zeitung* in 1926. Even the Communist Party got into the act with its highly successful *Arbeiter-Illustrierte-Zeitung* (*AIZ*). In 1930, the *Berliner Illustrirte* alone had a circulation of 1.85 million, and the *AIZ* a highly respectable 350,000.[5]

Readers who opened the pages of any of the magazines—including the communist *AIZ*—were taken on all sorts of adventures. They experienced (virtually, of course) the Pyramids from the air, a central African dance, the opening of the Indian parliament, or, in the middle of the German winter and in the company of a German film star, California's baking sun and lush vegetation. Other images brought home to Germany political conflict in China, an earthquake in Japan, the Oxford-Cambridge crew competition, a race in Shanghai, and the erection of the newest technological marvel, a radio tower that reached up to the sky. In and around the photographs, serialized novels, and sports reports streamed a flood of advertisements, even in the communist *Arbeiter-Illustrierte* (though in comparatively restrained form). Lifestyle products (as we would now call them) were especially prominent. Cigarettes, perfumes, health and beauty creams, lingerie, coffee, chocolate, champagne—everything one needed for the good life, and to make one look ten years younger, as the readers of the *Berliner Illustrirte* were so often advised. The men were always handsome, the women always beautiful and so often out shopping. Advertisers urged men to use various creams to keep their hair; they tutored women on how to keep slender and look youthful through a healthy lifestyle and, if all else failed, the proper lingerie.

Indeed, the house ethos at Ullstein, as the novelist and editor Vicki Baum noted in her memoirs, demanded photographs that expressed the joy of life (*Lebensfreude*). Virtually all the covers of the *BIZ* showed people smiling and laughing or enjoying the intensity of a sports match (fig. 6.2).[6] They were almost always young. Communists did not smile much, to judge by the covers of the *AIZ*, unless they were Russian. German Communists had too many tough political struggles ahead of them to laugh and smile, but they were often youthful and good-looking even when very determined. The *BIZ* provided politics lite—a photo spread of a new cabinet, a report on an international economics meeting, civil unrest somewhere far removed from Germany. The *AIZ*, in contrast, offered its readers a much heavier dose of politics and in proletarian style—demonstrations and clashes with the police in Germany, revolutionary uprisings in China, the great economic and educational advances in the Soviet Union.[7]

But what did this flood of images in the magazines signify?—aside from the fact that the photographs were enjoyable to look at. Did photographs constitute art? Or were they simply a crass form of commercialism? Did they capture reality better than any other medium—painting, sculpture, the written word—or alter the very forms of visual perception? Photography in particular raised these questions because it constituted the reproducible medium par excellence, and because by the 1920s, amateurs as well as professionals could be prolific and proficient wielders of the camera and manipulators of the negative. Photography blurred all the boundaries—between art and commerce, high and low culture, professionalism and amateurism: trends only accentuated by the establishment of photography as a formal profession in the mid-1920s. Photographers were not yet the paparazzi of Rome in

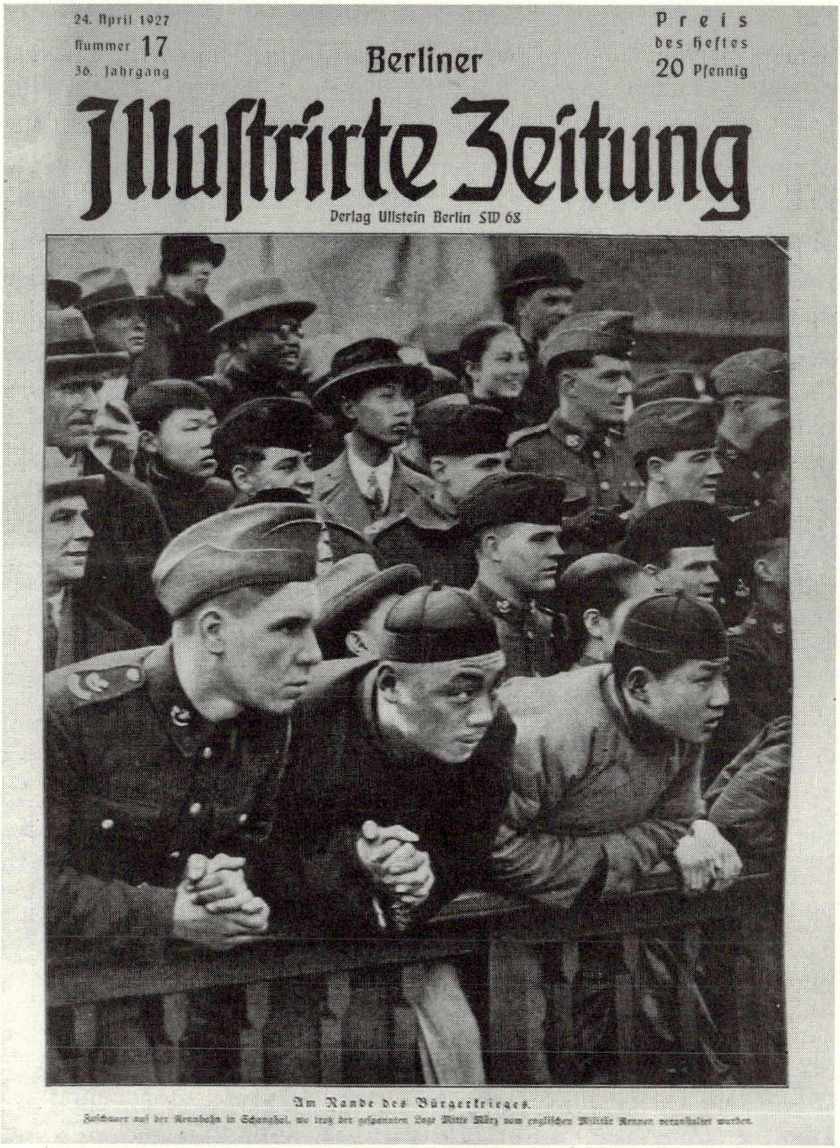

Fig. 6.2 Cover, *Berliner Illustrirte Zeitung*, 24 April 1927. "On the Edge of Civil War." Despite the tense situation in China, the *BIZ* reports, crowds still go to the races—typical for the weekly's sunny approach to life. No matter what, the fun goes on.

the early 1960s, immortalized (and not in a complimentary fashion) in Federico Fellini's film *La Doce Vita*, or those who incessantly hound present-day movie stars and other celebrities. But in the 1920s the photographic profession had already become a freewheeling, highly competitive, generally male enterprise. As a profession, it was open to new talent, even from among the lower classes or ethnic outsiders like Jews, very unlike the older, more hierarchical professions in the universities, the state bureaucracy, and the army. Most of the publishing houses in the 1920s hired freelance photographers and paid them a fee per photograph accepted—an employment structure that accentuated the competitive nature of the profession. Many photographers easily moved in and around journalism, advertising, and art, personifying the blurred lines that the medium itself signified. Ullstein produced in-house the vast majority of the advertisements that appeared in its pages, and the same photographers that might shoot the opening of a horse race also produced art photos that found their way into advertisements in the *Berliner Illustrirte* and out again into galleries or onto the covers of art magazines.[8]

Weimar-era photographers also broke new aesthetic and theoretical ground. Convinced that photography was *the* artistic medium of modernity, they used camera and pen to define its relationship to other art forms and to our ways of experiencing the world. Two of the greatest photographers of the Weimar period (and beyond) were László Moholy-Nagy and August Sander. Their aesthetic sensibilities and their conception of the medium could not be at greater variance. Together, they represent the artistic possibilities of photography in the 1920s and early 1930s.

Moholy-Nagy was born in Hungary in 1895. Though educated as a lawyer, he had already begun to move in progressive artistic circles before World War I. As Hungarian politics turned more repressive after the short-lived, post–World War I revolution, he decamped for Germany, as did many artists and intellectuals among his compatriots. He arrived in Berlin in 1920 and soon became involved with the Dadaists, though he never quite went for their deliberate absurdism and their constant efforts at provocation. Instead, he was attracted by their commitment to abstract art, their fascination with technology, their freewheeling borrowing from various genres, and the liberated spirit that animated their work.[9] Influenced by the Dadaists, Moholy-Nagy never restricted himself to any single medium. At various times he worked in painting, sculpture, architecture, typography, and film, along with photography. His varied, peripatetic artistry was matched by an outpouring of words. Few practicing artists have written so extensively and incisively about art. Through his entire career, including the exile years in the United States, Moholy-Nagy remained committed to abstract, nonrepresentational art and to the aesthetic possibilities of new technologies. His art probed light and form, more than color (though he did interesting paintings in color as well, and color photography did not come into its own until the later 1930s). The photographs reveal a keen attentiveness to geometric shapes—as individual elements, but even more as total compositions.

In 1922, Walter Gropius, the legendary founder and director of the Bauhaus, saw some of Moholy-Nagy's works at an exhibition and immediately recruited him to teach at the young institution. As discussed in the previous chapter, the Bauhaus, the school that would have so great an impact on twentieth-century art and architecture, was more than just a design aesthetic: it was a utopian ideology. Its founders and early participants believed that the modernist aesthetic could overcome the alienation that was the pervasive condition of modernity, and make humankind "whole" again.

Moholy-Nagy ran the metals workshop, but he also taught photography and much else besides, and edited the school's book publication series. Gropius must have sensed a kindred spirit, since Moholy-Nagy, though never very active politically, articulated similar kinds of utopian strivings in relation to art. He advocated the concept of *Gesamtwerk*, a total work. He distinguished his views from the composer Richard Wagner's famous notion of a *Gesamtkunstwerk*, a total work of art, in which opera would integrate all the various elements of art. Moholy-Nagy, like Gropius and so many others in the wake of war and revolution, raised the stakes even higher: he sought to break down the barriers between life and art (which Wagner's concept maintained) as well as among all the various genres and media of art. As he wrote in 1925:

> With its ramifications and its fragmenting action in every field, specialisation had destroyed all belief in the possibility of embracing the totality of all fields, *the wholeness of life*. . . . What we need is not the '*Gesamtkunstwerk*', alongside and separated from which life flows by, but a synthesis of all the vital impulses

> spontaneously forming itself into the all-embracing *Gesamtwerk* (life) which abolishes all isolation, in which *all individual* accomplishments proceed from a biological necessity and culminate in a *universal* necessity.[10]

An unrealistic perspective, with its belief in the possibility of eliminating all fissures in life, of creating one great harmonious, organic whole? To be sure. Slightly crazy? Yes. But very much in keeping with the aims of Gropius and his fellow architects Bruno Taut and Erich Mendelsohn and so many other artists of the Weimar era. These unrealistic, even utopian, ambitions led Moholy-Nagy to create works of enduring beauty that are also profound meditations on the light-space coordinates in which we live.

In a photograph of Berlin, "New Year's Morning," ca. 1930, we see the metropolis turned sparse (fig. 6.3). Instead of the usual crush of people and vehicles, we see a lone bicyclist and a couple walking. We are drawn to the three figures, who seem so strangely alone in the big city, but even more, to the lines and shadows. The image is taken at an elevation above street level (actually, from Moholy-Nagy's apartment).[11] It must be early morning, given the long shadows thrown by the bicyclist and the strollers. The figures and the shadows almost bisect the trolley lines, which make up the center of the photo and to which the sidewalks run parallel. They are also almost bisected by the shadows of the electrical lines that run overhead, which we do not see, only their shadows. "New Year's Morning" is a study in geometry and light, of lines and shadows.

Moholy-Nagy was especially drawn to shooting from an elevation. An untitled view from the Berlin radio tower, shot around 1928, composes all sorts of geometric forms (fig. 6.4).[12] We are drawn, first of all, to the soaring tower and the regular, repeating angular patterns of its steel-grid structure, which are replicated in the beginnings of its shadow. But the angular lines are offset by the concentric circles below, made up of outdoor tables and chairs and umbrellas set around a fountain. These then are offset by the angular arrangement of other tables and chairs around the rectangular base of the tower. One cannot see—again, it is early morning to judge by the shadows—but can imagine Berliners enjoying their beer and sausages in the sunshine, in the shadow of that great marker of modernity, the radio tower. But more important is the total sense of a variety of forms, of

Fig. 6.3 László Moholy-Nagy, "New Year's Morning," ca. 1930. The artist often shot his photos from an elevation. Here the usual bustling metropolis is quiet and becomes a study in lines and shadows. © 2006 Artist Rights Society (ARS), New York / VG Bildkunst, Bonn.

Fig. 6.4 László Moholy-Nagy, Untitled, radio tower, ca. 1928. Once again shooting from an elevation, Moholy-Nagy creates a study of various geometric forms, of repeating angles, grids, and circles. © 2006 Artist Rights Society (ARS), New York / VG Bildkunst, Bonn.

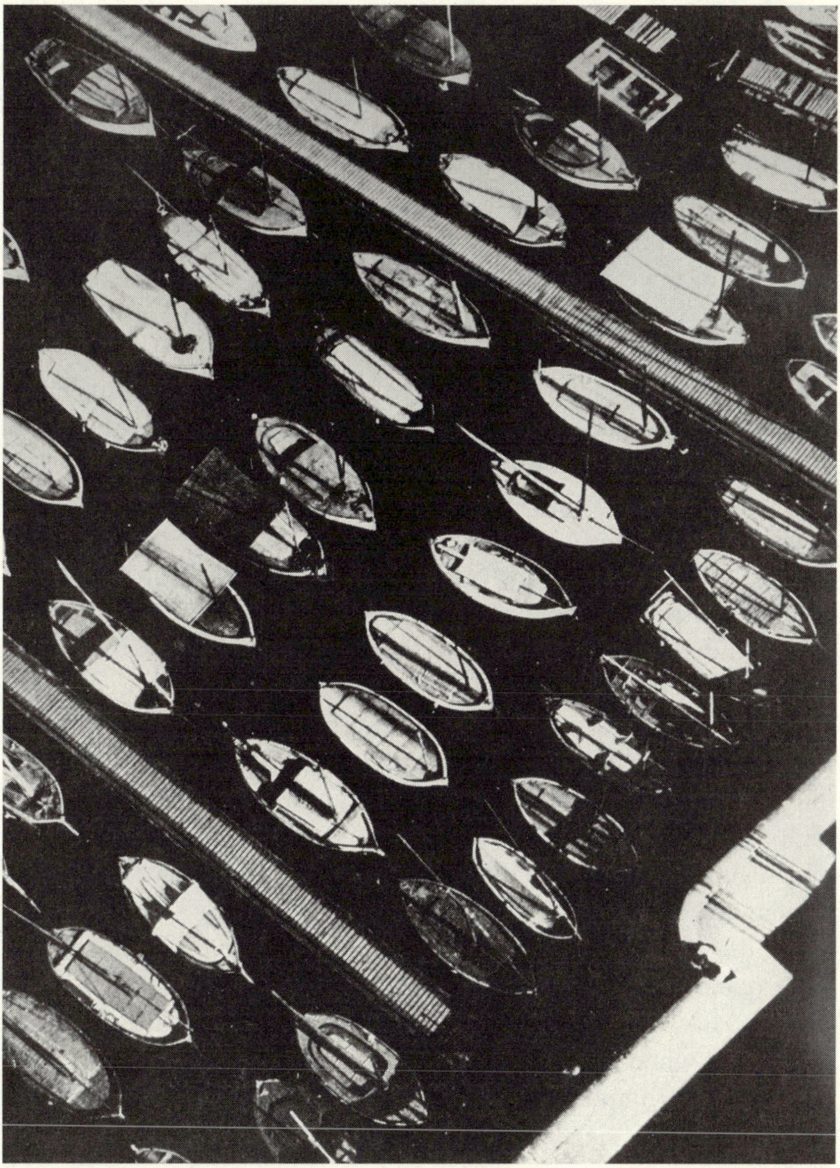

Fig. 6.5 László Moholy-Nagy, "Boats in Old Port of Marseilles," 1929. Moholy-Nagy's photographs are meditations on light and form. Here the repeating pattern of the boats is offset by varying shades of light. Some of the boats are so white that they almost leap off the print, others blend into the darkly-hued water in which they sit. © 2006 Artist Rights Society (ARS), New York / VG Bildkunst, Bonn.

angles, lines, and circles, that make up the entire composition, and, indeed, our lived world.

Finally, "Boats in the Old Port of Marseilles," from 1929, again shows Moholy-Nagy's preoccupation with repeating forms (fig. 6.5). The boats are all lined up in a more or less regular pattern, split into three groups by the piers. The lowered masts, set lengthwise in the middle of the boats, accentuate the regularity and the flow of the image from lower right to left, a sense of flow accentuated by the jagged pier in the lower right-hand corner. The masts set upright cast shadows that mimic the masts set horizontally. But here Moholy-Nagy worked with light to disrupt the regularity of forms. Some of the boats are so white that they almost leap off the printed image; others are so dark that they seem to blend into the darkness of the water. The bright white of the jagged pier adds to the contrastive effect.

Light and form: Moholy-Nagy's photographs play on those elements so intrinsic to living in the world that we barely think about them. And working with light and form, he created beauty. But he went further. In line with the Bauhaus ethos of finding beauty in the very materials used in composition, Moholy-Nagy argued fervently that photography is about the manipulation of light, hence the form most suited to the modern age.[13] (One can imagine that the dance of night lights in electrified Berlin had a profound impact on his thinking.) Painting was the medium of the past, photography that of the present and future. Painting was concerned with the static representation of color; photography rendered composition and movement, and expands our abilities to see far beyond what the naked eye could capture. Each medium has its own internal laws, Moholy-Nagy wrote, and when those of photography are finally understood, "representational composition will reach a peak and a perfection which could never be achieved by craft (manual) [i.e., painting] means."[14]

Photography, then, was not simply another creative medium; it opened up new vistas of life. "The traditional painting has become a historical relic and is finished with. Eyes and ears have been opened and are filled at every moment with a wealth of optical and phonetic wonders. A few more vitally progressive years, a few more ardent followers of photographic techniques and it will be a matter of universal knowledge that photography was one of the most important factors in the dawn of a new life."[15] Moholy-Nagy's lofty claims for photography's superiority over other media are charming (though probably not to a painter) and naive and, like many of his other pronouncements, rather over the top. But his ideas fueled his art, and without his belief in the life-possibilities of photography, without his drive to push the medium as far as possible, he would never have been able to create his great compositions. In that sense, he represents the very best of the Weimar spirit, the expressive utopianism that believed in the future and sought to penetrate the very meaning of modernity, in Moholy-Nagy's case, the meaning of photography, that most modern of media.

The photograms he produced in the mid-1920s are the very expression of this philosophy. Photograms are "camera-less" images created by a chemical process of layering different exposures on light-sensitive paper. At the very same time, Moholy-Nagy in Berlin, Man Ray in Paris, and El Lissitzky in Moscow were all experimenting with its possibilities. The medium enabled Moholy-Nagy to create images of perfect forms that seemed to float in the air, all demonstrating by their various exposure times the properties of light. His best photograms have an almost three-dimensional feel to them; sometimes the various forms are distinct, and sometimes they seem to fade into one another. Moholy-Nagy's near-obsession with light and form is evident in the total compositional effect of his photos and in the ethereal lightness of his photograms; they demonstrate his artistic brilliance and the possibilities of photography as a medium that does much more than promote the newest consumer products: it meditates on the coordinates of life (fig. 6.6).

Moholy-Nagy's somewhat older contemporary, August Sander (born in 1876), was no theoretician of art. He expressed himself mostly through his camera, and only rarely through writings, lectures, and teaching, the panoply of activities, in addition to the creation of art, that lent a certain manic air to Moholy-Nagy's life. Nor did Sander work in a variety of media. Sander had one great idea, and he spent forty years realizing it: he sought to photograph the entire spectrum of life among the German people. He began his project before World War I and kept at it through all the regime changes of twentieth-century German history. His great project was similar in ambition to Edward Steichen's Family of Man, first exhibited at the Museum of Modern Art in New York and a quintessential post– World War II, post-Nazi effort to depict the "oneness" of humanity in all its diversity.[16] Sander's oeuvre,

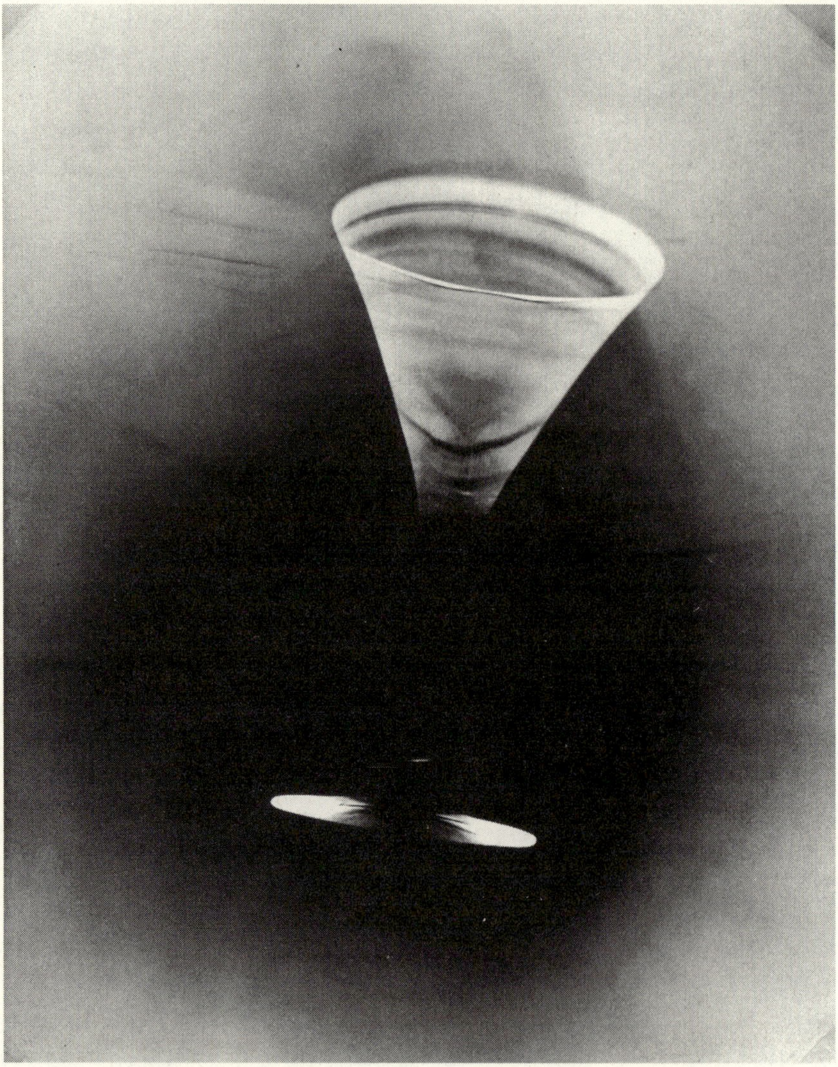

Fig. 6.6 László Moholy-Nagy, Photogram: wine glass, ca. 1926. One of the artist's camera-less photographs made by layering different exposures on light-sensitive paper. The result is an almost surreal image of ethereal lightness. © 2006 Artist Rights Society (ARS), New York / VG Bildkunst, Bonn.

though restricted to Germans, was even larger. It consisted of more than forty thousand negatives, which, tragically, were lost to a fire in 1946. Nonetheless, enough negatives and prints remained that his monumental labors can still be appreciated.

Sander had already had a successful career as a studio photographer in Cologne before World War I. His first publication brought his work to a much larger audience. *Antlitz der Zeit* (Face of Our Time), published in 1929 with an introduction by the great writer Alfred Döblin, was an immediate sensation.[17] In its grand ambitions, "Man of the Twentieth Century," Sander's title for his work, is a quintessential Weimar project—democratic in scope, grand in ambition—even though he had begun it before the war. Sander was a realist who despised the abstract work and theorizing of someone like Moholy-Nagy. In Sander's view, photography, better than any other medium, has the ability to capture people and landscapes "as they really are." In style and temperament, his approach accorded well with New Objectivity, the prevalent artistic style of the latter half of the 1920s, rather than with the expressionism of the immediate postwar years. New Objectivity emphasized realism, modulated tones, and clean lines. As Sander wrote in conjunction with an exhibition of his photos in Cologne in 1927:

> Nothing seemed to me more appropriate than to project an image of our time with absolute fidelity to nature by means of photography. . . . [Photography] can reproduce things with grandiose beauty, but also with cruel truthfulness; and it can also deceive incredibly. We must be able to endure seeing the truth, but above all we should pass it on to our fellow men and to posterity. . . . Nothing is more hateful to me than photography sugar-coated with gimmicks, poses, and false effects. Therefore, let me speak the truth in all honesty about our age and the people of our age.[18]

Sander believed unquestionably that he could depict the full panorama of the German people and thereby create an essential historical document. His photographs are marked by a strong humanitarian impulse. He depicted not only the respectable members of society, but also the handicapped, vagabonds, effete artists, Communists, androgynous women, and others. He issued no judgments in his photography, offered no pronouncements (figs. 6.1, 6.7, 6.8). He took people as they were. For precisely these reasons the Nazis banned his work: Sander showed all sorts of Germans who did not fit the Aryan ideal and whom the Nazis persecuted.

Sander's photographs are striking. At the same time, there is a certain

Fig. 6.7 August Sander, "Circus Workers," Düren, 1930. Sander did not shy away from photographing figures marginalized in German society, like these circus workers. As a result, he was persecuted by the Nazis. © 2006 Die Photographische Sammlung / SK Stiftung Kultur—August Sander Archiv, Cologne / ARS, NY.

Fig. 6.8 August Sander, "Unemployed Man," Cologne, 1928. Sander depicts the desperate circumstances of the unemployed, even before the onset of the Great Depression. © 2006 Die Photographische Sammlung / SK Stiftung Kultur—August Sander Archiv, Cologne / ARS, NY.

closed-off character to his work, a certain provincial element: all he could think about was Germany and Germans. A kind of national arrogance is at work, evident especially in the title, as if photographs of Germans sufficed to render a full picture of humankind in the twentieth century. And Sander's belief in physiognomy—that outward appearance revealed the inner essence of an individual and the group to which he or she belonged—while common enough in its day, has an uncomfortable affinity with Nazi racial ideology despite the firm anti-Nazi commitments of the Sander family, which resulted in the death of the eldest son in the Nazi prison to which he had been consigned because of his resistance activities. In many ways, Sander never really left his beloved Westerwald, the provincial, rural area in the far western part of Germany where he had grown up.

After World War II, Sander would be showered with honors, and his work continues to be exhibited in Germany and abroad. Moholy-Nagy, like so many of Weimar's great artists and intellectuals, had to leave Germany. He finally landed in Chicago, where he became a revered teacher at his own design school. But his efforts to establish a New Bauhaus foundered, and he never quite achieved the renown he deserved.[19] While Moholy-Nagy developed photography as an art of abstraction, an intellectualized engagement with light and form, the very elements of the medium and of life itself, Sander believed in the camera's ability to capture reality. Both were brilliant photographers, but it is Moholy-Nagy who probed more deeply and pushed further the possibilities of his chosen medium—and thereby personified the very best of Weimar Germany.

Photography was of course closely linked, technically and artistically, to that other medium of visual imagery, film. From the 1890s down to World War I, moving pictures were most often shown in small, dingy halls or in individual booths set up by traveling carnivals and circuses. Few Germans would claim proudly that they had seen the latest offering of a renowned studio or a popular film star. Watching movies still had a disreputable connotation, and the admission of attraction was something that deserved to be heard in confession, not in public.

But in Weimar, Germans descended in droves upon the movie houses. They watched melodramas, comedies, adventures, and news-

Fig. 6.9 Erich Mendelsohn, Universum Movie Theater, Berlin, built 1926–28. One of the great movie houses built in Berlin in the 1920s with signature features of Mendelsohn's style: the repeating bands of glass and the curved structure. Today it is a major theater, the Schaubühne. Author's photograph.

reels, and read reviews in the newspapers. They viewed films produced at the Babelsberg studios outside of Berlin, or in Hollywood, Moscow, and many other places around the world. Even in smaller towns movie theaters acquired a dramatic architecture and attracted crowds on a daily basis. In large cities like Berlin, movie halls became palaces. The Gloria-Filmpalast in Berlin, built like a baroque theater in a conscious attempt to win legitimacy for this new form of popular entertainment, seated sixteen hundred people. The Capitol-Filmpalast had space for fifteen hundred.[20] Erich Mendelsohn's Universum-Lichtspielhaus, built between 1926 and 1928, was a stunning example of modernist architecture joined to that most modern of entertainment forms, the cinema. Its striking functional design and curved exterior informed the building with a sense of dynamic movement (fig. 6.9). Inside, the sweep of the balcony and the seating provided a similar dynamism—exterior and interior design played off one another. "All lines and masses converge," Mendelsohn wrote, "as with a camera, towards the focus of the screen to which the whole audience is looking."[21]

The Universum mirrored exactly the innovative character of film, its qualities of dynamic movement, of displacement, of spectacle. Through film one is taken to dreamworlds far away from one's present circumstances. Cinema draws out the emotions—of fear, excitement, or love, or all at the same time. It entertains, and it may even create beauty. And it can make people think about their lives, and, beyond, about the meaning of reality. Weimar cinema did all this and more, and Germans responded. Like so many other people around the globe, they were attracted by the particular power of visual images, especially when displayed on a larger-than-life screen, which transported them to other worlds and stimulated their thoughts and emotions.

Today we remember the great films of the Weimar era—*The Cabinet of Dr. Caligari*, *Metropolis*, *M*, *The Blue Angel*, and many others. They broke new ground technically and artistically, and reflected the best of the Weimar spirit by probing individual and collective psychologies, passion and desire, the modern cityscape, and death. But in fact the vast majority of films that Germans viewed were simple melodramas, which played to packed houses around the country. Or Charlie Chaplin comedies. Or, especially in the early 1920s, dramas with a strong literary and historical dimension, in which German filmmakers sought to make movies out of classic books and heroic historical personages and events. But these historical and classical films did not work, not as movies. They were too tied to the high cultural tradition out of which they came, and to the formal structures of the theater. Cinema did not just entail moving a play from live performance to film. The camera's capacity to shoot rapidly and from different angles; the varied impact of lighting; the ability of directors to cut and paste the flow of images—all that opened up entirely new aesthetic possibilities, which the German film industry was slow to recognize.[22] Partly as a result, the very large and powerful Universal-Film-Aktiengesellschaft (Universal Film Company, or UFA) fell into bankruptcy and had to be bailed out in 1925 by MGM and Paramount, which gave the American companies substantial control over German film production. And MGM and Paramount wanted little competition for their American products, though they soon had to be bailed out as well. In 1927, the right-wing industrial magnate Alfred

Hugenberg bought out UFA. Now the largest German film-producing company received a substantial inflow of capital, though it still faced economic difficulties. Hugenberg was interested primarily in profits, of course, and sometimes artistic films—or at least films we now consider artistic—fit the bill.

Under UFA's banner as well as those of smaller production companies, Weimar cinema flourished. The early postwar films—before UFA's bankruptcy—have since come to be lionized as shining examples of expressionism. Not simple efforts to capture reality on film, films (and paintings and literature) in the expressionist mode probed the psychology of the protagonists—and of the audience. They emphasized emotional complexity and the layered levels of consciousness. Reality was not simple and certainly not readily apparent. What went on in the depths of consciousness, individual and collective, was often more "real," certainly more meaningful, than surface appearances.

The oft-cited, sterling example of expressionist filmmaking is *The Cabinet of Dr. Caligari*, which premiered in 1920. With its painted stage sets clearly culled from the theater, its innovative camera angles, and its rather creepy main figures, the movie presented viewers with a highly ambiguous picture of reality and motivation. Was the doctor or his patient responsible for the murder that takes place? Are dreamworlds more "real" than "reality"? To whom do we give up our autonomy as individuals? Is there such autonomy, or are we all enmeshed in the nightmarish dreamworld of Dr. Caligari? The director, Robert Wiene, offered no answers, and it is not even clear that audiences at the time thought about all of these questions as they took the streetcar home from the movie theater. Maybe they simply enjoyed the aura of mystery and fear the film aroused. But film critics from 1920 to the present have had a field day probing the inner meaning of *The Cabinet of Dr. Caligari*—sometimes, as with the great essayist and critic Siegfried Kracauer, seeing in films like *Caligari* a German unconscious longing for an authority figure that they would ultimately find in Adolf Hitler.[23]

Around 1924 filmmaking, like so many of the arts, moved from the hot emotionalism and psychological probings of expressionism to the cooler, more distanced tones of New Objectivity. New Objectivity had a more functional orientation and a concern with outward appearances and harmonies—of man with his built environment; of internal design, including furnishings, with external architecture; of human labor and machine production. It sought greater realism and less abstraction. It is no accident that New Objectivity emerged after the flush of revolutionary hopes had waned, after the chaos of 1918–19 and especially 1923 had been put to rest, as business principles of rationality and efficiency—rather than revolutionary demands for democracy and justice—took on greater urgency.[24]

On 23 September 1927, one of the greatest of the silent-era German films, *Berlin, Symphony of the City*, premiered in Berlin. Directed by Walter Ruttman, the film, through a montage of images, captures the speed and disorientation, and, at the same time, the regimentation and order, of the Weimar city. It opens with a train approaching Berlin, and the film viewer feels as if he or she is sitting in it, peering out the window as the rural landscape melts into the outskirts of the city and, finally, into the density of buildings that defines the metropolis. Slowly the city comes awake, and Ruttman tracks the parallel movements of people, animals, and machines as the day unfolds. Workers, businessmen, schoolchildren, female office workers, male machine operators—the full diversity of urban life is depicted in the film. The movements of life are matched by the engines of industry that start up slowly, then reach their rapid pace, and slow down again for lunch. But who is directing whom? Are the machines running human life, or are humans running the machines? It is not totally clear, but the film conveys more than a hint of the condition of alienation, of lives that have now lost their autonomy and free will. At the same time, Ruttman's direction plays on the wonder and beauty of industrial production. The regular rhythm of a machine's pistons is juxtaposed with repeating architectural forms, much as Moholy-Nagy's shot from the radio tower depicts the grid patterns of the structure. *Berlin, Symphony of the City* was not much acclaimed or even viewed in its day. Today we can see it as an artistic masterpiece, a celebration of the modern metropolis, with its pace and density and diversity, which, at least at some points, evinces its own kind of beauty—and a worrisome meditation on the power of the machine.

Menschen am Sonntag (People on Sunday), released in 1930, bears some similarities to *Berlin, Symphony of the City*. Another one of Weimar's great silent films, *Menschen am Sonntag* also captures the qualities of Berlin modern. The shots of the factories and bridges and trains take the viewer to the heart of the densely packed city. But it is not about the cityscape alone. In *Berlin, Symphony of the City*, there are no individuals. People are depicted most often as a mass—they are a part of the cityscape, not individuals with their own psychologies and desires and dramas. In *Menschen am Sonntag*, the focus is very much on a handful of young Germans, members of the new middle class, who make their way on the weekend from the city center to the Nikolassee, one of the lovely lakes on the outskirts of Berlin. Two men take up with two women, all seemingly in their twenties. At the lake they frolic and flirt, swim, picnic, and listen to music on the inevitable phonograph. The film has an erotic charge as the women and men dress and undress, run after each other, and develop sexual rivalries. The women both desire the more debonair of the two men; the other, a boorish clown, they try to ignore except when he amuses them. In a scene that must have moved and scandalized audiences of the 1920s, the debonair man and one of the women finally make love in the bushes, to the deep chagrin of her friend.

Menschen am Sonntag was written by Billy Wilder and directed by Robert Siodmak and Edgar G. Ulmer, and the cameraman was Fred Zinnemann—all of whom would go on to stellar Hollywood careers. Their film captured the lives of young, aspiring middle-class Berliners in the 1920s. They participate in the consumer society of their day, rushing to buy the newest records (and one of the women works in a record store). They are nicely attired in the style of the decade, the two women sporting short hair, short skirts, and lithe figures, the men handsomely dressed in jackets and ties even when heading for the beach on a Sunday. They all seem to live apart from their families—their social world consists of other people of their age and class, not the multigenerational family that encased people's lives in the past. They have casual relationships, sexual and otherwise, and have time and money on their hands—at least on the weekend. Like *Berlin, Symphony of the City*, *Menschen am Sonntag* has a bittersweet attitude toward Weimar modernity. Clearly, the four young Berliners want to enjoy life. But there is tension galore in the relationships, and at the end of the day they and thousands of others return to the city to start work anew on Monday. The film ends with the poignant line "The next week—four million wait." Life in the modern city has been segmented into the alienating work week, and the lovely weekend full of life and pleasure. Modernity means a fragmented existence, a condition that the filmmakers explored through visual representations, and that essayists and philosophers like Martin Heidegger and Siegfried Kracauer would probe so deeply in their writings.

Foreign films also had a powerful resonance among audiences and critics in Germany. Two of the greatest, Charlie Chaplin's *The Gold Rush* and Sergei Eisenstein's *The Battleship Potemkin*, premiered in 1926. *The Gold Rush* opened to immediate and enormous popularity; it was Chaplin's and the industry's most successful film to date. The German authorities tried to ban *Potemkin* as a work of Soviet propaganda, but after a long court fight and public debate, they were forced to relent. It had a more restricted audience, but critics recognized Eisenstein's great talent and stunning filmmaking. Both films were signs of the globalization—not just Americanization—of media in the 1920s. Communists, Soviet sympathizers, and, in some places, a broader public around the world viewed *Potemkin*. Chaplin, British-born, of course, was as popular in Tokyo as in Berlin and Paris, let alone all across the United States. All the commentary at the time spoke to the empathy he aroused among people who themselves had been battered by misery. The success of Chaplin and Eisenstein sharply defined the problem of most German cinema in the middle of the decade, its inability to understand the new aesthetics that cinema made possible, its "artificiality and literary atmosphere," as the present-day scholars Jost Hermand and Frank Trommler state. They echo the Weimar critic Axel Eggebrecht, who wrote in 1926:

> It was enough for us to come to the negative conclusion that film is fundamentally different from theater. But over there [America], unburdened by the past and with an amazing naïveté, they developed the cinema purely from the optical dimension. They didn't first have to throw out all the psychological drama; one didn't have to turn it into a "picture," but one worked from the sheer visual expression, even where in normal life it didn't make sense. Chaplin was possible only because they had no tradition there, and because one could project onto the screen—from the bottom up, in its entirety, materially and

> ideologically—the representational form of the machine age. Only there did cinema achieve that intimate connection between its creative power and the industrial bases of the form of life it represents. Only there could film become the complete, expansive art industry, an industry of representation.[25]

In Germany, another critic, Béla Balázs, wrote, everything had to be "deep," and "simplicity" on the order of Chaplin was seen as trivial.[26]

Both *The Gold Rush* and *Potemkin* contained scenes immortalized in cinematographic history. Chaplin was renowned for his character creations and his comic scenes, Eisenstein for the dramatic force and technical innovations of his filmmaking. In *The Gold Rush*, Chaplin is the impoverished tramp, off to seek his fortune in Alaska, who is reduced to eating his shoes. He draws out the scene brilliantly, applying fork and knife to the inedible leather, trying to deceive himself in the face of his desperate situation—and at the same time save himself from it.

In *Potemkin*, Eisenstein also draws out one scene after another packed with dramatic tension. The setting is the Russian Revolution of 1905, and sailors on the battleship mutiny after being forced to endure one more outrage visited upon them by their brutal officers—a soup made from rotten meat. On board, the top officers gather their loyal subordinates, order them to throw a tarpaulin over a group of the mutineers, and give the command to execute them. For endless minutes, Eisenstein plays out the situation. Finally, the revolutionary hero shouts at the armed officers and asks them, "Who are you shooting?" The sailors are Russians just like themselves. Discipline breaks, and the mutineers seize control of the ship. Eisenstein's camera moves back and forth between close-ups and large-frame shots, accentuating the dynamism and tension—something no live theater could ever produce. The camera gazes over individual men, determined revolutionary heroes, and swarms of them as they battle with the officers. The camera lingers over the ship's polished brass fittings, pounding pistons, and long, powerful guns, then moves back to give the viewer a glimpse of the ship at sea.

In Odessa the townspeople hear of the mutiny and head toward the harbor in sympathy with the sailors. Again, the camera moves back and forth between close-ups of individuals and large-frame shots of thousands of people moving down the long steps to the harbor. Men and women, young and old, the poor and the better-off are all united behind the revolution. Then, suddenly, the czar's troops appear. Moving down the steps in disciplined formation, they fire into the crowd, one round after another, shooting people in the back. Those who make it to the bottom are met by Cossacks, who beat them to the ground. A mother picks up her young son, shot by the troops and then trampled by the crowd. The camera focuses on her for minutes on end. She approaches the czar's soldiers, begging them to stop, only to be shot down herself. Another mother is shot, and, in the most famous scene of the movie, falls to the ground next to her baby carriage. Eisenstein's camera follows the carriage as it rushes, loosed from the hands of the mother, down the steps to certain disaster.

Eisenstein's dramatic flair showed how film could create scenes and dramatic tension in a manner distinctive to the medium. No theatrical play, no novel could evoke the emotions of fear and dread for the fate of a child as powerfully as the visual representation in film, or the tense standoff between the lone revolutionary ship, the *Potemkin*, and the squadron it faces. What Moholy-Nagy argued about photography—that it had its own laws as a medium, and had to be true to its own form and not mimic other genres—Eisenstein demonstrated with his direction. The scene on the steps was not "real" in the sense that it had actually happened in 1905, nor did he portray the mutiny completely accurately. But his film was "more real" in the sense that the scenes conveyed the tensions and emotions of a city in revolutionary turmoil, and the power of the masses as they converged on the docks to support the striking sailors. Both *Potemkin* and *The Gold Rush* signified Weimar Germany's immersion in an international culture whose sources lay on the fringes of Europe, in the United States and the Soviet Union—to the great dismay of the German Right, in both its respectable and radical forms.

All of these were silent films. Yet another aesthetic shift was required when the German film industry, finally, in 1929, began to make movies with sound—two years later than in America, even though the technology had been partly developed in Germany. The radio brought together the technological developments in sound amplification and transmission; "talking movies" brought together the auditory and visual revolutions into one very powerful new medium.

As in the United States, sound was the death knell for many silent actors and actresses, whose voices were anything but pleasant to hear. It also ended the careers of many directors who had a hard time discerning that sound was not simply an add-on, but in very significant ways changed the aesthetics of filmmaking. While UFA viewed the new technique as a vehicle to pull the company out of its ongoing fiscal crisis, sound also signified the growing nationalization of film industries worldwide. It was easy to replace the spare text in a silent film with a different language, much harder and more expensive to develop synchronization or subtitles.

In the few short years left before the demise of the republic, the German film industry managed to produce some highly popular films that would later be recognized as classics that influenced generations of film directors. Fritz Lang's *M* premiered in 1931. It is the story of a child murderer loose in the city. The spectacular direction conjured up an eerie aura. The setting is the very modern city, but it is made to appear as a place of danger, though also of transparency. In the most famous scene, the child murderer, played by Peter Lorre, is looking in a shop window—one of those broad window displays that flourished in the 1920s. "M" looks through the corner windows to his pursuers and notices on his back the "M" for murderer that somebody had chalked on his coat. He also sees himself reflected in the displayed knives. It is brilliant cinematic construction. And it raises thought-provoking questions: Does the transparency of the store windows allow one to "see" better? Do the multiple reflections reveal more about the innermost being of the character—to himself and to the audience—than would a cityscape that did not provide the possibility of such reflection? *M* is also social criticism in Brechtian fashion. As in *The Threepenny Opera*, the gangsters and the police get together, this time to chase down the murderer who has violated even the gangsters' code of morality, such as it is. But there is not much difference between those who uphold order and those who violate it through criminal pursuits.

That kind of moral ambiguity deeply irked the guardians of order. Clergymen, mayors, and city council representatives, trade union leaders and socialist politicians, all railed against the immoral and corrupting influence of cinema. They saw their own efforts to promote moral rectitude undermined by what they viewed as simply more "trash and dirt," now transposed from the penny novel to the large, attractive screen. They worried incessantly about the moviegoing experience, first because cinema did have a democratizing influence. Few if any workers could be found in Germany's opera houses or its legitimate theater. Few upper-class individuals patronized the rough bars and raucous entertainment that could be found in all German cities—unless they were deliberately slumming. But by the late 1920s, millions of Germans went to the movies. Tickets were inexpensive enough that only the very poor were excluded, and films had become suitably artistic and reputable to attract at least segments of those more educated and wealthy. The erotic element in cinema also deeply worried the guardians of morals, both because of what was displayed on the screen and because of the very experience of men and women sitting together in the dark. Cinema was the quintessential mass entertainment form. It brought all sorts of people together and undermined the claims of state and church, the wealthy and the educated, to establish the parameters of rectitude. Socialists could sound as puritanical as their conservative political opponents. In September 1919, for example, the USPD fraction in the Munich city council voted against allowing new film theaters to open, because film transformed their "less educated fellow Germans into anarchists and contributes to their intellectual and spiritual corruption," a view many did not relinquish through the entire history of the republic.[27]

No matter. Germans flocked to the movies whatever anyone said. Nothing could sap their popularity. In 1929 Germany had 5,600 movie houses, compared to only 2,400 ten years before. In Berlin alone more than four hundred million tickets were sold in 1924; in the mid-1920s, estimates ran that daily two million people went to the cinema in Germany.[28] The inveterate flaneur and commentator Franz Hessel depicted Berliners' love affair with the cinema:

> We Berliners are passionate filmgoers. The weekly show substitutes for all of world history that we have not experienced. The most beautiful women of both continents belong to us everyday; we see their smiles and tears in moving pictures. We have our great film palaces around the Memorial Church, on Kurfürstendamm, in the area around Potsdamer Platz, in the

> suburbs, and in the thousands of small theaters, bright, enticing lights in the half-dark streets of every neighborhood. Oh, and then there are the morning cinemas, nice, warm halls for body and soul. In the movie theater the Berliner is not so critical, not so dependent on the critics he reads in his newspapers, as is the case with the theater. He allows himself to be flooded by illusions. It is the substitute for life for millions, who want to forget the monotony of daily existence.[29]

"Official" Germans might wring their hands in despair, but a young female textile worker captured the mood of the population even better than Hessel did: "Say what you want, that the cinema is kitsch. In any case it relieves my worries and I happily laugh away."[30]

Illustrated magazines and films transported the viewers to faraway places, to the frigid north of Alaska, to the steps leading down to the Odessa harbor, to lion-populated savannas of Africa. The revolution in sound transmission in the 1920s brought distant speakers and performers right to the individual, whether in a crowd looking up to a podium, in a café, or in the privacy of one's home. We have photographs of Karl Liebknecht proclaiming, on 9 November 1918, a socialist republic from the balcony of the Royal Palace in Berlin. But how many people in the large crowd below actually heard his words? How many patrons of the Hofbräuhaus in Munich in the early 1920s, drunk or sober, could actually distinguish the phrases Adolf Hitler spoke during one of his speeches? We do not know, but a good guess is—not that many. Certainly, public speakers in the pre-amplification age had learned to project their voices powerfully, far more so than today. But virtually every photograph of a large public event from around 1930 onward shows the speakers standing before a microphone, broadcasting through loudspeakers, radio transmissions, or both. By the end of the 1920s, sound, whether of a speech or a concerto, had become electrified.

The microphone, phonograph, and radio were all, in part, related technologies. Microphones and loudspeakers developed first as components of telephones, amplifying sound between the telephone set and the speaker or listener, but technological innovations that could make sound audible over a far longer range were difficult and slow in coming. The scientific and engineering breakthroughs came, finally and rapidly, in the 1920s. The new technologies of sound amplification could be deployed in different combinations in all the various media and places of sound projection: public meetings, radio, phonograph, and film. In 1925, the new Deutsches Museum was dedicated in Munich. At the opening ceremony, the speeches and the musical performance were carried over loudspeakers. The crowd responded with awe and admiration. Quickly the new technology caught on, even in church—the priests in the very large Cologne Cathedral started using microphones and loudspeakers in delivering their sermons.[31] At the very least, their wayward parishioners could no longer claim that they could not hear the sermon, hence did not know they were violating God's (or the church's) strictures.

Also in 1925 the first phonograph was outfitted with an amplifier, the key technology in microphones as well, which permitted not only louder volumes but also the reproduction of a greater range of sound frequencies.[32] A plugged-in, amplified phonograph, though far from perfect, marked a huge improvement in power and quality over the old, cranked-up gramophone. The recording industry responded in kind, and not only in Germany. As with films, an international market emerged, and Germans bought jazz records produced in America and France, operas from Italy, and concertos from Austria. Domestically, the greatest volume of production consisted of light orchestral and vocal music, the pop standards of the 1920s. People listened to records in the privacy of their homes. But they also packed up phonographs and records and took them to the lakeside beach and the tavern in the woods. Cafés, hotel restaurants, and beer gardens played recorded music or offered live musicians the microphone and loudspeaker.[33] Train stations and sports stadiums quickly followed suit—who today can imagine a horse race or a boxing match without the announcer rapidly relaying the events into a microphone, or a German train station without the requisite refrain repeated over the loudspeaker, "The train is approaching. Be careful on the arrival. Please move back from the edge of the platform"?

Radio, by bringing together amplification with the transmission of sound over huge distances, marked the culmination of the auditory revolution of the Weimar period. And like cinema, radio was wildly popular. In 1931, there were 3.7 million registered radio sets in Germany. One probably needs to multiply that figure by at least ten to get even a rough idea of the number of radio listeners, which means a significantly greater figure than the two million Germans who daily went to the movies in the mid-1920s.[34] By 1932, probably one-fourth of all households had a radio, in the Berlin and Hamburg areas one-half.[35] While the density of radio ownership was clearly greater among urban, middle- and upper-class Germans, many young, working-class people banded together in clubs to build radios, and transmit and receive radio signals. The local tavern, whether in the city or the countryside, often added a radio to its offerings of food and drink. By 1932, enough transmission towers had been built that the country was pretty well blanketed with reception.

The initial sense of wonder was unlimited, as one person, interviewed many years later, remembered: "The first time that I heard the word radio . . . I may have been three or four years old. . . . Father said to my mother: 'Now there is something new and it's called radio. If they make music in Munich, Frankfurt, or even America, one can hear it by us [in Würzburg].' Mother's answer: 'You're crazy, music can't be so loud.' And to that father said, 'No, the music is cut up and turned into waves and comes through the air to us.' "[36] The communist writer Johannes R. Becher gave literary form to the sense of amazement and enthusiasm in his poem "Radio—Miracle of Daily Life," in which he wrote about the marvel of the "magical call," of hearing voices from beyond the distant ocean, from high mountains.

> Time and space are overcome,
> And the great miracle occurs:
> All the transmitters are connected,
> And they sing a rapturous song.

Radio was the signal of "our great, wonderful time!"[37]

At first, radios could be heard only through headsets or, less well, through large funnels, much like early gramophones. But in 1926, the first electric loudspeakers came on the market, and they were quickly integrated into radio sets.[38] Now listening to the radio could become even more of a collective experience. The complete individualization of listening developed only slowly, as with the introduction of television after World War II. Family members, neighbors and hobbyists gathered together around the big, boxy radios of the day. As one person remembered: "My father was the proud owner of the first radio in the neighborhood and even far beyond its borders. People came on the train or on foot . . . even people we didn't know at all. Everyone came and wanted to be convinced that they really could hear voices and music coming out of the ether. . . . Each person had a half hour, then came the next in line. In the next room more and more interested people waited their turn."[39] Bars, cafés, and excursion boats sometimes attracted patrons with their radios. Less successfully, people sometimes gathered in large halls to listen to radio broadcasts of lectures, but the initial fascination could usually not sustain the patrons in this setting—the reception at first was too poor, and a large hall needed a live presence to connect with the crowd. But when people listened to music broadcast over the airwaves, then the fascination was unbounded. To listen and dance to music transmitted from London or Paris while in a café or dance hall in Hamburg, Berlin, or Munich—that evoked a sense of wonder and pleasure at the offerings of the modern world. As a Bremen resident remembered, the owner of a coffeehouse had outfitted a room with a receiver and twelve headsets, "which hung on the wall over the tables, next to one another. The apparatus was mostly set to London. The guests sat on their chairs, still as mice, with a cup of coffee and listened with radiant faces to the new 'music of the spheres,' which came blowing through the air from England over the North Sea. Often there was a noise in the headphones, and many claimed that it was the sound of the sea."[40] In 1927, the journalist Otto Alfred Politzsch could write with only some exaggeration that the radio belonged to the normal inventory of a home, much like a potted plant or a cabinet. From its place in the corner came suddenly the sounds of a violin, or a man singing, or a landowner speaking about artificial fertilizer. "The world is wide and its tones many and diverse."[41]

Radios were still, in the 1920s, expensive items, and most sets were built by individuals alone or working together in clubs. One member of a workers' radio association, reflecting the widespread admiration of Henry Ford, even in working-class circles, complained, "Wo bleibt der deutsche Radio-Ford?"—in other words, where is the mass-produced radio, built with standardized parts and inexpensively priced?[42] A radio-Ford there was not until the 1930s; still, the medium captivated Germans. And precisely because of its popularity and its power, radio was too important to be left unregulated. Some of radio's more enthusiastic advocates touted its promise as a great force for democratization, a tool that would convey "culture," break down the barriers between classes and nations, or, in a different formulation, create an alternative, proletarian culture. Albert Einstein in 1930 waxed rhapsodic about radio as the voice of "true democracy" that can "reconcile the family of nations."[43] But others saw radio as another sign of dangerous, degenerate "mass" society, yet another medium of heightened nervosity and movement without deep content. And still others, especially in government, recognized radio's great potential and wanted it to be used to elevate the population. Like schools and the army, radio would be a medium of civic education designed to instill proper values among the population, in this case, the millions of people who gathered around radio sets.

The first "official" broadcast took place in Berlin on 29 October 1923. Quickly, governmental authorities, producers, and manufacturers began jockeying for control. By 1925, the state had assumed the dominant role by licensing both the production and the consumption ends, though programs were mostly privately produced. Legislation established a national broadcasting company that had a strong component of private investment, but the Reich Post Ministry maintained majority ownership of the national company, nine regional networks, and individual stations. The legislation spread out authority among the Post and Interior ministries and the federal states. Only state-approved broadcasts were allowed, and individual purchasers of radio sets had to register and pay a license fee. Local supervisory boards, generally composed of senior civil servants, had to approve every stage of the production of programs.[44] Efforts by the labor parties, Communist and Social Democrat, to establish their own broadcasting stations foundered, and the authorities leveled harsh penalties on those who broadcast and received without official licenses. Then a new law in 1932 provided for complete state control over the radio.

Those who had envisaged radio as a freewheeling, democratic medium (much as some computer enthusiasts saw their medium in the 1980s) in which virtually anyone could broadcast, or that would serve as a venue for the radical critique of capitalist society—their hopes were dashed. As one present-day historian sums up the situation at the end of the republic: "A public deprived of power: four million listeners pay and keep quiet."[45] Under state control programming became largely conventional, but also very popular. Radio stations broadcast a mix of popular and classical music, household advice, adventure and exotic travel stories, paeans to the wonders of high technology, religious homilies and sermons, lectures on science and nature, and dramas written especially for radio. The goal overall was to provide programs that were informative, moral, and uplifting, not, to be sure, more "trash and dirt." High, not low, culture was the guiding principle. Many of Germany's most famed authors read from their works, some designed specifically for radio, and listeners could also hear concerts by the Berliner Philharmonie and opera performances from the State Opera. In the last year of the republic, the state's new, highly conservative programming guidelines proclaimed:

> The radio participates in the life work of the German nation. The natural ordering of people in home and family, work and state is to be maintained and secured by the German radio. The radio does not therefore speak to the listener only as an individual, but also a member of this natural national order.
>
> German radio adheres to Christian beliefs and behavior and respects the sincere convictions of dissenters. That which degrades the Christian faith or endangers the custom and culture of the German people is excluded from German radio.[46]

Hence programming directed at women asserted the value of home life and women as mothers and housewives. They heard the typical mix of beauty tips, child-rearing guidance, and domestic advice. As the official journal of the national broadcasting network proclaimed: "[Radio] carries with it the possibility of binding together again that which is fettered and splintered. It can help [women] regain security in their place at the centre of the family. Domestic culture, which brings love and warmth to sons and daughters, husbands and friends, but which is endangered by the current crises and modern skepticism, can flourish again in the alliance between housewives and their radios."[47] Another journal saw a benefit in the fact that women could be connected to the outside world yet still remain in the home: "On top of the housewife's loneliness comes the fear that domestic cares, fragmentation and trivia will increase the distance from outside life, that she will no longer be able to keep up with her husband, and that she'll vegetate and become estranged from him. . . . Then radio offers itself as a *vade mecum*, which in contrast to the printed word, has the great advantage of not taking up any of the housewife's time."[48] And from a rather ungainly contraption with wires and antennae running everywhere, and listening at first limited to headphones, the radio with built-in loudspeaker became an elegantly designed piece of furniture, suitable for the living room of a good bourgeois household.

The authorities also believed at first that programming should be totally free of politics, but in this case they had to give in to pressure from their political masters, at least those of them who recognized the potential of radio. Listeners heard the first political broadcasts in 1924: speeches from the chancellor and a few cabinet members, then from representatives of the major parties concerning the upcoming Reichstag elections. In 1925, the two major candidates for president, Paul von Hindenburg and Wilhelm Marx, addressed radio listeners, though the censors banned the communist candidate Ernst Thälmann.[49] The quality of these broadcasts was terrible, and the politicians had not yet learned how to adjust their delivery to radio—they did not have to scream into the microphone as they had learned to do when addressing large crowds in the preamplification era. By the end of the decade, the programming authorities were airing political debates and speeches by the chancellor and other leading figures, and the first news reports. But no communist voices, nor, just yet, Nazi voices were heard on German radio. That, of course, would change once the Nazis had taken power and radio, like other media, came under their total control.

Yet programming evolved and did not always meet the strict standards envisaged by the authorities. At least some programs relayed the accomplishments of women in the professions. Despite strong reservations in some quarters, sports reporting also entered the scene and became very popular, and sometimes even included women's events.[50] The first live broadcasts took place in 1924 and 1925, and by the end of the decade, with technical improvements, had become feasible on a regular basis.[51] Oddly enough, some of the very first live sports reports were of sailing races, not exactly the stuff of exciting play-by-play commentary, but bicycle, soccer, and track events and horse races soon took pride of place. The censors, guardians of German culture, at first considered boxing too degenerate to pass muster. But even they had to concede to popular tastes. By the end of the decade fans could also hear boxing matches broadcast live, or transmitted with a few minutes' delay from America to Europe. In 1929, German listeners heard from the United States a very exciting heavyweight match between Max Schmeling and Paolino Uzcudun, which Schmeling won in fifteen rounds.

But sound amplification and transmission worried many people. Some commentators thought that the particular diction necessary for clarity over the radio already marked a transformation of culture: sound over vision, architectonic arrangement of voices and music over space, dramaturgical recitation over movement.[52] For someone like the great stage director and impresario Leopold Jessner, radio could convey only a weak shadow of the classic plays and operas, so dependent as they were on the live audience and the speech and movement of the actors. Instead, Jessner called for the development of a dramatic form, a new "species" of art, that was specific to the new, purely acoustical medium of radio.[53] Others were more critical: the medium was best suited to melodrama and rapid movement from scene to scene, topic to topic, a debasement of the high standards of Greek tragedy and the German classics. Without the visual presence of actors onstage, the narrative had to have excessive dramatic drive; the speaker had to convey even greater emotion in order to hold the listener's attention. In this view, the medium of radio created a debased culture.

Many composers and musicians were similarly concerned about the radio and recordings' impact on music. And there was no clear divide between modernists and traditionalists. The modernist composer Arnold Schönberg was a harsh critic of radio. He noted that radio "accustoms the ear to an unspeakably coarse tone, and to a body of sound constituted in a soupy, blurred way, which precludes all finer differentiation." Schönberg worried that radio music would become the standard, and the beautiful tones of various instruments would be lost. Radio gave music a "continuous tinkle" that in the end would mean that "all music has been consumed, worn out."[54] Indeed, in radio's early days, both the upper and lower frequencies could not be adequately captured, so violins and basses could barely be heard or distinguished. Some composers and performers, like Kurt Weill, began gearing at least some of their compositions specifically to the medium—paring down the orchestration and the sensuous quality of the music to create leaner works with an emphasis on clarity. Imperfections were also exposed—an opera singer's aria that was short of stunning might be covered over by his or her theatricality onstage. On radio and in recordings, it was pure voice, and nothing could hide the flaws.[55] Some musicians feared that, in general, radio and recordings had led to an emphasis on technique at the expense of interpretation.[56]

Other observers simply relished the possibility that the German classics and other worthy literature and music could be conveyed to millions more, so much more powerful a medium was radio than the printed page. Arno Schirokauer, active in publishing and radio, wrote: "Art is socialized. From a private possession it has been turned into the possession of everyone. Like the statesman, the artist is a public man. His production doesn't belong any longer to the one patron, to the best seller, to the consumer, but to the nine million radio listeners. The unique production of the artist becomes a common good through ingenious mechanisms of reproduction."[57] Schirokauer may have been a bit overenthusiastic, but he articulated the excitement that so many felt about the medium. Even the great philosopher Franz Rosenzweig noted that the radio and phonograph only marked the culmination of the trend that had begun in the late eighteenth century with the establishment of the concert hall, namely, the creation of "the public" as an audience for music, which stretched even beyond the spatial and temporal limits of the live performance in a hall.[58] The same virtues that Schirokauer lauded and Rosenzweig accepted—the widespread dissemination of a work of culture, its endless reproducibility—are precisely what worried so many others.[59]

Radio and recordings, photography and film opened up new worlds for Germans. The new media gave them some sense of connection to London or Amsterdam and even to America or China. They saw the images and heard the sounds of these distant places in ways that penetrated their consciousness far more deeply than was possible through the reading of a novel, story, or historical study—such is the power of our auditory and visual senses. They marveled at the rapidly moving images across the screen and the voices that came out of the "ether."

But did this mass media culture of the Weimar era change the way people listened and looked, the very way life was lived? Many people, from some of Weimar Germany's greatest intellectuals to government bureaucrats to the clergy and beyond, wrestled with this issue. On some level, all of them recognized that the changes wrought by the new mass media were profound at the deepest individual and collective levels. Radio, recordings, photographs, and movies not only enabled the transmission of existing works of literature or music to ever greater numbers of people. The new mass media also changed the way Germans experienced the world, indeed, changed the very nature of the world Germans experienced.

Most important, the encounter with a visual image or a collection of sounds was no longer based on the unique experience of live performance or viewing, the transforming moment of listening to a Beethoven sonata in the still quiet of a concert hall or of contemplating a masterpiece by the romantic artist Caspar David Friedrich in the solitude of a museum—or, if one were wealthy enough, in one's own drawing room. At the high intellectual level, the prevailing German philosophical and cultural traditions as they had developed since the late eighteenth century had emphasized the singular moment and the unique experience. But now, in the 1920s, visual images were reproducible, whether on Ullstein's ultramodern printing presses or in film studios. The images on-screen moved rapidly across the spectator's field of vision and were often made in faraway California. Recordings, too, were designed to be reproducible, the great and minor works of Germany's musical culture stamped out on brittle shellac discs. Recordings and live performances could now, with radio, also be transmitted over great distances. Who could possibly have a musical epiphany when the experience consisted of hearing the shallow, harsh tones transmitted through the airwaves or on disc? Who would be so moved by the sight of the Alps as Goethe had been, when he or she could sit in a movie theater or at home and experience the Alps on-screen or by leafing through the photographs in the *Berliner Illustrirte*?

There were no simple answers. Only one point was clear: Germans in the Weimar era were living through the greatest transformation of media culture since Johannes Gutenberg invented the movable-type printing press in the late fifteenth century. The inveterate observer Joseph Roth understood that the new technologies had altered the very nature of the sounds Germans heard and the images they saw. In an essay about an early form of electrified sound transmission, the wireless telephone [*Radiophon*], he wrote:

> There are no more secrets in the world. The whispered confessions of a despondent sinner are available to all the curious ears of a community, which thanks to the wireless telephone has become a pack. The tender love murmurs of a couple hidden in the park are made shamelessly loud and distinguishable to the vulgar passersby. The familiar chatter in the family circle is heard, dreadfully, by all the neighbors.
>
> There are no more secret conferences, no whispered consultations, no "seal of silence." The wireless telephone breaks it all open. Discretion has become loud, silence speaks, stillness cries.
>
> No one listened any longer to the song of the nightingale and the chirp of conscience. No one followed the voice of reason and each allowed himself to be drowned out by the cry of instinct.
>
> Does anyone know any longer how wonderful it rustles, when two blades of grass touch each other? Or when a butterfly flits its wings? Or when the supposedly silent blossoms fall in late spring?
>
> The wireless telephone is an invention we can be proud of, and which can make us modest.[60]

He was similarly worried about the photographic portrait, which presented not stability, not the capturing of a particular moment and person, as Sander thought. In Roth's view, the photograph, precisely because it was designed for the large public, shaped and exaggerated particular features of the subject.

> The new photographs are not "faithful" but are "full of expression." They don't reproduce the stability of a face, but its

> amazing capacity to change. [The photographer] takes portraits for display windows and newspapers, not for the album. Overall the modern portrait relies on various means to show the significance of light and shadows, the form of the hand, the glow of the iris, the perfection that the camera makes possible. . . . He doesn't portray a face, but particular situations of a face: the extended chin, the lowered forehead, the shadowed cheeks. . . . People who otherwise had only one face, suddenly have a profile. People who had completely ordinary eyes, all of a sudden obtain a look. The indifferent become thoughtful, the harmless full of humor, the simpleminded become goal oriented, the common strollers look like pilots, secretaries like demons, directors like Caesars.[61]

Presumably, a viewer could stand in front of a painted portrait of bygone days and contemplate the full range of human expressiveness. The photograph captured only one moment and one expression, and, often enough, an artificial one.

Roth exaggerated, to be sure. There were and are still secrets in the world. Photographic portraits and paintings can depict the subject with a rich range of emotional complexity or in a shallow and pretentious fashion. But Roth—who, after all, wrote for newspapers, another medium of modernity—was no doubt correct on some level. The very sounds and images of life had changed. Germans heard over the radio the ringing of the Cologne Cathedral's bells, live reporting of a horse race, and the sounds of a zeppelin landing and taking off. In cinemas they watched a race that had been run hundreds and even thousands of miles away and at another time, yet experienced the anticipation and the thrill of the competition. For the first time in human history and on a mass scale, one did not have to be within the space of sound—the natural range of church bells, the symphony hall—to hear its tones and coloration, or present at ringside or stadium to see a sporting event.

The expansiveness of sound and image in the 1920s, the chemical manipulation of light and the electromagnetic transmission of sound, challenged the rootedness of life that, previously, had been tied to the sounds, smells, and images directly experienced in a defined, bounded place and at a particular moment in time. Radio and recordings did alter the tonal qualities of the music that listeners heard over the airwaves or on disc—though the technology would evolve, enabling both to capture better the sounds experienced in a live setting. Film images moved consistently faster than people had previously experienced. The moving picture evinced a new kind of nervous energy. As Roth suggested, the new media had a particular affinity for emotional exaggeration and quick, unreflective thoughts.

But that was only part of the story. The reproducible sound and image also made possible new kinds of art and new forms of beauty. And they stimulated some of Weimar Germany's great creative figures to think about the meaning of the new media in which they worked, and, more generally, of life in modern times. László Moholy-Nagy and August Sander shot and printed photographs that even today we can linger over for a long time, pondering the play of forms and the lives reflected in the images, and wonder whether abstraction or realism is most meaningful. Or perhaps we can just take pleasure in both approaches and understand why each of the photographers believed that he was on the path to capturing best the lived world and penetrating its mysteries. Some of the great filmmakers of the Weimar era explored the ironies and complexities of the city, the very centerpiece and symbol of modernity. For Robert Siodmak, Edgar Ungar, Werner Ruttman, Billy Wilder, Fritz Lang, and many others, Berlin's powerful machines, churning trains, and racing population had their own kind of beauty, which they captured on film. The city could be a place of pleasure and satisfaction, and also a site of mystery, danger, and alienation. The advocates of radio and records loved the experience of hearing music and plays performed in faraway places, even as they worried about the degeneration of sound and the loss of image quality that accompanied the transmission and reproduction.

Weimar modernity was complex, contradictory, and contested; its greatest cultural figures understood that and used the media in which they worked—photography, film, radio, and recordings—to reflect upon the meaning of modernity. They were hardly alone. All across the developed world and beyond, the post–World War I era showered people with new sounds and images. Britons, too, flocked to the radio and the cinema, Argentines danced to recorded as well as live music, and wherever there was a movie projector and something resembling a screen, audiences laughed at Charlie Chaplin.

The electrified and reproducible sound and image internationalized culture in the 1920s as never before, and inspired and worried people all across the social spectrum.

But as with economics and politics, so with culture: there was something particularly vital and intense about Germans' engagement with these new media forms in the 1920s and early 1930s. Cinema, radio, illustrated magazines, and records offered Germans entertainment and relief galore from the troubles and tribulations of defeat in war and the burdensome legacies of reparations and inflation. The revolution inspired experimentation with everything new, from sound transmission to moving images. Many artists, writers, directors, and composers jumped at the chance to work in the new media precisely because they signified a break with the past and provided one more way to express rejection of pre-1918 imperial Germany with its kaisers, generals, nobles, and stuffy, rigid, and outmoded art academies.

However, the revolution's incomplete character, the failure of its proponents to destroy the bastions of power occupied by the elites, also ensured that there were voices aplenty to challenge the supposedly degenerate and dissolute influences of the new media forms like cinema and radio. No less than the constitution and social welfare policies, mass culture became a focal point of loud incessant conflict. The saddest irony is that almost all of the great artists who developed the new media forms of the 1920s and the great thinkers who pondered their significance for modern times would have to leave Germany, and the Nazis would become the master manipulators of the microphone, radio, and cinema.

7

Culture and Mass Society

The philosopher Ernst Bloch, writing in 1931 from Berlin to his lover (later to become his wife), Karola Piotrkowska, described an evening spent with his friend the composer Kurt Weill. He told of regaling Weill with a story he had read in a café about the last Arab storytellers, who had wandered around Turkey and the Middle East, learning and plying their trade. Now no one wants to listen to them anymore—people are reading newspapers instead—and the stories are dying out. Bloch worries that he faces the same fate: is he the last dreamer, the last metaphysician? Capitalism is destroying hope and making everything mundane and objective, including the newspapers read in Turkey and the Middle East; communism is also reducing everything to an arid and sterile materialism and a fog of lies. But he rouses himself. (One can imagine the bottles of wine or glasses of cognac—unmentioned by Bloch—consumed by the two of them as the evening and the story go on.) He may be the last dreamer of the old world, but he is also the first of the new one. His philosophical work—his metaphysics—is like a disturbing daydream, an explosive like a fairy tale that unsettles routine life, Bloch writes. But that is the purpose of his philosophy—to probe, to disrupt and, at the same time, to hold out the vision of a better future.[1]

A few years earlier, a young student, Hans Jonas, made his way to Freiburg and then Marburg to study philosophy with Martin Heidegger. Many years later, he described his first impressions. Heidegger's lecture dealt with the *Confessions* of St. Augustine. Jonas understood almost nothing, he claimed, but he had the "compelling feeling, that these were things of fundamental importance [*ums Ganze ging*] and he grappled profoundly with the matter." Something happened to Jonas at that moment of encounter with Heidegger. He still could not follow everything, but he never lost the feeling that Heidegger was presenting—and not just in that one lecture—something "that was immensely important, even when I did not understand it . . . an impression of profound thought." Jonas was moved by Heidegger's deep probing and creativity.

> All that exceeded my understanding, yet something of it touched my soul, namely, the conviction: that is philosophy on the move. . . . Heidegger's profound thinking was deeply creative, and not for a moment could one hold the suspicion that it was only an illusion. . . . All in all I felt that I was standing before a secret, and with the conviction that it would be worthwhile to join the cognoscenti.[2]

Bloch and Heidegger, and a young Jonas: that was Weimar culture at its best, a deep search for the meaning of the present and a belief in the possibilities of the future. The answers each provided would, of course, vary tremendously. Bloch was a Marxist; Heidegger later became a Nazi, though in the 1920s he accepted Jewish students like Jonas and Hannah Arendt and others who flocked to his lectures and seminars. Both philosophers refused to venture simple answers to the burning crisis of the present.

And what was the present that they and so many other leading Weimar cultural figures explored so deeply? It was, in a phrase, modern times—urban, industrial society, the mélange of sights, sounds, and thoughts connected with the city, with science and technology and layers of bureaucracy, with rational modes of thinking, with complex social hierarchies, the world of the bourgeoisie and proletariat uncomfortably situated amid the old nobility and a still-substantial peasantry, an urban demimonde of gamblers, thieves, cops, and prostitutes and an educated middle class desperately trying to maintain its stature and status. This was "mass society," a phenomenon that was both stimulating and unsettling. German artists and thinkers had been probing the meaning of this world since the middle of the nineteenth century. Now, in the shadow of war and revolution—the great disruptive events that left no life untouched—and the unceasing conflicts of Weimar politics, their probings ran more deeply, the burst of creative expression on page, stage, and canvas so vibrant that it is unmatched even by Paris in the 1920s or New York in the 1940s and 1950s.[3]

That was Weimar culture: the restless questioning of what it means to live in modern times, the search for new forms of expression suitable to the cacophony of modern life, and the belief in the possibilities of the future. Our guides into this world of culture will be a mere handful of the great writers, artists, and composers who flourished in the 1920s and early 1930s, and whose work we still read, view, and hear with deep engagement and appreciation: Thomas Mann, Bertolt Brecht, Kurt Weill, Siegfried Kracauer, Martin Heidegger, and Hannah Höch.

In the 1920s Thomas Mann was already a very famous man. His first novel, *Buddenbrooks*, the semiautobiographical chronicle of three generations of a great merchant family, had been published to acclaim in 1901. On 10 December 1929, he would be awarded the Nobel Prize for literature. Mann's novels and stories probed the psychological demands exacted by the refined and ordered life that he so prized and that characterized the bourgeois world from which he came. A life of order and rectitude was a fragile thing. Emotions and desires threatened constantly to burst the constraints that allowed business and art to flourish and the family, that centerpiece of bourgeois order, to maintain its status. In *Buddenbrooks*, Toni, after months of agonizing, agrees to marry the unattractive and somewhat dull businessman who will supposedly add his wealth and experience to the Buddenbrooks family. With flourish, she finally signs her name in the cherished family book, which records the marriages over generations. Toni has sacrificed herself for the family—but every sacrifice has its costs, and this one fails even to deliver on its promise. Toni's husband turns out to be a charlatan, and he helps drag down the firm and family. In *Death in Venice*, Gustav von Aschenbach travels to his beloved city only to find a pall of disease and decay. He has long sublimated his sexual desires into his art. In Venice, his longings for the lithe and handsome young boy Tadzio, though unconsummated, destroy the order he had so carefully constructed in his life. His shattered personal order mirrors the epidemic disaster spreading over the city.

As with individuals, so with societies. Society was also a fragile thing, always threatened by the instincts of men and women. Only the most concerted effort, the most heroic struggles to contain the desires for pleasure and death, made society possible—a theme also developed by Sigmund Freud in *Civilization and Its Discontents*.[4] Always, in individuals and societies, a war raged between the artistic, sensual, and erotic sentiments and the no less powerful claims for order and responsibility. For Mann personally, this was a conflict between north and south, between the great merchant city of Lübeck and artistic, sensual Munich and Italy; between his Protestant father, a bourgeois to the core, and his Catholic mother, born in Brazil of German and Spanish parentage; between duty and responsibility, art and licentiousness; between man and woman, or, more accurately, manly instincts and womanly instincts, since Mann constantly struggled with his own homoerotic desires; and, ultimately, between aestheticism and asceticism.[5]

Mann was a follower of Nietzsche, whose works he had read voraciously, and a Freudian before he had ever read Freud. But in contrast to Nietzsche's unruly politics and Freud's liberalism, the keen attentiveness to the conflict between eros and order turned Mann into a political conservative. During the war years he wrote *Reflections of an Unpolitical Man*, which he published in 1918. It is perhaps the least subtle, least compelling of his major works. Mann's conservative instincts found full expression here, as he gave complete support to the kaiser and the war effort. Some of the passages read like war propaganda issued by the General Staff, or the standard musings of right-wing ideologues. As his recent biographer, Hermann Kurzke, writes, war gave Mann (no less than so many others, one might add) a sense of purpose, and also freed him from a psychological and creative crisis. He could identify with those most manly of pursuits, war and violence, putting to rest, at least momentarily, his worries over his homoeroticism. Through his identification with the national cause and the attack on his liberal brother Heinrich, he would find, so he hoped, the great acclaim he desired and would become, in effect, the poet laureate of the nation. Indeed, war enabled Mann to join those polar tendencies, north and south, responsibility and passion, manliness and womanliness. Now the responsible thing to do was to be passionate about the nation at war.[6]

It was definitely not Thomas Mann's finest moment. But Mann was among those Germans who had come of age in the prewar era and were conservative by upbringing, intellect, and instinct, and then recognized in the 1920s the need to come to terms with mass society and the democratic era. They were labeled *Vernunftrepublikaner* (republicans by reason), and if not quite democrats at heart, they nonetheless gave the republic powerful intellectual support. On 15 October 1922, Mann delivered a remarkable speech that signaled the great distance he had traveled since *Reflections of an Unpolitical Man*.[7] The occasion was a homage to the great playwright Gerhart Hauptmann on his sixtieth birthday, and the audience consisted largely of conservatively inclined students. It was a curious talk. Mann drew on an unlikely pair, the great German romantic Novalis and the American poet Walt Whitman, to make his case in support of democracy and the republic.[8] These two romantic artists, Mann argued, had a similar approach to life—they sought to conserve the best of the past but understood that in the modern age a republic afforded men the opportunity for development. Without using the word, Mann invoked the German tradition of *Bildung*, the belief in self-cultivation that would come through engagement with great works of culture. *Bildung* had become the fashionable ideology of the German middle and upper classes, but by the turn into the twentieth century had also become laced with snobbishness and an air of self-satisfaction.[9] Mann sought to return to the true meaning of *Bildung* as education and cultivation, which Wilhelm von Humboldt had articulated in the early nineteenth century.

Only in the republic, Mann suggested, could men truly achieve *Bildung*. In the lavish language to which he was prone, peppered with extensive quotations from Novalis and Whitman, Mann had the courage not to spare his conservative audience his sharpest criticisms. The monarchy of old had fallen prey to an aggressive militarism wrapped in the mantle of the spirituality of the state, to a Nietzschean flight into pure power, which so many students had blindly followed. Only the republic now embodied the true meaning of the state, the true opportunity for human development, and that great ideal, Humanity. Mann endowed the republic with spiritual significance: in the republic, Germans, collectively and individually, would be able to develop their inner potential. The republic was the great medium, the synthesizer of the individual and the collective, the singular and the universal, the German and the European, Enlightenment and romanticism, and the very expression of Humanity. It was also an object of eroticism, of the tight bonds among men who gave it their devotion, and thereby created something great, a force of life over the force of death, even when the state sent its men to war.

It was good, of course, to have an intellectual of Mann's stature on the side of the republic. But one may well ask whether it was such a great service to foist onto the democracy of the 1920s the complex of ideas that conservatives in the nineteenth century had so lovingly applied to the Prussian and (after 1871) German state. Could any democracy, any republic, live up to Mann's lofty spiritual and erotic claims? That very basic task of any democratic state, to reconcile diverse interests, lay beneath Mann's concerns. He took the conservative German idiom of a *Kulturstaat* coupled with his own homoeroticism and applied it to Weimar, which must have struck many of his listeners as bizarre. Yet such was the magic of his intellect and erudition, drawing effortlessly on the classics of the German tradition as well as on Whitman, that he was able to carry along some of his listeners—at the least, the vocal expressions of opposition and dismay faded as his speech continued to unfold (and he must have spoken for a good two hours, to judge by the written text).

The war and postwar eras also provided Mann with the fertile basis to expound on the theme of decay. *Buddenbrooks* portrayed the rise and decline of a great merchant family in Lübeck. The cataclysm of the war with its millions of dead and the upheavals of the postwar era gave Mann a powerful impetus to think about decay on an even grander scale, not only that of a family or of German society, but of Western civilization itself. In 1925, he published *The Magic Mountain*, his greatest novel since *Buddenbrooks* and one of the classics of twentieth-century literature. It was instantly recognized as a masterpiece. Hans Jonas recalled that "everyone" in his Zionist and his academic-philosophical circles "of course read [the novel] . . . and could on any occasion quote or make references [to it], which were immediately understood."[10]

In *The Magic Mountain*, Hans Castorp visits his cousin, Joachim Ziemisch, in a sanatorium in the Swiss Alps populated by an array of patients suffering from tuberculosis and other diseases. The cold, refined air of the mountains and the watchful care of Hofrat Dr. Behrens provide their only chances for recovery. Dr. Behrens immediately notices that Hans, too, suffers from an ailment, and the three-week visit turns into a seven-year sojourn during which Hans, through a variety of interlocutors, contemplates the meaning of life and death. Our rather hapless protagonist bounces from one grand aspiration to another, from one set of beliefs to another. An engineer by training, at various times he expresses the ambition to be a pastor or painter, at other times a physician. He enthuses over the military bearing of his ill-fated cousin yet can never summon up the disciplined Joachim's stoic countenance in the face of death. Hans suffers the tongue-lashings of others like a little boy or wounded dog, head bowed and comments inarticulate. For endless months he watches the woman with whom he is infatuated, Clawdia Chauchat, she "with the Kirghiz eyes," unable to rally the courage to approach her. For unending pages, Mann, with his masterly sensibility, depicts the glances exchanged between them, the slightest movement of their hands and mouths, yet both Clawdia and Hans remain in their own worlds, without any words exchanged between them, until carnival and alcohol loosen Hans's restraint. But by then it is almost too late—Clawdia is leaving the next day (though she will return).

Hans moves among three men who represent the divergent strands of Western civilization. Each of them is, of course, ill. Why else would they while their time away on the magic mountain? Ludovico Settembrini is the great humanist who never tires of expounding upon the grand ideas of liberty and progress. His grandfather had belonged to the Carbonari, the conspiratorial Italian nationalist groups of the early nineteenth century; his father, also a humanist as well as a soldier in the Risorgimento, the movement that led to Italian unification in 1871. Settembrini tries to bring "Engineer," as he so often calls Hans, to the side of liberalism, to the ideas of the south, of Italy, of passion for liberty and belief in progress, of certainty about the greatness of man, versus the Teutonic penchant for order and discipline, though Settembrini is enough of a European, not just an Italian, to recognize the virtues of the German ideals. Yet there is an arid quality to Settembrini's rhetoric, filled as it is with quotations from obscure humanists of the sixteenth century and references to the grand achievements of the past. Liberalism's realm of action had been narrowed over the generations, from the activism of Settembrini's father and grandfather to his own penning of obscure encyclopedia articles and discussions among a few men in the rarefied atmosphere of the Alps. Settembrini's humanism, it seems, is an archaic remnant of the nineteenth century.

But his great antagonist, the Jesuit Leo Naphta, is even more of a relic. Naphta, of Jewish background, no less erudite than Settembrini, asserts the certainty of belief and the glories of medieval Christendom. He advocates the order the church imposes on society, the quietude of the beatific life, and the rigors of torture when necessary to defend Christendom. "Faith is the vehicle of understanding," he says; "the intellect is secondary."[11] Settembrini counters with the active life of accomplishment, of reason and labor and ever-advancing progress. Hans listens raptly as Naphta and Settembrini argue for hours on end. He is alternately captivated and repulsed by each of them.

Hans's third great interlocutor arrives rather late in the novel. He is a blustery, forceful figure, a Dutch colonial planter, Mynheer Peeperkorn, who has made a fortune overseas. He is physically large and rhetorically inarticulate, the very opposite of both Settembrini and Naphta, a powerful presence who is used to having his way. He is "*die Persönlichkeit*"—the grand personage—as Hans so often refers to him. Hans is again captivated, this time by the man of action who has made his way in the world and has accumulated great wealth and a penchant for issuing orders to those in his midst. In a night of indulgence, Peeperkorn gathers around him a dozen or more fellow patients and, through will and force, engages them in the dissipations of card playing, rich foods, and substantial quantities of alcohol. Half the sanatorium has a hangover the next day, thanks to the large appetite of "*die Persönlichkeit.*" Yet he, too, is ill, and—what is worse, from Hans's viewpoint—he arrives at the Berghof with Clawdia. They are "travel companions," in the quaint terminology of the prewar era.

Common people, "the masses," rarely appear in Mann's literature. When they do, they are shadowy figures, a driver or servant, who enable the lives and troubles of the protagonists to proceed, or they are anonymous crowds, captivated by the guile of a circus performer or a more sinister manipulator, as in the story "Mario and the Magician" or the *Dr. Faustus* trilogy. Mann is consumed with the travails of his own class, the *Bildungsbürgertum*, the educated middle class, that group so esteemed in modern German history. It is an elite, to be sure, defined by *Besitz und Bildung*, property and education, yet always confronted by the specter of the mass. In *The Magic Mountain*, Hans whiles away his seven years, careful about his expenditures yet able to meet the no doubt costly fees of the Berghof through the dividends he collects from his inheritance. *Besitz und Bildung* go along with a certain reserve and distance, a formality of relationships even among family members. Only upon his reckless departure from the Berghof—and the reader has a foreboding that he will return—does Joachim actually address his cousin by his first name, by "Hans," although they use the informal "you," *du*, with one another. On the same carnival- and alcohol-infused evening when he finally speaks to Clawdia, Hans addresses Settembrini with the informal "you," and the great humanist is not pleased. Indeed, Hans's breach of the bounds of respectability unleashes a tirade from Settembrini. Cultivated society, civilization itself, requires a certain formality and distance.

> For people to use informal pronouns or first names when they have no real reason to do so is a repulsively barbaric practice, a slovenly game, a way of playing with the givens of civilization and human progress, against both of which it is directed—shamelessly, insolently directed. Please, do not presume in calling you "my lad," I was addressing you in that fashion. I was merely quoting a passage from the masterpiece of your national literature. I was speaking poetically, as it were.[12]

Du might be the appropriate term among the masses—indeed, the labor movement consciously adopted it as a sign of egalitarianism and comradeship among its members. It was not appropriate for those who are the bearers of culture, and they must resist the blandishments of mass society through appropriate formality.

On that same evening and in an erotically charged encounter, Hans also uses *du* with Clawdia Chauchat. She claims (coquettishly?) to be offended by his familiarity, which also challenges the sexual order that cultivated society demands. Yet Clawdia's husband is somewhere "beyond the Caucasus," nowhere to be seen, and he allows his wife her liberties. Her very exoticism and the allure of her

"Kirghiz eyes," arouse Hans sexually, and he finally declares his love for her. Yet at his grand, decisive moment, he is still a somewhat pathetic character. She strokes his hair comfortingly, but it is as much a maternal as a sexual act. She parries his declaration of love and refers admiringly to his cousin. She finally leaves with a flourish, just as she always enters with a flourish, waving "Adieu" to the hapless Hans.

But perhaps, just perhaps, she invites him to her room, since she reminds him, softly, looking over her shoulder, to return the pencil he had borrowed from her.[13] The *du* of familiarity is also the *du* of the masses, and both threaten the ordered world of bourgeois society. Hans and Clawdia will eventually reunite, once she returns with Peeperkorn. But it is an ill-starred affair, finally destroyed by the shadow of Peeperkorn's suicide, who, for all his powers, is felled by his illness and by the knowledge of his companion's lack of love for him.

Hans Castorp is the middling embodiment of the bourgeois class, not as lost as Robert Musil's "man without qualities," yet, well, middling—intelligent, but not overly so; longing for great achievements, yet indecisive; ill, but not very seriously; mildly questioning, yet also quite self-satisfied. He takes easily to the languid pace of life in the sanatorium—the regular meals, five a day no less; the mandated, twice daily "lying cures," when the patients lie out in the cold air, wrapped in blankets, offering themselves to the thin, fresh air of the Alps; the periodic lectures, concerts, and excursions: all in a world where no one works, except for the staff of the Berghof. Like the other patients, Hans loses all sense of time: the weeks turn into months, the months into years, all punctuated by periodic obsessions that never last long—painting, anatomical studies, stargazing, skiing, the gramophone.

Yet what is one to make of it all? Did modern times signify only decay? Was there no way out of the crisis of civilization? Mann's tone in *The Magic Mountain* is, as ever, ironic and pessimistic and laced with strains of nostalgia for the safe, comfortable bourgeois world of the nineteenth century, so different from the conflict-strewn Weimar Republic of the 1920s and early 1930s. There are also moments of striking humor that relieve the despair that runs through so much of his novel. Yet for all that, for all the emotional and erotic tension of his writing, Mann was also a hardheaded realist who knew, especially after the cataclysms of World War I, that there was no road back to the simple optimism of Settembrini or to the religious mysticism of Naphta, not even to the hard-charging moneymaking of Peeperkorn. At the very end, Hans Castorp descends from the magic mountain to go off to war. So many of his companions die of their illness; he will most likely die in the battle for the nation, a cause that Mann had first supported so fervently but by the mid-1920s had come to view with greater distance.

Hans will die in war, but he had, earlier in the novel, chosen life. Off alone on a reckless skiing venture, he is caught in a snowstorm that suddenly swirls up around him. His vision is blinded, his sense of direction thrown awry. Finally he encounters a hut whose overhang provides at least some shelter. In a state of delirium, he dreams of a loving, peaceful place, bathed in sunlight as children play on the shore and young beauties, male and female, mount horses and dance in circles. His mind also conjures up a countervision of child-devouring monsters, a medieval scene of plague, pestilence, and warfare. Hans is about to give up his struggle and succumb to the harsh elements of the mountains and, symbolically, to the despairing side of his dream. A slice of blue sky breaks through the swirling storm and arouses Hans from his delirium. It seems like hours to him, but, in fact, only minutes have passed. The good weather jolts him back to his vision of sunbathed love and peace. "*For the sake of goodness and love, man shall grant death no dominion over his thoughts.*"[14] He mounts the snow and finds his way back to the Berghof: he has chosen life.

As with individuals, so with societies. Life was a complicated thing, threatened constantly by the pulls of desire and death. Order and stability were ephemeral achievements. Hans, the next morning, cannot so clearly remember the devotion to life and love that came to him in the snow. Mann's great novel captured, in complex and beautiful prose, those grand conflicts faced by his protagonist that were also the conflicts of Weimar modernity: between progress and tradition, order and desire, formality and hierarchy and the leveling tendencies of mass society. There are no easy answers, Mann tells us, and certainly no way back to the prewar world. He overcame great inner turmoil to arrive at his position in support of the republic. Even later, for all his anti-Nazi sentiments, it would take long deliberations and the strong pressure of his children, especially Erika and Klaus, before he threw caution to the winds to become the great antagonist of the Nazis. But like Hans in the snow, he did choose life.

The Magic Mountain was the literary event of 1925. *The Threepenny Opera*, written by Bertolt Brecht with music by Kurt Weill, was the theatrical sensation of 1928. It premiered on 31 August 1928 at the Theater am Schiffbauerdamm in Berlin. It was an immediate, smashing success, and it was also a trigger for the most profound loathing of everything modern. The audience and the critics recognized instantly the revolutionary character of the work. It took an art form that had become classical in the hands of Mozart, Verdi, or Strauss, deeply revered by its patrons for expressing the timeless truths of human existence in musical form, and made it popular. It took a stage form designed to express beauty, love, and tragedy and radicalized it, turned it into an exposé of the hypocrisies of capitalism. And into a music governed by a more or less standardized form since the late eighteenth century came the dissonant, subversive strains of jazz and cabaret. As the critic Herbert Ihering remarked: "What Brecht as author, Weill as composer . . . have achieved is to surmount the revue and make it into an entirely new art form. At the same time, they mix elements of Varieté to create a new, lively form of theatrical expression."[15]

The Threepenny Opera was the product of a creative collaboration between Brecht and Weill. Brecht was the more politically radical of the two, close to the Communists. Weill came from a bourgeois Jewish family and had had a rigorous classical music education. But he was keenly attuned to "the spirit of the age." He listened to jazz as well as the atonal compositions of Arnold Schönberg and Alban Berg. Like George Gershwin in the United States, he very consciously sought to integrate the pulse of the modern city into classical musical forms, very deliberately sought a wide audience for his music. Brecht was searching for a new language and form for the theater, a way to break through its tired conventions and limited appeal. In their parallel searches, Brecht and Weill eminently reflected the democratizing impulse of the Weimar years.

They first met in 1927 and collaborated on the song cycle *Mahagonny*. Mahagonny is a fictional city somewhere in America. It is populated with petty criminals, capitalists, cops, and prostitutes, with few if any characteristics distinguishing one from the other. The songs skewer the bourgeois values of order, discipline, and hard work. At the work's conclusion, the performers raised signs painted with anti-capitalist slogans. Weill's score was in and of itself revolutionary—he introduced a jazz-influenced ten-piece orchestra consisting of two violins, two clarinets, two trumpets, alto saxophone, piano, and percussion. Nothing like it had ever been performed at the German Chamber Music Festival in Baden-Baden, where it premiered. The audience was not pleased: its members booed and shouted; the performers blew whistles back at them. (Brecht had provided them with whistles in anticipation of just such a reaction.)[16] Through form, style, and content, Brecht and Weill, in one evening, had revolutionized musical theater in Germany—and beyond. The famous "Alabama Song"—sung that evening by Lotte Lenya, who would go on to a great career onstage and in film (and twice would be Weill's wife)—became a twentieth-century classic. (Those who know it only from the Doors' 1960s version believe it was written by Jim Morrison!)

Responding to criticism of *Mahagonny* from the very powerful Emil Hertzke, head of the Vienna-based musical publishing house Universal, Weill wrote:

> The reason I am drawn to Brecht is, first of all, the strong interaction of my music with his poetry. . . . I am convinced that the close collaboration of two equally productive individuals can lead to something fundamentally new. There can certainly be no doubt that at present a completely new form of stage work is evolving, one that is directed to a different and much larger audience and whose appeal will be unusually broad. . . . The task is to create the new genre which gives appropriate expression to the completely transformed manifestation of life in our time.[17]

Like Erich Mendelsohn and Bruno Taut in architecture, László Moholy-Nagy in photography, and many other Weimar figures, Weill and Brecht were consciously searching for forms and styles that reflected the fast pace, harsh conflicts, and popular aspirations of modern times. They wanted to create a new theatrical experience that would provoke and, at the same time, would have broad *public* resonance.

Brecht and Weill reworked the *Mahagonny* cycle into a longer full-fledged opera, but even that collaboration was, in a sense, the prelude to their work on a more extensive, even more earth-shattering piece, *The Threepenny Opera*. The story of the origins of *Threepenny* has been told many times. Brecht's companion, Elisabeth Hauptmann, had heard about the successful revival in London of an early eighteenth-century opera, *The Beggar's Opera*, by John Gay, with music by John Christopher Pepusch. That work incorporated the popular music, slang, and mix of street people of its day into a critique of upper-class English society. Its popular genre and political edge caught Brecht's attention. Brecht had only a few sketches of his adaptation ready to show an enterprising producer. *Scum*, as it was first titled, was commissioned in April 1928, with opening night scheduled some four and half months later. Not a note of music had been written for the opera; Weill might not even have been aware that Brecht had, in the contract, mandated his involvement in the project.

At some point, Brecht did, of course, inform Weill. In mid-May, the two of them, along with their wives, decamped for the Riviera and a few weeks of manic writing. But both the music and the text were still being rewritten as rehearsals began on 10 August. Conflicts on the set were rife; by opening night, everyone involved—author and composer, actors, producers, the great set designer Caspar Neher—expected a theatrical flop. The Weill scholar Jürgen Schebera describes what ensued: "Finally the evening of 31 August 1928 arrived, a date that was to go down in the history of twentieth-century theater. Up until the 'Kanonensong' (Cannon Song) the audience was rather reserved. But then came a breakthrough. The audience grew increasingly excited; approving murmurs and applause swelled to a crescendo. By the end, the triumphant success in which no one had believed had become a reality."[18] Brecht's hard-hitting language, peppered with street slang but also with comically baroque formulations, worked with Weill's incorporation of all sorts of musical elements, including parodies of traditional operatic forms laced with strains of jazz. Often, words that might appear to be most serious were given a kitschy or dissonant musical accompaniment that undermined their surface meanings. All along, Weill's compositions showed "artful refinement under the guise of simplicity," as Schebera writes.[19]

The story line depicts the interactions of a range of colorful characters: the beggar king, Jonathan Peachum; the inevitable (for Brecht) assortment of thieves, police officers, and prostitutes; Peachum's daughter Polly; and, of course, Macheath, better known as Mackie Messer (Mack the Knife). In Berlin in 1928, who could possibly have envisioned that Mackie's opening song would be turned into an American pop classic in 1959? Bobby Darin's rendition, whatever its virtues (or lack thereof), stripped the song of its political edge. Taken out of its context, it became an ode to a rather rakish character. Yet the Brecht-Weill collaboration is fundamentally about the depraved, degenerate, and exploitative nature of capitalism. Everyone lies; everyone cheats. The police are virtually indistinguishable from the criminals. The big-hearted prostitute has great dreams that are so often dashed. Sex is usually a business transaction of one sort or another. One of the biggest men in London makes his money by sending men and women out into the streets dressed as beggars. The wedding party is outfitted with goods stolen from all across London. The murderous rogue Mackie is ultimately pardoned by the queen herself, who ennobles him and grants him a castle and a lifetime pension.

So much for the bourgeois work ethic. The sharp political edge of *The Threepenny Opera* comes across clearly in particular lines: "First comes the fodder, then comes morality," or "Only the person with wealth lives comfortably," and especially in two great songs. In the fast-paced "Cannon Song," Mackie and police chief Tiger Brown wax nostalgic over their days slaughtering populations around the globe:

> The troops live under
> The cannon's thunder
> From the Cape to Cooch Bahar.
> When moving from place to place
> When they come face to face
> With a different breed of fellow
> Whose skin is black or yellow
> They quick as wink chop him into beefsteak tatare.[20]

No one could mistake the "Canon Song" for a celebration of German militarism, and it was only one of a number of powerful antiwar songs that Brecht and Weill wrote. They penned a deliberate affront to a Germany with a post-Versailles hobbled army but a still-powerful military culture.

And in "The Ballad of Sexual Obsession," Brecht and Weill satirized bourgeois sexual morality. The dirgelike quality of Weill's composition contrasts with Brecht's sharp-edged lyrics depicting both obsession and exploitation.

> Thus did many men see many men die,
> a great mind stranded in a whore!
> And those who looked on, whatever they swore,
> when they died, who buried them? Whores!
> Don't ask them if they want it, they're ready.
> That's sexual compulsion.
> This man follows the Bible, this one the Civil Code,
> this one's a Christian, this one an anarchist!
> At midday they force themselves to give up celery,
> in the afternoon they put their minds to higher things.
> In the evening they say "I'm in fine form."
> But before night falls they'll be on top again.[21]

The audience on opening night was enraptured, the critical reaction divided. Even the Communists missed the boat, claiming that *The Threepenny Opera* contained "no trace of social or political satire," while the conservative press lambasted it as "literary necrophilia" or "a political horror ballad." The Nazi *Völkischer Beobachter* used terms like "noxious cesspool" and "two-bit culture" that the police should simply sweep away.[22] But other critics remarked admiringly on its innovative character, and the production would have a long and successful run. It played the entire season in Berlin, and within a year had been staged by fifty-plus theaters in more than four thousand performances. By 1932 it had been translated into eighteen languages and performed to great acclaim in many European countries. The sheet music sold in huge press runs, and the lyrics and melodies were heard in cafés and dance halls.[23] The first recordings of *Threepenny* were issued in October 1928, just weeks after the opening, and the film version, directed by G. W. Pabst, came out in 1931. In this way, the new technologies of film and phonograph that flourished in Weimar contributed decisively to the success of *Threepenny*.

In all of his writing, Brecht questioned surface appearances. Moral pronouncements were exposed as mere platitudes or worse, social stature as a shell that hides a devious or depraved personality, the mask of one who made his way to the top through lies and exploitation. Brecht accepted nothing at face value. But he was not a cynic, as is so often claimed. A vibrant theater, in his view, would indeed shock its audience, but not just for thrills. Theater should force people to think, and if they see the true nature of society, the hypocrisies and injustices of the present, then there will be hope for the future. There was not the slightest trace of sentimentality here, no starry-eyed gaze into the future. Brecht was the toughest kind of writer, and he used jagged edges, punchy phrases, and dissonant elements to probe and provoke, to challenge any kind of simple, straight-line morality, any belief that any one individual or group embodied unadulterated virtue. As Brecht's great English-language critic, translator, and advocate John Willett wrote, Brecht sought "to attack, to judge, to startle, to demolish; thus showing the world itself as changeable, and the familiar as very odd."[24]

Brecht stripped the theater of many of its baroque excesses, the large, lavish productions, the pretensions of a dreamworld separated from daily life, that had been standard fare before 1914. He drew on the innovations pioneered by Erwin Piscator, Ernst Toller, and others, who brought onto the stage the features of modern times that the audience members encountered as they went about their routines on the streets and in the cinemas, music halls, and sports arenas of Berlin and any other German town or city in the 1920s and early 1930s. Following Piscator, Brecht sometimes splashed film clips or slide projections onto the background or had his cast march around with signs and shout slogans, mirroring the demonstrations and the pithy, sharp language that were so much a part of Weimar politics. He sought to reinvent the stage in the image of a boxing ring with harsh lights illuminating every corner and the crowd seated very close to the action and raucous in its behavior. His actors sometimes spoke directly to the spectators or sought audience involvement, a clichéd convention today, but revolutionary in the 1920s in its effort to break down the barrier between performers and viewers.

All this was Brecht's "epic theater," the term he himself adopted.[25] It meant, most basically and in the classical sense, a narrative form that was not bound to a particular time and place; instead, the narration consisted of a series of events loosely linked together, much like cinema with its sequencing of various scenes. Plot was less important, effect greater. But for Brecht, epic theater meant not merely visual or emotional impact. As he wrote in 1927, "the essential point of the epic theatre is perhaps that it appeals less to the feelings than to the spectator's reason. Instead of sharing an experience the spectator must come to grips with things."[26] And this meant that the actors should not try to enthrall the audiences, get them to identify with the character's emotions and psyche, but should confront and provoke the spectators, sometimes with a deliberately distanced way of speaking. Later, he would codify these thoughts into his notion of the "estrangement effect," the effort to make the spectators see the most common elements of life in a new, unfamiliar light, and thereby question all that has previously been embraced as truth or reality.

Weill's compositions fit perfectly with Brecht's epic theater. They dislodged the common and the familiar through parody and dissonance. Weill took standard musical forms and bent and reshaped them. The listener might at first nod with familiarity at a few bars of nineteenth-century opera or symphonic music, and then would find, perhaps disconcertingly, the conventional subsumed by the echoes of jazz and cabaret. At times Weill made the sense of the composition run against the lyrics of the song, as in "The Ballad of Sexual Obsession." Weill noted that in *Threepenny* he deliberately composed against the narrative. "I had a realistic plot, so I had to set the music against it, since I do not consider music capable of realistic effects. Hence the action was either interrupted, in order to introduce music, or it was deliberately driven to a point where there was no alternative but to sing."[27] Weill's music was deceptively simple while it also disrupted conventions.

The works of Thomas Mann and Bertolt Brecht and Kurt Weill were preeminent expressions of the Weimar spirit. All three of them sought to uncover the meaning of the present. But the cultural forms they championed were so very different. For Brecht, Mann was too refined, both in his personal manner and in his writing style, too preoccupied with the world of the past and unable to grasp artistically or intellectually the modernity of the 1920s. He was, simply, too bourgeois. Even though Brecht himself came from a bourgeois family in Augsburg, he reveled in the underworld and its harsh proletarian life—or at least claimed to revel in it. With his leather jacket and proletarian cap, he was a pioneer of "elegant slumming," in contrast to the always finely attired Mann. Brecht's language was hard and fast, almost American, while Mann's was languid and complex. Brecht's determination to develop an engaged theater, one that would consciously challenge and provoke its audience, marked an effort to find an aesthetic style appropriate to the unruly, conflict-ridden modern world of the 1920s.

Weill's brilliant compositions, drawing on so many musical genres and satirizing all of them, proved the perfect match. Mann, the reluctant republican, intuitively defended those of better breeding and culture. No one would ever expect someone of minimal education to read a Mann novel; Brecht and Weill had at least the hopes and pretensions that such people would flock to their productions. All three of them would end up in exile in the United States in the 1930s and 1940s. Brecht and Mann kept their distance from one another, their mutual loathing hardly a secret. Of the three, only Weill, with his love of American jazz and the pulsing rhythms of American life, would feel perfectly at home in exile. Yet although he wrote some lovely compositions, Weill's music in American exile lost the bristling creativity and sharp edges it had achieved in Weimar and through his collaboration with Brecht. It became sentimental instead of critical and innovative, something like Paul McCartney without John Lennon.

The philosophers and social theorists of the Weimar period who have had the most lasting impact are those who grappled directly with the meaning of the new, mass society on our thought processes and perceptions, of the impact of modernity on the very structures of thinking and seeing. Siegfried Kracauer and Martin Heidegger were polar opposites in terms of their sensibilities, political commitments, and career paths. But both of them sought to penetrate the surface appearances of the world, to probe behind the pulsing spectacles that modern society, and Weimar Germany in particular, offered up in so many guises and in such rapid-fire fashion. Kracauer lived the urban life of Berlin and Frankfurt, enthralled and repelled by its excitement and stimulation, its capacity for both alienation and emancipation.

For Heidegger, the modern world in which Kracauer immersed himself represented a shallow, hyperactive spectacle that made nearly impossible the deeper engagements that give true meaning to life. The modernity represented so thoroughly by Weimar had, according to Heidegger, privileged seeing over understanding. Modern man (and he did mean man) was a distracted, impoverished figure, one whose gaze roamed aimlessly and endlessly over mere sense perceptions. Life had been reduced to an unending succession of spectacles, that no longer permitted profound engagement with meaning. Film and the illustrated weekly, the focus of so many of Kracauer's essays, constituted, for Heidegger, the paradigmatic phenomena that established a tyranny of taste, a mass style, devoid of individuality, to which everyone aspired. Heidegger's response was not only intellectual but also personal: a retreat from urban society to his mountain hut among peasant compatriots, whence he delivered his thundering sermons critiquing modernity. Yet even for Heidegger, the fallen state of the present offered possibilities: thought could penetrate the contemporary moment and thereby find the path to the repossession of the self and the creation of a more authentic life.

Kracauer came from a lower middle-class Jewish family in Frankfurt. He had trained and begun work as an architect, and had also studied with the great social theorist Georg Simmel. He moved in the leading intellectual circles of Weimar Germany, those well established and those just beginning, a fellowship including Bloch (who had also studied with Simmel and the other great social theorist, Max Weber), Theodor Adorno, Georg Lukács, Walter Benjamin, Martin Buber, and others. Many of them, though certainly not all, were Jewish. Leaving architectural practice behind, Kracauer engaged in social and philosophical critique. He became a very prominent writer and editor for the *Frankfurter Zeitung*, one of Germany's preeminent liberal newspapers, for which he produced more than two thousand feuilleton pieces on all sorts of topics.

Like his friend Benjamin, Kracauer had a far more ambivalent attitude toward modernity than did Heidegger. Both Kracauer and Benjamin reveled in the sights and sounds of the city, and wrote trenchant analyses of the artifacts of modern culture, from the spatial layout of the city to film and photography. But they worried about the degeneration of the senses that came from all this rapid, hyperactive movement. In response, all sensory operations, tactile and visual, all the thought processes, were accelerated to respond to the fast-paced character of the city. Unlike the languid flaneur Franz Hessel (whom we met in chapter 2), who took his time strolling about the city, slowly taking it all in, Kracauer's flaneur has more the character of the modern cinema with its rapid-cut editing and quick shifting from one scene to another. Kracauer's flaneur walks briskly, speedily shifting his gaze from buildings to people to traffic. For Kracauer (and Benjamin), these new modes of perception were double-edged. The flaneur absorbs more, becomes, in a sense, a more developed person by taking in so much more than do Heidegger's peasants, whose world, if more coherent, is also profoundly limited by the rhythms of their cows, the seasons, and the weather. But the modern perceiver is also overwhelmed, like a circuit breaker that can no longer channel the current, and fragmented, like a capacitor sundered into pieces by an overly powerful burst of electricity. The perceiver is reduced to mere spectator, a helpless child who watches a flurry of events go by, but participates in none.

For Kracauer, the cinema mirrored rationalized labor in the factory: each is broken down into distinctive parts, then rapidly assembled. Neither the factory nor the cinema could be rejected: they were simply the facts of life of the modern world. But there was hope. Cinema, precisely because of its coordination with the factory, was not just debilitating (though it certainly could be); it was also potentially liberating. It enabled individuals (or at least the theorist) to grasp the nature of modernity, the first step in participation. Once the perceiver understands, he can move beyond mere spectatorship, and a world of possibilities, of freely chosen experiences, becomes available to him. The fragmentation produced by modernity was not the endpoint of history. By understanding its essence, the individual could transcend the present. The echoes of Hegel and Marx, and also of Brecht and Weill, are clear here.

"The Mass Ornament" is one of Kracauer's most brilliant and well-known essays. It was published in 1927, one among the cluster of great works produced in these years—*The Magic Mountain* in 1925, Heidegger's *Being and Time* (as we shall see) in 1927, "The Mass Ornament" in 1927, and *The Threepenny Opera* in 1928. Kracauer's subject here is not film but the "girl revues" of Weimar cabaret. The

Jackson Girls, the Tiller Girls, and many others were inspired by American-style performances, and achieved even greater precision and flair in Berlin. The thirty or so long-legged, scantily clad women moved in unison onstage in long rows and with precise movements. They were especially renowned for their high kicks.

To Kracauer (though many male viewers would probably have disagreed), there was nothing erotic about the girl revues. Instead, they joined together his two nightmare visions: Prussian militarism and the American factory. The highly organized, tightly disciplined movements of "the girls" evoked both the drill march of the Prusso-German army and Henry Ford's assembly line. They were the embodiment, not of desire, but of alienation, of the separation of men and women from all that made them human, including erotic sentiments. It was as if capitalist modernity had destroyed even that most basic element of human existence, replacing sexuality, through the Tiller Girls, with the symbolic replication of the machine gun's rapid fire and the relentless monotony of the assembly line. It was all very efficient, to be sure—whether in "real" form on the battlefield or inside the factory or as spectacle onstage—but it was also life-destroying. The girls, Kracauer wrote, are "products of American distraction factories [and] are no longer individual girls, but indissoluble girl clusters whose movements are demonstrations of mathematics."[28] They are "sexless bodies in bathing suits" and exist only "as parts of a mass." Modern communications and transportation—cinema, railroad, airplane—mean that they can be seen all around the world, in the tiniest village and on the most distant continent.[29] The Tiller Girls were a kind of globalization phenomenon before the thing itself had been named, with all the same ambivalences then and now: people everywhere can have the same experiences, resulting in a vast increase in their range of vision, but those same experiences are torn from their rootedness in a particular culture and society. A sense of loss and anonymity accompanies the broadening of experiences.

In a later essay, "Girls and Crisis," and writing about the Jackson Girls, Kracauer made the machine analogy even more explicit:

> The girls' poses recall the regular play of the pistons [of a ship's engines]. They are not so much of military precision as they correspond in some other way to the ideal of the machine. A button is pressed and the girl contraption cranks into motion,

> performing impressively at thirty-two horsepower. All the parts begin to roll, the waves fall into their cycles. And while the machine stamps, shakes, and roars like a sawmill or a locomotive, a smile drips a steady supply of oil onto the joints so that the cogs do not suddenly fail. Finally an inaudible signal brings the mechanical action to a stop, and the dead whole automatically decomposes itself into its living parts. A process of destruction that leaves behind the sad feeling that the parts are wholly incapable of existing further on their own.[30]

The loss of individuality that Kracauer sees in the machinelike activity of the Jackson Girls is profound. They exist only as a mass, and their only purpose is motion—manic, organized, and pointless motion. When the economy flourished, the spectator could hear "business, business" in the pounding of the dance girls' heels. "When they raised their legs with mathematical precision above their heads, they joyfully affirmed the progress of rationalization, and when they continually repeated the same maneuver, never breaking ranks, one had visions of an unbroken chain of automobiles gliding from the factory into the world and the feeling that there was no end to prosperity." But in the Depression's depths, the girls evince a "ghostly" air.[31] The factories have shut down, so the movement of the girl-factories has been hollowed of all substance.

Although Kracauer draws an explicit comparison with the capitalist production process, the Tiller Girls signify something even worse. Under capitalism—following Kracauer's Marxist-influenced thought—goods are produced and consumed solely for profit making (technically, for surplus value), not for any intrinsic value they might possess. The girl revues likewise have no intrinsic value; they only create an ornament that is consumed visually by the audience. It is, as the title of the essay suggests, a "mass ornament," so the individual girl has no distinctive character, just as the worker in the factory has no individual distinctiveness. The brilliance of Kracauer's analysis here is that it moves far beyond Marx's preoccupation with the world of production (though Marx did write about commodity fetishism) to the production and consumption of culture and the alienation *they* produce under conditions of capitalism—both for the enactors, the girls themselves, and for the spectators. Those involved cannot see the entire process, just as the proverbial worker-cog in the machine of capitalist production cannot see the total social meaning of his or her own labor. Indeed, even the parts of their bodies are disaggregated. The legs of the Tiller Girls capture the eyes of the audience and become the "abstract designation of their bodies."[32]

Still, these surface objects, the most superficial manifestations of the age, offer us the path to deeper understanding, according to Kracauer. The very objects of mass society, however petty and ugly, however devoid of meaning and sufficient unto themselves, provide evidence of the substance and spirit of the age. As he wrote in "The Mass Ornament": "The position that an epoch occupies in the historical process can be determined most strikingly from an analysis of its inconspicuous surface-level expressions. . . . [which] provide unmediated access to the fundamental substance of the state of things."[33] The perceptive critic can peer behind and underneath the surfaces of spectacle and display to discover meaning. He can discern the underlying pattern of life beneath the high kicks of the Tiller Girls, even when their kicks signify nothing more than linear and circular patterns.

Kracauer seeks meaning in the very ornamentations he describes as meaningless. Most important is his refusal to accept simple answers and draw facile conclusions. Kracauer's restless questioning and the fact that he relishes tensions and contradictions are traits that were also manifest in Mann's novels and essays, Brecht and Weill's operas and plays, and, as we shall see, Heidegger's philosophical ruminations and Hannah Höch's photomontages.

Kracauer was very much a part of the German mandarin tradition, which placed primacy on knowledge and self-cultivation and imagined the male, educated elite as the bearers of culture and the very embodiment of the German spirit.[34] That ideal helped create a superb system of higher education that, over the course of the nineteenth century, had become somewhat more open to Jews and others of nonelite backgrounds provided they were intellectually gifted. Kracauer also endowed the intellectual with primacy in the social world. If he adopted a critical stance, the intellectual could perceive the meaning of the Tiller Girls. He could understand the estrangement they signified; he could work through the mass ornament to transcendence, a nonalienated, utopian world.

For many mandarins, the worship of the intellectual ran hand in hand with a certain contempt for the common people of mass

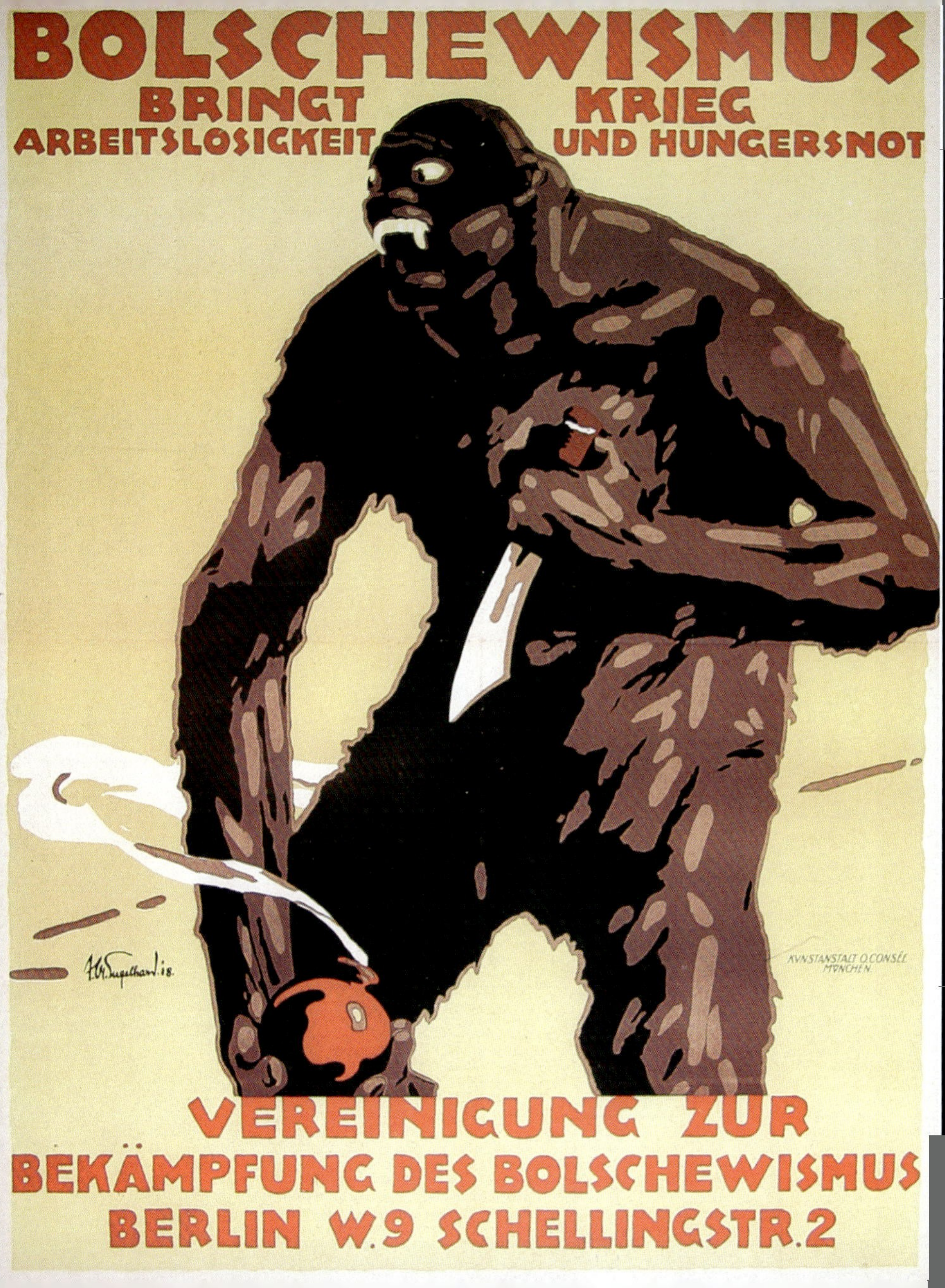
BOLSCHEWISMUS
BRINGT KRIEG
ARBEITSLOSIGKEIT UND HUNGERSNOT
KVNSTANSTALT O. CONSÉE
MVNCHEN
VEREINIGUNG ZUR
BEKÄMPFUNG DES BOLSCHEWISMUS
BERLIN W.9 SCHELLINGSTR.2

H.H.
DENKMAL II. 26
EITELKEIT

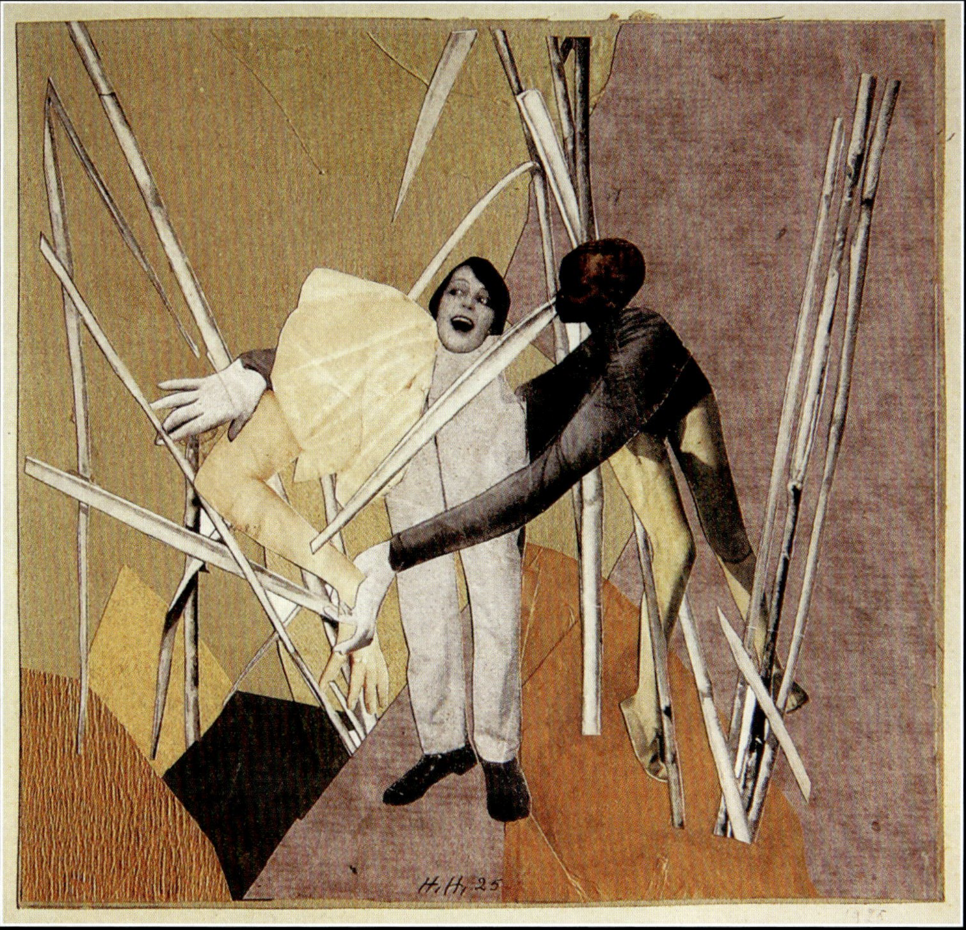

Plate 6. Hannah Höch, *Love in the Bush,* 1925. By the mid-1920s Höch's work had become sparser, more in tune with the prevailing style of New Objectivity. Yet her paintings, photomontages, and photo albums always retained a sharply critical edge. Here she disrupts standard racial and gender views by depicting an African man and a European woman about to make love, but the woman's head is placed on the torso of a man. These kinds of works enraged the Right. Many on the organized Left also rejected modern art; they wanted naturalist styles that depicted heroic male proletarians. © 2006 Artist Rights Society (ARS), New York / VG Bildkunst, Bonn.

Plate 5. Hannah Höch, *Cut with the Kitchen Knife,* 1919. Höch was a pioneer of photomontage. Here she cut and pasted images from the Berliner Illustrirte Zeitung and perhaps other periodicals, disrupting any sense that printed materials have a stable meaning. Heads and bodies are placed together incongruently. Individuals float around among the gears and ball bearings of industrial production. Crowds gather in mass demonstrations and political leaders are depicted in ironic fashion. Modernity is pulsing, exciting, and threatening in this work. Its busy, chaotic character is also typical of the Dada movement, with which Höch was associated in this period.

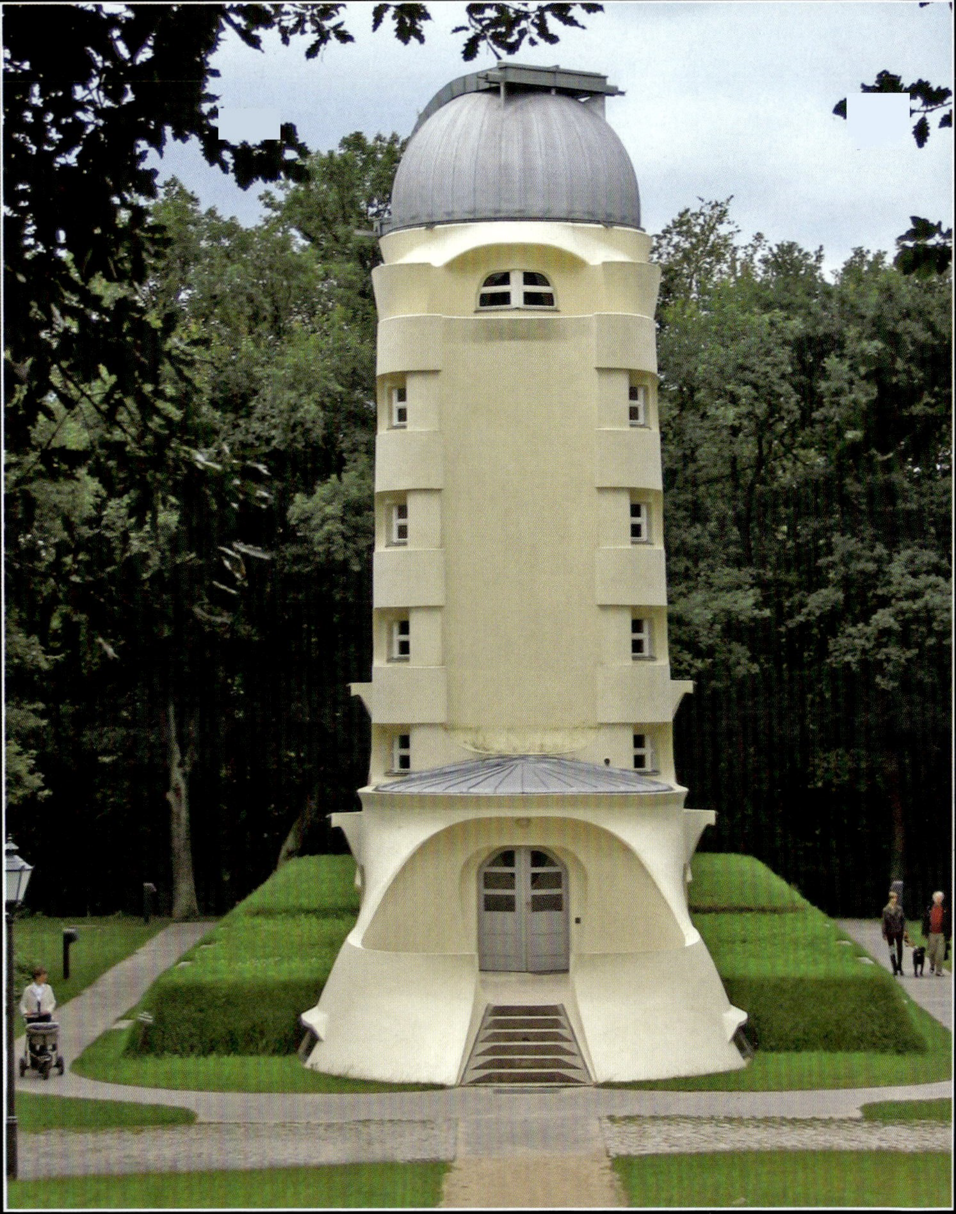

Plate 4. Erich Mendelsohn, Einstein Tower, built 1920–24. Mendelsohn was one of Weimar Germany's most prominent and successful architects. The Tower was built as a laboratory and observatory in which Einstein's theories would be tested. Mendelsohn sought to capture in form the essence of relativity theory. He might not have succeeded in that venture, but the smooth exterior, recessed windows, absence of ornamentation, and overall beauty mark the building as a strikingly original example of modern architecture. On his first visit, Einstein reputedly said in admiration, "Organic!" Here the building is shown following an extensive, very successful renovation in the 1990s. Author's photograph.

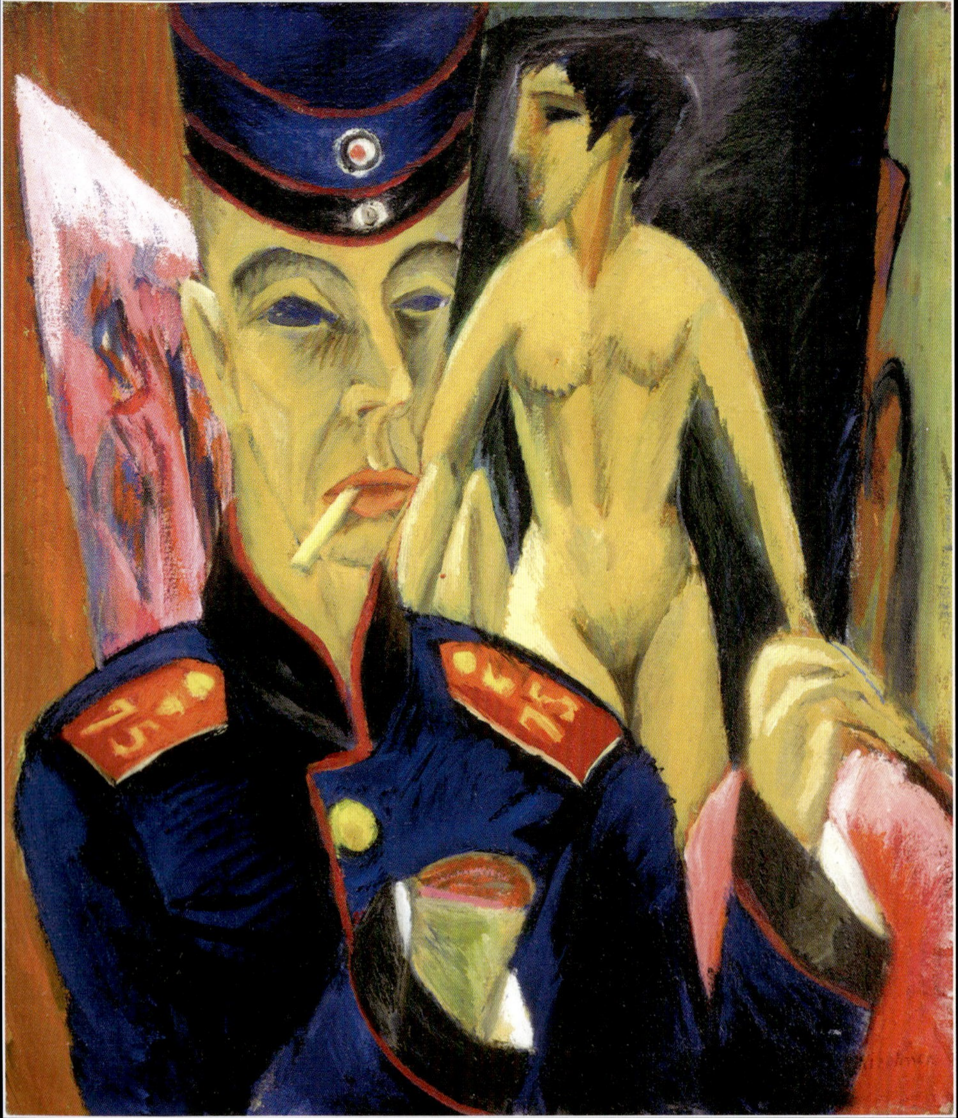

Plate 3. Ernst Ludwig Kirchner, *Self-Portrait as Soldier,* 1915. Kirchner served at the front in World War I and suffered a nervous breakdown. Here he painted himself in his army uniform and mutilated (though he had not been wounded physically). He has lost his painting hand, and the erotically-charged model in the background is unreachable, both on canvas and in life. Kirchner's face is drawn and tense. The themes of the painting and its angular shapes and bright colors are emblematic of Expressionism. Kirchner shows that the violence of war has disastrous, life-long effects. He never fully recovered from his breakdown and the combination of depressions and Nazi persecution led him to commit suicide in 1938. Allen Memorial Art Museum, Oberlin College, Ohio; Charles F. Olney Fund 1950.

Plate 2. "The Perfume of this Winter: Vogue" Consumer advertising came of age in the 1920s, and the image of the elegant, wealthy new woman sold everything from soap to perfume. Here she is bathed in jewelry and evokes an appealing scent. Note the clean lines of the typeface. ullstein bild / The Granger Collection, New York

Plate 1. "Women! Equal Rights - Equal Responsibilities. Vote Social Democratic!" The SPD tries to rally women voters by mixing the flaming red of socialism with the call for equality. But the male comrade is always a step ahead. Hessisches Landesmuseum Darmstadt.

society, especially women, and the pleasures they derived from the spectacle-world of the 1920s. Kracauer's contempt was especially patent and explicit. He wrote disparagingly of the "little shopgirls" who visit the cinema and become lost in the dreamworlds produced by Hollywood and its German counterpart, Bablesberg (located near Berlin).[35] To be sure, the major point of Kracauer's essay named for them—"The Little Shopgirls Go to the Movies"—is that cinema reproduces the values of capitalist society. As a business, the film industry is an inextricable element of capitalist production and would not dare to release movies that challenge the very value system of capitalism. Instead, it promotes cheap sentimentality and artificial crises, whose resolution takes the form of a vagabond's stumbling upon a fortune or a servant girl's finding a millionaire husband. And when a film does challenge the essence of capitalism, as did the Soviet film *Potemkin*, wrote Kracauer, critics in Germany and elsewhere talk only about its aesthetic virtues and cinematographic innovations, thereby depriving it of its revolutionary meaning.

But Kracauer's condemnation in the essay is not focused on capitalism alone. He also critiques the shopgirls for allowing themselves to be sucked in by the artificial dreamworlds of cinema. Kracauer summarizes the plot of a dozen or so cinematic melodramas, and ends each précis with a contemptuous reference to "the little shopgirls" who allow themselves to revel in dreams of finding their own millionaire husbands, or their "unexpected insights into the misery of mankind and the goodness from above," or the sentiments inspired by military uniforms.[36] "The little shopgirls learn to understand that their brilliant boss is made of gold on the inside as well; they await the day when they can revive a young Berliner with their silly little hearts."[37] Kracauer's sneering contempt is unsettling. What, one might ask, was so terrible about a few hours' diversion from the unrelenting supervision of foremen and bosses on the shop floor, at the sales counter, or in the office, and the poor pay and cramped living circumstances that defined the lives of so many German women?

"What is the meaning of Being?" The philosopher Martin Heidegger posed that most fundamental of all questions in *Being and*

Time. Published in 1927, it is, arguably, the most important philosophical work of the twentieth century. Heidegger did nothing less than throw overboard the entire corpus of Western philosophy since Socrates. He went back further, to the pre-Socratics, who were the last, he believed, to pose that searching question and had come closer to answering it than those who followed. Not that Heidegger ignored or disparaged the Western tradition. Hardly. But he did think that a fundamental theoretical error had entered into Western thinking and was reflected in the works of such luminaries as Plato, Aristotle, Aquinas, Descartes, Kant, and Hegel.

For Heidegger, that error consisted of a series of ruptures—of knowledge and being, of mind and body, of subject and object, of the knower and knowing, of true knowledge and everyday experience. The famous Cartesian line "I think, therefore I am" was fundamentally mistaken, according to Heidegger, because it presumed a radical separation of the individual from the world around him, including the world of objects that he perceives. Heidegger's effort at unraveling the meaning of Being (or *Dasein*, in German) involved, essentially, embedding man in the world, seeing a unity between man and his surroundings and between the moment of knowledge and the flow of time. There are objects "out there" that have an existence separate from their perception by humans, but they have meaning only after they are perceived, and to divine meaning is necessarily to engage in interpretation.

In Heidegger's philosophy, Being has a totalizing character. He was not writing about the being of individual objects or persons. "The 'universality' of 'Being,' he wrote in the introduction, "is not of a *class* or *genus*. . . . The 'universality' of Being '*transcends*' any universality of genus."[38] Heidegger talked about the very meaning of existence (though the term "existence" has a more debased connotation in his writing). There is a self-sufficiency to Being akin to the Hebrew Bible's nondefinition of God: "I am that which I am."[39] God is self-sufficient; God is totality; God is everything. So with Being. But how are we to understand its meaning? Heidegger was never able to arrive at an answer to his own question. The revolutionary character of Heidegger's philosophy lay in his posing of the question, the methodology he offered to try to answer it, and the creative combination of ideas and methods that, before Heidegger, existed as separate strands of philosophy. It may well be, even to Heidegger, that there simply is no final answer, but that the posing of the question at least brings one closer to authenticity, to Being.

Language is critical, and it is through the ur-language of philosophy, Greek, and its modern analogue, German, that we can begin to set out on the path to understanding. "Path" is a very Heideggerian metaphor, as are "light" and "illumination" and "clearing." On the path of questioning, we approach an illuminated spot or a clearing. Knowledge is revealed to us—we do not "grasp" or "appropriate" or "think" it. There is something primordial and experiential in our steps toward understanding.[40] Significantly, Heidegger often proposed that it is in nature and with nature—the clearing in the forest, the beam of light, the path through the forest that we traverse to those points—or in and with the process of labor, that we come closer to understanding. That understanding is in many ways an "uncovering," not a discovery of something new. The religious metaphors are patent: nature, revelation, illumination, the hints at transcendence that come from the understanding of Being. Heidegger had forsaken his Catholic upbringing, but not a Christian idiom.

At the same time, his philosophy is completely this-worldly: transcendence comes from knowledge of and action in *this world*, not an otherworld of the spirit. Indeed, it is in the this-world of everyday life, not in theorizing disconnected from the everyday, that one can begin to uncover meaning. But that does not mean one simply receives impressions from everyday occurrences. One has to probe what lies hidden, explore the connections, "think" the occurrences, to understand even the most common everyday events. The act of uncovering requires recognition of our relatedness to the world; there is no individual, no individuality abstracted from the world. At the same time, there is no essential meaning except that which we bestow on objects, hence the critical role of interpretation in Heidegger's philosophy.[41]

In *Being and Time*, Heidegger deployed very practical examples to explicate his ideas. The most famous is that of the carpenter and his hammer.[42] We could—and in fact, philosophy before Heidegger had done so—disaggregate the various elements: the discrete objects nail, hammer, and board, and the discrete motions of the arm and hand of the hammerer. But that is an impoverished understanding of what is really going on, Heidegger suggests. The objects and motions have meaning only when we think of them in combination. Yet even that thought-step provides only a very partial understanding. The hammer hits the nail at a discrete moment in time. Embedded in that moment is the past of the carpenter's accumulated skill and the future-directedness of the movement, which is not simply hammering a nail but creating a cabinet. We have to think of action and actor together, and of the flow of time in which the particular moment is embedded. Sometimes, it is only the disruption of the action-in-time—when the handle of the hammer breaks, or an unskilled blow bends the nail, or the expected supply of wood is not at hand—that allows us to see the totality of the relations, which is "lit up . . . [and] the world announces itself."[43] The example here is crucial: it is everyday experience, not abstracted thought, that allows us to understand the world, and the world is *revealed* to us (rather than thought) through our action-in-the-world. Yet at the same time, this revelation of the world, this "Being-in-itself" requires "interpretation."[44]

Thus, for Heidegger, things do not have a "true" essence that somehow stands behind that which we perceive or that unfolds in their practice. Rather, one can approach the meaning of Being only by understanding the inextricable links between objects and observer, things and agents, the embeddedness of all of them, their condition of *Dasein*, of being-there or being-in-the-world. Always, Heidegger challenged ruptures—of objects from knowing, of individuals from the world, of knowing from interpretation. In the modern wold, Heidegger suggests, we live in a state of mere existence, a state of unreflectiveness marked by a preoccupation with surface appearances and objects, with the technologies that devastate the earth. We live, in short, in a state of estrangement, a world that lacks *authenticity* and has lacked it for millennia. Being is authentic; existence is not.

By the proper questioning, man opens himself to Being and thereby becomes more human. Authentic questioning presumes an understanding of one's own embeddedness in the world, of *Dasein*, of being-there or being-in-the-world. Heidegger writes:

> Thus to work out the question of Being adequately, we must make an entity—the inquirer—transparent in his own Being. The very asking of this question is an entity's mode of *Being*; and

> as such it gets its essential character from what is inquired about—namely, Being. This entity which each of us is himself and which includes inquiring as one of the possibilities of its Being, we shall denote by the term "*Dasein*."[45]

The vast reach of Heidegger's intellectual ambition is evident here despite the circularity and obscurity of the language. In fact, the circularity is precisely the point. It is the way Heidegger strove to overturn the ruptures of subject and object that had governed so much of Western philosophy. The "entity" is the questing and questioning individual. By posing the fundamental question, one is engaged in Being. One gets one's essential character—Being—from asking about Being; one is there in Being, in the condition of *Dasein*. Asking about Being makes one more human. But that is a state one has to reach: *Dasein* is potential. "Dasein always understands itself in terms of its existence—in terms of a possibility of itself: to be itself or not itself."[46]

Heidegger's emphasis on authenticity via individuality forcefully echoed the German valuation of *Bildung* (education and cultivation) that has played such a prominent role in modern German history. No less than Mann and Kracauer, Heidegger stressed the role of the questing and cultivated man who has the potential to attain true knowledge of the ultimate, of Being. Although he was never explicit on the point, it does seem that only those cultivated men who are capable of serious reflection on the everyday can become "authentic" and thereby approach Being.

But in the present of the modern, inauthentic world, of Weimar Germany in particular, the anonymous mass, the "they," have taken over, and even the potential knowers of *Dasein* have lost their individuality. *Dasein* is the "I": "Dasein is an entity which is in each case I myself; its Being is in each case mine. . . . The question of the 'who' answers itself in terms of the 'I' itself, the 'subject', the 'Self.' "[47] But there is also the "they," "those from whom, for the most part, one does *not* distinguish oneself."[48] This point has a complex, even contradictory, character in Heidegger's opus. There is, as we have already seen, no completely abstracted "I" in Heidegger's philosophy. One is always with others: "Dasein in itself is essentially Being-with."[49] So there is a social character to the attainment of Being. But the others can also be the mass, which produces, instead of an individuated self (a *Dasein*), the world of conformity in which we do not reflect on the fundamental question of Being but simply exist subject to the will and desires of the mass.[50] The Moloch "they" stands over the "I," crushing the self.

Heidegger summons up as examples of the fearsome and delusive power of the mass those very modern technologies and communication forms, public transportation and newspapers, that flourished in Weimar. The passage is worth quoting at length:

> In utilizing public means of transport and in making use of information services such as the newspaper, every Other is like the next. This Being-with-one-another dissolves one's own Dasein completely into the kind of Being of "the Others", in such a way, indeed, that the Others, as distinguishable and explicit, vanish more and more. In this inconspicuousness and unascertainability, the real dictatorship of the "they" is unfolded. We take pleasure and enjoy ourselves as *they* take pleasure; we read, see, and judge about literature and art as *they* see and judge; likewise we shrink back from the "great mass" as *they* shrink back; we find "shocking" what *they* find shocking. The "they", which is nothing definite, and which all are, though not as the sum, prescribes the kind of Being of everydayness. . . .
>
> [T]he "they" . . . keeps watch over everything exceptional that thrusts itself to the fore. Every kind of priority gets noiselessly suppressed. Overnight, everything that is primordial gets glossed over as something that has long been well known. Everything gained by a struggle becomes just something to be manipulated. Every secret loses its force. This care of averageness reveals in turn an essential tendency of Dasein which we call the "leveling down" of all possibilities of Being.[51]

In their rhetorical power and vision of a debased world that crushes all individuality, all hope of authentic Being, these passages are the equal of those penned by other great critics of modern, mass society, from Karl Marx to Ortega y Gassett to George Orwell. For Heidegger, the origins of the fallen state lie not in the specifics of capitalism or of twentieth-century totalitarianism. The origins lie even more deeply and are more complex: in the errors of philosophy; in the power of conformity when the "they" preside over the individuated self; and in the condition of modernity, which places special emphasis on surface appearances and shallow hyperactivity, lends still greater power to the mass, and makes even wider the chasm of estrangement in which men live. The world of surfaces, of chatter rather than speech, of fear rather than a proper, thought-inducing *Angst*, marks this fallen world.[52] Life in the present is characterized by Inauthenticity.

However, the sense exists in *Being and Time* that the fall from a pre-Socratic state to the present is necessary and not to be mourned. There is a way back (even though neither Heidegger nor anyone else will actually find it). The return to Being occurs through stages of *Sorge*, of care for and concern with, of solicitude for others, for labor (or activity) in the world, for Being itself. And this entails as well a recognition of the finitude of life, of the nullity of death, of the irreducible individuality of death. We may have all kinds of emotions about the death of others, but ultimately our death is only our own. Recognizing that reality unleashes the freedom to approach Being, enables one to question seriously and thereby approach authenticity.[53] To get the question right is to have hope that there is an answer. As Heidegger writes:

> in what is asked about there lies also *that which is to be found out by the asking*. . . . Inquiry, as a kind of seeking, must be guided beforehand by that which is sought. So the meaning of Being must already be available to us in some way. . . . We do not *know* what "Being" means. But even if we ask, "What *is* 'Being'?", we keep within an understanding of the "is", though we are unable to fix conceptually what the "is" signifies.[54]

In the asking we awaken to the ecstasy or astonishment (depending on the translation) of Life: we abandon placidity and probe, with an air of wonder, the meaning of Being. But with hints in *Being and Time* and more explicitly later, Heidegger also links *Dasein* to the community, so that the organic national or racial community becomes the individual writ large: through an authentic community Being is accessible. That connection, the critique of modernity coupled with a plaintive plea for the individual to recognize his deep embeddedness in the national and racial community, was the common stuff of right-wing ideology of the Weimar period and accounts for Heidegger's later commitment to the Nazis.

The brilliance of *Being and Time* has much to do with Heidegger's unexpected and innovative combinations, which lent to his thinking, writing, and lecturing an astonishing freshness: his claim that understanding derives from everydayness yet, at the same time, requires interpretation; the great emphasis on the individuated self paired with an emphasis on the social through man's embeddedness in the world, composed as it is of nature, objects, and other human beings; the contention that the world is revealed to us, that understanding of Being is in some fashion primordial yet, again, requires interpretation. There are, indeed, as many would argue, contradictions galore in these couplings, and Heidegger's writing can be abstruse and circular. Call them contradictions; call them tensions: they enthralled Heidegger's students, like Hans Jonas, in the 1920s and continue to inspire thought, commentary, and debate.

For all of Heidegger's radical innovation in philosophy, for all of his unquestioned brilliance, he was also embedded in his own time and place, Germany in the 1920s and early 1930s. There appears to be no evidence in any of his writings, including personal correspondence, that suggests his intellectual breakthrough came as a direct result of the destructiveness of World War I and the postwar crises. Yet he had seen action on the western front, however briefly, and he was, without question, acutely estranged from the politics and culture of Weimar Germany. His voice was one more in the "crisis of civilization" chorus that dominated right-wing discourse in the 1920s (a topic to which we will return). Before he became famous, his call, in a letter to a friend (and perhaps lover), Elisabeth Blochmann, for a spiritual renewal echoed precisely the rantings of all sorts of people on the right, and sometimes on the left as well.

> Spiritual life must again become truly real with us—it must be endowed with a force born of personality, a force that "overturns" and compels genuine rising—and this force is revealed as a genuine one only in simplicity, not in the blasé, decadent, enforced. . . . Spiritual life can only be demonstrated and shaped in such a way that those who are to share in it are directly gripped by it *in their most personal existence*.[55]

Heidegger knew that he was the man to think his way to spiritual renewal; he was the man gripped by the force.

Heidegger rarely left southwestern Germany; he spent a good deal of his time at his retreat, little more than a hut, in the Black Forest. Jazz, expressionist art, the congestion of traffic and people, meandering around the city—all that was totally alien to his very being. Heidegger joined other conservative thinkers who despised so many aspects of modernity. Usually for them, the turning point had come with the French Revolution, which, in their understanding, had brought the masses onto the political stage and had adopted an ideology of liberal individualism that alienated human beings from their organic connection to the land and the nation or race. The modern factory and the modern city were the major manifestations of this alienation, and it was no surprise—according to the conservative way of thinking—that Jews played a prominent role in both. Heidegger shared these beliefs (though his anti-Semitism developed later, and he had a Jewish mentor in Edmund Husserl and, as noted, Jewish students) but found the origins of the alienation much further back in time than did most of his conservative counterparts. For Heidegger, it was not the political act of the French Revolution that had initiated the decline; rather, he traced its onset to classical Athens, when the fundamental error had entered into philosophy. There is an apocalyptic, theological tone to Heidegger's writing, a sense that man has lived in a fallen state since that time, and the only way out of the crisis is to rethink the fundamentals of Western philosophy. (Heidegger himself, despite his early theological training, would reject the assertion that his philosophy had a theological element.) It is this fallen state, *the lack of authenticity*, that so preoccupied Heidegger, and that also connects his views with those of other conservative thinkers.

Heidegger, after *Being and Time*, made an all-too-easy leap from the problem of understanding Being to postulating, somehow, an organic community that can arrive at understanding, a community whose language, German, has special affinities with the ur-language of philosophy, Greek. Only those languages, he suggested, could truly probe the meaning of Being. His organicism opens his writings up to all sorts of varied political inflections, especially since *Being and Time* explicitly rejects an ethical or moral content to understanding.[56] Yet at the same time, his philosophy is not simply conservative. His hermeneutical approach, the understanding that knowledge is, indeed, perspectival, dependent on the interpretation of the person, disrupts the certainties that conservative thought posits, the notion that there are fixed meanings that allow for no discussion, only political battles against the opponents.

While Thomas Mann, Siegfried Kracauer, Bertolt Brecht, and Kurt Weill fled Germany after 1933, Heidegger became a Nazi. As George Steiner argues so eloquently, the major issue concerning his political legacy is not so much his rectorship of Freiburg University under the Nazis, his pro-Nazi statements of the early and mid-1930s, and his acquiescence to the removal of Jewish faculty members, including his own mentor. Heidegger was no worse and no better than so many German intellectuals who believed the Nazis offered the resolution to the crisis of civilization. The more important issue, however, is his total silence after 1945.[57] He never, ever condemned National Socialism and mentioned Auschwitz only in one insipid comment that devalued the tragedy it represents. But as for his philosophy—that is a far more complicated matter. It had affinities with Nazi and other radical conservative thinking. At the same time, its hermeneutical approach also undermined—despite Heidegger's own political beliefs—those very same beliefs. One finds only very rarely in Heidegger irony or sarcasm, which serve to distance artists and philosophers from the events and ideas that they depict, whether in the novel, as with Mann, or in a modern, jazz-tinged opera in the case of Brecht and Weill.[58] For Heidegger, the crisis of philosophy was too serious, deadly serious, in fact.

For Heidegger, newspapers represented the idle chatter that he so detested, a sign of the fallen status of man in the age of modernity. For the artist Hannah Höch, they provided creative stimulation. Out of the typescript and images found in newspapers and magazines, Höch developed the new art form of photomontage. As with so much else in Weimar, the genre's lineage can be traced back before 1914, in this case to the late nineteenth century when designers patched together photos and drawings for advertising and picture postcards. In World War I, energetic entrepreneurs sold such postcards en masse to soldiers in the field so they could easily write their loved ones back home.

However, few observers before 1914 would have called these postcards or soap advertisements "art." "True art" represented timeless values and was displayed for contemplation in galleries and museums and in the drawing rooms of the wealthy. But during the war and, explosively, right afterward, modern artists began to use everyday items in their work. Rather than reject mass society and its artifacts, as did Heidegger and so many others, or react to it with deep ambivalence, as did Mann and even Kracauer, they embraced the products of the factory and the newspaper printing press. Höch was a pioneer who developed photomontage as one of the quintessential modern art forms. In her hands, photomontage also had a decisive critical edge. Her work both celebrated and critiqued Weimar modernity. And she was not alone. Her friends Kurt Schwitters and John Heartfield and the Soviet artist Kasimir Malevich, among others, were also innovators of the new art form, and all of them stood on the left, Heartfield and Malevich as members of their respective communist parties, Höch as a sometime sympathizer.

Höch and Heartfield both took photographic images and typescript from a wide variety of sources—newspapers, popular magazines, advertisements—and cut and pasted them together in wildly new and shocking ways. By taking images that had already been printed and disseminated and cutting and mixing them with other images, Höch and Heartfield boldly asserted the impermanence of things. What a newspaper or magazine or advertisement had tried to fix as a particular image, they rearranged, often with a whimsical or utopian sensibility. It is no wonder that Bloch responded so positively to photomontage: it was an aesthetic of emancipation that illuminated utopian possibilities.[59]

In the early postwar years, Höch and Heartfield were both affiliated with Dada, which proudly proclaimed the death of traditional art and the birth of a new "machine" art. In the famous Dada Manifesto of 1918, the Romanian-born French poet Tristan Tzara parodied every convention, every belief in tradition and timeless values. "DADA DOES NOT MEAN ANYTHING," he loudly proclaimed. It is ideals, knowledge, and nonsense, a rejection of the family, sexual prudishness, logic, memory, and archaeology. It celebrates spontaneity and folly. "Liberty: DADA DADA DADA;—the roar of contorted pains, the interweaving of contraries and all contradictions, freaks and irrelevancies: LIFE."[60] Dada was the first in a venerable line of twentieth-century art movements that mixed serious speculation and sheer provocation; that cried out against the violence, repressiveness, and authoritarianism of contemporary society and conventional art forms, yet sometimes found violence attractive; and that claimed that absolutely everything could be art, from the toilet bowl to the bicycle. Dada expressed the despair aroused by the violence of World War I, with its enormous scale of death and suffering, and the revolutionary hopes that emerged in the war's wake. It attracted followers from all across the continent, including Germany. The alliance between political revolutionaries like the Communists and aesthetic revolutionaries like the Dadaists was always tenuous, but between 1917 and 1923 both camps believed that they were on the same side. In its use of everyday objects in unlikely combinations, photomontage, at least in the early 1920s, was a quintessential Dadaist genre, though it would be adopted by other movements, like Soviet constructivism, which also influenced Höch.

Höch was born to a lower-middle-class family in Thuringia and in her twenties, just before the war, made her way to Berlin as an art student. In 1916 she began work as a pattern designer at the Ullstein publishing house, where she remained for much of the 1920s while she also pursued her own art. She lived the life of the new woman of the 1920s—a professional with a wide circle of friends of different nationalities, unmarried and involved in various relationships with men and women. She also lived what modern art propagated as its ethos, the movement back and forth between art and the everyday, art as protest and art as commerce. Her creations were displayed in galleries and studios, and also in the Ullstein mass-circulation newspapers and magazines.

Höch's photomontages celebrated modern life and also offered a searing critique. Their ambiguities and ambivalences in regard to race, gender, and technology make her best works extremely captivating. Like Brecht and Weill, Höch was enthralled by the signature features of modernity: speed, technology, mass communications, the possibilities of emancipation, the ethnic and racial diversity of the world. Her art is filled with the modernist symbols of the 1920s—skyscrapers, cinema, film stars, the new woman, the United States—and also with the European encounter with Asians and Africans.

There is a certain lightness especially to the works of the early 1920s. One feels the artist discovering new paths of expression and celebrating the possibilities of modern life, the lights, the consumption, the spectacles, the power of machinery, the optimistic hopes for a better, more just society. Female beauty clearly entranced her. Many of her works depict women in movement. As athletes and dancers, they often have an engaged and happy countenance, the very emblems of the liberated woman of the 1920s. But even the lightness of her early works is sometimes broken up with violent images, particularly the torn torsos of women. Höch celebrated women's emancipation and railed against the violence so often directed at them; she parodied the commodification of women, their use as points of attraction for the buying and selling of goods, from the mundane to the luxurious.[61]

In one of her most famous works, *Dada-Ernst*, from 1920–21 (fig. 7.1), the viewer is drawn to the image in the lower left corner of a female athlete, ready to leap. Above her is a stylized female seminude, and above her two male boxers. On the right-hand side is a skyscraper. But what does one make of the female legs that dominate the montage, with a cutout eye covering the pubic area, which is also partly covered by gold coins? The legs straddle a lithe woman in a gown with something like a dunce cap on her head. A sawlike machine part also dominates the center of the montage. Höch brings together here the discordant images of modernity. She celebrates the active body images of women and men (the boxers) that proliferated in the 1920s, but also seems to suggest that commerce (the coins) and violence (the legs separated from the rest of the body, the saw, boxing) are a part of modernity's reality as well, and particularly affect women. *Dada-Ernst* represents optimism and emancipation, fear and violence at one and the same time.

Another famous work of hers from this period, *Cut with the Kitchen Knife Dada through the Last Weimar Beer Belly Cultural Epoch of Germany* (1919–20) (see plate 5) is as chaotic as its title. The montage is composed of scores of images cut out of magazines and newspapers, its very density and busyness so expressive of the modernity it represents. One sees masses of people in a demonstration, the gears and ball bearings of industry, and the skyscrapers of the modern city. Circus performers share space with the icons of respectability,

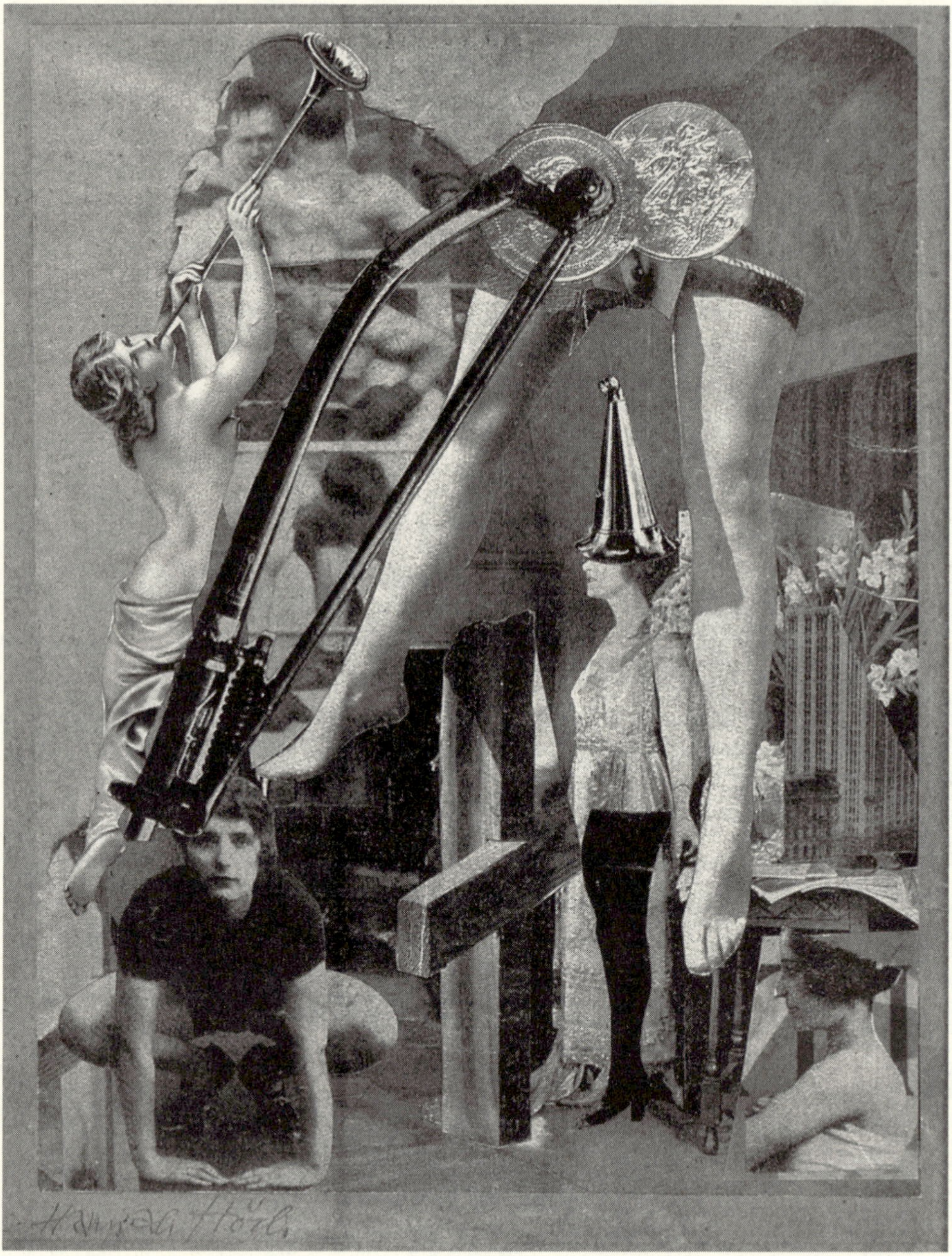

Fig. 7.1 Hannah Höch, *Dada-Ernst*, 1920–21. A photomontage from Höch's early Dada phase, it affirms women's strength, beauty, and independence and sees them threatened by the forces of modern life, notably the money and tools of capitalist production. © 2006 Artist Rights Society (ARS), New York / VG Bildkunst, Bonn.

bankers (it seems) and officers. Indigenous art holds up what looks like a trunk and a bank of cameras next to images of Marx and Lenin. Heads of women are connected to male bodies; in one instance, a woman seems to be flying through the montage. Various famous politicians and athletes grace the canvas. Reich president Friedrich Ebert appears in a not entirely complimentary depiction; ex-kaiser Wilhelm II and Field Marshal von Hindenburg are subjected to even greater ridicule. Well-known female actresses appear, along with Höch herself and a map of Europe showing the advance of female suffrage. The panoply of images is a controlled chaos, that of modernity itself. Höch represents the cacophony of modern life with all its varied elements, from bourgeois respectability to revolution, from the factory to the dance hall and theater stage, from illustrious individuals to people massed in demonstration. But Höch was not just a dispassionate observer: her ridicule of the iconic figures of imperial Germany and even of the political leadership of the republic, her representation of women in movement, and the appearance four times of the words "Dada" or "anti-Dada" show her commitment to aesthetic and political revolution.

From around the mid-1920s onward, Höch, in her own particular New Objectivity shift, gave her work a more somber tone and a sparer style. Gone for the most part are the cluttered, chaotic montages of the first postwar years. Technology is increasingly seen as the fearsome monster that fragments and destroys, rather than as the joyful liberator.[62] But the later montages also have a more decisive critical edge. Her best later works offer a scathing critique of the rabid racism of the Nazis and many other Germans. Her work also takes on more of a feminist edge, perhaps a reflection of her own difficulties as a female artist amid the overwhelmingly male and deeply misogynist Dada group (though she also had lifelong friendships with male artists, including Moholy-Nagy). Technology is the destroyer especially of women, and modernity also means the display of women as objects of commerce. In many works, she parodied the glamour of the new woman as she appeared in endless advertisements. Like many other European artists, Höch adopted aspects of a primitivist style and a belief that in the supposed naturalness and simplicity of non-Western peoples would be found the antidote to the pressures and fissures of modernity. In an era of mass advertising that commodified woman, she found beauty in those supposedly closer to nature, Africans and Asians.[63] In an age of stark racial ideology, she produced scandalous art mixing Africans and Europeans. It is easy to criticize this work as Orientalist—a European's fascination with and, at the same time, condescension toward "the primitive." But this later work evokes an admiration for the physical beauty of non-Europeans. While the photomontages of the early period demonstrated a radical, innovative mix of materials and objects, the later work continued this trend and also mixed Europeans and Africans or Asians, oftentimes in erotic fashion. The work disrupts the notion of races as distinct groups, hermetically sealed off from one other, each with its own particular, blood-based characteristics. Moreover, many of these works parody the display of "primitive cultures" associated with ethnographic and natural history museums—and with a more odious tradition, the *Völkerschauen*, the exhibitions of living non-Western peoples in traveling circuses and carnivals.

In *Love in the Bush* (1925), for example, Höch put together a white woman's face, mouth open, hair cut short, with the face of a black man (see plate 6). His oversized arms extend around the trouser-covered legs, which could be those of a man or a woman. Stalks jut out, representing the bush. *The Bride* (1933) shows a white woman's bare neck and shoulders connected to an African or Polynesian face, with lace on the top of the head and in the background representing a bridal gown (fig. 7.2). In *Monument II: Vanity* (1926) (see plate 7) Höch placed on a pedestal a white woman's lower torso and legs with the chest of a man and the masked head and headdress of an African "medicine man," the latter taken from a photo in the Ullstein publication *Uhu*. Through all of these images, Höch challenged conventional racial and gender ideologies with their notion of fixed identities. Most scandalously, she depicted the possibility of interracial love and sex and of androgynous or bisexual human beings. Some would argue that *The Peasant Wedding Couple* (1931) (fig. 7.3) only reinforces conventional racial views, indeed, is itself racist.[64] But it can also be read as satirical commentary on racial ideology and on the right-wing idealization of the peasantry. Nothing could be more outrageous to German conservatives than a peasant wedding depicted as the union of an African man and a woman with a caricatured gorilla face topped with the quintessential braided blond hair.

Fig. 7.2 Hannah Höch, *The Bride*, 1933. Again Höch challenges conceptions of race and gender by mixing European and African body forms. © 2006 Artist Rights Society (ARS), New York / VG Bildkunst, Bonn.

Höch's vision of unstable racial and gender identities and of mass society as multiracial and multiethnic was a powerful rejoinder to the racial ideology that prevailed almost everywhere in the Western world in the 1920s, and that would become Germany's official ideology under the Nazis. Höch's art used the objects of modernity, its representation in images reproduced in newspapers and magazines, to make art that was itself emblematic of modernism. And despite her accelerating fears of technology and her critique of the commodifica-

Fig. 7.3 Hannah Höch, *Peasant Wedding Couple*, 1931. The ultimate challenge to conservative Germans: the braids of a German peasant girl placed on an animal and the prospects of marriage between an African man and a German woman. © 2006 Artist Rights Society (ARS), New York / VG Bildkunst, Bonn.

tion of women, she continued to celebrate mass society with a vision of "the mass" that extended far beyond Germany to include Africans and Asians.

It is impossible ever "to prove" why, at a particular time and place, a culture flourishes, and artists, writers, and philosophers break through one boundary after another and create innovative forms of expression—whether on the stage, printed page, or canvas—that are immediately discussed and debated and resonate for decades afterward. But there can be no question that Weimar Germany was just such a place and time. Thomas Mann's *Magic Mountain*, Brecht and Weill's *Threepenny Opera*, Kracauer's essays, Heidegger's *Being and Time*, and Höch's photomontages are just a few of the pathbreaking works of the era. We read, view, and hear them today perhaps less as historical documents than as living cultural expressions; they still offer us insights into the condition of modernity and even, at times, perceptions of beauty—of language, thought, and image.

The great cultural figures of Weimar were, for the most part, the beneficiaries of Germany's phenomenal educational system as it had developed over the course of the nineteenth century. Even those like Mann who only completed Gymnasium (the elite high schools), not a university degree, had received a superb grounding in literature, philosophy, history, and classical and modern languages. Those who went on to university, like Kracauer and Heidegger, or to the art and music academies, like Weill and Höch, attained the very best the Western world had to offer in terms of knowledge and technical skills. Of course, only a tiny percentage of the age cohort were able to study at this high level. But those who were—and, by the turn into the twentieth century, they included Jews and some from middling social backgrounds—had the erudition to rethink, if they so chose, conventional categories and create new forms of expression.

They inhabited a social world that prized erudition and was not, after all, so very large. Brecht and Weill moved in theatrical, musical, and literary circles where, it seems, everyone knew everyone else. They and Bloch, Benjamin, Kracauer, and others sat in cafés together and talked; sometimes they lived in the very same neighborhoods of Berlin. Höch knew and was friends with some of the Bauhaus figures as well as the Dadaists. Mann lived in Munich during the Weimar years, but he traveled and lectured widely. And virtually all of them, like the modern architects discussed in chapter 5, were connected to a larger European world of cultural creativity. They spent time in Paris, and interacted with Dutch, Swiss, Italian, and Russian artists and writers who were forging their own, related brands of modernism. Only Heidegger, hiding out in the Black Forest, was something of an exception.

The Weimar cultural elite possessed erudition and comprised

a social-intellectual world that proved mutually inspiring and supportive. To be sure, this world was rife with petty jealousies and intellectual and political conflicts. Even friends could savage one another in print, as Kracauer did with one of Bloch's major philosophical treatises, let alone across the café table. But this high-strung, high-energy intellectual culture also proved immensely stimulating to its participants. They read, viewed, and listened to one another's works, and that critical engagement no doubt sharpened the thinking and the creativity of many of the participants. Heidegger was, again, something of an exception, but he too came of age in dialogue with the very significant philosophical work in neo-Kantianism and, especially, phenomenology that thrived in Marburg, Heidelberg, and Freiburg, all located in western Germany.

Like the philosophers and social theorists a generation older—Max Weber, Georg Simmel, Ferdinand Tönnies, those who had made their mark beginning in the 1890s—they sought to understand and critique modernity. They grappled with the meaning of the city, the factory, mass consumption, and mass politics. But *this* generation, the Weimar generation, also had to confront the meaning of mass violence and intense political conflict—war and revolution—on a hitherto unimagined scale. Those experiences, whether in the army or at home, gave an urgency to their intellectual engagements, an intensity perhaps greater than that experienced by their counterparts in Britain, France, or the Netherlands who lived in relatively more secure societies and polities. The Weimar intellectual generation sought to understand, critique, and locate in the present the possibilities of a better world in the future. Their answers, as mentioned, varied—when there were answers at all. The refusal to accept platitudes and simplicities, the drive to accept and render in art and thought the tensions and contradictions of modernity, constituted the defining features of Weimar culture.

It is no surprise, then, that the great figures of Weimar culture produced their best work in Germany in the 1920s and early 1930s. Yes, Thomas Mann wrote important novels and Bertolt Brecht significant plays after 1933. But *The Magic Mountain*, not the later novels and stories, remains one of the literary masterpieces of the twentieth century, *Threepenny* the breakthrough theatrical work of Brecht's entire career. Heidegger wrote other significant works, but nothing else of his had quite the defining character of *Being and Time*. Kracauer,

Weill, and Höch fell into near obscurity for a number of decades (to be rediscovered in the 1980s)—Weill known until then only for *Threepenny*, Kracauer only for his 1947 study of German film, *From Caligari to Hitler*.[65] Nazi Germany destroyed the intellectual and social milieu in which they all had flourished, even Heidegger the Nazi. That milieu could not be reproduced on the Pacific Palisades, as beautiful a setting as it was, nor on Manhattan's West Side, nor at any other place of exile where Mann, Brecht, Weill, Kracauer, and so many others landed, and certainly not in Freiburg under Nazi rule. Höch stayed in Germany and joined thousands of others in the "inner emigration," the retreat to their private studios and libraries. But without a public, how long can any artist remain creative?

Another group of Weimar intellectuals, somewhat younger than the individuals discussed here, would also go on to exile and, ultimately, a profound influence all over the Western world and beyond. Max Horkheimer, Theodor Adorno, and others associated with the Institute for Social Research (Institut für Sozialforschung), or the Frankfurt School, would complete their most significant writings in the 1930s and 1940s in American exile, and then partly in the 1950s after their remigration to West Germany. The German College for Politics (Deutsche Hochschule für Politik) spanned the Weimar generations, but younger social scientists who were on its faculty, like Franz Neumann, also had to flee Nazi Germany. They, too, would come to exert an important influence on American and, subsequently in the 1950s, German academic life. Significantly, both institutions were founded outside the formal universities; the deeply conservative academic disciplines and university structures had been barely affected by Weimar's democratizing impulses. While their greatest work would come later, after the demise of the republic, the intellectuals of both the Frankfurt School and the College for Politics were shaped throughout their lives by their Weimar experience. Their research and writings would always come back to the problems of modernity and, especially, of democracy and mass culture.

The great Weimar intellectual and creative figures were, then, preoccupied with the meaning of "the masses" and "mass society." As an intellectual and cultural problem, it had first been articulated in the 1890s by sociologists (sociology itself a new discipline and a direct reflection of the emergence of mass society) and philosophers. Some individuals, like Brecht, Weill, and Höch, found mass society liberating.

It spurred them on to create new aesthetic styles out of everyday languages, rhythms, and objects, and to write their plays and compositions and make their art in ways that—they hoped—would engage the common people. Heidegger reacted with nothing less than horror and retreated, literally and intellectually, from the pulsing forces of urban life. Yet the very existence of "the mass" served as a creative impulse for Heidegger as well, leading him to contemplate at the deepest levels the meaning of Being in contrast to surface banalities. Mann rarely wrote directly about mass society. But his lifelong concern with the dilemmas faced by educated and cultivated individuals, with the tensions between desire and order, between eros and logos, permeates all his literature and reflects an acute awareness of the always-threatening mass just outside the rarefied realms of the Buddenbrooks family or the bourgeois patients in a sanatorium in the Alps. Mann's high aesthetic style forcefully reasserted the importance of *Bildung*, but lurking all around were the threats, and sometimes the reality, of decay and degeneration. And for still others, like Kracauer, mass society was stimulus and narcotic at the same time; substantive meaning and banal surfaces. None of these figures, not even Heidegger, advocated a return to the styles and ways of thinking that had prevailed before 1914. They forged a new aesthetics in the hope of capturing the essence of an age so marked by the destructiveness of the Great War, the conflicts of revolution, and the hyperactivity of the modern city and modern capitalism.

8

Bodies and Sex

In 1926, the Dutch physician Theodor Hendrik van de Velde went on a lecture tour of Germany. He had recently published the first volume, *Ideal Marriage*, of an eventual trilogy on sex and marriage.[1] The book and his lectures were wildly successful. Velde's tone, combining the expertise of the physician with the reassurances of an experienced husband and father, captivated the German public—and, to judge by the forty-four reprintings between 1941 and 1966 of the American edition, others were equally enthralled.[2] In Berlin, a huge, diverse crowd filled the Philharmonie to listen to him. The press was present as well, including a reporter for the *Vossische Zeitung*:

> And there they stood and sat—the elderly, whom one would think don't need to learn anything more; couples and lovebirds, with happy and disappointed faces; the very young, who wanted to begin their coming-of-age with theory. When asked here and there, they all had come with reservations in mind.[3]

Is he sincere? they wondered. A charlatan? Under the veneer of science is he just a speculator and profiteer? "Or is he giving something out of the depths of his heart? And if he is offering something truthfully and honorably, can it help us?"[4] The crowd was tense and excited and even threatened to explode, because in parts of the hall Velde could not be heard. The reporter was not terribly impressed. People hungered for explanations and answers about the most basic yet intimate aspects of life, and got banalities in return: "Against the flu, hot compresses; the sweats, aspirin; against sexual misery, erotic techniques."[5]

Perhaps, but they bought his book and turned out in droves all over Germany to listen to his lectures. Many Germans, apparently, suffered from a widespread disease: sexual misery (*sexuelle Not*). Velde and legions of other reformers, mostly physicians, provided the diagnosis and the cure. With explicit descriptions of sexual techniques and friendly counseling, they would show Germans how to lead pleasurable and healthy sex lives. And that, in turn, would create a sound, flourishing, productive, and fertile society.

For Velde's German counterparts in the extensive and very loosely knit sex reform movement, the revolution and republic opened up vast new opportunities.[6] As in the fields of art and architecture, many of the protagonists had completed their professional training and begun their work before 1914. But with the collapse and overthrow of the imperial system, official censorship was largely abolished and the sex reformers had political allies in power, especially at the local level in Social Democratic–run municipalities. Moreover, war and revolution had caused a tectonic shift in moral and sexual values. For many Germans, the war dramatically demonstrated the ephemeral character of life. With so many men killed and ravaged by bullets, shells, and gas, so many women left without loved ones or reduced to caring for the seriously maimed—why not indulge life's pleasures when possible? Why wait for the official sanction of marriage to sample sex? Why limit oneself to only one partner? The revolution and the foundation of the republic also marked a grand new departure, a leap, so it seemed, into democracy and the modern world. Germans would leave behind the stuffy, rigid, and authoritarian society of imperial Germany dominated by royalty, nobility, and the military, and a constrained and hypocritical sexual morality. To be modern meant to be democratic, and it also meant a freer, more open attitude toward bodies and sex.

But the image of liberated sex and, especially, of the "new woman," the lithe, athletic, emancipated woman of the 1920s, also inspired visceral and vitriolic responses. Workers councils, strikes, the constitution, reparations, expressionist art, flat roofs—of all the flash points of conflict in Weimar Germany, none aroused so much deeply felt passion, so much debate, so much hostility, as the issues of sex and the family, and of women—what they did, how they looked—in particular. These issues lay at the very core of what Germans did and thought in their intimate and spiritual lives. And they struck at the heart of beliefs about how Germans should live together—whether, as some believed, a sober, sexually modest Christian family would undergird a moral society, or whether, as others advocated, sexual pleasure would help create the emancipated, open, and democratic Germany of the future. Between the defenders of the Christian family and the advocates of erotic fulfillment lay an unbridgeable chasm. On only one matter was there agreement: for both reformers and conservatives, sex was never simply a private matter, and no one, not even the most radical reformer, ever promoted pleasure for pleasure's sake. Good sex, even Christian good sex, had to have a social and political purpose.

Velde's book, *Ideal Marriage*, was typical of the many sex and marriage manuals published in the Weimar period. It articulated a deeply humanistic sensibility, a concern for the difficulties people faced in the most intimate aspects of their lives. They did not have to suffer in silence, Velde counseled. Science tempered by paternalistic solicitude would show them that their marriages, "often a hell of torment," could become a state of bliss. The key to "enduring happiness" in marriage lay in mutual, ongoing sexual pleasure.[7]

Men have to be the guides, according to Velde; that is their natural role in life. But he was scathing about the way most men made love. They were fast and sometimes even brutal, concerned only with their own orgasms.

> [Men] are naturally educators and initiators of their wives in sexual matters; and yet they often lack, not only the qualifications of a leader and initiator, but also those necessary for equal mutual partnership!
>
> They have no realization of their deficiencies. For the average man, of average "normal" genital potency, who performs his "conjugal duties" regularly and with physiological satisfaction to himself, still imagines that he has thereby met all the requirements his wife can make. And if she is not satisfied, and remains in a permanent condition of "suspended gratification," then, with regret or indignation according to his own type of

> temperament, he simply puts her down as one of those "sexually frigid" women . . . laments his bad luck, and drifts further and further apart from her.[8]

Men have to learn that "strictly within the bounds of *normality*," all sorts of variations are possible that "can banish the mechanical monotony of the too well-known from the marriage-bed." The husband has to learn that his wife's sexual rhythms are different, and that "the true lover achieves ecstasy by giving the joy of love." If he is not an "*erotic genius*" (and Velde clearly thought that few men were), then he needs "*explicit knowledge*." He must learn how to make love, and science will be the instructor.[9]

It is hard to imagine that Velde's readers lingered long over the first few chapters, almost the first half of the book, which precisely delineate male and female anatomy. They probably raced ahead to the ensuing chapters, which describe sexual techniques in great detail. Velde's highly clinical definitions and exact analyses of every stage of lovemaking—the kiss, the caress, genital kissing (as he terms it), coitus, various positions—are softened by a warm tone and affirmation of the joy of sex and the natural quality of sexual pleasure. To be sure, his instructions follow standard gender ideology: man is active, woman passive; man takes the initiative, woman responds; woman is completely a sexual being, man only partly so; woman's dependence on man is dictated by biology and nature. "Racially and reproductively," he wrote, "[man] has only to supply the fertilizing element to the woman. Sex is the essential element in woman; in man it is accessory."[10] In the sexual act maleness is the defining element for both partners.

> What both man and woman, driven by obscure primitive urges, wish to feel in the sexual act, is the essential force of *maleness*, which expresses itself in a sort of violent and absolute *possession* of the woman. And so both of them can and do exult in a certain degree of male aggression and dominance—whether actual or apparent—which proclaims this essential force.[11]

Unlike some reformers—Magnus Hirschfeld most famously—who accepted homosexuality and campaigned against homophobic legislation and prejudices, Velde advocated "normal" (as he termed it) heterosexual relationships. He assured men that if their wives had lesbian tendencies, "the husband can help his wife to conquer the abnormality, if he understands how to guide her thoughts and how, with skillful technique, to develop her sexual desires along normal lines."[12] Male homosexuality is a much greater problem, because sheer physical technique is less successful and would require the woman to take the initiative, normally the man's role.[13] His definition of intercourse is clinical-sounding and heterosexual in orientation and espouses the much-vaunted mutual orgasm. Perfection is achieved with simultaneous orgasm, and "the usual procedure is that the man's ejaculation begins and sets the woman's acme of sensation in train at once."[14] Velde included a diagram with this description, the scientific seal of proof of mutual orgasm. If, however, the woman fails to reach orgasm, the man has to take other steps; if all else fails, then—in Velde's phrasing, quaint and scientific at the same time—"*autotherapeutic measures* are probably better than none at all."[15]

While conventional in his definition of sex, Velde nonetheless always emphasized the importance of mutual pleasure in lovemaking. His advocacy of long and gentle foreplay is mirrored in his writing—just the description of the "erotic kiss" goes on for seven pages; his disquisition on the role of scent in sexual attraction occupies thirteen (in the English-language version).[16] After-play is no less important; a man's actions after his orgasm determine whether he is "*an erotically civilized adult.*"[17] He should not just turn over and go to sleep, but should gently kiss and caress his wife and express words of love. The man who neglects slow and gentle lovemaking "is guilty not only of coarseness, but of positive brutality; and his omission can not only offend and disgust a woman, but also injure her on the purely physical plane. And this sin of omission is unpardonably *stupid.*"[18] If women do not reach orgasm, it is most often because of the "inadequate technique" of their male partners. For such men Velde has harsh words: "Every considerable erotic stimulation of their wives that does not terminate in orgasm, on the woman's part, represents an injury, and repeated injuries of this kind lead to permanent—or very obstinate—damage to both body and soul."[19] Hence Velde railed against coitus interruptus as a means of birth control: it satisfied the man, but not the woman.

Velde's book, and other sex manuals, found large readerships in the Weimar period and, at the same time, influenced the sex reform movement. He and his fellow sex reformers believed deeply that the pleasurable sex they advocated would create better individual lives and, consequently, a more productive and humane society. Birth control—condoms primarily, but also diaphragms—would relieve couples of the anxiety of producing too many children, thereby resulting in more wholesome family lives and more enjoyable sex as well. The reformers believed that their work was of a piece with democratic governance, social welfare programs that protected workers from the vicissitudes of the business cycle, and the construction of well-built, sunlit affordable apartments. No less than the major drafters of the Weimar constitution and the architects of modern housing developments, the sex reformers played a central role in making Germany in the Weimar period a more modern, open, and humane society.

At the same time, many of the reformers found alternative models far from Germany. Wilhelm Reich, probably the most radical of the group, drew on Bronislaw Malinowski's idyllic portrait of the sex lives of Trobriand Islanders in the Pacific to show the dismal results of repressive bourgeois life. As Reich quotes Malinowski, Trobriand Islanders ridiculed white men's sexual performance because they reached orgasm too quickly, while the natives engaged in long lovemaking that was pleasurable to both partners.[20] Another reformer, Max Hodann, found an alternative model in "the Orient" and the gentle art of lovemaking, so he said, that the Indians, Japanese, and Muslims all practiced. "Naturalness" about sex "today still lives in the Orient," though it has been lost to Christian society.[21] In this view, the task of a democratic Germany was somehow to join the sex practices of traditional, non-Western societies with the fast-paced character of modern life.

And the reformers railed against the cramped and deprived sexual lives of so many Germans, the misery they detected throughout society. The reformers sounded the alarm, often in melodramatic prose. They wrote about a "specter" of sexual misery that one finds in alleyways and doctors' waiting rooms, in the hovels of the poor and the well-appointed dwellings of the rich. Syphilis, prostitution, illegal abortions, impotence, unhappy marriages—that is the reality, according to the four physicians and one criminologist who contributed to another major Weimar book, *Sexual Catastrophes*.[22]

Many of the reformers were left-wing doctors, including a substantial number of female physicians, and they knew the difficult conditions their patients faced. They lived in small, dark, overcrowded apartments where no one could find privacy, least of all a couple making love. Women were worn out by the burdens of housework, labor outside the home, and endless pregnancies. The level of ignorance about sex and biology was shocking. Terminated pregnancies, though illegal, were prevalent, and many women suffered the dire health consequences of back-alley abortions. A virtual epidemic of venereal diseases plagued the lives of men and women. Many reformers did not believe in sexual monogamy, and most advocated premarital sex. But they were often shocked by the casual sexual lives and the resultant cycle of unwanted pregnancies and illegal and dangerous abortions experienced by so many of the women they encountered.[23]

Reformers like Hodann also blasted their fellow physicians who moralized about the sanctity of life yet ignored the real conditions that trapped so many women and men, making every child a burden, and ensuring that quick and sometimes brutal sex was virtually the norm. Reich, perhaps the most radical of the sex reformers, argued that sexual repression was a "plague" that cut across all the class divisions of society, "shattering" individuals high and low and leading to serious neuroses.[24] The appropriate therapy was "the achievement of a gratifying sex life."[25] This was a simple enough prescription, but one whose actual implementation was terribly difficult.

Reich went still further. Sexual repression serves the interests of capitalism, he argued, so ultimately the only way to abolish neuroses was through psychoanalysis leading to good sex coupled with revolution to overthrow class society.[26] Hirschfeld, one of the best-known of the sex reformers and the founder, in 1919, of the Institute for Sexual Research, described in his three-volume *Sexual pathologie: Ein Lehrbuch für Ärtzte und Studierende* (Sexual Pathology: A Textbook for Physicians and Students) a huge range of sexual practices. The really horrific passages are those about the treatments that medical professionals and the authorities often meted out to individuals deemed perverse or sick, and those about the self-loathing and self-mutilation that so many people practiced and endured.[27] Hirschfeld wrote his magnum opus amid the mass slaughter of World War I and the revolutions and civil wars that followed. The violence of war depressed him greatly. Yet he still believed that "life-affirming love"—and for Hirschfeld, that meant, again, homosexual as well as heterosexual love—could counter war's rejection of life. It was the physician's task to show the way forward, to life rather than to death.[28]

The sex reformers counseled, wrote, and lectured in a highly politicized, highly activist environment. "Sexual misery," "marital misery," "the crisis of the family," "depopulation": this was the language that saturated public discussion, and every political group had its prescription. The reformers found critical support especially at the municipal level, where Social Democrats or at least the Weimar Coalition parties dominated many city councils and governments, and from a diverse popular movement. A huge expansion of family- and sex-counseling clinics resulted, even in small towns. Most were led by physicians, women activists, and officials of various sex reform leagues—often one and the same person performing multiple roles. The sex reform leagues had more than 150,000 members, and an influence far beyond their numbers through their publications, lectures, clinics, and sales of condoms and other birth control measures. The leagues included laypeople, health-care professionals, social workers, activists in the socialist and communist parties, and government officials.[29] Many of them were involved in the energetic public campaign against paragraph 218, the legal provision that criminalized abortion. On the streets, in the legislatures, in theaters, and in the press, a large popular movement emerged in 1931, and it was one of the very few of the Weimar era that cut across class, gender, and political lines. Hundreds of thousands of Germans demanded that women have the right to an abortion free of the fear of criminal prosecution and in safe, healthy conditions. The Communists, in a fit of enthusiasm for individual rights that they would soon renounce, launched the slogan "Your body belongs to you!" The campaign unfolded, amazingly, in the midst of the Depression, hardly an auspicious time. It failed to change the law, but it was one more sign of the acute body- and sex-consciousness of the 1920s and early 1930s, and of the prominent role played by sex reformers in Weimar politics and society.

Sexual misery could not be quantified, but statistics do tell one part of the story, and the facts they revealed greatly worried Germans. According to the 1925 census, there were 1,067 females for every 1,000 males, somewhat closer to equivalency than the 1919 figures, but still disturbing evidence of the toll of the war on men's lives and the resultant demographic imbalance.[30] Family size had dropped to an average of one child per family, and the household of working-class families on average amounted to only 3.9 persons. In 1933, Germany had the lowest birthrate in Europe: 14.7 per 1,000 people. The birthrate was half what it had been around 1900; in Berlin, it had declined from 43.1 per 1,000 in the 1870s to 9.89 in 1923. More than 35 percent of married couples in Berlin were childless in 1933. Meanwhile, the divorce rate had skyrocketed, and every year probably a million women (out of 31.2 million German women in total) had an abortion. The estimated deaths ran from 4,000 to 12,000 a year, with 50,000 women per year experiencing health complications from abortions.[31] For those who believed that national power rested on a large and vigorous population, and for everyone who lamented the dismal health conditions and life opportunities of so many Germans, the statistics were disturbing indeed.

But did people actually do anything differently in their private lives? Was there more sex? Better sex? Was homosexuality on the rise? It is always difficult to say, but at least in the major urban areas, and Berlin in particular, it does seem that a sexual revolution was under way. It was made possible by a variety of factors: the change in public attitudes prompted by the war and revolution; the proliferation of contraceptives, condoms in particular; and the outpouring of words and images about sex in books, brochures, lectures, clinics, magazines, and the movies. Someone must have been having sex and practicing birth control: the pharmaceutical industry produced annually 80–90 million condoms.[32] And gay bars and gay and lesbian underground publications flourished in Berlin, Hamburg, and other major cities.

The "new woman" was the most renowned symbol of the sexual revolution of the 1920s (fig. 8.1). She had short hair, the famed *Bubikopf*; she was slender, athletic, erotic, and amaternal. She smoked

Fig. 8.1 New Woman at the Romanische Café, ca. 1924. Elegantly dressed in the style of the day and out on her own. Bildarchiv Preussischer Kulturbesitz / Art Resource, NY

and sometimes wore men's clothes. She went out alone, had sex as she pleased. She worked, typically in an office or in the arts, and lived for today and for herself, as Elsa Herrmann wrote in yet another of the Weimar books, *So ist die neue Frau* (This Is the New Woman), devoted to the topic. The woman of yesterday lived for her husband and her children and sacrificed for the family. The new woman believes in equal rights, and strives to be self-reliant in economic terms. The war, argued Herrmann, brought women no substantive gains, but it did "awaken . . . them from their lethargy and laid upon them the responsibility for their own fate."[33]

This was, of course, an idealized image that few German women, even in Berlin, actually lived. Few women could attain Hollywood-style glamour or financial independence. In 1925, about one-third of all women worked in the paid labor force, the vast majority at low-paying factory and office jobs. The new woman was in large part a class-bound image, of middle- and upper-class women who had the independence and the means to pursue their interests and desires. For the preponderance of women, the sheen and glimmer of the good life lay very distant.

Though class-bound in its origins, as a style and a goal the new-woman image trickled down the social hierarchy and across the country, even into rural settings. Communists promoted their own version, short-haired and slender, but more sober, less erotic, and, of course, committed to the proletarian cause.[34] As hard as their lives were, at least some factory women displayed an independence and activism that signified a working-class version of the new woman. They were not totally beaten down by their hard working lives at home and in the factory. In the collection of autobiographical writings from 1930, *Mein Arbeitstag, mein Wochenende* (My Working Day, My Weekend), they described how they live for the weekends, when they have the opportunity to indulge their love of nature and companionship. "How beautiful nature is, one becomes so completely calm and happy inside," wrote one of them.[35] During their working hours they dream about a Saturday afternoon or Sunday walking in the woods and going for long hikes or bicycle rides. The foul factory air is dispersed, at least for a day, by the crispness of the forest. A few lucky ones even have a family hut out in the country that serves as a weekend retreat. Many of the younger women described excursions into the countryside with socialist youth groups; they relish the sense of comradeship that emerges as they sing songs and light campfires. Some volunteer for such community welfare organizations as the Workers Samaritan League; others serve on factory councils or in the trade union, and are preoccupied with securing health insurance or disability payments for their fellow workers. Occasionally they go to the theater or the movies, or read a book or the socialist press; they have an acute sense of the injustices under which they labor, and want to change the world around them.

But sometimes it was just too difficult. With work and housework, rushing everywhere, taking care of children and parents, toiling at the factory for eleven hours or so, where was the time or the setting for a fulfilling sexual life, daily exercise, political engagement, and cultural development? One woman wrote, "Often I am so tired and exhausted that I can't read or write. I need the time to sleep so I have the necessary energy for my physical exertions. *Intellect is the stepchild, always neglected.*" Nonetheless, she strives, despite work, "*to be a human being and live like one.*"[36] For this woman at least, all the words and images that conveyed a life of equality and fulfillment gave her the resources to imagine something better. Weimar culture generally, socialism in particular, enabled her to resist the automaton-like life at the textile mill and to strive "to be human," as she put it.

The image of the new woman—however limited its incarnation in real life—provoked a tidal wave of commentary, some supportive, some filled with loathing. The very notion that women could determine their own lives, might decide not to marry or might choose to have a variety of sex partners, and not all of them male, the display of female desire on the cinema screen and in pulp and even serious fiction—all that struck something very deep, in men and women. Like every other focal point of conflict in the 1920s and early 1930s, the disputes about the new woman were loaded onto the republic, which was seen as either the source of female emancipation (or at least its ally), or the very fount of immorality and evil. The hard-fought, often bitter discussions and commentary about the changing status of women raged on in every public venue, in newspaper columns and illustrated magazines, on the radio, from pulpits, and in the halls of government. The broad expansion of the public sphere in the 1920s and early 1930s, wrought by democratization and the new media, made the conflict over the new woman even more visible and contentious.

In 1929, some of Germany's leading literary figures published *Die Frau von Morgen: Wie wir sie wünschen* (The Woman of Tomorrow: How We Wish Her to Be), in which they reflected on the changes and imagined the future of women.[37] The contributors—all of them men, an irony that seems to have eluded these literary lights—lauded the great advances in female status and touted women as equal partners in society. Yet a certain uneasiness is evident in many of the contributions, a sense that maybe women had gone too far, had become too much like men and had given up their distinctive characteristics. Some of the writers were notably condescending toward women and wrote as if the grace of men had bestowed upon women the privileges that they now claimed as rights. Gender conflict was in the air and had become palpable on the printed page.

The lead contributor, the renowned author Stefan Zweig, had a different sensibility. He was clearly taken with the new woman—intellectually, politically, and, not least, erotically. In no previous period has such a "stormy and radical transformation of all moral and sexual relations in favor of women taken place as in our epoch."[38] Such a dramatic wave has to continue until its ultimate fulfillment: it cannot be stopped. Just a glance at an illustrated magazine of fifteen or twenty years ago, Zweig wrote, shows the difference.

> Did women really go about dressed in this fashion, so mummified and piled up, so ridiculously layered, so walled up and tied up, as in the Middle Ages? Like a historical object. . . . Laced up in corsets, covered to the neck with pleated cloth, tailored with skirts and petticoats, every movement and motion artificial—from this historical woman of yesteryear has emerged in one single generation the woman of today. The light clothing she wears moves like a wave over the line of her bright, free body. On this sunny day she takes in the wind and the air and every male glance—please, don't be frightened!—as previously women did only in certain houses, whose name we dare not speak. But she doesn't at all feel this new found freedom of the

> body, this freedom of the soul, as immoral, and neither do we. Just the opposite.[39]

Zweig was enraptured with the new woman:

> In this short period of time, women have triumphantly created an entirely new situation. The wonderful emancipation of woman in regard to her own body, to her blood, to her freedom, to her independence—all that won't be stopped just because a few old minds are shocked and a few late-blooming moralists are outraged.[40]

One thing was certain, Zweig continued: the woman of an older age, the aristocratic lady, the bourgeois housewife, the spinster—all of these types, encased in particular roles, each with its own particular hypocritical sexual morality—these "types" were all of a bygone age. "Companionship" is the marker of relations today. The woman stands next to her man as an equal, not a subordinate, independent by virtue of practicing her own profession. She makes her own decisions, of her own free will, whether to establish a long-term relationship or a brief affair, to enjoy sports and intellectual competition.[41] The newfound freedom signified also a new eroticism, limited only by fears of venereal disease and unwanted pregnancy. When medicine advances enough to provide safe preventive measures or remedies for both, Zweig predicted, full equality between men and women in sexual relations will emerge. That will be the end, finally, of sexual misery. Woman will be "master of her own Eros" and of her own morality.[42]

But other writers were far more ambivalent and were probably closer to the general popular mood than was Zweig. In the same volume, the playwright and poet Alexander Lernet-Holenia counseled the "woman of tomorrow" to be beautiful and not overly intellectual. She should live by her instincts, which will always prove right. Lernet-Holenia lauded the "gallantry" of men who understand women's desire to free themselves from their present, difficult condition.[43] An even more ambivalent perspective is evident in the contribution of the writer and journalist Axel Eggebrecht, who seems both attracted to and repelled by the vibrant presence of women in the public realm.

> Everywhere in daily life, we constantly run up against "the woman." She moves with self-confidence in all professions, official positions, offices, cafés, streets, parliaments, and theaters. She operates matter-of-factly; she works; she takes pleasure as we do. All these female competitors, comrades, and colleagues, all apparently genderless. Nonetheless at every moment they affect us as women, whether we like to admit it or not. Constantly there are those little excitements, which we barely notice now because they have become so frequent. Still, there is this general state of stimulation—no question about it. It's a kind of poison in the smallest doses, which one gets used to though it deadens the senses. Its dulling effect becomes apparent only when we experience an hour of conscious, open erotic stimulation.[44]

The sexual tension here is evident: all these women, all this arousal, yet it all ends up as a kind of poison. What really bothered Eggebrecht lay quite deep:

> In the meantime the single erotic result of this so-called emancipation has been eminently negative. The insecurity of the man in relation to the woman has become virtually unbearable. Today when a man comes together with a woman, he has no idea where this meeting will lead him. Even presuming clear and intense sexual desire, he doesn't know how far his own prowess extends, whether to fleeting excitement or continual fascination.[45]

Unlike Zweig, who was simply enthralled with the new woman, whose writing had an erotic charge, Eggebrecht was thrown into a state of sexual anxiety and self-doubt. All he could do was enter a pathetic plea that the old barriers between men and women be reestablished. Once again, men should exercise all of their charms and influence to win over women, and women "should each time feign just enough resistance to excite the man again and overcome his lack of stimulation."[46]

The new woman was the most visible, most talked about, most conflicted symbol of the moral and sexual revolution of the

1920s. But it was not the only one. Everywhere, it seemed, male and female bodies were in motion and on display as never before. They were more lightly and provocatively clad or altogether naked, and could be seen live onstage and at the beach, walking down the street (though not nude!), or in magazines and at the cinema. The difference between a Berlin street scene circa 1900—women corseted and covered, men so formally dressed—and 1926 would be patently clear to any observer, as Zweig noted (see fig. 2.4).

But what accounted for this change? As every commentator said: the war; to which we might add: the revolution. Both events seriously undermined deference to authority, including the prevailing moral and sexual standards of imperial Germany. For many people, body emancipation, whether in bed, on the streets, or at the beach, was one very powerful way to be modern and to display one's rejection of the confining world of pre-1918 Germany. But there is more: the mass media lived off the display of beautiful bodies. Movies, photography, magazines—all thrived because the visual image, whether as an advertisement or as an art form, resonates so powerfully with humans and in the 1920s had become so easily and extensively reproducible (as we saw in chapter 6). Moreover, a society that had become "mass" could now gather in the tens of thousands to watch spectacles of physical competition, whether boxing matches or soccer games, that would also be carried live on radio and reported in the newspapers. And perhaps, just perhaps, all the attention devoted in the 1920s and early 1930s to healthy, attractive bodies, female and male, may have been a kind of mass psychological reaction to the maimings of World War I, the very visible evidence all around of the war-wounded with missing limbs, blinded eyes, and faces partly blown away.

In any case, bodies were organized and liberated in that curious mixture that characterized so much of the Weimar experience. Germans danced as never before. Hotels and cafés, helped along by the dissemination of the radio and phonograph, hosted dances in the late afternoon, a startling innovation, while in the evenings large dance halls packed in hundreds of people. When did Germans work or take care of their families if they were filling the dance floors and, even worse, listening to American jazz and copying American styles like the fox-trot and Charleston? Dance revues were a regular feature of

Fig. 8.2 The Tiller Girls, one of a number of very popular female dance revues, renowned for their precision movements and high kicks.

Berlin cabaret. Like the famous Rockettes or the Cotton Club dancers in Harlem, the "girl" acts of the wildly popular Berlin cabaret featured lines of women in bodysuits, dancing with military precision—a curious combination of Prussian militarism and Weimar sexuality, as the critic and social theorist Siegfried Kracauer noted in one of his famous essays (discussed in chapter 7) (fig. 8.2).[47]

While so much of the debate in Weimar focused on women, men were hardly forgotten. Even the mainstream *Berliner Illustrirte Zeitung* devoted its pages to male beauty—certainly not naked men, but idealized images of the German male drawn from the cinema and racial stereotypes that sharply distinguished Aryans from Jews. A whole variety of images graced the pages of an article titled "The Magic of Male Beauty," from dark-haired mysterious types to open, charming ones (fig. 8.3).[48] None, though, was recognizably Jewish or non-European. One film star, Paul Richter, was described as having a *Siegfriedgestalt*; another, Ronald Colman, as a "modern type of beauty." Manly beauty as promulgated even by the liberal Ullstein publishing house was a conventional thing.

But it was also a tougher thing. Boxing was one of the sports that became a mass sensation in the 1920s. Thousands flocked to ringside to watch Max Schmeling and other icons pummel one another (fig. 8.4). The literary and cultural elite fawned over them, projecting upon the match and the boxer's body weighty philosophical meanings.[49] Bertolt Brecht, John Heartfield, George Grosz, and many other cultural luminaries, right and left, joined Schmeling's entourage and showered him with praise, hoping no doubt that they would absorb by osmosis some of his manliness. For so many Germans, the boxer marked the rejuvenation of heroic male competition and combat. In the ring, it was just man against man, a primal struggle of individuals. The boxer powerfully surmounted the degenerate male physique of the modern age, the indistinguishable mass of flabby, hunched-over bodies that moved through life in a herd, or had been terribly wounded in war. The boxer was not part of the mass; he rekindled the Greek ideal, in body and spirit. But he was also modern: hard, clean, fast, an Americanism made individual and powerful.

For some people, the Schmeling image was only a start. The body could be properly developed and celebrated only when it had shed its clothes. Nudism would reunite soul and body, man and nature. Shorn of constricting garments, Germans would exercise and frolic in forests and lakes and thereby recapture the spirit of primeval Germany. Hans Surén's fantastically successful *Der Mensch und die Sonne* (Man and Sun) went through sixty-one printings in just one year and sold 250,000 copies. It combined trite philosophy, clichéd romanticism, and melodramatic prose in its homage to nature and nudism:

> Hail to all of you who love nature and sunlight! Joyfully you wander through field and meadow, over hill and vale. Barefoot in

Nr. 26 Berliner Illustrirte Zeitung 1059

Bildnisse von Filmsternen zu dem Aufsatz: „Die Magie der männlichen Schönheit."

Paul Richter,
Siegfriedsgestalt, hohe Stirn, helle Adleraugen, verträumter Mund, leichte Melancholie, die zum mütterlichen Trösten auffordert, kraftstrotzend und ein wenig täppisch.
Phot. Becker & Maaß.

Ronald Colman,
moderner Schönheitstyp, ohne jede Süßlichkeit, sparsam in den Bewegungen, Neigung zum Saloppen, sympathisch, innerlich gespannt, kluge Augen, warmherzig, voll Mitleid.
Phot. Paramount.

Die Magie der männlichen Schönheit

Den antiken Frauen nahten ihre Götter in Wolken, den Frauen des bürgerlichen Zeitalters in den Nebeln der Phantasie, die aus den Romanen ihrer Zeit emporstiegen, den unserigen aber ward es vergönnt, ihre Götter zu sehen, nah zu nah, Angesicht zu Angesicht, ihr Lächeln, ihre kühnen Augen, die hohe Stirn, die Pracht der Glieder, den ausholenden Gang, die berückenden Posen und ihrer Heldentaten Zeugen zu sein.

Was war sonst ein Ritter? Ein Mann, der behauptete, in der oder jener Wüste einen Drachen erschlagen, in dem oder jenem finsteren Walde einen Löwen erlegt zu haben. Vor jener Stadt, die man nicht einmal vom Hörensagen kannte, erschlug er fünfhundert Sarazenen mit eigener Hand, und in der Höhle eines sagenhaften Zauberers hat er sich standhaft der Verführungen überirdisch schöner Nymphen erwehrt. Aber, wer konnte das alles kontrollieren? Wer bürgte dafür, daß der Mann nicht ein Hochstapler war? Sollte man ihm in jenem wilden Walde nachspionieren? Sollte man ritterliche Detektive recherchieren lassen? Man hätte sich selbst der Notwendigkeit ausgesetzt, gleichfalls in jenen unkontrollierbaren Gegenden gefährliche Abenteuer bestehen zu müssen.

Harry Liedtke,
Dichter und Bowlenbrauer, Schalk im Auge, Charme im Grübchen, Draufgänger, rätselhaft wechselnd zwischen Leichtsinn und Melancholie, goldiger Kerl, ewig jung und doch nicht mehr Junge.
Phot. Ufa.

Die schönen Leserinnen des 18. und 19. Jahrhunderts hatten es nicht minder schwer. Die faszinierenden Verführer, die blanken Offiziere, die Emigranten mit den melancholischen, dunklen Augen, die heldenhaften Verschwörer, die edelmütigen Räuber, die kühnen Seefahrer, ach, sie wurden in den vielbändigen Romanen der Zeit haargenau beschrieben und ihre Heldentaten füllten Hunderte von Seiten. Aber, was waren Worte gegen die Wirklichkeit! Wer soll den Glanz und die Bewegung eines menschlichen Auges beschreiben, wer kann nach einer bloßen Schilderung eine wirkliche Nase zeichnen? Immer mußte die Wirklichkeit bei diesen Phantasiebildern helfen, immer mußte ein lebendes Modell herhalten, damit die vagen Figuren des Buches Farbe und Gestalt gewannen. Und natürlich war dieses lebende Modell der Leserin in Wirklichkeit immer unerreichbar, sonst hätte sie eben nicht Romane gelesen, sondern selbst welche erlebt. Aber diese Unerreichbarkeit — was hatte sie anders zur Folge, als Bleichsucht, Ueberspanntheit, unglückliche Kompromisse, unverständige und unfruchtbare Sehnsüchte, Seufzer, Tränen, Hoffnungslosigkeit.

Hingegen heute! Da sind die Ideale greifbar. Da weiß man, an wen man sich zu halten hat, da kann man seinem Verehrer

Fig. 8.3 "The Magic of Male Beauty," *Berliner Illustrirte Zeitung*, 26 June 1927. Weimar society's body-fascination extended to men as well.

your linen smocks open at the neck, your knapsack at your back, you wander happily whether the skies be blue or storms rage. . . . But the joy of being is even more deeply felt when you have cast off your clothing by the bank of a stream or lake to bathe in sunlight and water. A marvelous feeling of freedom flows through

Fig. 8.4 The boxer Max Schmeling, an icon of manliness. Bildarchiv Preussischer Kulturbesitz / Art Resource, NY

> you and you exult in your work. Now you experience yourself, you experience your body! . . . There is a purity, a sacredness, in our natural nakedness. We experience a marvelous revelation in the beauty and strength of the naked body, transfigured by god-like purity shining from the clear and open eye that mirrors the entire depth of a noble and questing soul. . . . Therefore hail to all who love the sun in natural and healthy nakedness.[50]

Only in a climate that endures so many gray and rainy days would anyone write such atrocious prose about sunlight and nudity.

Over and over, Surén's book makes the same points: sun, nudity, health—these are the paths to happiness, both individually and collectively as a *Volk*. The ancient Greeks and Romans knew the virtues of sunlight and nudity, Surén claimed. They had faced harsh weather with only the lightest of clothing, had traveled great distances in little more than sandals. The Teutonic forefathers also knew this, but unfortunately, the triumph of Christianity had led to the loss of many of these fine traits. Surén even claimed that Greek culture was Germanic because the ancient Greeks descended from the Germanic tribes. However fanciful the history here, however bizarre the notion of a single Greek-German bloodline, this position enabled Surén to argue that by frolicking in the nude, contemporary Germans were reenacting the lives of their own forefathers. The return to the past will revive the *Volkskörper,* the health of the German racial collective.[51]

Naked male bodies running in the grass, at work absorbing the sun, skiing down a mountain slope, frolicking in a lake—the examples go on and on in *Der Mensch und die Sonne* (figs. 8.5, 8.6). Clearly, a strong element of homoeroticism, a worshiping especially of the naked, powerful, bronzed male body, runs through Surén's writing. However,

Fig. 8.5 Hans Surén, German Gymnastics. A wide variety of individuals and groups advocated nudity as the path to wholeness and, for those on the Right, the revival of the German spirit. Exercises in the nude, bathed in sunlight, would restore the individual and collective body and soul weakened by the corrupting influences of modern society. Surén's book, *Man and Sun*, was wildly successful. G. Riebicke, Galerie Bodo Niemann, Berlin.

Fig. 8.6 Hans Surén, My Sport Lime Bath. After strenuous exercise, time to frolic in the lime bath. Surén is the deeply bronzed figure on the right, benevolently observing his students. The homoerotic elements are obvious. G. Riebicke.

Surén also advises girls and women: "The woman must be strong and hardened, but must never lose what defines her essential nature—the female harmony of movement and body." Through rhythmic exercises to music, she will discover her own talents and abilities, which will then enable her to merge into the collective, strengthening both her own individuality and the larger society (figs. 8.7, 8.8).[52]

The kind of body culture Surén promoted had supporters all across the political spectrum, even if not all of them went as far as he did in advocating nudity. The health of the nation, so virtually every political movement or party proclaimed, rested on healthy bodies and an active communion with nature. Organized hikes in the mountains and in the woods on the outskirts of cities would replenish Germans weakened by the exertions required in the industrial age, who were stuck inside factories making repetitive motions and were subject to the smog and dirt of industrial cities. Active bodies would make individuals whole again and thereby repair the collective German body. Communists and socialists each had their nudist, bicycle, and hiking associations that promoted a healthy lifestyle and advocated mountain hikes and bicycle tours as a way to keep the proletariat sound in mind and body, and fortified for the class struggle. Everyone, from Communists to Nazis, promoted gymnastics—the liberal advocacy

Fig. 8.7 Hans Surén, from Dora Menzler, *The Beauty of Your Body*. Surén did not neglect women, and promoted an idealized form of female beauty.

Fig. 8.8 Hans Surén, the von Laban dance school. Women also had to engage in coordinated exercises and preferably in the nude, according to Surén.

reached far back into the nineteenth century—and images of sound, maternal woman.

Each and every political party also had a counterimage, the sick, debilitated, depraved bodies that represented the "other." Communist and Social Democratic propaganda depicted bosses as fat and soft, symbols of degenerate luxury and wealth, an old image that reached back into the nineteenth century and earlier. Communists made Social Democrats even more sickly looking. Having crossed the line separating proletarian and bourgeois worlds (in the communist view), Social Democrats were shown as bent and frail, the lackeys of bosses and bureaucrats, or pot-bellied and presumptuous. Women were often portrayed as oppressed and downtrodden, the victims of capitalist exploitation who required heroic men to elevate them out of their dire straits.

The communist representation of Social Democrats bore some striking affinities with two other images: the age-old anti-Semitic depiction of Jews and the languid, degenerate new woman. Both appear again and again as the very epitomes of danger. None of these bodies is shown erect. Either they are hunched over or they spill out across the background in a sexualized and possessive position. The new woman was modern, refined, and fashionable, and completely self-indulgent. In these images, she contributed nothing to the nation or race—not goods, not values, not nurture, and certainly not children. The anti-Jewish image, disseminated by every single party and movement on the right, became, if anything, even more virulent in the 1920s. Jews were inevitably hunchbacked, long-bearded, malevolent-looking. Their noses were stereotypically big; their eyes peered out from sunken sockets with a malicious gaze. Their limbs, more tentacles than arms or legs, spread over the earth or their unsuspecting victims, ensnaring them as they enacted the Jewish conspiracy of world domination. It was an ugly, degrading image, and the ultimate and tragic irony is that the Nazis, by depriving Jews of the resources of existence, would create the frail Jewish bodies that they depicted.

Sometimes, however, the threatening male image was not weak but hulking and powerful, a gorilla-like figure, often with caricatured African features, that threatened Germany. That was the way conservatives depicted French colonial troops who participated in the occupation of the Rhine and Ruhr (as discussed in chapter 3) and the Bolshevik soldier, who at any moment might overrun the nation (see plate 8).

The body culture of the Weimar period had a strongly militaristic hue. Communists marched in disciplined formation. Surén was hired to reform the Reichswehr's sports and physical education programs and then joined the Nazi party in 1933. The conservative right persisted in using heroic imagery drawn from the military tactics of a bygone age despite the realities of machine warfare and industrial-style death in World War I. The soldier on horseback, defending the nation; the infantryman with bayonet and musket drawn; the parade of gleaming uniforms, brass buttons and medals shimmering in the sun: a comforting image for a nation defeated in war and riven by civil conflicts.

The siren song of sexual pleasure and the bustle of bodies in motion also inspired deep misgivings. Even those on the left sometimes expressed fears about what all this frenetic movement signified.

Jazz and its accompanying dances, with their fast pace and wild movements, seemed to symbolize a world gone awry, a frantic search for meaning when its substance had been hollowed out, a sterile pursuit of the fashionable and new supplanting the timeless contemplation of the profundities of existence. Something has been lost, observed both Katharina Rathaus and Alice Gerstel in important intellectual journals, when "the strolling gait" of dances of a bygone era is replaced by the kinetic, frantic movement of the Charleston, when the dances accompanied by a jazz band have that "desperate, burned-out, light, unscrupulous, gasping, yet liberating step."[53] Loss and gain—the loss of the more ordered, predictable, slower-paced bourgeois world of the nineteenth century, the gain of emancipation via the liberating influences of jazz and America, the combination of primitive and modern represented, in German eyes, especially by African Americans.

The sexual revolution could exert its own kind of pressure, especially on women who moved in "progressive" and "emancipated" circles. Any refusal of a sexual offer could lead to a cascade of attacks drawn from the arsenal of psychology, a psychobabble of the 1920s about sexual inhibitions. As the author and journalist Grete Ujhely wrote in 1930 in one of Weimar's leading intellectual journals: "Have you ever said no to one of the lords of creation? . . . The result is a popular lecture for the next half hour from the angle of psychoanalysis, with primary emphasis on that nice, handy word *inhibitions*. When that stratagem comes to nothing, the man in his fine logical security concludes that you are either frigid or stupid. Usually both. The conclusion, which despite everything remains possible, that his nose perhaps does not appeal to you, has yet to be drawn."[54] Her conclusion? "Every woman has the right, but none the duty."

The critique penned by the great Weimar commentator Siegfried Kracauer was even more bristling. To Kracauer, all the preoccupation with the body was mere deception, a concern for surface appearances that disguised the repressive and inequitable character of capitalist modernity in the phase of mass consumption.

> The spread of sport does not resolve complexes, but is among other things a symptom of repression on a grand scale; it does not promote the reshaping of social relations, but all in all is a

> major means of depoliticization. . . . It is not just because of the many lakes that water sports are so popular in Berlin. Thousands of young employees dream about canoeing . . . [or] forsake every other pleasure for the sake of their sailing-boat. . . . The naked body evolves into the symbol of the human individual liberated from prevailing social conditions, and to water is ascribed the mythic power to wash away the dirt of the workplace. It is the hydraulic pressure of the economic system that overcrowds our swimming baths. But in reality the water just cleanses the bodies.[55]

Kracauer's brilliance is shadowed by a harsh coldness and a sneering contempt, as if there were something wrong with people's indulging in a few days or a few hours of pleasure.

> In the Luna Park, of an evening, a fountain is sometimes displayed illuminated by Bengal lights. Cones of red, yellow and green light, continually re-created, flee into the darkness. When the splendour is gone, it turns out to have come from the wretched, artilaginous structure of a few little pipes. The fountain resembles the life of many employees. From its wretchedness it escapes into distraction, lets itself be illuminated with Bengal lights and, unmindful of its origins, dissolves into the nocturnal void.[56]

Water to Kracauer, had no great spiritual significance; it just washes away dirt. Illumination dissipated into the void. Perhaps. But were all these distractions, all this body-consciousness, really so terrible? Was it so bad that Germans spent some hours dancing at a hotel, swimming in the Wannsee, watching a horse race or a boxing match, or lying in one another's arms? Even if next morning they were back on the shop floor, in the office, or at the sales counter.

But it was the churches in particular that thundered their opposition to all the sex talk and the public display of lightly clad bodies. All this, according to both the Protestant and Catholic churches, was the most blatant sign of the spiritual crisis of the age—a crisis, they believed, actively fostered by the republic. For all their differences and hostilities, both major churches, Lutheran and Catholic, sounded similar themes: the family was the foundation of society, and only families infused with Christian values could provide the basis for a healthy and fertile society and a moral and powerful state. The secular and atheist republic, both churches repeatedly charged, honored man rather than God, and thereby contributed to the dissolution of morals and the weakening of the family. Christians recognized that a healthy family life required a decent economic basis, and they condemned the impoverished circumstances of so many Germans. But the responsibility for the economic crises they also foisted on the republic; ultimately, they were most concerned with spiritual issues and the threat that "free love" posed to Christian teachings.

Parishioners heard these positions articulated almost every Sunday in church. Larger gatherings, like the regular national conferences held by the Lutheran and Catholic churches, provided another major forum for the reassertion of church teachings and for blistering attacks on the republic as the promoter of sexual immorality. At the 1924 Lutheran Church conference, D. Titius, a professor and one of the church's leading officials, sounded a familiar note by claiming that "*broad circles of our people have lost the living God* and have yielded to worldly pleasures and the worship of man."[57] Titius reiterated standard Lutheran themes concerning the family as the "living foundation" of church and state. "Nowhere else are God and man, nature and mercy so fervent as in Christian marital and family life."[58] Catholics made the same point at their 1929 conference, which convened around the theme "Saving the Christian Family":

> The decay of the family and the decay of the state are inseparable. By natural and sacred design, the family is the basis of the state. But when the foundation stones are hollowed out and crumble, then the entire building is threatened. . . . Without exaggeration, one can describe the problem of the family as the most acute social problem of our day.[59]

The sharp decline in the birthrate, the scandalous number of abortions, and the rapid increase in the incidence of venereal diseases were fearsome signs. In some areas of Germany, Protestants charged, premarital sex had become the new moral standard, the "unblemished beginning of marriage" an exception. Even the birth of a child out of wedlock was no longer seen as a sin.[60] Social order, "once so firmly constructed, has weakened and shattered, greatly endangering the protection and the dignity of the female sex. . . . [and threatening] the sense of honor and responsibility that defines the male sex."[61]

What had caused this moral crisis? Radical socialism and radical individualism, both encapsulated in the republic—according to church leaders. All these forces supposedly threaten the existing marital order. They support free love, which is certainly no basis for moral renewal. In fact, the advocates of free love and eroticism worship at the altar of lust and destroy the true meaning of love and marriage. In contrast, true love means patience with a spouse's weaknesses and mutual consideration and concern. True love means monogamy and faithfulness on the part of both individuals; true love regulates the passions. "Physically and morally, family life is in a state of the most severe convulsions," pronounced one leader at the 1924 Protestant conclave. "The recovery of the German people can occur only if there is a strengthening and renewal of marriage and family life. And that can happen only upon the principles of the gospel."[62]

Like Protestants, Catholics believed that the Christian family was threatened by virtually every aspect of Weimar culture and society. A veritable war had to be waged against rampant immorality and the drive of liberals, socialists, and Communists to influence Catholic youth.[63] Only the church militant and vigilant could save the family and ensure a proper Christian upbringing of young Catholics. At the 1929 conference, speaker after speaker reiterated the points about the holiness of marriage, the family as the core institution of society, the dangers facing the Catholic world. Threats to the family signified challenges to the well-being of state and society, since both rest upon that core institution, the family. The "fatal disease of the age," said Abbot Adalbert von Neipperg in the opening address, is the family's renunciation of God, its failure to stand under "God's miraculous light." Other participants roused to the chorus that "Modern life worships man . . . man worships himself."[64]

Both churches fought any effort to relax Germany's stringent divorce laws or to overturn the prohibition on abortion. Such reforms, Lutherans and Catholics argued, directly contravened Christian teachings on marriage as a sacrament and on the sanctity of human life. They also vigorously opposed various reform proposals that threatened to reduce or eliminate religious instruction in the public schools. As Titius stated at the Lutheran conference, "The moral recovery for which we strive is not to be found in a loosening of the marital relationship, but in its sanctification."[65] Only through Christian teaching and education in the home, in the church, and in the schools, only through a commitment to God and a reinvigoration of Christian morality in public and private life, can true family life be reestablished. The sharp decline in the birthrate indicated not only selfishness, but also a renunciation of God's will and the interests of the Fatherland.[66]

Women faced special responsibilities, as the 1929 Catholic conference proclaimed: "Every woman must know and understand that with the bond of marriage, she takes on the responsibility of being, first and foremost, the soul of the home. And with that she must recognize sacrificial love as her life's ideal."[67] A Catholic trade union official, Josef Gockeln, reaffirmed Catholic teaching about women's special character (*Eigenartigkeit*). "*For us the preservation and promotion of the genuine, natural character of women is more important than the achievement of formal-legal . . . rights. . . .* Whatever endeavors are undertaken in relation to women, we must not forget *the mothers*."[68]

For committed Christians, the republic was identical with sex talk, family-limitation strategies, the new woman, and the skyrocketing abortion and divorce rates. The republic lacked a moral center; in fact, it actively promoted the opposite, immorality.

The high seriousness with which sex was discussed in Weimar has an air of the comic about it, at least to later generations. After all, the sensations of pleasure are not exactly aroused by manifestos or learned tracts, written in scientific or bureaucratic prose, that officiously proclaim what is joyful. The German Association for the Protection of Mothers defended monogamy, yet also recognized that marriage cannot necessarily contain "all justified love relationships." The league defined its goal as the recognition of "human sexuality as a powerful instrument, not only for propagation but also for the progressive development of a joy in living." The organization went on to proclaim that "the human is a sensual emotional being whose intellectual and physical traits have the same right to a healthy and progressive development."[69] Thank you very much, one is tempted to respond. We now have learned that sex is normal and sex should be pleasurable.

Yet such a response would be unfair. Clearly, Germans worried about sex and the family and sufferered from their dysfunctions. They needed counseling, or at least so it seems from reading the countless sex and marriage manuals and the other writings of the Weimar period. The sex reformers, so many of them physicians, evinced enormous empathy for the limited, constrained, and sometimes brutal sex lives of their patients. Most reformers were on the left, and many were members of the SPD or KPD. They knew from their own practices the straitened circumstances and tragic stories of their patients. They attacked hypocrisy and the moral condemnation of sex, which left so many people adrift with feelings of remorse, guilt, and despair when they were only acting on normal human desires. The reformers believed that public education on sexual matters and more humanitarian laws would alleviate the misery of botched abortions, venereal diseases, and unhappy relationships. Improved living standards and sex education would allow couples the privacy to make intimacy and joyous sex part of everyone's life. In the professional world these reformers inhabited, inevitably they believed that they possessed the requisite knowledge and expertise to educate, advise, and treat, and that only through the enlightenment they provided could people become more fully human.

Conservatives all over Germany, the Protestant and Catholic churches in particular, loathed the sex and body talk and imagery of Weimar. To them, all this represented the victory of a hedonistic, atheistic, and materialistic worldview. They fought vigorously against it—and against the republic on which they foisted the blame for Germany's reigning degeneracy. Other Western societies in the 1920s and 1930s also heatedly debated the new woman and emancipated sex. But probably in no other country were the ties between these issues and the political system drawn so tightly as in Germany. While one side relished the republic's creation of opportunities for rich and fulfilling sexual lives, the other condemned it as the very fount of immorality, the cause of all that was wrong in German life.

"It's the war that has caused masses of women to abandon their deference toward the masculine ideal and, with that, also their faith in the traditional feminine model," wrote the novelist Robert Musil. "Women . . . have resolved to devise their own ideal."[70] And as Joseph Roth wrote, the revolution showed that what was once thought to be solid and eternal proved fragile and ephemeral.[71] That applied to moral values as well as political institutions. The war went a long way toward destroying deference toward received authority. The war also demonstrated how quickly life could be snuffed out, or a body once strong and vigorous could suddenly become hobbled and racked with pain. In such circumstances, life's pleasures were not to be delayed. For some Germans at least, the war, with all its deprivations, had also destroyed belief in prevailing sexual mores. The innovations fostered by the revolution ran from the workers and soldiers councils to the painter's canvas, the architect's blueprints, and women and men in bed, in various combinations.

It was not, however, all about wholeness and pleasure. The violence of World War I left everywhere visible traces of the war-wounded, some with ghastly body scars. Germans tried to avert their eyes, but they could not. Mutilated bodies sometimes inspired lurid fascination, often transferred from the wounded soldier to women of all sorts. On their canvases painters like George Grosz and Otto Dix depicted dismembered and bloodied female bodies, and authors associated with the paramilitaries expressed a primeval fear of women that they answered with the most brutal male fantasies and the ubiquity of right-wing violence.[72]

By the end of the republic, the fear for the family and male sexual anxieties had spawned an intense, unrelenting attack on women. All the social insecurities of the age were bound up with the charge that women were the cause of cultural degeneration and economic crisis. The new woman seemed to threaten the very existence of the nation or race. By pursuing her own pleasures, she revealed a self-indulgence that gnawed away at the core of the people: she should be having children, replenishing the population lost in the war.

With the deepening of the economic crisis in the early 1930s, women were no longer in a position to fight for equal pay; they had to fight for the very right to go to work. A univocal chorus arose—trade unionists, government officials, religious leaders, social reformers—calling upon women to leave the paid labor force in order to make room for men. There was little economic rationale to such demands, yet they had powerful resonance. Moreover, the vaunted ambitions of the Weimar welfare state were under attack from many sides, and "negative eugenics"—the notion that those with poor genetic characteristics should be prevented from reproducing—increasingly gained support.[73] "Women have become unpopular," as another Weimar observer, Hilde Walter, wrote. Perhaps "an unknown sexual fear" drove men to the irrational proclamation that the removal of women from the workforce would revive the desperately straitened economy.[74]

But the attacks on the new women went beyond economics. They became so virulent, especially in the last years of the republic, because the new woman seemed to personify the Weimar spirit, and it is no surprise that the republic's opponents blended together in their propaganda the image of the new woman with that of Jews and Bolsheviks. Sexually emancipated women, Jewish businessmen, communist revolutionaries—all rolled into one, the nightmare vision of the Right.

And yet Weimar did offer a different, emancipatory vision. Most of the sex reformers had been trained before World War I, and some, like Hirschfeld, had been writing and lecturing for years. Weimar Germany gave them the chance to reach a much broader audience: it was the opportunity of a lifetime. The openness of Weimar society gave their ideas a wider hearing; Weimar politics—health and welfare legislation on the national level, crusading municipalities, hundreds of partly public, partly private associations and clinics—provided an institutional locus for their work, far more extensive than prevailed in other European countries in the same period. The reformers advocated pleasurable and responsible sex as a critical component of modern life.

But even in its most drawn-out fantasies about communion with nature and bodily pleasures, Weimar modernity had its limits: it could never quite leave the individual, or the couple, alone. There had to be a social and political purpose to good sex, namely, the physical, moral, and cultural health of the nation. On that point, at least, all sides—the advocates of the sexually modest Christian family, the promoters of erotic fulfillment—could agree. Yet every speech, every article, every visual image of the emancipated woman and joyful sex aroused the utter fury of so many Germans, including those beyond the circles explicitly committed to the Protestant or Catholic church or the political Right. There was a virulence to their reaction that suggests deep-seated psychological and sexual anxieties. Many societies no doubt live with such tensions. In Weimar, however, those anxieties developed a very specific political articulation. For its many and varied opponents, the republic was the "system," as they called it, that sold Germany to foreign powers, destroyed the healthy German economy, opened the gates to Jews and other supposed foreigners—and promoted sexual degeneracy.

Still, later generations can applaud the efforts and engagement of the sex reformers, whatever their limitations, and wonder whether, in sexual matters, we have really traveled all that far from the 1920s.

9

Revolution and Counterrevolution from the Right

The founding of the republic, the constitution, stunning examples of modern architecture, philosophical and literary musings on the meaning of modernity, dazzling theatrical productions and engaging films, women's emancipation, sexual experimentation, new social welfare programs—all the great achievements of Weimar were bitterly contested every step of the way. The opponents were a diverse lot. There were the Communists, who supported some of these developments and, at the same time, contributed to the sense of disarray that prevailed through most of Weimar's existence. But Communists never had anything close to the resources and support required to seize power. Whatever their own delusions and the fears of a good part of the population, Germany was not Russia.

Instead, the republic's most dangerous antagonists always came from the Right. Some of them were well established and lodged in the most powerful institutions of society—the army, the Protestant and Catholic churches, the state bureaucracy, industry and finance, schools and universities. Only in public service had the Weimar governments been able to effect some shift in personnel, opening up the ranks to new people committed to the democracy. Even here, though, the success was only partial. Elsewhere, at the middle and top levels of the major institutions, there existed significant personnel continuities with the pre-1918 imperial system and the brittle antidemocratic inclinations of clerics, officers, civil servants, professors, and businessmen. But Weimar's opponents were also a ragtag collection of displaced World War I veterans, disgruntled teachers and shopkeepers, street-corner agitators, and lay Catholics and Protestants. They built new organizations—parties, associations, publishing houses, paramilitary bands—that promoted a new, violent brand of politics, which contributed greatly to the frenetic, chaotic quality of Weimar society. Ultimately, Weimar's opponents, the established conservatives and the radical Right, would come together in a grand coalition under the rubric of the Nazi Party. They would destroy the republic and all the opportunities it had offered for cultural efflorescence, social progress, and personal emancipation.

The rapprochement of the established and the radical Right was not easy and was never complete. The radicals created, literally, hundreds of organizations until the Nazis absorbed most of them in the early 1930s. The members of the radical Right were often too unpredictable, violent, and lower-class, too lacking in deference, for the generals, archbishops, estate owners, bankers, professors, and state secretaries who comprised Germany's traditional conservative elite. They pined for a return to the ordered, authoritarian past of imperial Germany. At the same time, total war and revolution had changed the established conservatives. They had, by and large, abandoned faith in the monarchy and recognized the power of mass mobilizations. They had supported massive violence against revolutionary forces all over central and eastern Europe in the years right after World War I, and had become, in many cases, more actively anti-Semitic. In the 1920s and early 1930s, they hungered for a powerful leader who could march Germany out of what they considered the morass of corruption and immorality that defined the republic.

The old, established elite was willing, in short, to countenance new ideas and practices to fight the republic, and behind them was a large middle class that longed for nothing so much as order and stability. Ultimately, it took the combined political and economic crisis of the Depression, coupled with the dynamism of the Nazi Party and Hitler's personal magnetism, to bring together the diverse grave-diggers of the republic. However tenuous and tension-ridden the coalition, all through the Weimar period the established and the radical Right shared certain ideas and values and worked with a common language that enabled them to unite at critical moments. Members of both camps supported the Kapp Putsch in 1920, responded gleefully to the assassinations of Mathias Erzberger and Walter Rathenau, worked in coalition against the Young Plan, and, ultimately, supported or accepted the Nazi assumption of power.

Certain keywords and key phrases comprised the shared language of the Right—*Volkstum*, *Deutschtum*, *Überfremdung*, *Dolchstoß*, *Diktat von Versailles*, *Schieberrepublik*, *Schmährepublik*, *Judenrepublik*, *Kampf*, *Drittes Reich*, *Führer*, to mention just some of the most prominent. They were thundered from the pulpit; printed in the press, leaflets, and novels; declaimed in parliament; displayed on placards; and spoken around the dinner table at estates in East Prussia and well-appointed houses all over Germany. They conveyed a belief in some kind of German essence, a supposedly moral, hardworking, sober, and creative people, whose upstanding characteristics were based on shared "blood" (*Volkstum*, *Deutschtum*). This racial sense of German-ness infiltrated the language of even those institutions like the churches that formally rejected racial ideology. In this line of argument, the German people were threatened by a variety of enemies. The country and its people, its bloodline, were being infiltrated by diverse foreign elements, most notably Jews but also Poles and other Slavs. They were flooding Germany (*Überfremdung*), exploiting its people, becoming rich off their misery, and destroying the nation's racial purity. These were the people who had undermined Germany from within during the great trial of World War I, stabbing it in the back (*Dolchstoß*), and they continued their nefarious work in every realm of society. They were in league with Germany's enemies abroad, France in particular, who had imposed the Treaty of Versailles upon the country and established the republic, a system of usury and exploitation (*Schieberrepublik*) that defamed the German people (*Schmährepublik*) and that was, finally, the republic of the Jews (*Judenrepublik*). It was foreign and alien to the very essence of the Germans; what the people needed now was a new, third empire (after the medieval Holy Roman Empire and the pre-1918 imperial Germany), a Third Reich (*Drittes Reich*) presided over by a leader (*Führer*) who embodied the essence and destiny of the German people. This great personality would take up the struggle (*Kampf*) against all the dissolute and degenerate people and ideas represented by the republic, and would lead the Germans to the Elysian fields of prosperity, cultural achievement, and—not least—national grandeur.

The Nazis deployed all of these words and phrases, and the language resonated with large segments of the population because of the series of crises that battered the republic. But the words and phrases were by no means Hitler's private invention. They constituted the common language of the Right, established and radical, of the Weimar period. The Nazis became their most adept purveyors, but intellectuals and clerics provided their most developed articulation. Through countless meetings and publications of both the Protestant and Catholic churches and the outpouring of words in learned tracts as well as in crass propaganda, the keywords and key phrases of the Right diffused through Weimar society. By the time Hitler was granted the chancellorship of Germany on 30 January 1933, his language, the language of the Right, was utterly familiar to the population.

The "conservative revolutionaries," as they were already dubbed in the 1920s, played a key role in the development of the right-wing mind set. As the oxymoronic phrase indicates, they merged certain old-style conservative tenets, like the commitment to a hierarchical order and desire for one great leader, with the modern emphasis on technology, propaganda, and the power of popular mobilizations. Many of the leading figures—Edgar Jung, Martin Spahn, Carl Schmitt, Oswald Spengler, Ernst Jünger—were brilliant intellects who had benefited from Germany's superb elite educational system. The notion that right-wing politics generally and Nazism in particular were the work only of material-minded, self-interested elites coupled with a collection of thugs and brutes is one of the major misinterpretations that has managed to prevail over the decades. In fact, Germany's conservative revolutionaries were, in many cases, serious thinkers and writers, who also happened to be profoundly antidemocratic and, in many but not all instances, anti-Semitic as well.[1]

Oswald Spengler's *The Decline of the West* was one of the foundational texts of the Right, established and radical, and its great popularity extended even far beyond those circles. The first volume was published in 1918, just at the crisis moment of Germany's defeat in the war, the second volume in 1922 amid the harsh reality imposed by the Versailles Treaty. Spengler's elaborate effort to show that all cultures flourish and decline according to immutable laws struck a chord with the public in Germany and abroad. The theories were debated, often refuted by experts, but that had little impact on Spengler's popularity. By 1926 the volumes had sold more than one hundred thousand copies in Germany alone, a remarkable figure.[2] The English translation issued by the esteemed publisher Alfred A. Knopf won the book acclaim in the United States and Britain, and the work was translated into many other languages, including Arabic. The Heidegger student and philosopher Hans Jonas, reminiscing years later, recalled that he had "lapped up" the second volume of *Decline*, whose treatment of the ancient world accorded with Jonas's own views in his first book. Jonas had written that Spengler, despite being an academic outsider, had revealed characteristics of the ancient world that others had completely missed.[3] The left-wing writer Arnold Zweig (later a member of the Communist Party) declared that *Decline* was "the most exciting [*spannendes*] book, that I have found in a long time." Even if he did not understand Spengler's mathematics and considered what Spengler wrote about Kant nonsense, "there are fabulous perspectives and wonderful observations in it, so that one sits before it with heart beating and can neither eat nor drink."[4]

Reading Spengler in our day, one is at pains to see why Jonas, Zweig, Knopf, and many others were so taken with the work. *The Decline of the West* certainly demonstrates great knowledge of history and philosophy, but it is also replete with contradictions, unsubstantiated "laws" about the rise and fall of cultures and civilizations, and arbitrary and bizarre applications of mathematics and natural science to the flow of history. It reads like the work of an erudite crank, perhaps even an idiot savant. Yet *The Decline of the West* clearly captured something of the mood in Germany and beyond after World War I. Its prevailing pessimistic tone coupled with grandiose visions of rebirth and revival; the mix of psychology and history; and its expansive ambition—not only to capture the total span of human history but to predict the future as well—resonated with the sense of despair and the longings that many Germans felt.

It also utilized language and articulated ideas that comprised the standard fare of the Right, a fact that seemed not to worry liberals like Jonas and Knopf and leftists like Zweig. Spengler defined people in terms of races, even though he believed, in opposition to most on the right, that a shared destiny rather than common biological traits defined individual races. Nonetheless, distinct races, closed off from one another, characterized the human species, and the relationship among them was constituted most fundamentally by war. "War is the primary politics of *everything* that lives, . . . battle and life are one, and being and will-to-battle expire together."[5] In *Preußentum und Sozialismus* (Prussiandom and Socialism), written between the two volumes of *Decline* and published in 1919, Spengler was even blunter: "War is the eternal form of higher human existence and states exist for war: they are the expression of the will to war."[6]

This Darwinian view of life as constant, violent struggle between competing groups, led by their respective states, of unending warfare, was music to the ears of the veteran who found his way into the right-wing military bands after World War I, the Reichswehr officer who chafed under the military restrictions imposed by the Versailles Treaty, and the aspiring demagogues like Hitler who sought to overturn both the republic and the Versailles system and make Germany again a world power ready to expand its territorial boundaries. Whatever his quirkiness, Spengler expressed the fascist mentality with its celebration of violence and death.

The Decline of the West often exudes a pessimistic tone. Cultures develop and then they fall. The race becomes soft, no longer capable of the heroic achievements that derive from grand struggle. But Spengler did not just despair; he also offered hope: the moment when a leader appears who embodies the destiny of the race and drives it on to greater glories. The great man is not an intellectual or priest, someone who is merely contemplative, but a man of action who moves by intuition, somehow finding the correct course, and joining his will to Destiny. When a great man appears out of the depths, Spengler argued, the entire people will follow him.[7] All of this would take place in a new empire, the Third Reich, a term that had common currency on the right and was popularized especially by Arthur Moeller van den Bruck and his book of that name. But Spengler, too, lent his name to the term.[8] Between the passages marked by a spirit of despair, Spengler offered a heady, powerful vision of a triumphant race led by a great man lording over the world.

Spengler adopted and further developed another powerful linguistic innovation—the melding of nationalism and socialism. The true German socialist revolution, he wrote, took place not in 1918–19, but in August 1914 when Germany went to war.[9] Socialism for Spengler signified national unity and the national struggle imbued with the Prussian qualities of discipline, self-sacrifice for the greater good, productivity, and creativity. These qualifies were present all over Germany, he argued, not just in the territory of Prussia.[10] Spengler was hardly alone in reworking the meaning of socialism and nationalism in this fashion. But he did it well and acquired a large readership. Stripped of its Marxist and internationalist meanings, the word socialism developed a broad-based appeal because it connoted unity, collective destiny, and creative labor; when joined to the "nation," it made the boundaries of the community clear and fostered the belief, already quite strong, in German superiority over its neighbors to the west and the east. Finally, by writing about socialism and revolution, Spengler helped free the Right from its connections to traditional conservatism, even though he remained committed to a vital nobility (but not the monarchy). The new Right became a revolutionary Right, and in its drive to obtain state power it would garner support among established conservatives who found the language of national socialism quite apt.

The Spenglerian way out of the German crisis meant unending warfare, the militarized state and society of World War I perpetuated as an ongoing, normal condition of life. It was a vision that glorified the actions of those Germans who thrilled after violent combat, whether in formal battle or in riots and street brawls against Communists and Jews. Even though Spengler rejected the Third Reich—among other choice phrases, he called it "the organization of the unemployed by those who shy away from work"—it is no wonder that so many Nazis considered Spengler one of their own.[11]

With his kind of spiritual, otherworldly fulminations, Spengler suggested that no middle way was ever possible for Germany, that there had to be either total triumph or utter disaster. In this view, Weimar was merely the continuation of Allied victory over Germany and the very symbol of Germany's annihilation. Spengler spoke to the many Germans who believed that a great figure would lead them out of their travails to that higher, virtually cosmic level of personal and collective German grandeur. It was a seductive and dangerous gift that Spengler offered, an easy solution—the one great man in whom Germans could vest all their hopes. It was also a gift replicated in other venues in Weimar, like the circle around the poet Stefan George, who attracted many conservative intellectuals and other elite members of society.

Though a cantankerous and quirky individual, Spengler had many counterparts who also helped develop the common orientation of the Right. Other men also wrote about national socialism and the glory of warfare. Even in the age of mass, anonymous slaughter on the battlefields of World War I, they ennobled male combat, male camaraderie, and mass killings. They created an aesthetics of death, destruction, and mass murder. For every Erich Maria Remarque, the soldier turned pacifist author of *All Quiet on the Western Front*, there was at least one exponent of bellicose aesthetics: Ernst Jünger, for example, the prolific and immensely popular novelist, memoirist, and essayist whose postwar writings continually returned to the theme of heroic combat, ennobling death. Jünger's books *In Stahlgewittern* (*Storm of Steel*), *Das Wäldchen 125* (*Copse 125*), and many, many others depicted the war as an uplifting, heroic struggle that gave meaning to life. Copse 125 was a tiny hill, its lack of renown, its utter meaninglessness, precisely what attracted Jünger, who then made the battle for its domination into the very essence of masculinity and the national cause. Jünger depicted in this work the great idealism of war, a struggle of youth against the tired security of the older generation.[12]

In Jünger's depiction, the life force that flows through these new romantic heroes is the blood of the race, which connects directly to the guns they carry and that other life force, nature. Machine and man, war and nature: in Jünger's hands violence is aestheticized and technology naturalized. The rapid fire of machine guns is described as "glow worms"; an airplane dances like "a pretty butterfly"; an intruder is "a small bright dragon-fly."[13] The landscape of battle is awash in beauty. Treeless, the land is drenched by the hot morning sun; wildflowers "bathe the trenches in a hot stream of scent"; the "spirit of annihilation [is]" carved into the land. Amid the evidence of battle and death, "there is utter peace, and only nature speaking to itself."[14]

Jünger gave an erotic sensibility to the practice of killing. In one chapter after another, he depicted the kill in loving detail, like an artist describing every brushstroke of his masterpiece.[15] For Jünger, the beauty of nature can be perceived only amid the reality of death and acts of violence; manly virtue is possible only through the act of killing. Violence is the means to a higher existence, the test of virtue and the mark of distinction. Like Spengler, Hitler, and so many others, Jünger believed that rejuvenation could come only through war, and those who sought to avoid this fundamental law of nature were only "ridiculous," the "pests of civilization," whose beliefs led to civilization's decay.[16] The glorification of war in an age of industrial killing fit exactly with the Nazi idealization of virile violence as the way to surmount the lowly, traitorous Weimar Republic and create the bright Aryan future.[17]

Radicals like Jünger and oscillators like Spengler, who moved back and forth between the established and the radical Right, were, for the most part, fundamentally anti-Christian. Nonetheless, the language and ideas they propagated had many affinities with the anti-Weimar fulminations that constantly emanated from the churches, Protestant and Catholic alike. Perhaps more than anything else, the rhetoric deployed by the Christian establishment made the Nazis *salonfähig*, that is, acceptable in polite society.

The churches' distaste for Weimar reflected their ongoing unease with the modern world—and Weimar politics, the Weimar "spirit," were, indeed, the very epitome of modernity. Family and sexual matters were major elements of the churches' hostility toward Weimar, as we saw in chapter 8. But there were other issues as well. Protestants and Catholics alike evinced a nostalgia for a bygone age when, supposedly, order existed and Christian spirituality permeated every sphere of life. In the churches' view, Germans had forsaken a deep connection with God and nature; instead, the modern society they inhabited was mechanistic, rationalist, egotistical, individualist.[18] The Catholic Church complained that parishioners were worn down by the fast tempo of modern life and constant concerns about providing for the family. At the end of the day, they flop exhausted onto the couch and listen to the radio, whose "nighttime music is the sleep narcotic."[19] Spiritual concerns were neglected, and the father had no time for his children. He might provide for the family, but he was "no longer the patriarch in his family community. No longer friend, comrade, and counselor. No longer the source and center of a rich and deep religious-moral, spiritual-soulful, and pleasant-intimate family life."[20] All of this was the result of the "rationalist-enlightenment" ideas of the present day and its selfish orientation, which placed the single individual, not God, at the center of all things.[21]

Catholics and Protestants remained deeply divided during Weimar, but they spoke in the same disparaging voice about Weimar politics and Weimar society. They reaffirmed traditional Christian teachings on the close link between church and state, yet also warned the state—and they meant the Weimar state—that it should not reach too deeply into the life of the church.[22] Despite Christianity's long-standing theological affirmation of the state as God's vehicle on earth and a major force for order in society, both churches kept their options open throughout the Weimar period. If the existing state continued down its immoral path, if it failed to provide for the people and protect the family, then the churches would renounce their loyalty. By making their support conditional, Protestants and Catholics decisively weakened the Weimar state and, indeed, opened the path for others, like the Nazis, to create their vision of a new order.

Christian theology was certainly opposed to racial ideology. But both the Lutheran and Catholic churches easily and frequently used the word *Volkstum*, which by the 1920s carried profound racial connotations. The word signified that defined characteristics lay "in the blood," that German *Volkstum* was something innate and transmitted through the generations.[23] Nor did the churches shy away from specific attacks on Jews and Judaism. At the 1924 Lutheran conference, one major speaker, Paul Althaus, noted that the "Jewish spirit" threatened the German people. While "wild anti-Semitism" was unhealthy, Althaus claimed, the church had to take a clear stand against "the Jewish threat to our national character," against the Jewish influence in the economy, press, art, and literature. Christians were called " 'to fight consciously against such immoral influences.' " It was not about hatred of Jews, not about blood, not even about the religious beliefs of Judaism, he charged, but "the threat posed by a totally degenerate and degenerating urban spirit, whose bearer is first and foremost the Jewish race."[24] Althaus expressed the hatred every conservative, established and radical, felt toward the republic and its culture. Weimar was urban, modern, degenerate, and Jewish, all in one. The "reasonableness" of Althaus's anti-Semitism—it was not even against Judaism, he claimed—made it all the more dangerous.

At the conference, his speech met "with loud applause" from the delegates and words of high praise from the vice president.[25] Like so many others, Althaus cleared the path for the reconciliation of Christianity and Nazism. They would be able to deceive themselves about the Nazis' hostility toward Christianity because on so many other points they were on common ground. The belief in the "unity of Christendom and German-ness," the greatest achievement of the German people, would lead many Christians down the path to Nazism.[26]

Oswald Spengler, Ernst Jünger, Paul Althaus—these were men from the bourgeois middle class of German society. Althaus was a professor and served his church in high positions. Many of the men who applauded him were professors, pastors, and mid- and high-level government officials—as a glance at the conference participants list shows. Spengler and Jünger were the beneficiaries of Germany's fine Gymnasien and universities and were widely read by the literate public. All of these men promoted the views associated with the radical Right. But they were by no means isolated, marginalized radicals. They stood at the very center of German society.

All of them articulated an alternative to Weimar's secular, modernist democracy. Their views were by no means the same, their relations with the Nazis ambivalent and sometimes hostile. But all three wrote in and spoke a common language that was also, in very significant ways, the language of Nazism. They talked about race, German-ness, degeneration, rebirth, the leader, hard struggle, and the enemies whose influence had to be eliminated. Their unforgiving hostility to the republic and everything it represented effectively served the Nazis' first aim: destroy the republic from within by unrelenting attacks and by creating an alternative vision of a racially based national community.

The Nazis invented nothing ideologically or rhetorically. Hitler spoke the same language, used the same words and phrases as did Spengler, Jünger, Althaus, and all the other forces on the right, only did so more radically and more fervently, less knowledgeably and gracefully, than the others. When he wrote in 1924 in *Mein Kampf*, "Was there any form of filth or profligacy, particularly in cultural life, without at least one Jew involved in it?" his words were all too similar to Althaus's speech at the Protestant conference.[27] When Hitler charged that Jews brought "Negroes" into the Rhineland with the aim of ruining the white race through miscegenation, his words evoked the DNVP's political poster against the Locarno treaties (chapter 3, fig. 3.7) and the right wing's intense campaign against the French occupation.[28] The notion that Germany was involved in an existential struggle against the varied enemies at home and abroad merely repeated the overheated anti-Versailles and anti-Weimar rhetoric that Catholics and Protestants heard at their respective conferences and from their respective pulpits. When Hitler spoke about Jews becoming rich off Germany, he reiterated the language that had become so prevalent in the war and inflation about the speculator and the profiteer, who was always identified as a Jew. Constantly, this rhetoric—of Hitler and the others—was linked to the "Versailles dictate" and the "enslavement of Germany," conjuring up a vast world of conspiracy directed at Germans in every single aspect of their individual and collective lives, from the ability to maintain a family to the territory of the nation. Every single problem was a result of *der Jude*, the Jew, who took on mythical, otherworldly powers in this discourse.[29]

The Nazis spoke the common language of the Right. Their innovations were tactical and strategic. They developed a consistent (at least from 1926 onward), aggressive political strategy that placed primacy on constant action; built alternative institutions in the party, its paramilitary units, and its youth organization; and, in Adolf Hitler, promoted a brilliant rhetorician and political tactician. And more fervently and consistently than any of the established conservatives, they targeted the particular, singular enemy whom they identified as the cause of all of Germany's travails—the Jew.

Hitler had learned from the fiasco of the 1923 putsch. He would never again fully trust the established conservatives and decided that the road to power lay through the democratic procedures of the Weimar Republic. Never again would he attempt an armed putsch. Instead, the Nazis would use the freedom of the press, assembly, and speech that Weimar offered to build a mass following, and the electoral system to win the chancellorship or presidency of Germany. In the years before the Depression the Nazis constituted a tiny party on the fringes of German politics and society. But they used these years to good effect by building a party of supremely dedicated followers and by establishing Hitler's role as the preeminent leader, the embodiment, supposedly, of the German people's destiny. The party was also for some a revolving door—many people joined and left. But those who stayed developed into highly committed activists.

Who were they? A diverse lot. Over time and especially after they were in power, a greater proportion of the party membership would come from well-established and elite backgrounds. But the most salient point is that the Nazis formed Germany's first *Volkspartei*, that is, a people's party with members from all across the social spectrum. Every other major party had a particular social or confessional profile—the Social Democrats and Communists had predominantly working-class memberships; the Center Catholics; the German National People's Party estate owners, businessmen, and peasants. The Nazis attracted people from every class and virtually all Christian denominations. That said, the party did include an overrepresentation of people from lower-middle- and middle-class backgrounds: clerks, teachers, civil servants, shopkeepers. Workers and Catholics joined the party too, but they were underrepresented because so many of them were already well organized into the milieus of the socialist labor movement or the Catholic Church, which the Nazis had a difficult time penetrating.

But whether Lutheran or Catholic; working-, middle-, or upper-class; urban or rural, they all were attracted by the Nazi Party's dynamism, impassioned anti-Marxism, and unrelenting hostility to the republic. They believed that National Socialism would achieve for Germans prosperity and power, a grandeur greater than Germans had ever known before. Some of them were fervent anti-Semites, others indifferent to the so-called "Jewish question." But if not anti-Semitic beforehand, those who joined the NSDAP and became the party faithful learned that Jews were the source of all of Germany's problems.

One other thread holds together the members of the Nazi Party—they were, predominantly, men who constituted the Weimar generation. The very top leadership was slightly older and comprised many World War I veterans, like Hitler, Ernst Röhm, Rudolf Hess, Hermann Goering, and Reinhard Heydrich. But just below them were those who felt that the great challenge of war, the great opportunity to test their manhood and commitment to the Fatherland, had passed them by because of their late birth. Some of them were footloose young men who, in the difficult economic and social conditions of Weimar society, had never established a "normal" path into a steady job and a settled family life. Some were street toughs who enjoyed the opportunity for brawls, or cashiered army officers who felt comfortable only in military-like settings. Still others were highly educated men of the middle class who had come to believe that Germany had, indeed, been betrayed by the enemies at home and abroad, that race was the way of the world, and that Germany needed a full-scale revolution that would drive out the traitors, make war against the foreign oppressors, and create the racial society everywhere that Germans ruled.

Werner Best and Joseph Goebbels were typical of this latter group.[30] Best came from the well-established middle class, Goebbels from a lower-class family. But both saw their families fall on increasingly hard times as a result of World War I and the upheavals of the early Weimar years. They had early traumas: as a young boy Goebbels suffered an illness that resulted in his clubfoot; Best, when he was fifteen, lost his father in the first months of World War I. Best and Goebbels were smart, ambitious, and seething with resentments at their own straitened circumstances, and at Germany's defeat in World War I and national malaise in the postwar world. They quickly found their way into right-wing politics and joined the Nazi Party early, Goebbels in 1926, Best in 1930. Both would go on to powerful careers in the Third Reich. Goebbels became propaganda minister; Best served in many posts, notably as Reinhard Heydrich's deputy in the Reich Main Security Office of the SS and in the German occupation administration in France and Denmark. Goebbels was the shrill ideologue who relished mobilizing the party and, later, German society to violent campaigns against Jews, Communists, and foreign powers. Best was a cool, efficient administrator and intellectual who provided much of the rationale for the expansion of police powers in the Third Reich. Race was their idée fixe: Aryan superiority was an unquestioned fact, and Aryan power needed to be established through political revolution. Jews constituted the main threat; only through their elimination would Aryans be able to flourish. An all-powerful state with its one great leader would create the racial utopia of the future through hard, bitter struggle. The Nazi Party and the Third Reich needed them both: the loud, unsavory propagandist who rallied the multitudes, and the clearheaded bureaucrat and intellectual who got things done, united in their hatred of Weimar and their determination to establish the racial state and society.

What did Best, Goebbels, and the thousands of other committed Nazis do in the 1920s and early 1930s? They agitated. They spread the language of the radical Right in unending rounds of speeches and articles, and organized countless meetings, rallies, and demonstrations. Constant, frenetic activity was their strategy. Goebbels and Best moved among various groups on the right, established and radical, before throwing in their lot with the Nazis. For Best, already at the age of fifteen, "not to be able to fight as my father did, as a soldier for the German victory, became the trauma of my youth, which in the succeeding years created in me an inner drive—often unconscious—to set to work actively, wherever I found a possibility."[31] In the student movement of the 1920s he fought for the "*völkisch* line," which meant, most immediately, the exclusion of Jews, and quickly moved into its leadership. In the Rhineland he organized and agitated against the French occupation, finding support, financial and otherwise, from the varied elements of the German conservative-national right wing: the student movement, businessmen, wealthy notables, and some government officials. Best railed against "the Versailles dictate" and for a popular mobilization and a *levée en masse* in this "final struggle of the world war" against the French enemy and all the "defeatists" at home who again wanted to "betray Germany." Like the Irish against the English, the German people had to take up arms against the occupier, Best argued.[32] Goebbels ran up and down the Rhineland speaking before comrades and the larger public and scheming for his own advance within the party. After some early hesitations, he fawned over Adolf Hitler and, adept propagandist that he was, helped forge the image of the nearly superhuman *Führer*, no doubt part of the reason that Hitler soon made Goebbels party leader in Berlin.

All the motion and activity paid off, even before the Depression and the explosion of Nazi support. By working so tirelessly, men like Goebbels and Best developed an entire rank of dedicated cadres, mostly young, always male, who then also spread the word.

Affinghausen, a village in Lower Saxony, provides a good example. Starting in 1928, a Nazi activist came from a neighboring town and spoke about the dire conditions of the peasantry and about the Nazi movement. Like the villagers, he was a peasant, so he knew their concerns and knew how to talk to them. And he came back, every few months and then more often. Then other Nazi leaders came. They attracted new members, and when the initiates had absorbed Nazi doctrine, they fanned out to neighboring villages, replicating the process.[33] None of the other parties had anything like this kind of organizational depth or the determination to mobilize and organize in villages and areas that were essentially uncharted politically.

In cities all over Germany, Nazis displayed their activism and aggressiveness by seeking out confrontations with Communists, Social Democrats, and Jews. Goebbels was particularly skillful at fomenting such activities. In February 1927, the local Nazi Party organization held a rally in Wedding, a communist stronghold in Berlin, with Goebbels as the featured speaker. This was, of course, a deliberate provocation. According to an internal party report, one thousand people showed up, four-fifths Nazi storm troopers, one-fifth Communists, and more people filled the streets outside. First the Communists tried to prevent the meeting from proceeding as planned, then people in the crowd started heckling the Nazi speaker, and suddenly "a savage fight" erupted. Chairs, beer mugs, and tables flew through the air. The party report claimed that eighty-five Communists were wounded, but only about fifteen Nazis. It was a great victory, the party press trumpeted: "Marxist terrorism has been bloodily suppressed."[34] The Nazis exaggerated the triumph and meaning of this incident. In itself, it hardly made a dent in communist support. But it did demonstrate vividly the Nazis' commitment and determination, and that, of course, was the point.

The Nazis infused neighborhoods, villages, and towns with their presence, blanketing them weekly and even more often with leaflets, demonstrations, and stern-faced, disciplined storm troopers. In Thalburg, a midsized Hannoverian town, the Nazis in 1930 held a meeting virtually every other week, which they promoted with themes like "The German Worker as Interest-Slave of International Capitalists," "Saving the Middle Class in the National Socialist State," "Eleven Years Republic—Eleven Years Mass Misery," or "Marxists as

Murderers of the German *Volk* in the Pay of the Enemy."[35] The slogans spoke directly to the town's largely middle-class residents. As in Berlin-Wedding, the Nazis were deliberately provocative and timed their rallies and demonstrations to challenge similar efforts by the SPD or KPD. The Nazi SA and the Reichsbanner, the SPD's paramilitary force, both armed with clubs, brass knuckles, and small firearms, fought one another in the streets, in bars, and at rallies. For middle-class elements already hostile to "the Marxists"—which meant in this town Social Democrats, since there were few Communists—it was easy to attribute the disorder and chaos to the workers who supported the SPD. As one housewife remembered: "The ranks of the NSDAP were filled with young people. Those serious people who joined did so because they were for social justice or opposed to unemployment. There was a feeling of restless energy about the Nazis. You constantly saw the swastika painted on the sidewalks or found them littered by pamphlets put out by the Nazis. I was drawn to the feeling of strength about the party, even though there was much in it which was highly questionable."[36] Here and in other towns, a few individuals who were well established joined the local party organization early on and made it respectable for others to follow.

During election campaigns—and there were many in the last years of the republic—Nazi agitation became even more fervent. Thalburg was typical. For election rallies, the Nazis mobilized all of their supporters in the surrounding area, who descended on the town in full force. Marching together in uniform with banners flying and the storm troopers raining down leaflets from trucks, the Nazis projected a powerful image. At especially important rallies, local Nazis recruited well-known party leaders or military officers who were willing to lend their name to the cause. Most important of all was a visit from Hitler. The local Nazis spent weeks in preparation, plastering the town with posters and drafting additional help from Nazis in the environs. Everything was precisely planned—the route of the motorcade, the storm troopers who stood guard, the lineup of speakers, all leading to the crescendo of Hitler's speech. The spectacle was enticing for many Germans—the sea of swastikas held aloft, the sheer press of people, the seats reserved for war veterans and for Nazis who had supposedly been wounded in battles with Socialists and Communists, the sight of Hitler's airplane as it descended from the clouds to land in a field nearby, the enthusiasm and devotion of the crowd when Hitler rose to speak.[37]

The Nazis in all these settings not only looked young; they seemed very modern with their adoption of the most innovative technologies. Hitler was the first German politician to travel extensively by airplane in electoral campaigns. At large rallies the party loyalists assiduously set up microphones and loudspeakers. Later on, Hitler would use the radio, Goebbels films, all to great effect. By sound amplification and transmission, and the automobile and airplane—the new media and transport technologies of the 1920s—the Nazis maintained a constant, vivid presence in the public realm.

But the Nazis did not just talk and fight. They also provided material help to the poor and the unemployed by establishing soup kitchens and charity drives. The social work programs, like everything else the Nazis did, were largely self-financed. They raised money through the contributions of their own members and the small admission fees they charged at their rallies, plus larger gifts from wealthier supporters. For their charity work, they received donations from local merchants and peasants in the surrounding countryside. In Thalburg at the end of 1931, the Nazis were feeding two hundred people a day.[38] And to youth they offered great opportunities for play in a nonreligious, nonsocialist setting. As one Thalburger remembered his reasons for joining the Hitler Youth in 1930:

> I joined [the Hitler Youth] . . . simply because I wanted to be in a boys club where I could strive towards a nationalistic ideal. The Hitler Youth had camping, hikes, and group meetings. . . . There were boys from all classes of families though mainly middle class and workers. There were no social or class distinctions, which I approved of very much. There was no direct or obvious political indoctrination until much later. . . . Without really trying to get new members, the Thalburg Hitler Youth grew rapidly. . . . Most of the other boys joined for the same reason I did. They were looking for a place where they could get together with other boys in exciting activities.[39]

A young man who joined the party in Bad Harzburg described a similar surge of enthusiasm: "For me this was the start of a completely new life. There was only one thing in the world for me and that was service to the movement. All my thoughts were centered on the movement. I could only talk politics. . . . My only interest was agitation and propaganda."[40]

The Nazi Party was new, vital, and dynamic. It projected an image of youth and offered boys and young men opportunities for enjoyable and thrilling activities. (Less so before 1933, decisively in the Third Reich, it would offer the same to girls and young women.) It promised to rectify the "national shame" and the real-life problems that so many Germans had experienced through the succession of crises that beset the republic. The Nazi Party fomented disorder, yet—in a very nice game—successfully presented itself as the party of law and order against the Communists and "alien elements" so many Germans feared. Nazis spoke in the common language of the Right, yet with an unmatched radicalism and determination. And the party identified the enemy whose suppression would make Germany and Germans great again.

But none of this sufficed to bring the Nazis to power. For that, two other factors were required: the support of the established Right and the Depression.

In 1928, at the height of the "golden years" of the Weimar Republic, the Social Democrats returned to the government in a large coalition. There were worrisome signs—employers locked out workers in the Ruhr iron industry, the Nazis were gaining some support in depressed rural areas, a very large number of splinter parties had entered into the election—but the revival of the SPD's electoral fortunes, the loss of votes on the extremes of the political spectrum, and Stresemann's generally successful foreign policy all boded well for the republic.

Then came the onset of the world economic crisis, beginning with the stock market crash in the United States in October 1929. The impact spread very quickly to Germany, and by spring 1930 its economy was in a tailspin. The collapse of stock values soon precipitated a banking crisis, particularly as American financial institutions demanded repayment of their short-term loans to German businesses and governments. Capital evaporated, leading to a rapid decline in production and then, finally, a demand crisis as both consumers and businesses lacked the resources to purchase goods in the marketplace. By the late spring of 1930, a full-scale economic depression was under way in Germany, its most visible signs shuttered factories and throngs of unemployed workers. In one generation, Germans lived through three social catastrophes: total war, hyperinflation, and, now, depression on a scale that no one had ever experienced previously.

The political ramifications were immediate. The SPD-led coalition government broke up over the issue of unemployment insurance. With tax revenues declining drastically and ever increasing numbers of workers lining up for unemployment insurance payments, the government faced a severe budgetary shortfall. The Social Democrats and some Catholics wanted to preserve and even expand benefits. Conservatives wanted payment levels cut and access to benefits made more restrictive. Each of the parties retreated to its own base; consensus and compromise were not possible. In this situation, the president, Field Marshal Paul von Hindenburg, named a new chancellor, Heinrich Brüning from the Center Party, who formed a new government with some of the same figures, but without the Social Democrats. And also without Gustav Stresemann, the most effective advocate of foreign policy compromises, who had died in the fall of 1929, just before the onset of the Depression.

Brüning sought to lead Germany out of the Depression by following deflationary policies, which meant balancing the state budget through drastic cutbacks in personnel and services (as we saw in chapter 4). The state's model should be carried over into the private sector, Brüning believed. Businesses should expect no aid from the government and would have to let their own purchases and investments fall to the level where a market equilibrium was reached. At that point, businesses would again find it profitable to invest and produce and could then hire more workers. In a time of unprecedented misery, Brüning believed that only financial rigor in the public and private sectors could restore Germany's economy. Internationally, Brüning's policy evolved: Stresemann's policy of fulfillment, he came to believe, had made far too many concessions to the Western powers. While Brüning kept up negotiations, he was also determined to overthrow the Versailles Treaty and revive Germany's great-power status. By the last months of his chancellorship, Germany would be headed toward the confrontational path that it had abandoned after the hyperinflation crisis.

However, Brüning could find no legislative consensus for his policies. The Reichstag remained deeply divided. In a remarkable display of self-delusion and political myopia, he called for new elections, fully expecting that he would get widespread support in the polls. It was a most foolish act: of course the population, sliding ever deeper into depression, was not going to come out in droves to support a man and a government that had no active policy to redress their misery. Suddenly, in a national election on 14 September 1930, the Nazi Party surged ahead, winning 18.3 percent of the vote and 107 seats in the Reichstag. The shock was huge as newspapers trumpeted the Nazi success in big, bold headlines.

From a small sect on the margins of the political system, the Nazi Party had now become a major force. Germany already faced an extremely difficult political situation because of the large numbers of parties represented in the Reichstag and the deep social and political divisions among them. Now it became ungovernable through normal parliamentary mechanisms. The Nazis never had any intention of working productively within the system. They simply used all the legislatures in Germany, from the Reichstag to the Landtage to city councils, as arenas of propaganda.

The situation, a disaster for those Germans committed to democracy, presented Brüning with a wonderful opportunity. He wanted to use his office to overthrow the republic and create some kind of authoritarian political system. He happily deployed the powers granted to him by President Hindenburg. The basis of Brüning's rule was article 48 of the Weimar Constitution. It gave the president the power to declare a national emergency, in which case the chancellor could rule by decree, so long as his orders did not violate the constitution. The framers envisioned article 48 as a provision that would be used only in the rarest instance when the republic itself was threatened. Instead, article 48 became a regular means of governance because the Reichstag could come to no agreement on anything of substance. For the next two and one-half years, Germany still had a Reichstag with which Brüning had to consult and constitutional liberties remained in force. But in essence Germany was governed under a presidential dictatorship. Politically, the republic had been overthrown well before Hitler came to power.

Brüning relied on President Hindenburg to renew periodically the emergency situation declaration, which Hindenburg did willingly. His elections to the presidency in 1925 and 1932 were Weimar fiascoes. The Center and Right adored him as a figure of masculine prowess, order, and stability, and a link to the bygone imperial age. The most that can be said of him is that he did not actively undermine the republic during his presidency, and he took seriously his oath to the constitution. But the election of a general who, in his most fundamental beliefs, was hostile to democracy made a travesty of the republic. Moreover, by the time of his reelection in 1932, Hindenburg was well into his eighties and beset by senility. An image of leadership that had a comic-opera quality to it in 1925 lost any levity with the onset of the Great Depression and the accompanying political crisis. Weimar needed at its helm a vigorous, committed democrat, not an octogenarian, semilucid field marshal.

All through the latter half of 1930 and 1931 and on into 1932, Brüning issued one decree after another that led to the firing of large numbers of civil servants and cutbacks in unemployment and other social welfare benefits. People looked high and low, but there was no sign of an economic revival. Instead, Germany slipped deeper into depression and the political system into paralysis. By the summer of 1932, nearly one-third of the labor force was unemployed, according to official statistics. But the real numbers were even higher. Women were often the first fired, and relatively few received unemployment benefits. The common view was that the position of the male breadwinner should be preserved: women would be "double-dipping" if their husbands were employed or received unemployment insurance and they did as well.

Meanwhile, the Nazis kept up their agitation and constant stream of attacks on the republic. They were winning an ever increasing number of supporters. Newspapers reported daily on brawls involving the Nazis. Germany was in crisis, Germans were suffering, and there seemed no way out. Social Democrats, the most faithful supporters of democracy, were now identified with a system that was failing. Many SPD members fought vigorously against the Nazis and wanted to engage in full-blown opposition, perhaps in coalition with the KPD (which that party would have countenanced only if the alliance were on communist terms). But the SPD leadership could think of nothing better than to defend the republic, even as its substance was being hollowed out by Brüning and his successors. In the Reichstag SPD delegates tolerated Brüning's government, and in the presidential election of spring 1932, the party advocated support for

Hindenburg as the lesser evil. It was a sad situation for Social Democrats to be seen supporting antidemocratic figures, one connected to the authoritarian bastions of the crown and army (Hindenburg) and the other in quest of a modern, twentieth-century dictatorship (Brüning). A mood of demoralization swept through the ranks of the SPD.

Brüning's policies were also failing, and, finally, he lost the support of Hindenburg and other conservatives. Two factors were decisive. His interior minister decided that the Nazis were becoming too bold and too disruptive. He wanted to rein them in a bit, so he issued an order banning marches of the storm troopers. That did not go over well with the many conservatives who wanted to use the Nazis to overthrow the republic. More important, Brüning, in his drive to cut the state budget, sought to eliminate government subsidies to estate owners in Prussia. This was a program of welfare payments to the most elite group in Germany, Prussian nobles, including the president. A small group of advisers around Hindenburg convinced him that Brüning had to go, and he was duly fired on 30 May 1932.

Hitler had made his second bid for power (the first was the putsch attempt in 1923) in the spring of 1932 by running against Hindenburg for the presidency. He was most hesitant to undertake the campaign, but was pushed along by Goebbels and other top Nazis. Hitler understood that the Nazi Party was an engine that had to keep accelerating. It kept its supporters in a high state of agitation and mobilization. It had no intention of participating in the normal work of governance; power was its immediate goal and the raison d'être of its existence. If he did not make his move in 1932, just as Germany's political and economic situation was reaching its nadir, his political support could evaporate. He tried and he lost. He did force Hindenburg into a runoff election, but in the end Hindenburg trumped him (figs. 9.1, 9.2).

A distraught Hitler and a chastened Nazi Party: that seemed like the perfect situation for established conservatives who wanted to use the Nazis to help them overthrow the republic but had no intention of fully turning power over to them. They were still too uncouth, too unpredictable to trust completely. Enter Franz von Papen, a Catholic noble from Westphalia and onetime member of the Center Party whom Hindenburg tapped as Brüning's successor. Papen, too, believed that the path out of the Depression lay through deflationary

Fig. 9.1 Germans were inundated with politics in the Weimar period. Here is Potsdamer Platz in spring 1932 during the Reich presidential election. The poster for Hindenburg reads, "Elect a Man, Not a Party!" while one of the Hitler posters proclaims "The Reich President is named Adolf Hitler." Below the political advertisements people go about their business; some will patronize the vegetarian restaurant under the Hindenburg poster, others will enter the pastry shop below the Hitler posters. ullstein bild / The Granger Collection, New York.

policies. Papen, even more fervently than Brüning, also wanted to overthrow the republic and the Versailles system, and he thought the Nazis could serve his purposes. In July 1932, he threw out the elected government of Prussia, a bastion of Weimar democracy, and

Fig. 9.2 Politics reached deep into society, into villages and even the buildings within a neighborhood. During a rent strike in Berlin-Wedding in 1932, some apartments fly Nazi flags, others the communist hammer and sickle. Scrawled on the wall is the slogan, "First food — then rent." ullstein bild / The Granger Collection, New York.

installed his subordinate in its place. Fool that he was, Papen repeated Brüning's mistake: he called elections, believing that he would find powerful support in the populace that he could then use to implement his program. But in the middle of a depression, the population was unlikely to support a sitting government whose policies offered no immediate redress of their grievances.

Germans went to the polls on 31 July 1932. The Nazis received 37.3 percent of the vote, the highest they would ever achieve in a free election. They now became Germany's largest party and had 230 delegates sitting in the Reichstag. They celebrated their triumph, but it is worth underscoring the fact that they did not achieve, and never would achieve, a majority in a freely contested election. They received a very large chunk of the vote, more than one-third. But the German people never elected the Nazis to power. Nearly two-thirds of the electorate cast their votes against the Nazi Party.

Still, as leader of the largest party in Germany, Hitler made another bid for power. He believed the chancellorship was rightfully his. He had an audience with Hindenburg, that man who embodied the bearing and beliefs of the Prussian officer corps. To him, Hitler was a lowly, uncouth rabble-rouser, who in four years of army service during World War I had risen only to the rank of corporal. Hindenburg received him but refused to name him chancellor.

Papen ruled as caretaker until the new parliament convened in September 1932. Like Brüning, he governed by decree. But the Nazis thought they had been double-crossed by Papen, because he, rather than Hitler, had received the bid to serve as chancellor. The Reichstag met in early September with Hermann Goering presiding as the parliamentary leader of the largest party. The Nazis entered a motion of no confidence in the government, which the Communists supported. Papen's government fell before it had even begun, and new elections had to be held, the third major election in 1932—not exactly a situation to inspire confidence in the republic.

Germans voted on 6 November 1932, and the results are notable. The Nazi surge had broken. Their share of the vote fell to 33.1 percent, their number of deputies to 196. Germany was no closer to political consensus, nor was there any clear path to power for the Nazis. In fact, the party descended into disarray. Hitler had made two bids for power in 1932 and had failed both times. The party coffers were empty, and a great deal of grousing and opposition against

Hitler had emerged in the party's ranks. In the late fall of 1932, a Nazi assumption of power was only a possibility—by no means whatsoever a foregone conclusion.

Weimar Germany's third chancellor in 1932 was a close aide of President Hindenburg and another army general, Kurt von Schleicher. He claimed that he had a plan for dealing with the combined economic and political crisis. He believed that behind his program for government-supported jobs creation, he could put together a coalition that ranged from the social democratic trade unions on the left to the anti-Hitler Nazis on the right. Schleicher, too, suffered from delusions: the cleavages between the political parties were much too deep for his idea ever to become reality.

Meanwhile, in early January 1933, secret negotiations began between Papen and Hitler, prompted by a small circle of advisers around President Hindenburg. The established conservatives now entered into serious negotiations with the radicals. Every other plan and government in the course of 1932 had failed. The officers, nobles, and high state officials around Hindenburg, supported by a few other businessmen and bankers, believed they could use the Nazis to carry out their goal of overthrowing the republic from within. The Nazis believed they could use the conservatives for the same purpose. They all shared the same language and enough of the same goals that the engineering of the grand, anti-Weimar coalition became, in the final weeks, a fairly simple matter. All of them despised the republic. They wanted an authoritarian system domestically and a revival of Germany's great-power status internationally. They sought to promote a *völkisch* politics that meant, most immediately, severe restrictions on Jews. Trade unions, socialism of all stripes, modern art, sexual reform movements—all of these were to be driven from public life. The coalition was antidemocratic, antisocialist, and anti-Semitic. The established Right was not enthralled with Hitler and the Nazis, who remained too radical and unpredictable. But after all the failed plans and with Germany still, formally, a republic, still mired in depression, still living under the strictures of Versailles, Hitler and the Nazis had become acceptable to the established conservatives and large segments of the middle class.

So in January 1933, Hindenburg's advisers presented him with a plan for a new government. Adolf Hitler would preside as chancellor, Franz von Papen would serve as vice-chancellor. Of the ten other members of the government, only two were Nazis. Hindenburg, reassured by the presence of so many conservatives, overcame his distaste for Hitler. On 30 January 1933, in a constitutionally legal manner, he named Hitler chancellor. Weimar Germany was finished.

Weimar's demise was, in the final accounting, the result of a conspiracy of a small group of powerful men around the president who schemed to place Adolf Hitler in power. There was nothing inevitable about this development. The Third Reich did not have to come into existence.

To be sure, the Nazis were extremely successful in presenting themselves as a dynamic party that would resolve the Depression, reestablish morality, and restore German grandeur. In Hitler they had an enticing and clever figure in whom so many Germans chose to place their hopes. But Hitler would have been just another Weimar crank, the Nazi Party just another tiny grouping on the radical fringe, had not Weimar's succession of crises given them an opening. The toll of the war and the Versailles Treaty, hyperinflation, and, finally, the Depression had left a battered population that, by the winter of 1932–33, was desperate for some sort of solution. Moreover, the long-standing "democratic deficit" in Germany, the persistence of authoritarian structures and mentalities going back to the founding of the state in 1871, provided a strong basis for right-wing politics of all sorts in the post–World War I era.

But for all the Nazis' innovative activism, for all of Hitler's personal magnetism, however desperate the situation in the last years of the republic, the Nazis never achieved majority support under democratic conditions. Without the established conservatives, without the support of elite officers, businessmen, civil servants, and nobles, the Nazis would never have come to power. Their victory, like everything else about Weimar, was deeply contested, and the controversies would be resolved only by their willingness to use immense violence against any and all of their opponents, real and imagined.

The Nazi assumption of power was a counterrevolution in the sense that it overthrew the great achievements of the revolution of 1918–19. Universal and equal suffrage, political liberties, elections, popular participation in all sorts of institutions—all that was quickly destroyed by the Nazis, obliterating the republic and the constitution, even though neither was ever formally abolished. The revolution had also fostered more than a decade of exciting innovation in the arts and all sorts of strivings for personal and collective emancipation. That, too, the Nazis eviscerated, even if they retained some of the outward forms of modernism in architecture and other genres. And it was a counterrevolution because the elites who were under attack in 1918–19 and were forced into all sorts of political, economic, and social concessions returned with a vengeance in 1932–33 to destroy the republic. The timidity and shortsightedness of the Social Democrats in the revolution, their slogan of "no experiments" and their refusal to challenge the social and economic bases of elite power in the army, churches, economy, universities, and state bureaucracy, would hound them and haunt them for the twelve long years of the Third Reich.

But the Nazi assumption of power was also a revolution. The conservatives who engineered and accepted Hitler's appointment as chancellor would quickly be outflanked by the Nazis. They got a lot more than they had anticipated, and in the end, it was the Nazis who went a long way toward destroying Germany's old conservative elite. The complete power that the Nazis sought to wield over every individual and every realm of society marked the most radical departure possible from standard conservative, as well as from liberal thinking. And the replacement of Weimar's democratic conception of citizenship with a racial state and society was the deepest and deadliest revolution imaginable.

On 30 January 1933 and in the days following, the Nazis marched through towns and cities around Germany in huge torchlight parades. Luise Solmitz, an upper-middle-class woman married to an army officer, exulted:

> Hitler . . . is Chancellor of the Reich! And what a Cabinet!!! One we didn't dare dream of in July. Hitler, Hugenberg [head of the DNVP], Seldte [head of the veterans' organization, the Stahlhelm], Papen!!!
>
> On each of them depends part of Germany's hopes. National Socialist drive, German National reason, the non-political Stahlhelm, not to forget Papen. It is so incredibly marvelous. . . . for

> when has Germany ever experienced a blessed summer after a wonderful spring? Probably only under Bismarck. What a great thing Hindenburg has achieved! . . .
>
> Huge torchlight procession in the presence of Hindenburg and Hitler by National Socialists and Stahlhelm, who at long last are collaborating again. This is a memorable 30 January![41]

In Berlin, Betty Scholem wrote a few days later to her son, the great Jewish scholar Gershom Scholem, who years before had emigrated to Palestine. She wrote about the family printing business, the difficulties with contracts and customers and so on, the comings and goings of acquaintances and family members, the harsh winter weather. She seemed not overly concerned about the Nazi victory. "A flu wave and Heil Hitler dominate the market," she noted on 7 February 1933. Two weeks later, in another letter, she wrote that, as always, political changes have a bad impact on business. People become more cautious about spending money and pull back their contracts. She also remarked about a wonderful production of *Faust* that she had seen at the State Theater.[42]

They both were deceived. Solmitz would learn that the Nazis fully intended to implement a right-wing revolution in Germany. Her cherished conservatives, who brought Hitler to power and, for the most part, continued to support him throughout the Third Reich, were quickly trumped by the Nazis. Scholem would also discover the deadly seriousness of the Nazis. They took her prized possession, the family printing business. As a woman in her sixties, she left for exile in 1939, finally finding a place with her daughter in Australia, where she soon received the news that another son, the ex-Communist Werner, had been murdered by the Nazis in Buchenwald.

CONCLUSION

Weimar's glow has lasted these many decades since its demise. We are drawn to the Greek tragedy of its history—the star-crossed birth, the conflicted life, the utter disaster as the curtain falls. And like a Greek tragedy, Weimar causes us to ponder the meaning of human action—the striving for something new and wonderful encountering absolute evil, well-meaning ineptitude alongside the recklessness of those who should have known to be more careful.

Weimar had few heroes or heroines in the political realm, and no innocents, no children of Medea here, though nearly everyone, from army officers to Communists, claimed the mantle of violated innocence. But Weimar did have committed activists and brilliant talents, who created new forms of cultural expression, worked valiantly to build a more humane society, and pondered deeply the meaning of modernity. They planned new housing developments that alleviated the miserable conditions in which so many Germans lived. They wrote and lectured about sex and established counseling clinics, convinced that every woman and man deserved a fulfilling sex life. They reduced the length of the inhumane workday that had prevailed in industry before the war. They composed music, wrote novels and philosophical tracts, took photographs, made photomontages, and staged theater productions with riveting creativity and profound contemplation about the meaning of modern times. Sometimes, they even created breath-stopping beauty, which one can still experience by lingering over a paragraph written by Thomas Mann or, on a lovely summer day, gazing at Erich Mendelsohn's Einstein Tower.

These were Weimar's very great achievements. Over the long length of the twentieth century, few places and periods can match 1920s Berlin and its outposts in Dessau, Munich, and even Freiburg,

Heidelberg, and Marburg for their sparkling brilliance and longer-term cultural and intellectual effects. Heidegger's *Being and Time* was the most influential text for post–World War II existentialism and late twentieth-century postmodernism. Weimar architecture, wonderfully creative in its own right, played a key role in the development of the modernist international style after 1945. After the long, dreary detour into high-rise apartment blocks, planners and architects have gone back to Bruno Taut's best creations of the 1920s, which showed that housing developments could be planned on a humane scale. Thomas Mann's elegant engagement with the spectrum of nineteenth-century ideas and values continues to have meaning for our own time. Avant-garde directors return time and again to Bertolt Brecht and his idea of epic theater.

Weimar did not just foster a few creative talents. It produced an entire generation of probing, searching artists and intellectuals. There are no definitive answers to the question of why this particular moment, this particular place, proved so creative. But part of the reason was certainly the sense that the old society had proved its utter bankruptcy in World War I, the revolution had cleared more of the detritus, and, at least for a time, the future seemed unbounded and open—and not only in Germany, but all across the continent. Weimar's great talents emerged in a Europe-wide context of upheaval and revolution and in continual conversation with their artistic and intellectual colleagues in many different countries.

The sentiment of unlimited possibilities would not, could not, last. The constraints of politics and economics quickly came to the fore. But for a time, it seemed indeed that it was possible to create something utterly new, and that sentiment energized the creative spirits of Hannah Höch, Bruno Taut, Erich Mendelsohn, László Moholy-Nagy, and so many others. Their own work became more restrained in the subsequent years. But this does not mean that the artists lived two distinctive lives, two distinctive periods. They built upon the imaginative and creative breakthroughs of their earlier periods. It may well be that their greatest creations came when they had learned to temper the fire of their revolutionary enthusiasms—but there would have been no tempering without the initial blast of heat, no New Objectivity without first expressionism.

Weimar was a tense place, no question about it. The many upheavals, the all-too-brief periods of stability, the absence of consensus—that was Weimar society. The lost war placed particular burdens on German politics and economics and cast a psychological pall over the entire nation. But the war provides only part of the explanation. Weimar's tense, highly conflicted character was also a result of its status between East and West—not in the geographic sense, but in the fact that Weimar Germany, no less than Soviet Russia, was profoundly shaped by revolution. Yet its revolution was incomplete. It created a constitutional order on the Western model and left intact elites who were fundamentally opposed to the democracy.

Weimar was a difficult place to live, but it also produced vibrant creativity. Sedate, somnambulant, self-satisfied societies—and there are such things—do not question, do not probe. Most of Weimar Germany's great artists and intellectuals had had their training and had produced their initial work before World War I. They were poised for bursts of creative activity once they returned from military service or sought to reconstitute their lives in the wake of the war's disasters. Most of them were on the left, but there are also examples from the right, like Ernst Jünger and Martin Heidegger. They despised the republic, but their work was also nourished in its midst.

The younger generation also felt freed from the constraints of the past. The historian Felix Gilbert—who came of age in the shadow of the lost war and amid the turbulence of revolution, civil war, and inflation—looking back sixty years later, wrote, "[T]he one certainty we had was that nothing was certain." A scion of the great Mendelssohn family, prominent in so many spheres of Prussian and German life in the nineteenth century, Gilbert remembered how conscious he and his friends were of their generational ties.

> We felt strongly that the postwar generation was something new. We enjoyed shocking our elders by not wearing hats in the summer, by not wearing tuxedos when we went out in the evenings, and by sitting for long hours on high chairs in bars instead of going to suitable wine restaurants. We wanted to live our own lives, not bound to fit, tight schedules.[1]

Their attitude toward sex was simple: let people do what they want, be honest, and do not make moral judgments. That, apparently, extended to homosexuality, despite its proscription by law. Berlin was a free city, they felt, at least freer than many others.[2]

The freedoms that Gilbert and his friends relished were not just the product of some indefinable postwar mood or sensibility. They were a political creation, the results of the revolution of 1918–19, which established political liberties, opened up new avenues of representation, proclaimed the equality of women, and, for the most part, abolished censorship. These great accomplishments went beyond the formal political system; they also enabled many people to live more freely chosen, more emancipated lives, whether in formal groups like liberal nudist associations or communist radio clubs, or informally as friends going out together to clubs and dance halls.

But these freedoms were also deeply contested. Modern art, the new woman, and casual sex were all flash points of conflict that were piled on top of the plain hatred of democracy that the large, multitudinous right wing continually articulated. Ultimately, the opposition would prove too great for Weimar freedom. But Weimar did not just die as if there were some anonymous process at work, as if there is some undefined moment when a volume of social conflict reaches a crescendo and everything comes crashing down. Weimar did not just collapse; it was killed off. It was deliberately destroyed by Germany's antidemocratic, antisocialist, anti-Semitic right wing, which, in the end, jumped into political bed with the Nazis, the most fervent, virulent, and successful opposition force. Weimar may indeed have had too few democrats, too few people willing to stand up and defend the republic. Weimar suffered more crises than any democracy can legitimately be expected to bear. The radical Left certainly did not help matters. The KPD's attacks on Social Democrats and the Weimar system contributed to the general sense of despair that weakened the democracy. But the Communists had nowhere near the resources of any kind—human, material, military—that would have enabled them to launch a successful assault on the republic. They had already attempted to overthrow the system three times in the early years of the republic and had failed miserably. Their prospects were no better in the early 1930s than they had been in 1919, 1921, and 1923.

The Right did have major resources. It had intellectual capital in the form of well-placed professionals and cultural figures who spoke and wrote in the same language as the Nazis. It had spiritual capital in the many pastors and priests who thought Nazism was at least acceptable. The Right occupied governmental offices and military commands and controlled great segments of the industrial and financial resources of the country. To be sure, not every businessman or pastor was pro-Nazi, and among those who engineered the final destruction Hitler was more tolerated than loved. But the collective hostility of those who commanded Germany's resources, staffed its major institutions, and found a democratic, socially minded, and culturally modern and innovative society intolerable—those are the people who destroyed the republic and without whom the Nazis would never have come to power. Their attacks on Weimar, coupled with the Nazis' formidable political instincts, undermined the system. In their wake came the large, varied German middle classes and many from the lower classes as well, who found disorder deeply disturbing, and understandably so. Germans could not be sure that they would be able to earn reasonable livings for their families, or that hard work would pay off in savings whose value would remain stable or even increase; at moments of civil war and political street brawls, they could not even be certain that they could walk their neighborhoods safely. On that basic level of security, the first task of any governmental system, Weimar did not fare well. In the ensuing years, the members of the right-wing elite and many other people realized that they had gotten far more than they had bargained for in 1932 and 1933. Their Nazi partners were not to be controlled. But that was the bed that they had made for themselves.

Weimar's history does show us that a society lacking consensus, a society in which no set of ideas and no group constitute hegemony, can be a dangerous place. A democratic political system cannot long endure a situation in which virtually every issue becomes magnified to an ideological contest over ultimate meanings. But it especially cannot endure when its elites seek to undermine the democracy from within, when they whine incessantly about a system in which they still exercise privileges and still dispose of immense resources.

Weimar cautions us about the conditions in which democracy can flourish. It would be hard to think of more inauspicious circumstances for the founding and flowering of a democracy than those of post– World War I Germany. The burdens of the lost war, revolution and civil war, economic crisis—even in a society with a well-rooted democratic culture, such conditions would put democratic convictions and democratic practices to hard tests. People desire security—protection of their very lives and of their economic well-being. When a democratic system cannot provide those basic requirements, even the best democrats may edge away from it and look to more authoritarian solutions.

Weimar also demonstrates the limits of elections as a criterion for democracy. Weimar had its elections, to be sure, and they were democratically contested. But it also had a highly conservative judiciary that rarely punished right-wing militarists and terrorists, while it gleefully interned and convicted left-wing activists. Weimar had a bureaucracy that, despite the influx of Social Democrats and liberal Catholics, remained in many offices deeply opposed to democracy. And it had a business class whose commitment to the republic was tenuous at best. Democracy needs democratic convictions and a democratic culture that ripple through all the institutions of society, not just the formal political ones. That was hard to find in many of the key institutions of the republic. Weimar's problem was not so much a popular democratic deficit, because the bastions of the republic were to be found primarily among workers, reform-minded Catholics, artists and writers, and some members of the professions. The major institutions like the churches, the army, schools and universities, and industrial organizations were largely hostile or recklessly indifferent to the republic, and those institutions were at the upper levels populated by the well connected and the powerful.

So many of the creative and dedicated people mentioned in this book would suffer very personally from the demise of the republic. Rudolf Hilferding—a Jewish physician turned economist, one of the greatest theoreticians of Marxian social democracy, the republic's finance minister at the time of the hyperinflation—fled Nazi Germany for exile in France, where he was arrested by the Vichy government in 1941. He was slated to be turned over to the Gestapo but died in custody, probably a suicide because he knew the fate that awaited him in

Gestapo hands. Many others who fled into exile could never quite find their footing again. Neither Bruno Taut nor Erich Mendelsohn ever again had the flourishing careers they had achieved in the 1920s and early 1930s. Taut had no commissions in Japan and Turkey, and none of Mendelsohn's later designs have quite the glory of his best Weimar buildings. Walter Gropius landed at Harvard and did have a successful career, but too many of his post–World War II buildings evoke the worst of sterile, planned modernism, buildings constructed in accordance with functionalist theory but on an antihuman scale. Kurt Weill loved the freedom of America, and he scored some excellent Broadway productions, but he, too, is best remembered for his Weimar creations. Only a few of the exiles who were already well established in Weimar, like Thomas Mann and Bertolt Brecht, maintained a high level of piercing creativity. Even on the right, the conservative intellectuals of the Weimar era had checkered careers afterward, politically and intellectually. Ernst Jünger and Martin Heidegger were not always so pleased with the Nazis they sometimes embraced or worked under. While both continued to write for decades afterward—Jünger died in 1998 at the ripe age of 102—they, too, are remembered best for their Weimar publications, *Storm of Steel* and *Being and Time*.

Weimar still speaks to us. Its sparkling creativity and emancipatory experiments, politically and culturally, are still capable of inspiring thoughts that a better, more humane, more interesting condition of life is possible. It reminds us that democracy is a fragile thing, society an unstable construction, each threatening to spin wildly out of control. Weimar shows us the dangers that can develop when there is no societal consensus on any of the fundamental issues of politics, social order, and culture. Democracy can be fertile soil for all sorts of interesting debates and for the efflorescence of the cultural spirit. But when virtually every debate becomes a live-or-die question about the essential features of human existence, from the intimacy of the bedroom to the structure of the business world, when every issue is seen to carry earth-shattering significance, when there is no overarching system of belief to which most people give their loyalty, a democracy cannot long endure. And it especially cannot endure when powerful groups in that society seek at every turn to undermine and destroy its very being. The threats to democracy are not always from enemies abroad. They can come from those within who espouse the language of democracy and use the liberties afforded them by democratic institutions to undermine the substance of democracy. Weimar cautions us to be wary of those people as well. What comes next can be very bad, even worse than imaginable.

Notes

Introduction

1. Over the last generation scholarly work especially in social and gender history and in cultural studies has enriched our understanding of Weimar politics and society. Many older works and recent ones in more straightforward political and economic history are also extremely valuable. I have chosen not to engage the arguments of these works in the text but have included a bibliographic essay after the notes.

1. A Troubled Beginning

1. Friedrich Ebert, "Ansprache an die Heimkehrenden Truppen," 10 December 1918, in *Politische Reden III: 1914–1945*, ed. Peter Wende (Frankfurt am Main: Deutsche Klassiker, 1994), 94–95. Translations throughout are mine, unless otherwise noted.

2. Ibid., 95.

3. Statistics from Richard Bessell, *Germany after the First World War* (Oxford: Clarendon, 1993), 5–6, and Willibald Gutsche, Fritz Klein, and Joachim Petzold, *Der Erste Weltkrieg: Ursachen und Verlauf* (Cologne: Pahl-Rugenstein, 1985), 292.

4. Letter exchange, Daniela Mueller and H. Arndt from Elkenroth, July 2005, information based on "Ehrenchronik unserer Gemeinde Weltkrieg 1914–1918" (ms.) and the war memorial in the town.

5. Figures from ibid. and *Sozialgeschichtliches Arbeitsbuch III: Materialien zur Statistik des Deutschen Reiches 1914–1945*, ed. Dietmar Petzina, Werner Abelshauser, and Anselm Faust (Munich: Beck, 1978), 27–32.

6. *Chronik der Stadt Essen* (ms., Stadtarchiv Essen) 1917, 67, and Hubert Schmitz, "Ausgewählte Kapitel aus der Lebensmittelversorgung der Stadt

Essen in der Kriegs- und Nachkriegszeit," *Beiträge zur Geschichte von Stadt und Stift Essen* 58 (1939): 135–36.

7. *Chronik der Stadt Essen* 1919, 99, and Schmitz, "Ausgewählte Kapitel," 126–27.

8. Interview with Theo Gaudig, Essen, 28 May 1980.

9. Historisches Archiv der Fried. Krupp GmbH, Werksarchiv (hereafter HA Krupp WA) 41/6-4, 6-5, and K. Wandel, "Die Arbeiterschaft der Kruppschen Gußstahlfabrik: Zur Denkschrift 'Die Firma Krupp im Weltkriege,'" (ms., n.d.), HA Krupp WA/VII/ff1105/Kd75/table2.

10. Alfred Döblin, *A People Betrayed. November 1918: A German Revolution*, trans. John E. Woods (New York: Fromm International, 1983), 99. Döblin began writing the multivolume novel in the 1930s; it was first published in three parts between 1948 and 1950.

11. Quotations from Belinda J. Davis, *Home Fires Burning: Food, Politics, and Everyday Life in World War I Berlin* (Chapel Hill: University of North Carolina Press, 2000), 100–103.

12. The sculpture was placed in a German military cemetery near Ypres, where her son Peter was buried. Kollwitz's grandson, also named Peter, was killed in World War II, fighting with the Germany army in the Soviet Union. The statue now sits in the Neue Wache in Berlin. In 1993, Chancellor Helmut Kohl declared *Mother and Son* the central memorial to the victims of the two world wars, including the Holocaust. That decision has been a source of controversy ever since because it seems to gloss over the specificity of the Holocaust.

13. Gunther Mai, *Das Ende des Kaiserreichs: Politik und Kriegführung im Ersten Weltkrieg*, 3rd ed. (Munich: DTV, 1997), 144.

14. Ibid., 146.

15. Wilson's speech to Congress, 11 February 1918, in Woodrow Wilson, *War and Peace: Presidential Messages, Addresses, and Public Papers (1917–1924)*, ed. Ray Stannard Baker and William E. Dodd (New York: Harper and Brothers, 1927), 177–84, quotation 180.

16. Mai, *Das Ende des Kaiserreichs*, 157.

17. Quoted in Peter Longerich, *Deutschland 1918–1933: Die Weimarer Republik. Handbuch zur Geschichte* (Hannover: Fackelträger, 1995), 50.

18. Bessell, *Germany after the First World War*, 79.

19. Wilhelm Berdrow, "Die Firma Krupp im Weltkrieg und in der Nachkriegszeit," 2 vols. (ms., 1936), HA Krupp, Familienarchiv Hügel IV/E10, 287, 293.

20. Prussia, Ministerium für Handel und Gewerbe, *Jahresberichte der preussischen Reigierungs- und Gewerberäte und Bergbehörden* (hereafter *Jahresbericht*) 1920: 656.

21. Ibid.

22. *Jahresbericht* 1921:549.

23. See, for example, the leaflets and orders issued by the Essen Workers and Soldiers Council in Stadtarchiv Essen Rep. 102/Abt. I/1093.

24. Döblin, *A People Betrayed*, 52.

25. Erich Maria Remarque, *All Quiet on the Western Front*, trans. A. W. Wheen (German original 1928; New York: Fawcett Crest, 1975), 294.

26. For the Munich example, see Martin H. Geyer, *Verkehrte Welt. Revolution, Inflation und Moderne: München 1914–1924* (Göttingen: Vandenhoeck and Ruprecht, 1998), 67–79.

27. Ibid., 70.

28. Ibid., 70–75, quotation 72. British officers on an inspection mission to Berlin also noted the dance craze: Gerald D. Feldman, *The Great Disorder: Politics, Economics, and Society in the German Inflation, 1914–1924* (New York: Oxford University Press, 1993), 99–102.

29. Rainer Maria Rilke to Clara, 7 November 1918, in *Weimar: Ein Lesebuch zur deutschen Geschichte 1918–1933*, ed. Heinrich August Winkler and Alexander Cammann (Munich: C. H. Beck, 1997), 44–45.

30. Oswald Spengler, quoted in ibid., 57–58.

31. Betty Scholem to Gershom Scholem, 7 January 1919, in ibid., 63–65.

32. Betty Scholem to Gershom Scholem, 13 January 1919, in ibid., 65–66..

33. Arnold Zweig, "Freundschaft mit Freud: Ein Bericht" (1947/48) in *Arnold Zweig, 1887–1968: Werk und Leben in Dokumenten und Bildern*, ed. Georg Wenzel (Berlin: Aufbau, 1978), 103–4, quotation 103.

34. Arnold Zweig to Helene Weyl, 4 April 1919, in Arnold Zweig, Beatrice Zweig, Helene Weyl, *Komm her, Wir lieben dich: Briefe einer ungewöhnlichen Freundschaft zu dritt*, ed. Ilse Lange (Berlin: Aufbau, 1996), 149–51, quotation 150.

35. Arnold Zweig, "Theater, Drama, Politik" (10 January 1921), in Wenzel, *Arnold Zweig*, 115–18, quotation 117.

36. Max Cohen, "Rede für die Nationalversammlung vor dem Allgemeinen Kongress der Arbeiter- und Soldatenräte," 19 December 1918, in *Politische Reden III*, 97–121.

37. Ibid., 109 (italics in the original).

38. Ernst Däumig, "Rede gegen die Nationalversammlung vor dem Allgemeinen Kongress der Arbeiter- und Soldatenräte," 19 December 1918, in *Politische Reden III*, 122–41, quotation 122 (italics in the original).

39. Quoted in Longerich, *Deutschland 1918–1933*, 89.

40. Friedrich Ebert, *Rede zur Eröffnung der Verfassunggebenden Nationalversammlung*, 6 February 1919, in *Politische Reden III*, 244–53.

41. Ibid., 246 (italics in the original).

42. Ibid., 247–48.

43. Margaret MacMillan, *Paris 1919: Six Months That Changed the World* (New York: Random House, 2001), 460.

44. Ibid., 460–61.

45. Quoted in ibid., 464.

46. For the quotation and slightly varying interpretations, see ibid., 463–65, and Erich Eyck, *A History of the Weimar Republic*, vol. 1: *From the Collapse of the Empire to Hindenburg's Election* (German original 1954; Cambridge: Harvard University Press, 1964), 92–95.

47. Philipp Scheidemann, "Gegen die Annahme des Versailler Vertrages," 12 May 1919, in *Politische Reden III*, 254–71, quotation 254–55.

48. Ibid., 255, 256, 259.

49. Arthur Graf von Posadowsky-Wehner, "Gegen die Unterzeichnung des Friedensvertrages," 22 June 1919, in *Politische Reden III*, 272–87, quotations (in order), 273, 287, 277–78, 284–85.

50. See, for example, the speeches by the socialist delegates, Gustav Bauer, "Zur Unterzeichnung des Friedensvertrages," 22 June 1919, and Hugo Haase, "Für die Unterezeichnung des Friedensvertrages," 22 June 1919, in *Politische Reden III*, 263–71 and 288–302.

51. Quoted in Longerich, *Deutschland 1918–1933*, 99.

52. For the most recent account, see Macmillan, *Paris 1919*, 459–83. The older account of Eyck, *History*, 1:80–128, is still valuable.

53. Quotations from Geyer, *Verkehrte Welt*, 76.

2. Walking the City

1. Peter Fritzsche provides a very interesting though somewhat different tour of Berlin in *Reading Berlin 1900* (Cambridge: Harvard University Press, 1996).

2. Franz Hessel, *Spazieren in Berlin* (1929), in *Sämtliche Werke in fünf Bänden*, vol. 3: *Städte und Porträts*, ed. Bernhard Echte (Oldenburg: Igel, 1999), 9.

3. Ibid., 103.

4. *Potsdamer Platz: Drehscheibe der Weltstadt*, ed. Günther Bellmann (Berlin: Ullstein, 1997), 111.

5. Ibid.

6. Franz Hessel, "Ich wähle 'Käse,'" in *Potsdamer Platz*, 103–10, quotation 110.

7. "Einhundertfünfzig pro Minute," *Berliner Tageblatt*, 4 September 1928, in *Potsdamer Platz*, 121–24, quotation 121–22.

8. Ibid., 123.

9. T. Koch, quoted in Alex De Jonge, *The Weimar Chronicle: Prelude to Hitler* (New York: Meridian, 1979), 125.

10. Hessel, *Spazieren in Berlin*, 103.

11. Felix Gilbert's comments in *A European Past: Memoirs, 1905–1945* (New York: Norton, 1988), 58–59.

12. Joseph Roth, "Lebende Kriegsdenkmäler," 25 August 1920, in *Berliner Saisonbericht: Unbekannte Reportagen und journalistiche Arbeiten 1920–39*, ed. Klaus Westermann (Cologne: Kiepenheuer and Witsch, 1984), 85–90, here 85.

13. See Horst Mauter, "Der Potsdamer Platz im Wandel der Zeiten," in *Potsdamer Platz*, 13–42, here 32.

14. Inge von Wangenheim, "Das Hinterteil der Muse," and Kurt Pomplun, "'Ach Willy, ach Willy, um sechs im Piccadilly,'" in *Potsdamer Platz*, 127–39, 167–70.

15. Quoted in Siegfried Kracauer, *The Salaried Masses: Duty and Distraction in Weimar Germany*, trans. Quintin Hoare (German original 1930; London: Verso, 1998), 91.

16. Hans Ostwald, "Alle Tische besetzt," in *Potsdamer Platz*, 57–64.

17. "Einhundertfünfzig pro Minute," *Berliner Tageblatt*, 4 September 1928, in *Potsdamer Platz*, 122.

18. Ostwald, "Alle Tische besetzt," in *Potsdamer Platz*, 59.

19. Ivan Goll, "The Negroes Are Conquering Europe," in *The Weimar Republic Sourcebook* (hereafter *WRS*), ed. Anton Kaes, Martin Jay, and Edward Dimendberg (Berkeley and Los Angeles: University of California Press, 1994), 559–60.

20. Christopher Isherwood, *Goodbye to Berlin*, in *The Berlin Stories* (1935; New York: New Directions, 1945), 14.

21. See Ilse Nicolas, "Name und Gesicht gewechselt," in *Potsdamer Platz*, 141–58, here 146.

22. See George L. Mosse, *Confronting History: A Memoir* (Madison: University of Wisconsin Press, 2000), 8–11.

23. Hessel, *Spazieren in Berlin*, 26.

24. Ibid., 29.

25. Ibid., 27.

26. Ibid., 27–28.

27. Ibid., 9.

28. Joseph Roth, "The Orient on Hirtenstrasse" (1921), in idem, *What I Saw: Reports from Berlin 1920–1933*, ed. Michael Bienert, trans. Michael Hofmann (New York: Norton, 2003), 31–34.

29. Roth, "Refugees from the East" (1920), in *What I Saw*, 35–39.

30. Hessel, *Spazieren in Berlin*, 58.

31. Figures and quotation from Adelheid von Saldern, *Häuserleben: Zur Geschichte städtischen Arbeiterwohnens vom Kaiserreich bis heute* (Bonn: J.H.W. Dietz Nachfolger, 1995), 121, 123.

32. See ibid., 153–61.

33. Hessel, *Spazieren in Berlin*, 110.

34. Thomas Mann, "Wälsungenblut," in *Berlin erzählt: 19 Erzählungen*, ed. Uwe Wittstock (Frankfurt am Main: Fischer Taschenbuch, 1991), 7–39, quotation 19.

35. Ibid., 35.

36. Hessel, *Spazieren in Berlin*, 15–17.

37. Carl Zuckmayer, "Die Affenhochzeit," in *Berlin erzählt*, 111–59, quotation 144.

38. Hessel, *Spazieren in Berlin*, 110. The "Berlin room" was the corner room in larger Berlin apartments. It had a small window that looked onto the courtyard, and two doors, one leading to the front hallway and rooms and the other to the servant quarters, kitchen, and back stairs. It became quite the fashion toward the end of the nineteenth century. I thank my colleague Gerhard Weiss for this information, and for help with these translations from Hessel.

39. Ibid., 111.

40. Isherwood, *Goodbye to Berlin*, 3.

41. Ibid., 1.

42. Ibid., 14–15.

43. Hans Eisler, Erich Weinert, and Ernst Busch, "Roter Wedding," Nova recording 8 85 004.

44. Isherwood, *Goodbye to Berlin*, 100, 101.

45. Ibid., 123.

46. Carola Sachse, *Siemens, der Nationalsozialismus und die moderne Familie: Eine Untersuchung zur sozialen Rationalisierung in Deutschland im 20. Jahrhundert* (Hamburg: Rasch and Röhring, 1990), 122.

47. See ibid., quotation 145, and Wilfried Feldenkirchen, *Siemens 1918–1945* (1995; Columbus: Ohio State University Press, 1999), 345–59.

48. See Sachse, *Siemens*, 151–68, statistics 158.

49. Hessel, *Spazieren in Berlin*, 17–18.

50. Ibid., 18.

51. Ludwig Finckh, "The Spirit of Berlin," in *WRS*, 414–15 (italics in the original).

52. Wilhelm Stapel, "The Intellectual and His People," in *WRS*, 423–424.

53. Ibid., 424–25.

54. Joseph Goebbels, "Around the Gedächtniskirche," in *WRS*, 560–62, quotation 561–62.

55. Erich Kästner, "Besuch vom Lande," in *Potsdamer Platz*, 119.

56. Kurt Tucholsky, "Berlin and the Provinces," in *WRS*, 418–20.

57. Matheo Quinz, "The Romanic Café," in *WRS*, 415–17.

58. Harold Nicolson, "The Charm of Berlin," in *WRS*, 425–26.

3. Political Worlds

1. Joseph Roth, "Kaisers Geburtstag," 20 January 1925, in *Berliner Saisonbericht: Unbekannte Reportagen und journalistiche Arbeiten 1920–39*, ed. Klaus Westermann (Cologne: Kiepenheuer and Witsch, 1984), 306–9.

2. See, for example, "Programm der Sozialdemokratischen Partei," Görlitz, 23 September 1921, in *Deutsche Parteiprogramme seit 1861*, ed. Wolfgang Treue, 4th ed. (Göttingen: Musterschmidt, 1968), 111–16.

3. About political posters, see, especially, *Politische Plakate der Weimarer Republik*, ed. Hessisches Landesmuseum Darmstadt (Darmstadt: Hessisches Landesmuseum, 1980), and Peter Paret, Beth Irwin Lewis, and Paul Paret, *Persuasive Images: Posters of War and Revolution from the Hoover Institution Archives* (Princeton: Princeton University Press, 1992).

4. "Programm der Deutschen Demokratischen Partei," 13–15 December 1919, in Treue, *Deutsche Parteiprogramme*, 135–40, quotation 136.

5. See Martin Spahn, "Die sterbende Mitte," in idem, *Für den Reichsgedanken: Historisch-politische Aufsätze 1915–1934* (Berlin: Ferd. Dümlers Verlag, 1936), 370–85, and Larry Eugene Jones, "'The Dying Middle': Weimar Germany and the Fragmentation of Bourgeois Politics," *Central European History* 5:1 (1972): 23–54.

6. "Richtlinien der Deutschen Zentrumspartei," 16 January 1922, in Treue, *Deutsche Parteiprogramme*, 140–49, quotation 147.

7. See Eric D. Weitz, *Creating German Communism, 1890–1990: From Popular Protests to Socialist State* (Princeton: Princeton University Press, 1997).

8. "Grundsätze der Deutschen Volkspartei," 19 October 1919, in Treue, *Deutsche Parteiprogramme*, 127–35, quotations 128, 129.

9. Ibid., 130.

10. "Grundsätze der Deutschnationalen Volkspartei," in Treue, *Deutsche Parteiprogramme*, 120–27, quotation 122.

11. Ibid., 120–27, quotations 122–23, 126.

12. The argument of Klaus Theweleit, *Male Fantasies*, trans. Stephen Conway in collaboration with Erica Carter and Chris Turner, 2 vols. (Minneapolis: University of Minnesota Press, 1987–89).

13. Quotations from Eduard Stadtler, a founder in 1918 of the Vereinigung für nationale und soziale Solidarität, in Erwin Könnemann, "Die völkische Komponente in der Ideologie rechtsextremistischer Organisationen nach der Novemberrevolution (1918–1923)," (ms., n.d.), 15–16.

14. Quoted in ibid., 18.

15. Quoted in ibid., 19–20.

16. Quoted in ibid., 20.

17. Quoted in ibid., 28.

18. This and the previous quotation from Klaus Epstein, *Matthias Erzberger and the Dilemma of German Democracy* (Princeton: Princeton University Press, 1959), 388–89. With the help of well-connected authorities in Bavaria, the two assassins fled to Hungary, then returned in triumph to Nazi Germany in 1933. After the war they were tried and convicted, but were soon released on parole.

19. Joseph Wirth, "Reichstagsrede aus Anlass der Ermordung Rathenaus," 25 June 1922, in *Politische Reden III: 1914–1945*, ed. Peter Wende (Frankfurt am Main: Deutscher Klassiker, 1994), 330–41, quotations 331, 333, 341.

20. Quoted in Erich Eyck, *A History of the Weimar Republic*, vol. 1: *From the Collapse of the Empire to Hindenburg's Election*, trans. Harlan P. Hanson and Robert G. L. Waite (German original 1954; Cambridge: Harvard University Press, 1962), 167.

21. Ibid., 131. The gold standard had been abolished on 4 August 1914.

22. Example from Gerald D. Feldman, *The Great Disorder: Politics, Economics, and Society in the German Inflation, 1914–1924* (New York: Oxford University Press, 1993), 225.

23. This is Hans Mommsen's argument, presented with verve in *The Rise and Fall of Weimar Democracy*, trans. Elborg Forster and Larry Eugene Jones (Chapel Hill: University of North Carolina Press, 1996).

24. Margaret F. Stieg, "The 1926 German Law to Protect Youth against Trash and Dirt: Moral Protectionism in a Democracy," *Central European History* 23:1 (1990): 22–56, quotation and comment 46.

25. Luke Springman, "Poisoned Hearts, Diseased Minds, and American Pimps: The Language of Censorship in the *Schund und Schmutz* Debates," *German Quarterly* 68:4 (1995): 408–29, quotation 415.

26. Quoted in *Chronik des 20. Jahrhunderts: 1926*, ed. Brigitte Beier and Petra Gallmeister (Gütersloh: Chronik Verlag, 1995), 192.

27. Stieg, "1926 German Law," 52.

28. *Chronik des 20. Jahrhunderts: 1927*, ed. Brigitte Beier (Gütersloh: Chronik Verlag, 1986), 120.

29. Figure and payment schedule from *Chronik des 20. Jahrhunderts: 1929*, ed. Brigitte Beier (Gütersloh: Chronik Verlag, 1988), 98–99.

30. Erich Eyck, *A History of the Weimar Republic*, vol. 2: *From the Locarno Conference to Hitler's Seizure of Power*, trans. Harlan P. Hanson and Robert G. L. Waite (German original 1956; Cambridge: Harvard University Press, 1963), 37.

31. Gustav Stresemann, "Rede zum Eintritt Deutschlands in den Völkerbund," 10 September 1926, in *Politische Reden III*, 466–71.

32. Franz Hessel, *Spazieren in Berlin* (1929), in *Sämtliche Werke in fünf Bänden*, vol. 3: *Städte und Porträts*, ed. Bernhard Echte (Oldenburg: Igel, 1999), 71–72.

33. The figure of two hundred comes from Könnemann, "Völkische Komponente," 14.

34. Uwe Lohalm, *Völkischer Radikalismus: Die Geschichte des Deutschvölkischen Schutz- und Trutz-Bundes* (Hamburg: Leibniz Verlag, 1970), 89–91.

35. Eyck, *History*, 1:158.

36. At least according to Carl Severing, quoted in Eyck, *History*, 1:275.

37. Quoted in *Chronik des 20. Jahrhunderts: 1925*, ed. Antonia Meiners (Gütersloh: Chronik Verlag, 1989), 95.

38. From Stresemann's diary, quoted in ibid., 95.

39. *Chronik 1926*, 68.

40. Quoted in *Chronik 1927*, 150.

41. *Chronik des 20. Jahrhunderts: 1928*, ed. Brigitte Beier (Gütersloh: Chronik Verlag, 1987), 12.

42. Quoted in *Chronik des 20. Jahrhunderts: 1929*, ed. Brigitte Beier (Gütersloh: Chronik Verlag, 1988), 13.

43. I am following Hans Mommsen's argument in *Rise and Fall of Weimar Democracy*.

44. Kurt Tucholsky, "Der Löw' ist los-!" in *Berlin erzählt: 19 Erzählungen*, ed. Uwe Wittstock (Frankfurt am Main: Fischer Taschenbuch, 1991), 66–70, quotations 68, 69.

4. A Turbulent Economy and an Anxious Society

1. Walter Rathenau, "Rede auf der Tagung des Reichsverbandes der Deutschen Industrie," 28 September 1921, in idem, *Gesammelte Reden* (Berlin: S. Fischer Verlag, 1924), 241–64, quotation 264.

2. To extend the metaphor of Martin H. Geyer's study of the inflation to the entire Weimar period: *Verkehrte Welt. Revolution, Inflation und Moderne: München 1914–1924* (Göttingen: Vandenhoeck and Ruprecht, 1998).

3. For good analyses of the economic trends of this period, see Werner Abelshauser and Dietmar Petzina, "Zum Problem der relativen Stagnation der deutschen Wirtschaft in der zwanziger Jahren," in *Industrielles System und politische Entwicklung in der Weimarer Republik*, ed. Hans Mommsen et al. (Düsseldorf: Droste Verlag, 1974), 57–76; Werner Abelshauser and Dietmar Petzina, "Krise und Rekonstruktion: Zur Interpretation der gesamtwirtschaftlichen Entwicklung Deutschlands im 20. Jahrhundert," in *Historische Konjunkturforschung*, ed. Wilhem Heinz Schröder and Reinhard Spree (Stuttgart: Klett-Cotta, 1980); and Detlev Peukert, *The Weimar Republic: The Crisis of Classical Modernity*, trans. Richard Deveson (New York: Hill and Wang, 1989).

4. For a good summary, see Theo Balderston, *Economics and Politics in the Weimar Republic* (Cambridge: Cambridge University Press, 2002), 19–33, and for a more elaborate discussion of the intertwining of inflation and reparations, see Gerald D. Feldman, *The Great Disorder: Politics, Economics, and Society in the German Inflation, 1914–1924* (New York: Oxford University Press, 1993).

5. Balderston, *Economics and Politics*, 25–26.

6. Ibid., 20.

7. Ibid., 27–28.

8. Ibid., 36–53, summarizes very well the debate on the causes of the inflation, both at the time among contemporaries and more recently by economic historians. I largely follow his analysis, as well as that of Feldman, *Great Disorder*, on both the causes and the effects of the inflation.

9. Figure in Horst Möller, *Weimar: Die unvollendete Demokratie*, 4th ed. (Munich: DTV, 1993), 154.

10. Table printed in Feldman, *Great Disorder*, 613.

11. See Feldman's comments in ibid., 504–7.

12. Figures from ibid., 669.

13. See the table from the official Reich statistical office reproduced in ibid., 782.

14. Ibid., 783.

15. For many examples, see ibid., 582–83.

16. Testimony by the head of the Reich Health Office to the Reichstag, in *The German Inflation of 1923*, ed. Fritz K. Ringer (New York: Oxford University Press, 1969), 115.

17. Quoted in Geyer, *Verkehrte Welt*, 162.

18. Feldman, *Great Disorder*, 546.

19. Quoted in ibid., 548.

20. See Geyer, *Verkehrte Welt*, 130–66.

21. Stresemann before the Nobel Prize Committee, 29 June 1927, quoted in *Chronik des 20. Jahrhunderts: 1927*, ed. Brigitte Beier (Gütersloh: Chronik Verlag, 1986), 102.

22. See the comments of the professor and Reichstag deputy Georg Schreiber, in Ringer, *German Inflation*, 103–9.

23. Hermann Kurzke, *Thomas Mann: Life as a Work of Art*, trans. Leslie Wilson (Princeton: Princeton University Press, 2002), 326–27.

24. Geyer, *Verkehrte Welt*, 251–52.

25. The economist Moritz Julius Bonn, in Ringer, *German Inflation*, 101.

26. Feldman, *Great Disorder*, 185.

27. See, especially, Geyer, *Verkehrte Welt*, 243–77.

28. Quoted in ibid., 245.

29. Quoted in ibid., 246.

30. Quoted in Feldman, *Great Disorder*, 717.

31. Quoted in ibid., 718.

32. Ibid., 807.

33. The important work here is Gerald D. Feldman, *Iron and Steel in the German Inflation, 1916–1923* (Princeton: Princeton University Press, 1977).

34. Payment schedule from *Chronik des 20. Jahrhunderts: 1929*, ed. Brigitte Beier (Gütersloh: Chronik Verlag, 1988), 98–99.

35. Feldman, *Great Disorder*, 406.

36. Ibid., 350.

37. Ibid., 377–84.

38. Quoted in ibid., 835.

39. See the summary of conditions of the agrarian sector in ibid., 839–40.

40. Balderston, *Economics and Politics*, 80.

41. *Sozialgeschichtliches Arbeitsbuch III: Materialien zur Statistik des Deutschen Reiches 1914–1945*, ed. Dietmar Petzina, Werner Abelshauser, and Anselm Faust (Munich: C. H. Beck, 1978), 61.

42. Quoted in Feldman, *Great Disorder*, 851.

43. Ibid., 850–51.

44. Reproductions of the Kaloderma and Mont Blanc advertisements and the cover of *Die Neue Linie* in Frederic V. Grunfeld, *The Hitler File: A Social History of Germany and the Nazis, 1918–1945* (New York: Random House, 1974), 43–45.

45. *Die Gartenlaube: Illustriertes Familienblatt* 29 (21 July 1927): 4 of frontmatter.

46. *Gartenlaube* 30 (28 July 1927): 4 of frontmatter.

47. *Gartenlaube* 32 (11 August 1927): n.p.

48. Hans Kropff, "Women as Shoppers," in *The Weimar Republic Sourcebook*, ed. Anton Kaes, Martin Jay, and Edward Dimendberg (Berkeley and Los Angeles: University of California Press, 1994), 660–62, quotation 660.

49. Mary Nolan, *Visions of Modernity: American Business and the Modernization of Germany* (New York: Oxford University Press, 1994), 133.

50. See, especially, ibid.

51. Quoted in ibid., 30.

52. Quoted in ibid., 37, 94.

53. For many examples, see ibid., 83–107.

54. Quoted in *Chronik des 20. Jahrhunderts: 1928*, ed. Brigitte Beier (Gütersloh: Chronik Verlag, 1987), 65.

55. Figures in Eric D. Weitz, *Creating German Communism, 1890–1990: From Popular Protests to Socialist State* (Princeton: Princeton University Press, 1997), 119–20.

56. Wolfram Fischer, "Bergbau, Industrie und Handwerk 1914–1970," in *Handbuch der deutschen Wirtschafts- und Sozialgeschichte*, vol. 2, ed. Hermann Aubin and Wolfgang Zorn (Stuttgart: Ernst Klett, 1976), 805.

57. *"Mein Arbeitstag—mein Wochenende": Arbeiterinnen berichten von ihrem Alltag 1928*, reprint, ed. Alf Lüdtke (1930; Hamburg: Ergebnisse Verlag, 1991).

58. Ibid., 132, 133.

59. Ibid., 46 (italics in the original).

60. Ibid., 124–25 (italics in the original).

61. Ibid., 130–31.

62. Ibid., 135 (italics in the original).

63. Auszug aus dem Soko [Sozial Kommission], Protokoll No. 65, 11 September 1929, Betriebsarchiv der Leuna-Werke 1340.

64. Quoted in Weitz, *Creating German Communism*, 120.

65. Quoted in ibid., 122 (italics in the original).

66. And through émigrés, would strongly influence American sociology of the 1950s. From Emil Lederer and Hans Speier there is a direct link to C. Wright Mills, David Riesman, and others who analyzed the American middle class and the dangers of "anonymous" society and totalitarianism.

67. Hans Speier, *German White-Collar Workers and the Rise of Hitler*, trans. idem (German original written in 1932, first published in 1977; New Haven: Yale University Press, 1986), 2, 33.

68. Figures calculated from Statistisches Reichsamt, *Statistisches Jahrbuch für das Deutsche Reich* 46 (1927) (Berlin: Reimar Hobbing, 1927), 20–21.

69. Ibid.

70. Siegfried Kracauer, *The Salaried Masses: Duty and Distraction in Weimar Germany*, trans. Quintin Hoare (German original 1930; London: Verso, 1998).

71. Ibid., 33–44.

72. Statistics in Speier, *German White-Collar Workers*, 53.

73. Kracauer, *Salaried Masses*, 76–79, quotation 79.

74. Ibid., 79.

75. Quoted in ibid., 89.

76. Ibid., 83.

77. *Sozialgeschichtliches Arbeitsbuch III*, 55.

78. Feldman, *Great Disorder*, 189–93.

79. Elizabeth Bright Jones, "Landwirtschaftliche Arbeit und weibliche Körper in Deutschland, 1918–1933," in *Ort. Arbeit. Körper: Ethnografie Europäischer Modernen*, ed. Beate Binder et al. (Münster: Waxmann, 2005), 469–76.

80. On these issues, see ibid., as well as other works by Elizabeth Bright Jones: "A New Stage of Life? Young Farm Women's Changing Expectations and Aspirations about Work in Weimar Saxony," *German History* 19:4 (2001): 549–70, and "Pre- and Postwar Generations of Rural Female Youth and the Future of the German Nation, 1871–1933," *Continuity and Change* 19:3 (2004): 347–65.

81. Balderston, *Economics and Politics*, 79–81.

82. See, for example, Hans Ungelehrt, *Das Ende der Arbeitslosigkeit* (Renningen: Isis-Verlag, 1932), one of probably thousands of brochures published by self-styled reformers. Typically, the author imagined a closed economic system in which job-creation schemes would be self-financing. The revival of production would enhance tax revenues and thereby resolve the budget crisis.

83. Figures in Feldman, *Great Disorder*, 849.

84. I am referring to the "Borchardt debate" prompted by the prominent economic historian Knut Borchardt, who argues that the Weimar economy was overburdened by high wages and social welfare costs. For entries into the debate, see Knut Borchardt, "A Decade of Debate about Brüning's Economic Policies," in *Economic Crisis and Political Collapse: The Weimar Republic, 1924–1933*, ed. J. Freiherr von Kruedener (New York: Berg, 1990), 99–151, and Balderston, *Economics and Politics*, 68–71, 93–96. For one of many contemporary examples that place the blame for the crisis squarely on the backs of supposedly overpaid and unproductive workers and civil servants, Peter Schlösser, *Die Erwerbslosenfrage als nationales Problem* (Breslau: Wilh. Gottl. Korn Verlag, 1932).

85. Marie Jahoda, Paul F. Lazarsfeld, and Hans Zeisel, *Marienthal: The Sociography of an Unemployed Community* (German original 1933; Chicago: Aldine, 1971).

86. Ibid., 22, 26.

87. Ibid., 66.

88. Ibid., 76–77.

89. Quoted in Kracauer, *Salaried Masses*, 57.

90. Speier, *German White-Collar Workers*, 41–42.

5. Building a New Germany

1. Hermann Finsterlin, 3 February 1920, in *The Crystal Chain Letters: Architectural Fantasies by Bruno Taut and His Circle*, ed. and trans. Iain Boyd Whyte (Cambridge: MIT Press, 1985), 53.

2. See the lovely bilingual German-English edition, the first reissue since the original, *Bruno Taut: Alpine Architektur*, ed. Matthias Schirren (Munich: Prestel, 2004), with extensive commentary by the editor.

3. Bruno Taut, 24 November 1919, in *Crystal Chain Letters*, 21.

4. Quoted in Taut, 23 December 1919, in ibid., 23–25.

5. Wenzel Hablik, January 1920, in ibid., 37–38.

6. Hans Scharoun (n.d.), in ibid., 42–46, quotation 45.

7. Taut, 5 October 1920, in ibid., 154–57, quotation 155.

8. Taut, quoted in Franziska Bollerey and Kristiana Hartmann, "Bruno Taut: Vom phantastischen Ästheten zum ästhetischen Sozial(ideal)isten," in Barbara Volkmann, *Bruno Taut 1880–1938: Ausstellung der Akademie der Künste vom 29. Juni bis 3. August 1980* (Berlin: Brüder Hartmann, 1980), 15–85, quotation 60.

9. Bruno Taut, "The Earth Is a Good Dwelling," in *The Weimar Republic Sourcebook* (hereafter *WRS*), ed. Anton Kaes, Martin Jay, and Edward Dimendberg (Berkeley and Los Angeles: University of California Press, 1994), 456–59, and idem, "A Program for Architecture," in *WRS*, 432–34.

10. Adelheid von Saldern, *Häuserleben: Zur Geschichte städtischen Arbeiterwohnens vom Kaiserreich bis heute* (Bonn: J.H.W. Dietz Nachfolger, 1995), 121, and Barbara Miller Lane, *Architecture and Politics in Germany, 1918–1945* (1968; Cambridge: Harvard University Press, 1985), 90–103, statistic 102. Lane states that 14,000 new units in Berlin were designed by "radical architects," meaning modernists like Taut (103).

11. See Saldern, *Häuserleben*, 123–38.

12. On the Onkel Tom Siedlung, see Michael Braum, ed., *Berliner Wohnquartiere: Ein Führer durch 70 Siedlungen*, 3rd ed. (Berlin: Dietrich Reimer, 2003), 130–33; Martin Wörner, Doris Mollenschott, and Karl-Heinz Hüter, *Architekturführer Berlin*, 5th ed. (Berlin: Dietrich Reimer,

1997), 430–33; Helge Pitz and Winfried Brenne, eds., *Die Bauwerke und Kunstdenkmäler von Berlin: Bezirk Zehlendorf. Siedlung Onkel Tom* (Berlin: Gebr. Mann, 1980); and Bollery and Hartmann, "Bruno Taut," 70–81.

13. Bruno Taut, "Colour" (1931), in Pitz and Brenne, *Bauwerke und Kunstdenkmäler*, 151–56.

14. Ibid.

15. Ibid., 155.

16. In fact, his earlier efforts in Magdeburg, where he had many buildings painted, were widely derided. See Bollerey and Hartmann, "Bruno Taut," 65–68.

17. Braum, *Berliner Wohnquartiere*, 122–25; Wörner, Mollenschott, and Hüter, *Architekturführer Berlin*, 386–87; and Bollery and Hartmann, "Bruno Taut," 70–81.

18. Bruno Taut, "The New Dwelling: The Woman as Creator," in *WRS*, 461–62.

19. Ibid.; Grete Lihotzky, "Rationalization in the Household," in *WRS*, 462–65; and, generally, Saldern, *Häuserleben*, 178–88.

20. Paolo Portoghesi, "Presentation," in Pitz and Brenne, *Bauwerke und Kunstdenkmäler*, 15–25, quotation 19.

21. First lecture in Philippson salon, in Ita Heinze-Greenberg and Regina Stephan, eds., *Erich Mendelsohn: Gedankenwelten* (Ostfildern-Ruit: Hatje Cantz, 2000), 14–20, here 14.

22. Eighth lecture in Philippson salon, 1919, in ibid., 38–44, here 44.

23. Ita Heinze-Greenberg and Regina Stephan, eds., *Luise and Erich Mendelsohn: Eine Partnerschaft für die Kunst* (Ostfildern-Ruit: Hatje Cantz Verlag, 2004), 109.

24. Quoted in Heinze-Greenberg and Stephan, *Erich Mendelsohn: Gedankenwelten*, 7.

25. Erich Mendelsohn, "Die internationale Übereinstimmung des neuen Baugedankens oder Dynamik und Funktion" (1923), in ibid., 48–53, here 49–50.

26. Erich Mendelsohn, "Harmonische und kontrapunktische Führung in der Architektur" (1925), in ibid., 54.

27. Erich Mendelsohn, "My Own Contribution to the Development of Contemporary Architecture" (lecture at UCLA, 17 March 1948), in *Eric Mendelsohn: Letters of an Architect*, ed. Oskar Beyer, trans. Geoffrey Strachan (London: Abelard Schuman, 1967), 161–74, quotation 165.

28. Mendelsohn, "Internationale Übereinstimmung," 48–49.

29. Erich Mendelsohn, "Das neuzeitliche Geschäftshaus" (1929), in Heinze-Greenberg and Stephan, *Erich Mendelsohn: Gedankenwelten*, 96–103, here 103.

30. Mendelsohn, "Internationale Übereinstimmung," 48–49.

31. Ibid., 50–51.

32. A point rightly emphasized by Norbert Huse, "Facetten eines Baudenkmals," in *Mendelsohn: Der Einsteinturm. Die Geschichte einer Instandsetzung*, ed. idem (Stuttgart: Karl Krämer, 2000), 14–27, here 21–23.

33. Or so Mendelsohn claimed, in "My Own Contribution to the Development of Contemporary Architecture," 166.

34. Erich Mendelsohn, "The International Consensus on the New Architectural Concept, or Dynamics and Function" (1923), in *Erich Mendelsohn: Complete Works of the Architect: Sketches, Designs, Buildings*, trans. Antje Fritsch (German original 1930; Princeton: Princeton Architectural Press, 1992), 22–34, here 33; also, in slightly altered fashion, in Mendelsohn, "My Own Contribution to the Development of Contemporary Architecture," 166 and 172.

35. Huse, "Facetten eines Baudenkmals," 23–24, and Mendelsohn, "My Own Contribution to the Development of Contemporary Architecture," 166–67.

36. Paul Westheim, quoted in Huse, "Facetten eines Baudenkmals," 24–25.

37. See, especially, Huse, *Mendelsohn*. By today's standards, Mendelsohn did not use enough steel for the material to qualify as reinforced concrete. See Gerhard Pichler, "Die Baukonstruktion, oder: Warum bleib der Einsteinturm ein Pflegefall?" in Huse, *Mendelsohn*, 91–101, here 96.

38. For an analysis of the design and construction, see Tilo Richter, *Erich Mendelsohns Kaufhaus Schocken: Jüdische Kulturgeschichte in Chemnitz*, ed. Evangelischer Forum Chemnitz (Leipzig: Passage-Verlag, 1998), 67–93, including Mendelsohn's own comments, 80–81, and Mendelsohn, "My Own Contribution to the Development of Contemporary Architecture," 168.

39. See Mendelsohn, "Neuzeitliches Geschäftshaus."

40. Mendelsohn, "International Consensus," 28.

41. See Erich Mendelsohn to Luise Mendelsohn, 5 November 1924, in Beyer, *Eric Mendelsohn: Letters of an Architect*, 71–74, and Mendelsohn's homage, "Frank Lloyd Wright"(1926), in Heinze-Greenberg and Stephan, *Erich Mendelsohn: Gedankenwelten*, 83–86.

42. Quoted in Lane, *Architecture and Politics*, 45.

43. Walter Gropius, *The New Architecture and the Bauhaus* (London: Faber and Faber, 1935), 52.

44. Walter Gropius, "Program of the Staatliches Bauhaus in Weimar," in *WRS*, 435–38, quotation 436.

45. Ibid., 435.

46. Walter Gropius, "The Theory and Organization of the Bauhaus" (1923), in *Bauhaus 1919–1928*, ed. Herbert Bayer, Walter Gropius, and Ise Gropius, rev. ed. (1938; New York: Museum of Modern Art, 1975), 20–29, quotation 27.

47. Gropius, *New Architecture and the Bauhaus*, 26–29. Here Gropius was referring specifically to houses, but the point holds for other types of modern buildings.

48. Ibid., 43–44.

49. Gropius, "Theory and Organization of the Bauhaus," 20.

50. Quoted in Lane, *Architecture and Politics*, 67.

51. Gropius, *New Architecture and the Bauhaus*, 85.

52. Gropius, "Theory and Organization of the Bauhaus," 20.

53. Gropius lauded the application of factory methods to the building site in *New Architecture and the Bauhaus*, 34–43.

54. Quoted in Dennis Sharp, *Bauhaus, Dessau: Walter Gropius* (London: Phaidon, 1993), 25–26.

55. Mendelsohn, "Internationale Übereinstimmung," 51.

56. Ibid., 52.

57. Mendelsohn, "My Own Contribution to the Development of Contemporary Architecture,"167.

58. Edgar Wedepohl, "The Weissenhof Settlement," in *WRS*, 466–68.

59. Marie-Elisabeth Lüders, "A Construction, Not a Dwelling," in *WRS*, 468–69.

60. For an extensive discussion, see Lane, *Architecture and Politics*, 69–86.

61. See ibid., 125–47, quotation 136–37.

62. Quoted in ibid., 138.

63. Quoted in ibid., 139.

64. Paul Schultze-Naumburg, in Walter Gropius and Paul Schultze-Naumburg, "Who Is Right? Traditional Architecture or Building in New Forms," in *WRS*, 439–45, quotation 445.

65. Braum, *Berliner Wohnquartiere*, 134–37, and Wörner, Mollenschott, and Hüter, *Architekturführer Berlin*, 191.

66. Saldern, *Häuserleben*, 184–85, based on numerous oral history studies, emphasizes the positive recollections expressed by those who had lived (and, sometimes, continued to live) in the new housing.

67. Brochure, "Die Europäische Mittelmeerakademie" (1933), in Heinze-Greenberg and Stephan, *Erich Mendelsohn: Gedankenwelten*, 126–33.

68. See the excerpts from Luise Mendelsohn's unpublished autobiography, "My Life in a Changing World," in Heinze-Greenberg and Stephan, *Luise and Erich Mendelsohn: Eine Partnerschaft*, 95–98, 110–13.

1. On Ullstein's printing presses, see Peter Fritzsche, *Reading Berlin 1900* (Cambridge: Harvard University Press, 1996), 211–12.

2. The image is one of Sander's most famous.

3. On the history of roll film and the introduction of the Leica, I have relied on S. F. Spira, with Eaton S. Lothrop, Jr., and Jonathan B. Spira, *The History of Photography as Seen through the Spira Collection* (New York: Aperture, 2001), 96–109, 146–65.

4. The essay by Walter Benjamin, "The Work of Art in the Age of Mechanical Reproduction" (1936), in idem, *Illuminations*, ed. Hannah Arendt, trans. Harry Zohn (New York: Schocken, 1968), is the classic engagement with the revolutionary and problematic character of the reproducibility of art images in the modern world.

5. Figure from Maud Lavin, *Cut with the Kitchen Knife: The Weimar Photomontages of Hannah Höch* (New Haven: Yale University Press, 1993), 51, 55.

6. See Vicki Baum, *Es war alles ganz anders: Erinnerungen* (Berlin: Ullstein, 1962).

7. These examples from the *BIZ* 36:1–51 (2 January–18 December 1927) and the *AIZ* (1928–32).

8. Lavin, *Cut with the Kitchen Knife*, 56.

9. See Krisztina Passuth, *Moholy-Nagy*, trans. Éva Grusz et al. (London: Thames and Hudson, 1985), on the influence of Dada, 19–21. Later he would also be influenced by the Soviet constructivists, like El Lissitzky.

10. László Moholy-Nagy, *Painting, Photography, Film*, trans. Janet Seligman (German original 1925; Cambridge: MIT Press, 1967), 17.

11. Andreas Haus, *Moholy-Nagy: Photographs and Photograms*, trans. Frederic Samson (New York: Pantheon, 1980), 64.

12. Apparently there are at least four other similar images that Moholy-Nagy shot. See ibid., 66.

13. László Moholy-Nagy, "Photographie ist Lichtgestaltung," *Bauhaus* II/I (1928), in Passuth, *Moholy-Nagy*, 302–5. Here the translation is "Photography is Creation with Light," but others use, more accurately, "manipulation." See, for example, the same text in slightly different translation in Haus, *Moholy-Nagy*, 47–50.

14. Moholy-Nagy, *Painting, Photography, Film*, 34.

15. Ibid., 45. He could also be witheringly critical of those who sought to mimic painting in their photography. See his comment on an Alfred Stieglitz photo, "New York," from 1911: "The triumph of Impressionism or photography misunderstood. The photographer has become a painter instead of using his camera *photographically*." Ibid., 49.

16. Edward Steichen, *The Family of Man* (1955; New York: Museum of Modern Art, 1997).

17. August Sander, *Antlitz der Zeit: Sechzig Aufnahmen deutscher Menschen des 20. Jahrhunderts* (1929; Munich: Schirmer/Mosel, 2003).

18. Quoted in Robert Kramer, "Historical Commentary," in *August Sander: Photographs of an Epoch* (New York: Aperture, 1980), 24, 27.

19. See Sibyl Moholy-Nagy, "Moholy-Nagy: The Chicago Years" (lecture to the Museum of Contemporary Art, Chicago, May 1969), in *Moholy-Nagy: An Anthology*, ed. Richard Kostelanetz (New York: Da Capo, 1970), 22–26.

20. *Die Chronik Bibliothek des 20. Jahrhunderts: 1926*, ed. Brigitte Beier and Petra Gallmeister (Gütersloh: Chronik Verag, 1995), 24.

21. Erich Mendelsohn, "My Own Contribution to the Development of Contemporary Architecture" (lecture at UCLA, 17 March 1948), in *Eric Mendelsohn: Letters of an Architect*, ed. Oskar Beyer, trans. Geoffrey Strachan (London: Abelard Schuman, 1967), 168. The exterior of the building can still be appreciated. It is now the Schaubühne, an important theater on the Kurfürstendamm in Berlin. But the interior did not survive World War II bombings.

22. See Jost Hermand and Frank Trommler, *Die Kultur der Weimarer Republik* (Munich: Nymphenberger, 1978), 261–98.

23. Siegfried Kracauer, *From Caligari to Hitler: A Psychological History of the German Film* (Princeton: Princeton University Press, 1947).

24. On the shift, see the classic work of Peter Gay, *Weimar Culture: The Outsider as Insider* (New York: Harper and Row, 1968).

25. Both quotations in Hermand and Trommler, *Kultur der Weimarer Republik*, 276.

26. Ibid., 278.

27. Quoted in Martin H. Geyer, *Verkehrte Welt. Revolution, Inflation und Moderne: München 1914–1924* (Göttingen: Vandenhoeck and Ruprecht, 1998), 75.

28. Figures in Heinrich August Winkler, *Der Schein der Normalität: Arbeiter und Arbeiterbewegung in der Weimarer Republik 1924 bis 1930* (Berlin: J.H.W. Dietz Nachf., 1988), 138–39.

29. Franz Hessel, *Spazieren in Berlin* (1929), in *Sämtliche Werke in fünf Bänden*, vol. 3: *Städte und Porträts*, ed. Bernhard Echte (Oldenburg: Igel, 1999), 131.

30. *"Mein Arbeitstag—mein Wochenende": Arbeiterinnen berichten von ihrem Alltag 1928*, reprint, ed. Alf Lüdtke (1930; Hamburg: Ergebnisse Verlag, 1991), 21.

31. Ernst Weiß, "Audio Technologie in Berlin bis 1943: Mikrophon," in *50 Jahre Stereo-Magnetbandtechnik: Die Entwicklung der Audio Technologie in*

Berlin und den USA von den Anfängen bis 1943, ed. Audio Engineering Society (Darmstadt: Berlebach, 1993), 37–54, here 44.

32. Klaus Harder, "Audio Technologie in Berlin bis 1943: Verstärker," in ibid., 73–102, here 90.

33. Ibid., 91.

34. Inge Marßolek and Adelheid von Saldern, eds., *Zuhören und Gehörtwerden*, vol. 1: *Radio im Nationalsozialismus. Zwischen Lenkung und Ablenkung* (Tübingen: Edition Diskord, 1998), 13.

35. Carsten Lenk, *Die Erscheinung des Rundfunks: Einführung und Nutzung eines neuen Mediums 1923–1932* (Opladen: Westdeutscher Verlag, 1997), 14.

36. Quoted in ibid., 65.

37. Johannes R. Becher, "Radio—Wunder der Alltäglichkeit!" (1933), in *Radio-Kultur in der Weimarer Republik: Eine Dokumentation*, ed. Irmela Schneider (Tübingen: Gunter Narr, 1984), 58–59.

38. Lenk, *Erscheinung des Rundfunks*, 108–14.

39. Quoted in ibid., 79.

40. Quoted in ibid., 76.

41. Quoted in ibid., 13.

42. Quoted in ibid., 118.

43. Quoted in Christopher Hailey, "Rethinking Sound: Music and Radio in Weimar Germany," in *Music and Performance during the Weimar Republic*, ed. Bryan Gilliam (Cambridge: Cambridge University Press, 1994), 13–36, quotation 14.

44. Kate Lacey, *Feminine Frequencies: Gender, German Radio, and the Public Sphere, 1923–1945* (Ann Arbor: University of Michigan Press, 1996), 28.

45. Winfried B. Lerg, *Rundfunkpolitik in der Weimarer Republik* (Munich: DTV, 1980), 524.

46. Quoted in Lacey, *Feminine Frequencies*, 51.

47. Quoted in ibid., 41–42.

48. Quoted in ibid., 43.

49. Lerg, *Rundfunkpolitik*, 389–94.

50. See Lacey, *Feminine Frequencies*, 57–95.

51. Joachim-Felix Leonhard, ed., *Programmgeschichte des Hörfunks in der Weimarer Republik*, vol. 1 (Munich: DTV, 1997), 454–66.

52. See, for example, Theodor Csokor, "Mein Hörspiel 'Ballade von der Stadt'" (1928), in Schneider, *Radio-Kultur*, 156–57.

53. Leopold Jessner, "Rundfunk und Theater" (1929), in Schneider, *Radio-Kultur*, 163–70.

54. Quoted in Hailey, "Rethinking Sound," 13, 14.

55. See ibid., especially 32–36.

56. Robert Hill, "'Overcoming Romanticism': On the Modernization of Twentieth-Century Performance Practice," in Gilliam, *Music and Performance*, 37–58.

57. Arno Schirokauer, "Kunst-Politik im Rundfunk" (1929), in Schneider, *Radio-Kultur*, 86–91, quotation 86.

58. Franz Rosenzweig, "The Concert Hall on the Phonograph Record" (1928–29), in *Cultural Writings of Franz Rosenzweig*, ed. and trans. Barbara E. Galli (Syracuse, NY: Syracuse University Press, 2000), 116–52, here 116–17.

59. And it was the same point that Walter Benjamin would make, with greater philosophical depth, and would turn into one of the signal features of modernity in his 1936 essay "The Work of Art in the Age of Mechanical Reproduction."

60. Joseph Roth, "Radiophon," 22 March 1922, in idem, *Berliner Saisonbericht: Unbekannte Reportagen und journalistiche Arbeiten 1920–39*, ed. Klaus Westermann (Cologne: Kiepenheuer and Witsch, 1984), 185–87.

61. Joseph Roth, "Alte und neue Photographien," 14 September 1929, in *Berliner Saisonbericht*, 323–25.

7. Culture and Mass Society

1. Ernst Bloch to Karola Piotrkowska, 9 April 1931, in Ernst Bloch, *Das Abenteuer der Treue: Briefe an Karola 1928–1949*, ed. Anna Czajka (Frankfurt am Main: Suhrkamp, 2005), 88–94, here 89–91.

2. Hans Jonas, *Erinnerungen*, ed. Christian Wiese (Frankfurt am Main: Insel, 2003), 82–83.

3. See also Peter Gay's classic work, *Weimar Culture: The Outsider as Insider* (New York: Harper and Row, 1968).

4. Sigmund Freud, *Civilization and Its Discontents*, trans. and ed. James Strachey (German original 1930; New York: W. W. Norton, 1961).

5. Hermann Kurzke, *Thomas Mann: Life as a Work of Art*, trans. Leslie Wilson (Princeton: Princeton University Press, 2002), 16, 55–56, and passim.

6. Ibid., 217–20 and passim.

7. Thomas Mann, "Von Deutscher Republik," 15 October 1922, in *Politische Reden III: 1914–1945*, ed. Peter Wende (Frankfurt am Main: Deutsche Klassiker, 1994), 342–83.

8. See also the way Wolf Lepenies plays out the theme of Novalis and

Whitman in his important book *The Seduction of Culture in German History* (Princeton: Princeton University Press, 2006).

9. See Fritz Ringer, *Decline of the German Mandarins: The German Academic Community, 1890–1933* (Cambridge: Harvard University Press, 1969).

10. Jonas, *Erinnerungen*, 101.

11. Thomas Mann, *The Magic Mountain*, trans. John E. Woods (New York: Knopf, 1995), 390. The original German is somewhat different: "Der Glaube ist das Organ der Erkenntnis und der Intellekt sekundär" (Thomas Mann, *Der Zauberberg* (Frankfurt am Main: Fischer Taschenbuch Verlag, 545). "Organ" has a more forceful and more intimate connotation than "vehicle."

12. *Magic Mountain*, 322. The German original is, again, both more forceful and more poetic:

> Das "Du" unter Fremden, das heißt unter Personen, die einander von Rechtes wegen "Sie" nennen, ist eine widerwärtige Wildheit, ein Spiel unter dem Urstande, ein liederliches Spiel, das ich verabscheue, weil es sich im Grunde gegen Zivilisation und entwickelte Menschlichkeit richtet—sich frech und schamlos dagegen richtet. Ich habe Sie auch nicht "Du" genannt, bilden Sie sich das nicht ein! Ich zitierte eine Stelle aus dem Meisterwerk Ihrer Nationalliteratur. Ich sprach also poetischerweise. (Mann, *Zauberberg*, 452–53)

Note Settembrini's use of the noun "Menschlichkeit" and the phrase, "das ich verabscheue," both of which are lost in the translation.

13. Mann, *Magic Mountain*, 337–38.

14. Ibid., 487 (italics in the translation). And in German: "Der Mensch soll um der Güte und Liebe willen dem Tode keine Herrschaft einräumen über seine Gedanken" (*Zauberberg*, 679).

15. Quoted in *Die Chronik Bibliothek des 20. Jahrhunderts: 1928*, ed. Brigitte Beier (Gütersloh: Chronik Verlag, 1987), 142.

16. I am drawing on Jürgen Schebera, *Kurt Weill: An Illustrated Life*, trans. Caroline Murphy (New Haven: Yale University Press, 1995), 89–102.

17. Quoted in ibid., 101–2.

18. Ibid., 111–12.

19. Ibid., 114. The author is referring to the "Moritat von Mackie Messer," but the point can be generalized.

20. Lyrics from *The Threepenny Opera*, RIAS Berlin Sinfonietta, London cd 430 075-2.

21. Lyrics from *Ute Lemper Sings Kurt Weil*, London cd NL 425 204-2. This particular song was incorporated into the production only after the premiere.

22. Quotations from Schebera, *Kurt Weill*, 117–18.

23. Statistics in ibid., 120.

24. John Willett, *The Theatre of Bertolt Brecht: A Study from Eight Aspects*, 2nd ed. (London: Methuen, 1959), 78.

25. See ibid., 168–87.

26. Quoted in ibid., 170.

27. Quoted in Schebera, *Kurt Weill*, 111–12.

28. Siegfried Kracauer, "The Mass Ornament," in idem, *The Mass Ornament: Weimar Essays*, ed. and trans. Thomas Y. Levin (Cambridge: Harvard University Press, 1995), 75–86, quotation 75–76.

29. Ibid., 76.

30. Siegfried Kracauer, "Girls and Crisis," in *The Weimar Republic Sourcebook*, ed. Anton Kaes, Martin Jay, and Edward Dimendberg (Berkeley and Los Angeles: University of California Press, 1994), 565–66.

31. Ibid.

32. Kracauer, "Mass Ornament," 84.

33. Ibid., 75.

34. See Ringer, *Decline of the German Mandarins*.

35. Siegfried Kracauer, "The Little Shopgirls Go to the Movies," in idem, *Mass Ornament*, 291–304.

36. Ibid., 295.

37. Ibid., 300.

38. Martin Heidegger, *Being and Time*, trans. John Macquarrie and Edward Robinson (German original 1927; New York: Harper and Row, 1962), 22.

39. Exod. 3:14. On this point, see George Steiner, *Martin Heidegger* (1978; Chicago: University of Chicago Press, 1987), 61–63.

40. Richard Wolin stresses and critiques the primordial elements in Heidegger's thinking. See *Heidegger's Children: Hannah Arendt, Karl Löwith, Hans Jonas, and Herbert Marcuse* (Princeton: Princeton University Press, 2001).

41. See also the commentary by Dorothea Frede, "The Question of Being: Heidegger's Project," in *The Cambridge Companion to Heidegger*, ed. Charles Guignon (Cambridge: Cambridge University Press, 1993), 42–69, here 54–56, 66.

42. Heidegger, *Being and Time*, 98–100.

43. Ibid., 105.

44. Ibid., 106.

45. Ibid., 27. See also Steiner, *Martin Heidegger*, 70–71.

46. Heidegger, *Being and Time*, 33.

47. Ibid., 150.

48. Ibid., 154.

49. Ibid., 156.

50. Ibid., 164. In this quotation and others, I have eliminated the original German terms in brackets that the translators provide.

51. Ibid., 164–65.

52. Steiner, *Martin Heidegger*, 93–95.

53. Ibid., 105–7.

54. Ibid., 24–25.

55. Heidegger to Elisabeth Blochmann, 15 June 1918, quoted in Wolin, *Heidegger's Children*, 211.

56. It is precisely this point that has led many critics to link his philosophy to his political support of National Socialism. See Steiner, *Martin Heidegger*, xxxiii–xxxiv, and the quotation from Ernst Cassirer and the commentary provided by Wolin, in *Heidegger's Children*, 176–77.

57. See Steiner, *Martin Heidegger*. But for harsher critiques that exposed more completely Heideigger's National Socialist politics, see the two major works that set off the "Heidegger controversy" in the 1980s: Hugo Ott, *Martin Heidegger: Unterwegs zu seiner Biographie* (Frankfurt am Main: Campus Verlag, 1988), and Victor Farias, *Heidegger and National Socialism*, trans. Paul Burrell and Dominic Di Bernardi (Philadelphia: Temple University Press, 1989). More recently, see Wolin, *Heidegger's Children*, and Charles Bambach, *Heidegger's Roots: Nietzsche, National Socialism, and the Greeks* (Ithaca: Cornell University Press, 2003), both of whom, though to different degrees, argue for a direct link between Heidegger's philosophy and his commitment to National Socialism. For a good collection of Heidegger's own writings and commentary on the controversy, see *Martin Heidegger and National Socialism: Questions and Answers*, ed. Günther Neske and Emil Kettering, trans. Lisa Harries and Joachim Neugroschel (New York: Paragon House, 1990).

58. One of the very few examples is in his parenthetical critique of *Lebensphilosophie*: "(this expression says about as much as 'the botany of plants')." *Being and Time*, 72.

59. Maud Lavin, *Cut with the Kitchen Knife: The Weimar Photomontages of Hannah Höch* (New Haven: Yale University Press, 1993), 74–75, and Ernst Bloch, *The Utopian Function of Art and Literature*, trans. Jack Zipes and Frank Mecklenburg (Cambridge: MIT Press, 1988).

60. Tristan Tzara, "Dada Manifesto," 23 March 1918, <http://www.391.org/manifestos/tristantzara_dadamanifesto.htm> [27 June 2005].

61. Her lover and fellow Dadaist, Gustav Hausmann, advocated women's emancipation, including their sexual emancipation—and also sometimes hit Höch. See Lavin, *Cut with the Kitchen Knife*, 25–27.

62. Even in another early work, *Das schöne Mädchen* (1919–20), the female bather seems encased by the products of technology. Her head is

replaced by a lightbulb, and the prominent timepiece symbolizes the rationalized factory world that regulates and dominates everyone within sight. Unlike the active and vital women depicted in some of her other early works, the female bather in *Das schöne Mädchen* just sits in place and absorbs a punch from a cutout of the American boxers Jim Jeffries and Jack Johnson. See Maria Makela, "The Misogynist Machine: Images of Technology in the Work of Hannah Höch," in *Women in the Metropolis: Gender and Modernity in Weimar Culture*, ed. Katharina von Ankum (Berkeley and Los Angeles: University of California Press, 1997), 106–27, here 114–16.

63. This is perhaps especially true of the images in her unpublished scrapbook, though the scrapbook also contains many more standard images of film stars and athletes. See Lavin, *Cut with the Kitchen Knife*, 71–121.

64. See, for example, Lavin's discussion in ibid., 151–55.

65. Siegfried Kracauer, *From Caligari to Hitler: A Psychological History of the German Film* (Princeton: Princeton University Press, 1947).

8. Bodies and Sex

1. Theodore H. van de Velde, *Die vollkommene Ehe* (Leipzig: B. Konegen, 1926). The subsequent volumes were *Die Abneigung in der Ehe* [Sexual Tension in Marriage] (Leipzig: B. Konegen, 1928) and *Die Fruchtbarkeit in der Ehe und ihre wunschgemässe Beeinflussung* [Fertility and Sterility in Marriage: Their Voluntary Promotion and Limitation] (Leipzig: B. Konegen, 1929).

2. Th. H. van de Velde, *Ideal Marriage: Its Physiology and Technique*, rev. ed., trans. Stella Browne (German original 1926; New York: Random House, 1930).

3. "Van de Veldes Rezept: 'Erotisierung der Ehe,'" *Vossische Zeitung* 47 (24 February 1928): 5–6. See also "Der vollkommene Ehemann: Dr. Th. Van de Velde am Votragspult," *Berliner Tageblatt* 92 (23 February 1928, evening edition): 4. He published his lecture in extended form: Th. H. van de Velde, *Die Erotik in der Ehe: Ihre ausschlaggebende Bedeutung* (Stuttgart: Benno Konegen, 1928). This book affirmed the importance of eroticism but lacked the explicit technical instructions about sex that are contained in *Die vollkommene Ehe*.

4. *Vossische Zeitung* 47 (24 February 1928): 5.

5. Ibid., 6.

6. The key work here is Atina Grossmann, *Reforming Sex: The German Movement for Birth Control and Abortion Reform, 1920–1950* (New York: Oxford University Press, 1995).

7. Velde, *Ideal Marriage*, 1, 2.

8. Ibid., 7–8.

9. Ibid., 7–8, 9.

10. Ibid., 115; also, Th. H. van de Velde, *Sexual Tensions in Marriage: Their Origin, Prevention and Treatment*, trans. Hamilton Marr (German original 1928; New York: Random House, 1931), 78–79.

11. Velde, *Ideal Marriage*, 159.

12. Velde, *Sexual Tensions in Marriage*, 99.

13. Ibid., 100.

14. Ibid., 181.

15. Ibid., 192.

16. Ibid., 151–58, 26–39.

17. Ibid., 250.

18. Ibid., 148.

19. Ibid., 190.

20. See Wilhelm Reich, "The Imposition of Sexual Morality" (1932), in Wilhelm Reich, *Sex-Pol: Essays 1929–1934*, ed. Lee Baxandall, trans. Anna Bostock et al. (New York: Random House, 1966), 123–24. Reich's effort to combine Marxism and Freudianism and his blatant advocacy of sex won him very few friends and got him into trouble with all sorts of people, including the moral police of the Weimar Republic, his professional psychiatric colleagues, and his communist comrades, who threw him out of the party in 1932.

21. Max Hodam, *Sex Life in Europe: A Biological and Sociological Survey*, trans. J. Gibbs (German original 1929; New York: Gargoyle Press, 1932), 17–18.

22. See, for example, Ludwig Levy-Lens, "Vorwort," in *Sexual-Katastrophen: Bilder aus dem modernen Geschlechts- und Eheleben*, ed. idem (Leipzig: A. H. Payne, 1926), ix–x.

23. Grossmann, *Reforming Sex*, 68–69.

24. Reich, "Imposition of Sexual Morality," 94, 95.

25. Ibid., 93.

26. Ibid., 111.

27. Magnus Hirschfeld, *Sexualpathologie: Ein Lehrbuch für Ärtzte und Studierende*, 3 vols. (Bonn: A. Marcus and E. Webers Verlag, 1920–21).

28. Ibid, 3:327.

29. Grossmann, *Reforming Sex*, statisic 14.

30. *Die Chronik Bibliothek des 20. Jahrhunderts: 1926*, ed. Brigitte Beier and Petra Gallmeister (Gütersloh: Chronik Verlag, 1995), 124.

31. Statistics in Grossmann, *Reforming Sex*, 4, 101–2.

32. Ibid, 15.

33. Elsa Herrmann, "This Is the New Woman," in *The Weimar Republic Sourcebook* (hereafter *WRS*), ed. Anton Kaes, Martin Jay, and Edward Dimendberg (Berkeley and Los Angeles: University of California Press, 1994), 206–8, quotation 207.

34. See Eric D. Weitz, *Creating German Communism, 1890–1990: From Popular Protests to Socialist State* (Princeton: Princeton University Press, 1997), 188–232.

35. *"Mein Arbeitstag—mein Wochenende": Arbeiterinnen berichten von ihrem Alltag 1928*, reprint, ed. Alf Lüdtke (1930; Hamburg: Ergebnisse Verlag, 1991), 18.

36. Ibid., 46.

37. *Die Frau von Morgen: Wie wir sie wünschen*, ed. Friedrich M. Huebner (Leipzig: E. A. Seemann, 1929).

38. Stefan Zweig, "Zutrauen zur Zukunft," in *Die Frau von Morgen*, 7–17, quotation 8.

39. Ibid., 8–9.

40. Ibid., 9.

41. Ibid., 11.

42. Ibid., 14.

43. Alexander Lernet-Holenia, "Die Frau aller Zeiten," in *Die Frau von Morgen*, 103–8, quotation 103, 106–8.

44. Axel Eggebrecht, "Machen wir uns nichts vor: Ein aufrichtiger Brief," in *Die Frau von Morgen*, 109–26, quotation 121.

45. Ibid.

46. Ibid., 122.

47. Siegfried Kracauer, "Girls and Crisis," in *WRS*, 565–66.

48. "Die Magie der männlichen Schönheit," *Berliner Illustrirte Zeitung* 36:26 (26 June 1927): 1059–61.

49. See David Bathrick, "Max Schmeling on the Canvas: Boxing as an Icon of Weimar Culture," *New German Critique* 51 (1990): 113–37.

50. Hans Surén, *Der Mensch und die Sonne* (Stuttgart: Dieck and Co., 1925), 14–17. For this passage I have used the translation in *WRS*, 678–79 (though I have changed "exalt" to "exult"). The ones that follow are my own translations.

51. For some choice phrases, see Surén, *Der Mensch und die Sonne*, 5, 28, 34, 78–80, 82.

52. Ibid., 184–87.

53. Alice Gerstel, "Jazz Band," and Katharina Rathaus, "Charleston: Every Age Has the Dance It Deserves," in *WRS*, 554–55 and 558–59, quotations 554 and 558.

54. Grete Ujhely, "A Call for Sexual Tolerance," in *WRS*, 710–11, quotation 711.

55. Siegfried Kracauer, *The Salaried Masses: Duty and Distraction in Weimar Germany*, trans. Quintin Hoare (German original 1930; London: Verso, 1998), 95.

56. Ibid.

57. D. Titius, "Evangelisches Ehe- und Familienleben und seine Bedeutung in der Gegenwart," in *Verhandlungen des ersten Deutschen Evangelischen Kirchentages 1924*, ed. Deutschen Evangelischen Kirchenausschuß (Leipzig: Reichardt, 1924), 85–103, quotation 86 (italics in the original).

58. Ibid.

59. Priest and professor Heinrich Weber, in *Die 68. Generalversammlung der Deutschen Katholiken zu Freiburg im Breisgau 28. August bis 1. September 1929*, ed. Sekretariat des Lokalkomitees (Freiburg im Breisgau: Verlagsbuchhandlung Herder and Co., n.d.), 105.

60. *Verhandlungen des ersten Deutschen Evangelischen Kirchentages 1924*, 95.

61. Ibid., 88.

62. Ibid., 88, 89.

63. See newspaper reports on the conference, e.g., "68. Generalversammlung der Deutschen Katholiken," *Germania* 398 (28 August 1929, morning edition): 1–2; "Der Freiburger Katholikentag," *Germania* 404 (31 August 1929): 5–7; "Der Freiburger Katholikentag," *Germania* 406 (1 September 1929, morning edition): 9–11; "Glanvoller Abschluß in Freiburg," *Germania* 407 (2 September 1929, morning edition): 7–10; and "Rettung der christlichen Familie," *Germania* 408 (3 September 1929, morning edition): 7–10.

64. *68. Generalversammlung der Deutschen Katholiken*, 72, 80.

65. *Verhandlungen des ersten Deutschen Evangelischen Kirchentages 1924*, 91.

66. Ibid., 97.

67. As stated in one of the final resolutions of the conference: *68. Generalversammlung der Deutschen Katholiken*, 85.

68. Ibid., 226–27 (italics in the original).

69. "Guidelines of the German Association for the Protection of Mothers," in *WRS*, 697–98.

70. Robert Musil, "Die Frau gestern und morgen," in *Die Frau von Morgen*, 91–102, quotation 100–101.

71. Joseph Roth, "Kaisers Geburtstag," 20 January 1925, in *Berliner Saisonbericht: Unbekannte Reportagen und journalistiche Arbeiten 1920–39*, ed. Klaus Westermann (Cologne: Kiepenheuer and Witsch, 1984), 306–9.

72. See Klaus Theweleit, *Male Fantasies*, trans. Stephen Conway in collaboration with Erica Carter and Chris Turner, 2 vols. (Minneapolis: University of Minnesota Press, 1987–89).

73. See Detlev Peukert, *The Weimar Republic: The Crisis of Classical Modernity*, trans. Richard Deveson (New York: Hill and Wang, 1989), and David F. Crew, *Germans on Welfare: From Weimar to Hitler* (New York: Oxford University Press, 1998).

74. Hilde Walter, "Twilight for Women?" in *WRS*, 210–11, quotations 211.

9. Revolution and Counterrevolution from the Right

1. For a sampling of the very large literature on the conservative revolutionaries, see the following: Walter Kurt Sontheimer, *Antidemokratisches Denken in der Weimarer Republik: Die politische Ideen des deutschen Nationalismus zwischen 1918 und 1933* (Munich: Nymphenburger Verlagshandlung, 1964); Walter Struve, *Elites against Democracy: Leadership Ideals in Bourgeois Political Thought in Germany, 1890–1933* (Princeton: Princeton University Press, 1973); Jeffrey Herf, *Reactionary Modernism: Technology, Culture, and Politics in Weimar and the Third Reich* (New York: Cambridge University Press, 1984); and a number of articles by Larry Eugene Jones, including "Edgar Julius Jung: The Conservative Revolution in Theory and Practice," *Central European History* 21:2 (1988): 142–74.

2. "Biographical Note," in Oswald Spengler, *Today and Destiny: Vital Excerpts from "The Decline of the West" of Oswald Spengler*, ed. Edwin Franden Dakin (New York: Alfred A. Knopf, 1940), 355. On the critical reception, see also H. Stuart Hughes, *Oswald Spengler: A Critical Estimate* (New York: Charles Scribner's Sons, 1952), 89–97.

3. Hans Jonas, *Erinnerungen* (Frankfurt am Main: Insel Verlag, 2003), 150. Spengler wrote back a very complimentary letter, saying that Jonas was the only one who understood what he was saying.

4. Arnold Zweig to Helene Weyl, 22 January 1920, in Arnold Zweig, Beatrice Zweig, Helene Weyl, *Komm her, Wir lieben Dich: Briefe einer ungewöhnlichen Freundschaft zu dritt*, ed. Ilse Lange (Berlin: Aufbau-Verlag, 1996), 175–79, quotation 178.

5. Spengler, *Today and Destiny*, 28–29. On his understanding of the concept of race, see 162.

6. Oswald Spengler, *Preußentum und Sozialismus* (Munich: C. H. Beck, 1920), 53.

7. Spengler, *Today and Destiny*, 32–38, and idem, *Preußentum und Sozialismus*, 12.

8. See, for example, *Decline of the West*, 1:363. See also Hughes, *Oswald Spengler*, 123.

9. Spengler, *Preußentum und Sozialismus*, 12.

10. Ibid., 29.

11. Quotation in Joachim Fest, *Hitler: Eine Biographie* (1975; Berlin: Ullstein, 2004), 636.

12. Ernst Jünger, *Copse 125: A Chronicle from the Trench Warfare of 1918* (London: Chatto and Windus, 1930), ix, 2.

13. Ibid., 9.

14. Ibid., quotations 28–30.

15. For examples, see ibid., 125, 106–24, and 202–64.

16. Ibid., 50, 57.

17. For analyses of violence, see Klaus Theweleit, *Male Fantasies*, trans. Stephen Conway in collaboration with Erica Carter and Chris Turner, 2 vols. (Minneapolis: University of Minnesota Press, 1987–89), and Omer Bartov, *Murder in Our Midst: The Holocaust, Industrial Killing, and Representation* (New York: Oxford University Press, 1996).

18. See, for example, *Verhandlungen des ersten Deutschen Evangelischen Kirchentages 1924*, ed. Deutschen Evangelischen Kirchenausschuß (Leipzig: Reichardt, 1925), 109, and *Die 68. Generalversammlung der Deutschen Katholiken zu Freiburg im Breisgau 28. August bis 1. September 1929*, ed. Sekretariat des Lokalkomitees (Freiburg im Breisgau: Verlagsbuchhandlung Herder and Co., n.d.), 94–95.

19. *68. Generalversammlung der Deutschen Katholiken*, 206–18, quotation 206.

20. Ibid., 206.

21. Ibid., 206–8.

22. Dr. Simons, in *Verhandlungen des dritten Deutschen Evangelischen Kirchentages 1930*, 247.

23. See, for example, Paul Althaus, "Kirche und Volkstum," in *Verhandlungen des zweiten Deutschen Evangelischen Kirchentages 1927*, ed. Deutschen Evangelischen Kirchenausschuß (Wittenberg: Herrose and Ziemsen, 1927), 204–24.

24. Ibid., 216, 298.

25. Ibid., 224–25.

26. Ibid., 211.

27. Adolf Hitler, *Mein Kampf*, trans. Ralph Manheim (Boston: Houghton Mifflin, 1943), 57.

28. Ibid., 325.

29. See Martin H. Geyer, *Verkehrte Welt. Revolution, Inflation und Moderne: München 1914–1924* (Göttingen: Vandenhoeck and Ruprecht, 1998), 278–318.

30. See Ulrich Herbert, *Best: Biographische Studien über Radikalismus, Weltanschauung und Vernunft, 1903–1989* (Bonn: J.H.W. Dietz Nachfolger, 1996). My account of Best is based on this impressive biography.

31. Quoted in ibid., 48.

32. Ibid., 74–76, quotations 75.

33. *Nazism 1919–1945: A Documentary Reader*, vol. 1: *The Rise to Power, 1919–1934*, ed. Jeremy Noakes and Geoffrey Pridham (Exeter: University of Exeter Press, 1983), 49.

34. Ibid., 53–54.

35. William Sheridan Allen, *The Nazi Seizure of Power: The Experience of a Single German Town, 1930–1935* (Chicago: Quadrangle Books, 1965), 25, 31, 40. In this first edition, Allen used the pseudonym "Thalburg" for the town. Quickly, reporters identified it as Nordheim, so he used that designation in the subsequent edition.

36. Quoted in ibid., 25.

37. See Allen's description in *Nazi Seizure*, 117–19, and the diary entry of Luise Solmitz, an upper-middle-class Hamburg housewife married to an army officer, in Noakes and Pridham, *Nazism*, 74.

38. Allen, *Nazi Seizure*, 70–71.

39. Quoted in ibid., 73.

40. Quoted in Noakes and Pridham, *Nazism*, 51.

41. Quoted in ibid., 129.

42. Betty Scholem–Gershom Scholem, *Mutter und Sohn im Briefwechsel 1917–1946*, ed. Itta Shedletzky (Munich: C. H. Beck, 1989), 273–80, quotation 270.

Conclusion

1. Felix Gilbert, *A European Past: Memoirs, 1905–1945* (New York: Norton, 1988), 65.

2. Ibid., 67–68.

Bibliographic Essay

The literature on Weimar Germany is vast, and the following essay makes no effort to be complete. It lists some important works as a guide to further reading. I have limited the entries to works that have appeared in English.

Any historian who approaches Weimar Germany has to engage with three masterworks: Peter Gay, *Weimar Culture: The Outsider as Insider* (New York: Harper and Row, 1968); Detlev Peukert, *The Weimar Republic: The Crisis of Classical Modernity*, trans. Richard Deveson (New York: Hill and Wang, 1989); and Hans Mommsen, *The Rise and Fall of Weimar Democracy*, trans. Elborg Forster and Larry Eugene Jones (Chapel Hill: University of North Carolina Press, 1996). I was introduced to *Weimar Culture* years ago in one of the first German history courses I took as an undergraduate. I have gone back to it many times since. It remains a poignant and eloquent essay, enriched and influenced by the author's contacts with many of the émigré Weimar intellectuals who were still active in the 1950s and 1960s. Peukert's *Weimar Republic* provides one of the most sophisticated and complex analyses of the myriad, intertwined crises faced by German society after World War I. Mommsen's *Rise and Fall of Weimar Democracy* offers the most acute political history of the ill-starred republic.

The Weimar Republic Sourcebook, ed. Anton Kaes, Martin Jay, and Edward Dimendberg (Berkeley and Los Angeles: University of California Press, 1994), is a superb collection of primary materials that surpasses even collections in German. The University of California Press's series of which it is a part, Weimar and Now: German Cultural Criticism, has published many significant volumes, largely though not exclusively in cultural studies. A different but also important collection of primary documents is *Nazism 1919–1945*, vol. 1: *The Rise to Power, 1919–1934*, ed. Jeremy Noakes and Geoffrey Pridham (Exeter: Exeter University Publications, 1983), the first of four volumes.

Erich Eyck's *A History of the Weimar Republic*, trans. Harlan P. Hanson and Robert G. L. Waite, 2 vols. (German original 1954–56; Cambridge: Harvard University Press, 1962–63), is still very much worth reading. Eyck was a prominent liberal political figure as well as a historian. His two volumes, written with literary flair, bring the events to life. Charles Maier's *Recasting Bourgeois Europe: Stabilization in France, Germany, and Italy in the Decade after World War I* (Princeton: Princeton University Press, 1975) is a classic in historical political economy. Gerald D. Feldman's many works, including *The Great Disorder: Politics, Economics, and Society in the German Inflation, 1914–1924* (New York: Oxford University Press, 1993), are also essential reading for anyone trying to grapple with the complex interplay of politics and economics in Weimar Germany. Theo Balderston provides a briefer and very useful survey in *Economics and Politics in the Weimar Republic* (Cambridge: Cambridge University Press, 2002). Richard Bessell, *Germany after the First World War* (Oxford: Clarendon, 1993), is an important study of demobilization, and David Abraham, *The Collapse of the Weimar Republic: Political Economy and Crisis*, 2nd ed. (New York: Holmes and Meier, 1986), remains a very important study on the end phase of the republic. Mary Nolan, *Visions of Modernity: American Business and the Modernization of Germany* (New York: Oxford University Press, 1994), is an important study on rationalization and Americanization.

Three edited collections that cover the long course of modern German political history have important chapters on the Weimar period: *In Search of a Liberal Germany*, ed. Konrad Jarausch and Larry Eugene Jones (Oxford: Berg, 1990); *Between Reform, Reaction, and Resistance: Studies in the History of German Conservatism from 1789 to 1945*, ed. Larry Eugene Jones and James Retallack (Oxford: Berg, 1993); and *Between Reform and Revolution: German Socialism and Communism from 1840 to 1990*, ed. David E. Barclay and Eric D. Weitz (Providence: Berghahn, 1997). Hans Mommsen, *From Weimar to Auschwitz*, trans. Philip O'Connor (Princeton: Princeton University Press, 1991), collects many of his major essays. For a different approach from Mommsen's, see William L. Patch, *Heinrich Brüning and the Dissolution of the Weimar Republic* (New York: Cambridge University Press, 1998). Peter Fritzsche, "Did Weimar Fail?" *Journal of Modern History* 68:3 (1996): 629–56, engages in a learned manner with many of the critical questions concerning the fate of the republic. Volker R. Berghahn has an insightful treatment of Weimar in *Modern Germany: Society, Economy, and Politics in the Twentieth Century*, 2nd ed. (Cambridge: Cambridge University Press, 1987). The first volume of Ian Kershaw's major biography, *Hitler, 1889–1936: Hubris* (New York, 1999), is indispensable. Geoff Eley's many writings contain important insights on Weimar politics and society, as in *Forging Democracy: The History of the Left in Europe, 1850–2000* (New York: Oxford University Press, 2002) and *From Unification to Nazism: Reinterpreting the German Past* (Boston: Allen and Unwin, 1986).

On the major political tendencies, Eric D. Weitz, *Creating German Communism, 1890–1990: From Popular Protests to Socialist State* (Princeton: Princeton University Press, 1997), and Donna Harsch, *German Social Democracy and the Rise of Nazism* (Chapel Hill: University of North Carolina Press, 1993), are important reevaluations of the Left. Stefan Berger provides a significant comparative study in *The British Labour Party and the German Social Democrats, 1900–1931* (Oxford: Oxford University Press, 1995), and Larry Eugene Jones, *German Liberalism and the Dissolution of the Weimar Party System, 1918–1933* (Chapel Hill: University of North Carolina Press, 1988), is the major study of liberalism. Along with Jürgen Falter's work in German, Thomas Childers, *The Nazi Voter: The Social Foundations of Fascism in Germany, 1919–1933* (Chapel Hill: University of North Carolina Press, 1983), demonstrated once and for all that the Nazis secured support all across the social spectrum. Childers's article "The Social Language of Politics: The Sociology of Political Discourse in the Weimar Republic," *American Historical Review* 95 (1990): 331–58, is also enlightening. Julia Sneeringer has written an important study of the role of women in Weimar politics, *Winning Women's Votes: Propaganda and Politics in Weimar Germany* (Chapel Hill: University of North Carolina Press, 2002). Robert G. Moeller, *German Peasants and Agrarian Politics, 1914–1924* (Chapel Hill: University of North Carolina Press, 1986), is also important on rural life and politics for Weimar's first phase. Shelley Baranowski, *The Sanctity of Rural Life: Nobility, Protestantism, and Nazism in Weimar Prussia* (New York: Oxford University Press, 1995), explores the interplay of religion, rural life, and conservative politics.

Atina Grossmann, *Reforming Sex: The German Movement for Birth Control and Abortion Reform, 1920–1950* (New York: Oxford University Press, 1995), is the most important work on the politicization of sex and the family in Weimar. Cornelie Usborne, *The Politics of the Body in Weimar Germany: Women's Reproductive Rights and Duties* (Ann Arbor: University of Michigan Press, 1992), can also be read with profit. The essays in *When Biology Became Destiny: Women in Weimar and Nazi Germany*, ed. Renate Bridenthal, Atina Grossmann, and Marion Kaplan (New York: Monthly Review Press, 1984), pathbreaking in their time, are still important, and most of the authors went on to write books that elaborated upon their topics. Michelle Mouton, *From Nurturing the Nation to Purifying the Volk: Weimar and Nazi Family Policy, 1918–1945* (New York: Cambridge University Press, 2007), makes a major contribution by working across the divide of 1933 and by exploring the implementation of family policy at the local level. On the earlier period, Belinda J. Davis, *Home Fires Burning: Food, Politics, and Everyday Life in World War I Berlin* (Chapel Hill: University of North Carolina Press, 2000), is an important study of women's activism. A number of articles by Elizabeth Bright Jones are notable for revealing the little-known experiences of women in the agricultural sector: "A New Stage of Life? Young Farm Women's Changing Expectations and Aspirations about Work in Weimar Saxony," *German History* 19:4 (2001): 549–70, and "Pre- and Postwar Generations of Rural Female Youth and the Future of the German Nation, 1871–1933," *Continuity and Change* 19:3 (2004): 347–65, among others. Klaus Theweleit's unruly yet classic study, *Male Fantasies*, trans. Stephen Conway in collaboration with Erica Carter and Chris Turner, 2 vols. (Minneapolis: University of Minnesota Press, 1987–89), is central to an understanding of the gendered ideology of the radical Right.

David F. Crew, *Germans on Welfare: From Weimar to Hitler* (New York: Oxford University Press, 1998), and Young-Sun Hong, *Welfare, Modernity, and the Weimar State, 1919–1933* (Princeton: Princeton University Press, 1998), are two important studies of social welfare. Konrad Jarausch, *The Unfree Professions: German Lawyers, Teachers and Engineers, 1900–1950* (New York: Oxford University Press, 1990), is a major study of these significant groups. William Sheridan Allen, *The Nazi Seizure of Power: The Experience of a Single German Town, 1930–1935* (Chicago: Quadrangle Books, 1965), is a pioneering and still valuable work on the creation of the Nazi surge. Rudy Koshar, *Social Life, Local Politics, and Nazism: Marburg, 1880–1935* (Chapel Hill: University of North Carolina Press, 1986), is a later and also significant exploration of how the Nazis won support. Peter Fritzsche, *Reading Berlin 1900* (Cambridge: Harvard University Press, 1996), is an important cultural and social history that is more expansive than the "1900" of the title would suggest.

Fritz K. Ringer, *The Decline of the German Mandarins: The German Academic Community, 1890–1933* (Cambridge: Harvard University Press, 1969), remains the most distinguished work on the professoriat, a critically important group in German society. Jeffrey Herf, *Reactionary Modernism: Technology, Culture, and Politics in Weimar and the Third Reich* (Cambridge: Cambridge University Press, 1984), deserves the many accolades it has won over the years. Richard Wolin, *Heidegger's Children: Hannah Arendt, Karl Löwith, Hans Jonas, and Herbert Marcuse* (Princeton: Princeton University Press, 2001), is critical for an understanding of Heidegger's appeal. Walter Struve, *Elites against Democracy: Leadership Ideals in Bourgeois Political Thought in Germany, 1890–1933* (Princeton: Princeton University Press, 1973), is still valuable.

Barbara Miller Lane, *Architecture and Politics in Germany, 1918–1945* (1968; Cambridge: Harvard University Press, 1985), has a great deal to offer, as does Michael Brenner, *The Renaissance of Jewish Culture in Weimar*

Germany (New Haven: Yale University Press, 1996). Walter Laqueur, *Weimar: A Cultural History, 1918–1933* (London: Weidenfeld and Nicolson, 1974), is encyclopedic. Peter Jelavich, *Berlin Cabaret* (Cambridge: Harvard University Press, 1993), and a number of works by John Willett, including *The Theatre of Bertolt Brecht: A Study from Eight Aspects*, 2nd ed. (London: Methuen, 1959), are critical to an appreciation of the vibrant theatrical world of Weimar. Patrice Petro, *Joyless Streets: Women and Melodramatic Representation in Weimar Germany* (Princeton: Princeton University Press, 1989); Maria Tatar, *Lustmord: Sexual Murder in Weimar Germany* (Princeton: Princeton University Press, 1995); and Richard W. McCormick, *Gender and Sexuality in Weimar Modernity: Film, Literature, and "New Objectivity"* (New York: Palgrave, 2001), are all major studies of culture and gender. Barbara McCloskey, *George Grosz and the Communist Party: Art and Radicalism in Crisis, 1918 to 1936* (Princeton: Princeton University Press, 1997), is a significant work. W. L. Guttsmann, *Workers' Culture in Weimar Germany: Between Tradition and Containment* (New York: Berg, 1990), is very important for its discussion of the large and varied cultural movements attached to the labor parties.

Acknowledgments

This book has been long in the making and the debts are many. The Arsham and Charlotte Ohanessian Chair in the College of Liberal Arts at the University of Minnesota provided generous resources for my research and writing. The History Department at Minnesota has provided a most stimulating and engaging setting for this work. Over the last eight years, I have learned a great deal from my colleagues, those whose interests are close to mine as well as those whose work is far removed from my own. I was very fortunate to have three excellent Minnesota graduate students, Daniele Mueller, Eric Roubinek, and Edward Snyder, serve as my research assistants. Elizabeth Jones, Mary Jo Maynes, and Jack Zipes read the entire manuscript, Gary Cohen and Anna Clark specific chapters. I have benefited greatly from their comments and thank them for their efforts. Gerhard Weiss helped with some particularly difficult translations. Three anonymous reviewers for Princeton University Press provided serious and engaged criticisms that were very helpful in the final stages of writing. Carol, Lev, and Ben have always been there, even when I have disappeared, whether to Berlin or to my study, and Carol's talents helped greatly with the images.

Prof. Dr. Erwin Könnemann was an endless source of knowledge and bibliographic advice. After a visit to him and his family in Blankenburg or Halle, I always left with a pile of books and new ideas. I have also learned a great deal about Weimar and other matters from Martin Geyer and Thomas Lindenberger. The years that we taught together the Trans-Atlantic Summer Institute in German Studies, sponsored by the Center for German and European Studies at the University of Minnesota, the Zentrum für Zeithistorische Forschung in Potsdam, and the Ludwig-Maximilians-Universität in Munich, were very stimulating.

It has been a great pleasure to work again with Princeton University Press. Lauren Lepow is a superb copyeditor, and the entire production staff has been creative and efficient. I want especially to thank the History editor, Brigitta van Rheinberg. This book originated out of an e-mail exchange and phone conversation we had quite some years ago. Along the way we have discussed and debated many points about Weimar Germany. Brigitta read every word I wrote, sometimes more than once. She has been a most supportive editor and my most discerning reader. Whatever virtues this book may have are a result also of her high standards and incisive criticism. The errors are, of course, my own.

Index

re invited to
unsigned, after rea